AUTOS TRANSIT AND CITIES

A TWENTIETH CENTURY FUND REPORT

The Twentieth Century Fund is an independent research foundation that undertakes policy studies of economic, political, and social institutions and issues. The Fund was founded in 1919 and endowed by Edward A. Filene.

AUTOS
TRANSIT
AND
CITIES

John R. Meyer / José A. Gómez-Ibáñez

A Twentieth Century Fund Report

Harvard University Press

Cambridge, Massachusetts
&
London, England
1981

Library of Congress Cataloging in Publication Data
Meyer, John Robert.
   Autos, transit, and cities.
   "A Twentieth Century Fund report."
   Includes bibliographical references and index.
   1. Urban transportation policy—United States.
I. Gómez-Ibáñez, José A., 1948-   . II. Title.
HE308.M49   388.4′0973   81-6477
ISBN 0-674-05485-7   AACR2

Foreword

Urban transportation problems have frequently been touched upon in the many urban policy studies sponsored by the Twentieth Century Fund. But it was not until a few years ago, when John R. Meyer and José A. Gómez-Ibáñez submitted a proposal for a thorough assessment of urban transportation policies, that the Fund was presented with an opportunity to sponsor and supervise a project that focused directly on the role of transportation in our cities. The Fund's Trustees, who had decided and very individualistic views about the "mess" in urban transportation—as does everybody who has ever been stuck in traffic on congested streets or has suffered the foul air and crowded conditions of urban subways—recognized the value of the proposed study. They also were reassured that the project directors were not only immensely knowledgeable about their subject but also levelheaded, unlikely to be swayed by new panaceas in an area where policy makers have adopted plans that were billed as panaceas but that have all too frequently been found wanting.

Meyer, a respected economist and an authority on transportation (he is a professor at Harvard University) and Gómez-Ibáñez, associate professor at the Kennedy School of Government at Harvard, made a very effective team, both for analyzing urban transportation policy since World War II and for making their own recommendations for the future. Their clear and comprehensive examination reveals that public policy with other specific objectives—promoting home ownership, for example—had a marked influence on urban transportation. They also point out that policy makers concerned with transportation policies have frequently behaved like generals fighting their last war over again; repeatedly, their response to changing developments has been to propose (usually expensive) programs that because of changing conditions are outmoded almost before they are implemented and to swing from one extreme in strategy to another.

Above all, this study provides fresh and compelling documentation of the pervasive role of the automobile. Despite the energy crisis, and despite the loss of the competitive edge once held by the American automobile industry—which pioneered in mass production and which has had so great an economic, social, and cultural influence on our society—Americans continue to rely, perhaps excessively, on the automobile. Certainly, our attachment to the automobile has been accompanied by multiple problems for our cities—street and highway congestion, high levels of gas consumption that have contributed to air pollution and affected our balance of payments, and high accident and casualty rates that have increased insurance premiums and resulted in tragedy for those involved. The public policy response to these and other problems—which has involved billions in expenditures—has been either ineffective or inadequate.

It is the thesis of Meyer and Gómez-Ibáñez that the automobile will remain the nation's dominant form of urban transportation and that transportation programs that fail to assume—and accept—its continued significance cannot work. Their own policy recommendations are directed at taming and containing the automobile and its role, in part by redesigning and reengineering the automobile itself. They also consider the options available in the form of mass transit facilities and other, more modest, arrangements. But they make a strong case that critical attention must be paid to civilizing the automobile. This solution may itself seem tame or (if I may be permitted a pun) pedestrian. In reality, though, it may be the beginning of wisdom for getting out of the transportation mess.

The Fund is indebted to John R. Meyer and José A. Gómez-Ibáñez for their painstaking research and for their thoughtful analysis. Their work will inform the public policy debate on the role of the automobile in urban America for this decade and beyond.

M. J. Rossant, Director
The Twentieth Century Fund

Acknowledgments

In 1964 Harvard University Press published *The Urban Transportation Problem* by John Meyer (one of the present authors), John Kain, and Martin Wohl. Although the passage of time has treated many of its arguments kindly, urban transportation policy and problems have changed markedly since then. Specifically, a number of new public policy concerns have come to the fore—energy conservation, air quality, environmental blight, safety, and mobility for the handicapped. This book provides a fresh and current overview of urban transportation policy, tendered in the same spirit and intended for much the same audience as the original work.

We have received a great deal of assistance in our efforts, most notably from the Twentieth Century Fund, which was the principal source of financial support for the writing and research. The 1907 Foundation (now the United Parcel Service Foundation), through its generous endowment of the chair occupied by the senior author, provided substantial aid for the project, including funds for research assistance, clerical, and other such help. Similarly, earlier research that provided most of the basic materials for Chapters 4 and 5 was funded by a grant from the Urban Mass Transportation Administration (UMTA) to the Division of Research of the Harvard Business School. The Harvard Business School Division of Research also provided invaluable logistical and administrative support throughout the project.

Several of our faculty colleagues provided much-appreciated encouragement and advice during the course of this project. Professors John Kain, Greg Ingram, Gary Fauth, Don Pickrell, David Segal, and Arnold Howitt all allowed us to borrow freely from their important research results and gave us valuable counsel. Professor Martin Wohl of Carnegie Mellon University was one of the first to see the need for a new book in this area, and made helpful comments on early thoughts and drafts.

Editing and organizing our manuscript proved to be a major effort, and we received important aid from several sources. Especially helpful were Murray Rossant, director of the Twentieth Century Fund, the late Walter Klein of the Fund's staff, and Max Hall, who had "shepherded" the earlier book through the Harvard University Press; they reviewed early manuscripts and suggested numerous ways to shorten and focus our arguments so that the book would be clearer and more readable. Pamela Gilfond of the Twentieth Century Fund did a superb job in editing the final manuscript; she shortened the text, improved the prose, and carefully ferreted out many inconsistencies and errors.

We are also indebted to several of our former students and others who provided research assistance during the course of this project. The statistics on urban travel trends in Chapter 2 were painstakingly collected from obscure reports by Peter Stump, Robert Emslie, Leslie Meyer, and Sally Ferris. Robert Emslie also gathered materials for Chapters 11 and 13, while Robert Dewer collected information used in Chapters 5, 10, and 12.

Last but by no means least, we would like to thank Eleanor Lintner, who served as the principal secretary and coordinator for the project. Mrs. Lintner typed many drafts with constant good cheer, kept track of the manuscript chapters despite our tendencies to lose them, and assisted us in finding missing facts and citations.

Even with the help of all these friends, the manuscript undoubtedly still contains many errors. The responsibility for these rests, of course, with us.

John R. Meyer
José A. Gómez-Ibáñez

Contents

PART I
ANTECEDENTS

1

The Evolution
of Public
Concerns and
Policies

Urban transportation in the United States is dominated by the private automobile. By the 1980s, no matter how measured, well over 80 percent of all trips in American cities (beyond the house or workplace) were made in automobiles, and there seems little prospect that this will change much in the near future. Indeed, folklore has it that the most distinctive aspect of the American culture of the twentieth century is dependence on the automobile. Through the automobile, in this view, Americans find status, romance, and access to all that is worthwhile—and much that is not. Perhaps the finest succinct summary of the interdependence between American life and the automobile was made by Secretary of Defense Charles Wilson, when he stated that what was good for his former employer, General Motors, "was also good for the country." No one particularly challenged this statement on its merits; rather, outrage was expressed at its brazenness.

Critics of the American automobile, both domestic and foreign, come in droves. Perhaps the most strident complainers about the industry have taken aim at its marketing practices, specifically at the fact that it historically has garnered some of its best profit margins from nonutilitarian frills. The tail fins of the late 1950s were perhaps the most blatant and commonly resented of such effects. Many critics have suggested that such frills diverted the industry's energies from more constructive pursuits, such as improvements in technology and safety. The industry, of course, has had its answers. One of the most famous was that voiced by Boss Kettering, also of General Motors, when he asserted: "It isn't that we are such lousy car builders, but rather that they are such lousy car customers."

Whoever may be at fault, it is clear that extensive reliance on the automobile has posed serious problems for the nation's urban areas. The public policy response, unfortunately, has been largely ineffectual. These policies, moreover, have often involved billions of dollars in expenditures, making the failures all the more difficult to accept.

The essential difficulty is that governments have grossly oversimplified the problem and have tended to lurch from one panacea to another. Urban transportation is one small part of the complex and highly interdependent systems that constitute the large urban conurbations of modern industrial society. Changes in one sector almost invariably affect many others, often in ways that are little understood or anticipated. To devise better solutions to the problems posed by extensive use of automobiles requires an understanding of the workings of these systems in order to define how and where different policies, of *all* kinds, can contribute. Some policies may make only limited contributions but nevertheless may be well worth the effort. Other, frequently expensive, policies may be found to contribute little or nothing once their indirect as well as direct effects are understood. No simple or easy solutions are likely to emerge. Instead, a comprehensive, multifaceted attack— mainly consisting of nibbling at many small margins—offers the best hope of making urban transportation policies work more efficiently and equitably.

Only one conclusion is absolutely undeniable: solving problems created by the automobile will require modifications in both the use and design of the automobile itself. Nothing less will suffice. Other policies, such as improving alternative types of transit, can help, but cannot do the job alone.

AUTOMOBILES AND SUBURBANIZATION: 1920–1955

The automobile emerged into preeminence on the American transportation scene somewhat slowly, the process being seriously disrupted by the Great Depression and World War II. The number of cars per thousand of population reached an early peak around 1929–1930 (just under 200 automobiles per thousand of population) and remained more or less stable over the next fifteen years. During the early 1930s, high unemployment rates arrested the growth of automobile ownership. During World War II, the automobile supply was limited as manufacturers concentrated on armaments production, and automobile ownership declined both absolutely (by almost four million vehicles) and in relation to population (from over 200 per thousand of population just before the war to about 190 as the war ended).[1]

A surge in incomes during World War II, coupled with wartime controls that constrained consumption, led to a substantial accumulation of personal savings and many unrequited demands for consumer durables. This set the stage for rapid consumer investment following the war, not only in automobiles, but also in housing, where production also had backed up because of the Great Depression and World War II. Housing starts had peaked as early as 1925 and did not regain the same level until 1946. The home construction industry, always characterized by many small and highly adaptable suppliers, apparently made the postwar transition easily and rapidly· housing starts tripled between 1945 and 1946.[2]

During the Great Depression and World War II, many young couples had postponed marriage, or, if they married, had tended to live with parents and postpone having children. After the war, they began to form their own households and made a start on what was later to be known as the "great postwar baby boom." Home construction was boosted, too, by government programs that offered housing loans to veterans at lower-than-market interest rates—even lower than those available from previously established government housing programs.

All this "catching up" in demography and housing had enormous effects, among which was the increased importance of the American suburb. New households that had young children and that were well financed through savings and government loan programs were clearly ideal candidates to buy new suburban housing. In the late 1940s, too, job opportunities began to migrate toward suburban and even exurban locations.[3] The manufacturing industry, for example, decentralized because the suburbs offered open land sufficient for sprawling single-level plants. Restaurant and hotel services decentralized as the airplane became an increasingly popular means of travel.

The automobile industry, rather than creating these trends toward decentralization, as has often been suggested, actually lagged in its response. It took about three years after World War II for automobile production and sales to reach their prewar level (in sharp contrast to the quick expansion of the housing industry). By 1949, though, the industry was producing and selling cars at annual rates well above anything ever before experienced.[4] Herbert Hoover's "chicken in every pot and two cars in every garage" was finally on its way to realization—for better or worse.

THE HIGHWAY ERA: LATE 1950s AND EARLY 1960s

With the proliferation of suburban housing and the rise in automobile ownership in the late 1940s and early 1950s, cities as systems were seriously disequilibrated. In particular, existing urban streets and highways proved quite inadequate. An increase in the number of cars per capita and in the number of miles traveled by the typical metropolitan dweller further compounded the problem.

The result, of course, was traffic congestion. The seemingly obvious solution at the time was to build more streets and highways. In particular, a need was perceived for high-performance urban highways, expected to relieve congestion either by directly augmenting existing street capacity or by providing bypasses around high-density areas. In ways that curiously reflected differences in local customs and attitudes, these high-performance highways were called turnpikes (and charged tolls) in some parts of the United States, whereas in others they were called expressways, freeways, or even thruways.

Prototypes for these high-performance urban highways existed, and showed how helpful such facilities could be. In the late 1930s, California developed the urban freeway, which allowed for improved urban highway speeds, particularly during the nonrush hours. Other high-performance urban highways were built just before the outbreak of World War II and in the early 1950s in Connecticut, New Jersey, and New York State; these provided important bypasses and connections around and through New York City, Buffalo, Newark, and Jersey City. By 1956, about 480 miles of high-performance urban highways were complete or under construction in central U.S. cities, of which 290 miles were in New York City, Los Angeles, and Chicago.[5]

Thus, to many, the high-performance highway had been tested and had proved effective as a means of alleviating traffic congestion. Furthermore, there was evidence, especially in the eastern part of the United States, that motorists were willing to pay the cost of constructing such facilities. Turnpike and thruway authorities were established in the northeastern states on a self-financing basis, and revenues collected at toll booths were generally sufficient to cover all building and operating costs. However, certain particularly high-cost urban highways, such as some "urban-only" toll roads like Chicago's Calumet Skyway, did not realize revenues equal to their costs. In the postwar euphoria, though, these local problems were generally overlooked.

The political issue at that time was not whether to build more and better urban expressways, but how to finance them. Should they be "free" (in the sense of being paid for through gasoline or other vehicle-related excise taxes) or toll roads? As might be expected, the eastern states that had already built or were building toll roads tended to favor the toll concept, while western states without toll roads preferred financing through gasoline and similar excise taxes. Even more predictably, the railroad industry gave strong support to the concept of toll roads, while trucking interests preferred the excise-tax approach.[6]

The issue of highway financing was essentially decided in 1956 with the enactment of the Interstate and Defense Highway Act. The act provided for the construction of about 41,000 miles of high-performance "interstate highways" at an estimated cost of $27 billion (revised to $41 billion in 1958, $89 billion in 1975, and $104 billion in 1977). Of the original $27 billion, about $15 billion was to be spent on urban portions, representing about 8,000 miles of the total system. Ninety percent of the cost of these interstate highways was to be paid through a federal highway trust fund financed by a 3-cents-a-gallon federal tax on vehicle fuels, an 8-cents-a-pound tax on tires, and special excises on heavy trucks. Clauses were written into the act to compensate, at least partially, those northeastern states that had already built major portions of the projected interstate systems as toll roads. At the time of its passage, the Interstate Highway System was the largest public works program ever undertaken in the United States.

But the high expectations for the interstate highway program were never realized. For one thing, the system was not finished on time. Originally scheduled for completion in 1972, it remained incomplete in 1980, with the prospect that certain portions might never be built. The costs greatly exceeded original projections, in part due to inflation and to design changes. Significantly, the unfinished portions of the system, and those most likely never to be completed, are in major urban areas where communities did not take kindly to the notion of an interstate highway proceeding through their terrain. Such routing often led to the displacement of residences and businesses, the diminution of property tax rolls, and increased air and noise pollution. The greatest disappointment with the interstate highway program, though, was that it did not seem to achieve its major objective of reducing traffic congestion.

Many explanations were advanced as to why this was so. Highway builders argued that the benefits of urban high-performance highway systems became apparent only as full completion approached. It was therefore unfair to judge systems that were incomplete because time or funding had not permitted finishing the construction or because local community objections had totally prevented the undertaking.

Another explanation was that the new urban interstates had improved performance, but not so dramatically as to be appreciated by the commuting public. Typically, rush hour commuting speeds would only rise from, say, 25 to 35 miles per hour on both expressways and surface streets when new expressways were completed. The improvement in the nonrush hours with the completion of an expressway was almost invariably more dramatic: speeds of 50–60 miles per hour were not uncommon. Needless to say, dashing across a major metropolitan area at such high speeds during the off-peak hours could be an exhilarating experience. By contrast, a mere improvement from 25 to 35 miles per hour or so during the rush hour was a disappointment.

A particularly underappreciated improvement brought about by the new urban interstates was a shortening of the peak congestion periods in most metropolitan areas. Without a very substantial increase in capacity, to levels that often would be deemed excessive, a few central portions in almost every city's highway network will be congested for at least a few minutes every day. In a sense, the phenomenon is much like that experienced on highways or streets surrounding a football stadium just after the termination of a big game: few would expect that the nearby streets would not be congested for a short period after the final whistle. Much the same holds true for streets surrounding major employment centers at, say, 5:00 P.M. In such intensive traffic, the impact of additional highway capacity is simply to shorten the duration of the congestion. The level of congestion measured by mileage per hour during the height of the rush hour peak thus would often be little affected, and commuters going home from work at the peak hours might not be aware of a change. The new highways helped, but not in ways that were necessarily noticeable to those commuters traveling to or from work during the peak rush periods.[7]

Furthermore, regardless of efforts to curtail congestion, the typical commuter trip by automobile in medium-sized cities in the United States has remained in the range of 20–25 minutes (one way). This constancy of the average commuter trip in the face of substantial additions to urban expressway capacity strongly suggests that many people have been trading a longer commuter trip for an improvement (within income or budget constraints) in their housing. This concept has been cited in the economics and city-planning literature by several authors.[8] In essence, the new highway improvements made it easier to develop and market good housing at lower-cost locations.

Suburbanization and growth in automobile ownership in the early postwar years thus reinforced each other and, in turn, created a demand, even a need, for more urban highway capacity, which fed back to augment the demand for suburbanization and automobile ownership.

These feedbacks manifested themselves on the urban highway networks as lesser reductions in congestion than might first have been expected from highway improvements. In essence, an effective reduction in urban traffic congestion proved an elusive goal that did not yield easily to the simple expedient of building more and bigger highways.

"BALANCED" TRANSPORTATION:
THE MIDDLE AND LATE 1960s

When it became increasingly clear in the 1960s that more urban highways might not be the answer to all the transportation problems of American cities, new solutions were sought. By far the most popular of these was what came to be known as "balanced transportation."

To achieve balance, federal funds were to be made available not only for urban highways but also for improving mass transit—travel by bus or on rails. The Urban Mass Transportation Act of 1964 was the first important legislative recognition of this goal. Under this legislation, federal grants were to be provided to help solve local transit problems, to be made on a two to-one matching basis (two-thirds federal, one-third local). Aid was restricted to capital acquisitions on the grounds that operating subsidies for local transit districts would be very difficult to control and would intrude the federal presence into decisions better left to local governments. The act discouraged the use of fare increases as a means of financing local transit and established substantial incentives for public authorities to acquire any private transit companies still in operation.

This federal support for local transit was sold on many grounds, but a basic consideration was that of parity or balance between transportation modes. If the federal government funded 90 percent of urban interstate costs, but provided no help for transit, public transit would be shortchanged relative to highways.

Another, rather more tacit, argument for federal involvement in urban transit was that it seemed an uncontroversial way to provide federal financial aid to America's increasingly troubled cities. In the 1960s, urban problems were coming to the fore as the result of many developments, the most obvious manifestation being race riots. Other forms of federal financial aid to local governments were regarded, probably correctly, as more controversial or politically difficult to implement than public transit subsidies.

The most persuasive of the arguments for federal aid for public transit, though, was congestion relief. Many automobile commuters were in favor of public transit improvement as a means of getting *other* people off the road. Improved transit was a good idea, even if never used by oneself, because it would make one's own automobile commute simpler, by diverting other commuters from automobiles to transit.

This diversion was to be achieved by making public transit both faster and more comfortable. High hopes were expressed that, with a major infusion of capital, transit could acquire comforts and convenience not too dissimilar from those of the automobile. Buses and rail transit were to be air-conditioned; better-designed and more comfortable interiors were advanced as ways of making transit more enticing.[9]

The major immediate effect of the capital grant program was a sharp rise in sales of new transit buses, from 2,200 a year in the early 1960s to 3,400 a year in the early 1970s. Public transit systems in major U.S. cities were thus reequipped, the average age of transit buses dropping from a median of 9.6 years in 1961 to 8.3 years in 1977.

The 1964 act also promoted plans for new rail transit. Some large cities had made a start on extending or introducing rail transit systems even before federal funds became available. The largest-scale example of this was the Bay Area Rapid Transit (BART) system under development in the San Francisco area. Local financing had also been provided for extensions or improvements of existing rail transit systems in New York, Boston, Cleveland, Philadelphia, and Chicago. When federal funds became available, more plans sprang up. In a few cities, these plans moved fairly quickly. Cleveland, Chicago, Philadelphia, Boston, and New York, for example, all extended their rail transit systems in important ways during the middle and late 1960s with federal help. In San Francisco, many of the BART system's "completion pangs," including cost overruns, were relieved by federal aid. Later, Washington, D.C., Baltimore, Miami, and Atlanta began building new systems, while Honolulu and Los Angeles proceeded with feasibility studies.

Balanced transportation was about as simple in concept as the earlier urban highway approach—and was motivated by many of the same considerations. Essentially, balanced transportation was a bit more of much the same: increase expenditures on capital improvements so as to relieve congestion. It was thought that with enough expenditures on new equipment and facilities, properly balanced between the different modes, the basic congestion problems of urban areas would be relieved.

The new approach was no more successful than the highway program. As with the highways, cost overruns and late completion were the rule. Almost without exception, the rail extensions and new systems did not live up to their passenger-demand projections, and their discernible impact on urban congestion was a good deal less than expected.

The brand-new rail systems were a particular disappointment. Criticism of these became almost endemic, and some of the most cogent critiques originated with people who had once been among the ardent advocates of rail transit.[10] Once again, a great deal of public money had seemingly been spent on urban transportation improvements to accomplish remarkably little.

MATURITY AND COMPLEXITY: THE 1970s

By the early 1970s, the American public had completed two cycles of experience with oversimplistic solutions to urban transportation problems, both ending in frustration. It is not surprising, therefore, that a recognition grew that perhaps urban transportation problems were more complex than originally expected, requiring in turn more complex solutions.

This feeling of complexity was further fed by important environmental and other political perceptions of the late 1960s. Urban transportation policy became increasingly intertwined with issues about the quality of the urban environment and mobility opportunities for special groups such as racial minorities, the poor, the aged, and the handicapped.

The emergence of these new concerns coincided with growing skepticism about the possibility, perhaps even the desirability, of relieving congestion as such. Certainly by the early 1970s it was appreciated that relief of traffic congestion could be a very elusive goal. Furthermore, the major method of achieving congestion relief—investing more capital in the various urban transportation modes—might have its own undesirable side effects. The adverse impact on neighborhoods was perceived fairly quickly, especially when elevated structures were used. Similarly, improving high-performance rail or highway connections between the suburbs and central business districts may have expedited the decentralization of some urban activities rather than help preserve the urban core. As an irony of ironies, moreover, the main beneficiaries of building high-performance facilities were increasingly found to be high-income property owners or suburbanites rather than rank-and-file central-city dwellers.[11]

Almost every aspect of federal aid for urban transportation improvement came into question. Was such aid regressive in that it helped the rich more than the poor? Did such aid promote racially segregated neighborhoods by improving mobility in urban areas and making more remote residential locations possible? Would improvements in public transit actually help with some of the special problems of those most dependent on urban transportation—the aged and the handicapped? Did the high percentages of federal contributions to local transportation projects badly distort local decision making by creating an illusion that expensive capital facilities really cost only 10 to 20 cents on the dollar, thereby inducing investments of little value? Did an emphasis on capital improvements create artificial incentives to substitute capital for labor? Would expansion of capacity in urban transportation facilities ever reduce congestion, since these new facilities seemingly created as much demand as they served?

With the adoption of more ambitious objectives, and a better understanding of the inherent complexity of the problem, public policy shifted. In the late 1960s, and to an even greater extent during the early 1970s, the major federal agency involved in urban transportation, the Urban Mass Transportation Administration (UMTA), began to experiment. Express bus services were specially designed for linking well-defined clusters of residential origins with workplace destinations. Dial-a-ride, a crossbreed between jitney and taxicab service, was tested. Vanpooling, a form of do-it-yourself jitney for employees with a common workplace, was introduced. Experiments were conducted in which highway and street lanes were reserved exclusively for buses and carpoolers. Fresh attention was given to the possibility of using lightweight rail vehicles instead of always assuming that heavy rail vehicles would be best. "People movers" and special shuttle buses for downtown distribution were investigated and in some cases tried. More attention was given to the needs of minority groups who, living in central residential locations but working at the city periphery, made so-called inside-out commutes. Several different alternatives for providing transit to the handicapped were tested.

Environmental issues also came to the fore. Legislation was enacted in 1970 mandating strict limits on the pollutants that automobiles could emit. The Environmental Protection Agency (EPA) developed plans for reorienting or restricting traffic in ways that might reduce air pollution in urban areas. These plans varied from city to city, but generally included restrictions on automobile use in very high-density central business districts—restrictions such as prohibitions on automobile entry into central areas, conversion of certain city streets into pedestrian or transit malls, and lower downtown speed limits.

Restrictions on automobile use and characteristics took on an added dimension, and urgency, after the Organization of Petroleum Exporting Countries (OPEC) made energy a concern in the mid-1970s. Automobiles were not only required to limit their pollutants, but legislation was passed specifying certain mileage-per-gallon standards to be achieved on average by all new cars sold in the United States.

These proposals, whether originating with UMTA, EPA, or energy concerns, were striking in two respects. First, they represented an important step away from making congestion reduction the more or less exclusive target of urban transportation policy and planning. Second, many of the plans stressed operating changes and did not involve major capital outlays by government agencies.

In keeping with this reduced emphasis on public capital improvements, the 1970s also saw transit *operating* subsidies incorporated for the first time into the federal support program. A local community no longer had to buy a new bus or a new terminal or build a new rail system in order to qualify for federal aid. Funds now were available for direct subsidy of operating losses in certain circumstances. This shift toward operating support was mainly motivated by a desire to provide more immediate and direct financial aid to hard-pressed urban transit systems and was only loosely linked to the achievement of the newly emerging policy goals.

The major objection to operating subsidies all along, of course, was the danger that they would become open-ended or unlimited. As a natural accompaniment to the introduction of operating subsidies, the federal authorities became more concerned with problems of productivity in urban transit operations. UMTA, for example, initiated efforts to develop better operating methods, further extending the agency's involvement in the managerial complexities of the industry.

CONCLUDING OBSERVATIONS

In broad perspective, public policy developments over the past few decades can be viewed as codifying what was always the underlying reality of urban transportation—that these functions are executed as part of the larger and very complex reality that constitutes modern urban conurbations.

This lesson has not been learned easily. Public policy in urban transportation has all too often been based on highly oversimplified diagnoses, without any recognition of the interactions among various urban transportation policies and other public policy goals. Specifically, public policy has tended to shift from one simple panacea to another, first building express highways and then rail transit systems.

As a consequence of these policies, a great deal of money has been spent on various public works. A few of these have been well conceived and may have achieved all the goals sought. Others were not as cogent but nevertheless have resulted in facilities of some utility and durability. Still others have contributed virtually nothing of worth, certainly nothing commensurate with their costs.

Unfortunately, the need all along has not been for large-scale attempts to solve the urban transportation problem at one swoop but rather for a sustained, systematic, simultaneous effort on many fronts. This effort, moreover, must include an undertaking to make the automobile a more acceptable and civilized part of the urban scene; problems created by the dominance of the automobile in urban transportation cannot be solved by seeking a solution through indirect expedients. Again, for the automobile as for the broader issues, coordination, comprehensiveness, and consistency are apt descriptions of what is required. Proliferation of policy goals in recent years has only heightened these needs.

A related and also very essential element of any solution must be a careful reduction in the extent to which urban transportation is subsidized and mispriced. Some of the problems of the automobile—such as congestion or air pollution—can be attributed in part to the fact that the motorist does not always pay his way and in particular does not pay the full social costs of automobile use. Civilizing the automobile therefore often involves reducing explicit or implicit subsidies—for example, by making automobiles using central-city expressways pay more nearly the costs or by eliminating employer provision of free parking spaces. Unfortunately, government subsidies to competing modes such as rail transit have done little to offset the problems caused by the automobile and often cause added problems of their own. With subsidies and mispricing, as with other elements of transportation policy, changes again must be carefully implemented and coordinated.

Abandoning simplistic notions about urban transportation policy is, of course, not likely to be easy. Complex policies are more difficult to design and implement than simple ones. A major obstacle to applying many of the policy lessons learned from earlier failures has simply been the administrative burden of doing so. Greater recognition of interdependencies can inhibit and frustrate as well as enlighten. Nevertheless, such understanding is absolutely indispensable to good policy design, and that understanding begins with a recognition of the underlying locational and travel trends that have been shaping and reshaping modern cities.

2

Metropolitan
Location and
Travel Trends

RESIDENTIAL AND EMPLOYMENT LOCATION PATTERNS

For several decades, cities in the United States and around the world
have been suburbanizing and decentralizing because of increasing
urban populations, rising real incomes, and falling real transportation
costs.[1] Urban overcrowding has been relieved through expanding the
geographic boundaries of cities; in particular, people have used some of
their increased real income to separate themselves from others. This
tendency is universal and long standing: it is discernible as far back as
reliable data are available (approximately the mid-nineteenth century)
and in virtually all parts of the world—developed and underdeveloped,
with and without widespread ownership of automobiles.[2]

Technological innovations that required large land areas for their
implementation (such as air travel and the single-story manufacturing
plant) made it increasingly attractive for employers to move to the
edge of the city where land was usually cheaper as well as more available. The growth of industries that did not require much intercity
transportation for their execution (for example, services and lighter
manufacturing that did not need access to centrally located ports and

rail marshaling yards) also contributed to employment decentralization.[3]

Some data on the mid- to late 1960s suggested that this tendency toward employment decentralization in the United States was leveling off.[4] Careful analysis indicated, however, that the slowdown in decentralization was probably as much a result of the business cycle as of any basic change in the underlying trends.[5] When the very substantial economic boom generated by the "guns and butter" policy of the mid-1960s hit its peak in 1967–68, manufacturing lofts, old office space, and otherwise less-than-attractive workplaces in central cities were fully occupied; they were rapidly evacuated, however, when business expansion subsided in 1970 and 1971.

A comparison of the 1960 and 1970 U.S. censuses confirms that central-city employment has continued to decline. Between 1960 and 1970, the absolute number of central-city jobs fell in almost half of the metropolitan areas with populations of one million or more, as the total number of central-city jobs in these areas fell by 287,000, and the proportion of metropolitan workers employed in central cities dropped from 64 to 41 percent. The older central cities in the Northeast and North Central regions were the hardest hit. Indeed, some metropolitan areas in the West and South have recorded substantial gains in absolute numbers of central-city jobs (see Table 2.1), but even in these regions central-city employment declined relative to employment in the suburban rings. Furthermore, the central city is usually a very broadly defined geographic area (as the percentage employment numbers would indicate). If reliable figures, therefore, were available on employment in the central business districts of large central cities, declines would probably be even more universally evident.

During the 1960s, employment also decentralized at a more rapid rate than residences, as central-city jobs either declined more rapidly or grew more slowly than central-city populations in the country as a whole (see Table 2.1). Similarly, suburban jobs expanded more rapidly than suburban populations. However, these tendencies were most pronounced in the older and larger metropolitan areas of the Northeast and North Central states.

A study of manufacturing plant relocations between 1971 and 1976 shows a continuation in this pattern of employment decentralization, with a remarkably high percentage of manufacturing relocations originating in major cities. Depending upon the particular measure employed—for example, employment or number of establishments—between one fifth and one fourth of manufacturing plants that relocated in the early 1970s apparently originated in the New York City area alone; Chicago, Los Angeles, Boston, Philadelphia, Detroit, San Fran-

TABLE 2.1. Population and workplace changes in the 33 Standard Metropolitan Statistical Areas (SMSAs) with populations above one million, 1960–1970.

	Percentage change in population			Percentage change in jobs			Absolute change in jobs (in thousands)		Percentage of SMSA residents working in central city	
	Total SMSA	Central city	Suburban ring	Total SMSA	Central city	Suburban ring	Central city	Suburban ring	1960	1970
All 33 SMSAs	17	−1	26	18	−2	54	−287	4,528	64	51
By census region:										
Northeast	8	−1	17	3	−0	24	−513	738	63	51
North Central	13	−7	33	18	−11	79	−464	1,712	67	50
South	32	9	57	40	14	100	332	1,016	70	55
West	27	−1	60	28	12	51	359	1,063	59	48
By individual SMSA:										
New York	8	1	28	−2	−10	32	−307	237	80.9	74.4
Los Angeles/ Long Beach	16	−17	73	14	2	29	28	276	56.9	51.1
Chicago	12	−6	36	12	−15	70	−229	495	69.1	52.9
Philadelphia	11	−3	23	5	−11	28	−97	177	57.5	48.4
Detroit	12	−9	28	14	−22	61	−156	325	56.7	38.6

TABLE 2.1. (Cont.)

	Percentage change in population			Percentage change in jobs			Absolute change in jobs (in thousands)		Percentage of SMSA residents working in central city	
	Total SMSA	Central city	Suburban ring	Total SMSA	Central city	Suburban ring	Central city	Suburban ring	1960	1970
San Francisco/Oakland	17	-3	31	10	0	23	1	104	39.5	36.4
Washington, D.C.	38	1	60	44	2	117	9	322	63.8	45.2
Boston	6	-10	12	7	-9	20	-36	103	44.5	37.8
Pittsburgh	0	-12	4	3	-5	2	13	12	35.9	36.4
St. Louis	12	-19	30	22	-15	80	-61	209	60.6	42.0
Baltimore	15	-3	34	22	-6	77	-22	154	66.0	50.9
Cleveland	8	-15	28	12	-15	83	-71	152	71.8	54.0
Houston	40	32	56	67	49	165	177	11	84.3	75.1
Newark	10	-4	14	8	-19	22	-33	75	33.2	24.8
Minneapolis/St. Paul	22	-7	57	30	0	25	1	158	49.9	36.1
Dallas	39.0	23	64	46	38	73	114	72	75.6	71.1
Seattle/Everett	28.4	-2	65	28	20	48	53	58	69.0	55.9
Anaheim/Garden Grove/Santa Ana	101.8	53	136	117	*	*	*	*	*	16.9
Milwaukee	9.8	-3	28	19	-11	110	-36	116	75.6	56.9
Atlanta	36.7	3	68	46	13	124	33	131	68.4	52.4

Cincinnati	9.2	-10	22	29	0	83	0	101	65.7	51.2
Paterson/Clifton/Passaic	14.5	0	19	20	-10	35	-10	72	33.2	25.0
San Diego	31.4	20	46	29	-8	89	-21	93	73.0	60.6
Buffalo	3.2	-14	15	4	-17	31	-43	61	56.1	44.6
Miami	35.6	14	45	38	-1	83	1	121	54.3	39.6
Kansas City	15.0	9	19	26	-4	56	-22	72	63.5	52.8
Denver	32.1	-5	63	39	20	82	45	84	69.4	59.8
San Bernardino/Riverside/Ontario	40.9	36	43	29	8	43	8	64	40.8	34.1
Indianapolis	17.6	4	116	58	31	201	66	81	84.0	69.6
San Jose	66.0	118	42	72	46	92	38	101	42.9	36.4
New Orleans	15.4	-5	60	17	-3	114	-8	55	82.3	67.7
Tampa/St. Petersburg	31.1	9	93	33	17	71	27	50	69.9	61.0
Portland/Oregon-Washington	22.5	3	38	25	8	57	15	57	65.1	56.3

Source: David Miller, ed., *Urban Transportation Fact Book, Part 1,* study prepared by Barton-Aschman Associates, Inc., and sponsored by the American Institute of Planners and Motor Vehicle Manufacturers Association of the United States, Inc. (Detroit: Motor Vehicle Manufacturers Association, 1974), pp. 1–9 and 1–14 through 1–18.
* Not available.

cisco, Newark, and the immediate environs of New York City (Long Island and Westchester County) accounted for nearly one fourth to one fifth more of the mover originations. Thus, roughly one half of all manufacturing plants that relocated between 1971 and 1976 were originally located in either greater New York City or the seven other major cities cited above. Almost half of these moves involved the relocation of headquarters facilities, a process in which the big loser was Manhattan and the big winner was Fairfield County, Connecticut.[6] Most of these were short-distance relocations, involving a move from the central city to not-too-distant or even neighboring suburbs (only modestly offset by some return flow into the older and larger central cities).

In short, urban decentralization is clearly a pervasive and widespread phenomenon. As two leading scholars of urban population trends have summarized the situation: "There appears to be no country in which the trend [toward decentralization] has not been pervasive and persistent during many decades. No serious observer of urban affairs can possibly believe that suburbanization was a post–World War II U.S. invention or that it is mainly the result of automobile commuting or central city racial tensions."[7] And decentralization is not limited to housing alone: in the United States, at least, employment has apparently been suburbanizing as fast as or faster than residential populations.

POSTWAR URBAN TRAVEL PATTERNS

Basic trends. Decentralization of employment and residences does not necessarily reduce travel to and from a central city or its central business district. More trips might be made by those residents who remain, or there might be an increase in the number of people shopping or conducting other business in the center of the city. For transportation planning there is thus no substitute for actual observations of tripmaking in and through central areas, particularly during the rush hours, when the strain on urban transportation facilities is greatest.

Unfortunately, remarkably few data are available on these critical aspects of travel behavior. The 1960 and 1970 U.S. censuses provide some insights, but for worktrips only. There remains the major question of how travel for purposes other than commuting might have offset or exacerbated any changes in commuter behavior.

To fill this void, various postwar surveys of household travel behavior (which usually cover nonworktrips as well as worktrips) have been conducted in most large U.S. metropolitan areas. But only a few metropolitan areas have completed more than one survey, and even when a metropolis has conducted several surveys the numbers generated in the different studies may not be readily comparable, due to differences in methodology or orientation. As a result, reasonably comparable and comprehensive trip data at different points in time are available for only nine major U.S. metropolitan areas.

In all nine of these, the number of persontrips increased rapidly, often doubling within fifteen years (see Table 2.2). In Chicago, for example, the number of average weekday persontrips increased from about 9.9 million in 1956 to 18.6 million in 1970. In Denver, between 1959 and 1971, weekday persontrips increased from 1.8 to 3.1 million. Urban travel for shopping, personal business, social, recreational, and other nonwork purposes has increased more rapidly than urban commuting. In Chicago, the number of worktrips increased by 36 percent between 1956 and 1970 while the number of nonworktrips increased by 101 percent.

Population growth accounts for only a fraction of this postwar increase in urban travel. In Chicago, between 1956 and 1970, where the population increased by only 34 percent, the number of persontrips grew by 88 percent. In the nine metropolitan areas for which data are available, the average number of weekday trips per capita increased from about two in the 1950s to almost three in the early 1970s, suggesting that, even if there had been no population growth, urban tripmaking would have increased by about 50 percent.

This increase in tripmaking per capita is partly attributable to postwar gains in real household incomes. As incomes rise, households can afford more shopping, social, and recreational activities. Worktrips have also increased—mainly due to increased labor force participation—but at rates only slightly higher than the rates of metropolitan population growth.

Decentralization may also have encouraged the increase in tripmaking per capita. If shops, recreational facilities, workplaces, and other destinations are widely dispersed, it may become difficult to accomplish several purposes with a single trip. Longer distances between destinations also may have forced some travelers to switch from walking, usually not counted in household travel surveys, to trips by automobile or public transportation, which are tabulated.

The average postwar urban trip also increased in length. Between 1956 and 1970 in the Chicago metropolitan area (for which the most complete statistics are available), the number of weekday miles of travel increased by 128 percent, while the number of persontrips increased by only 87 percent. The length of the average trip in Chicago

TABLE 2.2. Postwar growth in trips and population in selected U.S. metropolitan areas.

| Metropolitan area | SMSA population 1970 (thousands) | Years of travel studies | Study area population | | Weekday persontrips | | | | | |
| | | | Number (thousands) | Percent change | All trips | | Worktrips | | Nonworktrips | |
					Number (thousands)	Percent change	Number (thousands)	Percent change	Number (thousands)	Percent change
Chicago	6,978	1956	5,170	34.4	9,931	87.5	2,033	36.3	7,898	100.6
		1970	6,946		18,616		2,770		15,846	
Detroit	4,436	1953	3,093	29.2	6,392	53.8	1,738	22.2	4,554	69.3
		1965	3,997		9,832		2,123		7,709	
Dallas/Ft. Worth	2,378	1950–51	534	241.0	1,232	363.1	326	193.9	906	424.1
		1964	1,821		5,706		958		4,748	
Baltimore	2,071	1945	*	*	1,195	117.9	*	*	*	*
		1962	*		2,604		*		*	
Minneapolis/ St. Paul	1,965	1949	*	*	1,633	106.2	370	55.7	1,263	121.0
		1958	*	*	3,367	47.8	576	43.9	2,791	48.6
		1970	*		4,977		829		4,148	
Denver	1,239	1959	817	37.0	1,819	70.6	*	*	*	*
		1971	1,119		3,103		*		*	
Kansas City	1,274	1957	857	28.7	1,870	33.9	385	11.7	1,485	39.7
		1963	1,103	*	2,504	51.6	430	*	2,074	*
		1970	*		3,797		*		*	
Phoenix	969	1947	162	*	576	75.5	*	*	*	*
		1957	*		1,011		*		*	
Wichita	389	1951	238	33.6	638	37.1	184	7.6	454	49.1
		1960	318		875		198		677	

Source: Figures compiled by the authors from various origin-destination surveys.
* Not available.

went from 4.2 to 5.1 miles (one way), with a greater increase in the length of worktrips (from 5.3 to 7.0 miles) than of nonworktrips (from 3.8 to 4.5 miles).

The reasons for this increase in trip length are multiple and complex. Decentralization of residences and workplaces certainly played a role, as did an increase in the geographic spread of the typical metropolitan area as populations grew.[8] Increasing rates of labor force participation may also have been a factor. With an increasing number of workers living in households where two or more persons are employed, residential location cannot so easily be selected to minimize commuter trip lengths.

The decentralization of urban travel. Almost all of the growth in urban worktrips has been to and within suburban areas (see Table 2.3). During the 1960s, worktrips to the central city increased slightly in the South and West, but declined in the large metropolitan areas of the Northeast and North Central regions. Meanwhile, worktrips ending outside the central city grew everywhere.

The decline in trips to the central city becomes even more pronounced when nonworktrips are considered and when the metropolitan center is defined as a one- or two-square-mile downtown commercial zone in the heart of the metropolitan area (see Table 2.4). In the seven U.S. metropolitan areas for which data are available, the proportion of all urban trips that originated or terminated in the downtown district declined from about 10–20 percent in the 1950s to about 3–5 percent in the early 1970s. Downtown travel fell everywhere in relative terms and fell in absolute terms in all but one metropolitan area (Dallas/Ft. Worth).

Growing dominance of the automobile. Virtually all growth in urban travel has been in automobile and truck traffic. The volume of automobile traffic on urban roads more than tripled between 1950 and 1977, increasing from 182 to 666 million vehicle-miles. During this same period, urban truck traffic more than quadrupled, rising from 33.8 to 153 million vehicle-miles, or almost 19 percent of all urban highway use. Urban highway use by buses, on the other hand, increased by only about 35 percent between 1950 and 1977, from 2.0 to 2.7 million vehicle-miles, accounting for only about 0.3 percent of all urban highway use.[9]

Patronage on most forms of urban public transportation has also declined (see Table 2.5). Between 1950 and 1972, transit patronage declined by 62 percent, the most rapid losses taking place in the 1950s. After 1972, total transit ridership stabilized and even increased slightly. The traffic carried by commuter railroads also fell between

TABLE 2.3. Changes in worktrip distribution between central cities and suburbs, 1960–1970.

Area	Worktrip begins and ends in central city		Worktrip into central city from SMSA ring		Worktrip into SMSA ring from central city		Worktrip begins and ends in SMSA ring	
	Net change (thousands)	Percent change	Net change (thousands)	Percent change	Net change (thousands)	Percent change	Net change (thousands)	Percent change
All 33 SMSAs with populations above one million[a]	−1,227	−11	940	24	904	79	3,624	50
By census region:								
Northeast	−599	−14	86	9	79	27	659	23
North Central	−670	−21	206	16	390	119	1,322	71
South	−35	−2	367	56	190	121	826	97
West[a]	78	4	281	31	246	67	817	48

Source: David Miller, ed. *Urban Transportation Factbook, Part 1*, study prepared by Barton-Aschman Associates, Inc., and sponsored by the American Institute of Planners and Motor Vehicle Manufacturers Association of the United States, Inc. (Detroit: Motor Vehicle Manufacturers Association, 1974), pp. 1–14 through 1–18.
[a] Does not include the SMSA of Anaheim/Garden Grove/Santa Ana, California.

1951 and 1977, but less precipitously than for mass transit, specifically by about 6 percent.[10] Taxi patronage, on the other hand, increased slightly during the 1950s and 1960s, and reached about 2.4 billion passengers per year in the 1970s.[11]

Mass transit use has always been concentrated in the larger, older, and denser metropolitan areas, but heavy postwar ridership losses in small metropolitan areas have made this pattern even more pronounced. By 1972, 38 percent of the nation's mass transit ridership was concentrated in the urban area comprising New York and northern New Jersey, an area that contained only 8 percent of the nation's population; 53 percent of the nation's transit ridership was concentrated in four urban areas (New York, Chicago, Boston, and Philadelphia), which contained only 15 percent of the nation's population. By contrast, urban areas with fewer than 50,000 persons, and rural areas— which together constitute about 42 percent of the nation's population—reported only about 5 percent of the nation's transit patronage in 1972.[12]

The public modes of transportation may also have held their position better on worktrips than on nonworktrips and for trips to and from centers of metropolitan areas. Table 2.6 shows postwar changes in the number and percent of worktrips and nonworktrips by public transportation in four metropolitan areas for which reasonably reliable data are available. In each of the four areas, the percent of worktrips made by public transportation fell less than the percent of nonworktrips. In Chicago, for example, the share of worktrips carried by public transportation fell from 33 to 19 percent, while the share of nonworktrips fell from 22 to 7 percent. Still, the drop in worktrips by public transportation was larger absolutely in two cases (Detroit and Dallas/Ft. Worth) than the drop in nonworktrips by public transportation, largely because nonworktrips by all modes were growing so rapidly during that period.

Postwar trends in public transportation trips to or from the downtown area are also shown in Table 2.6 for the eight metropolitan regions for which reliable data are available. Downtown travel by public transportation has declined in all of these areas. Public transportation's share of trips to or from downtown has fallen much less, however, than its share of all metropolitan trips. In Minneapolis/St. Paul, for example, the share of downtown trips carried by public transportation dropped from 39 to 17 percent between 1949 and 1970, while the share of all trips in the metropolitan area by public modes declined from 26 to 3 percent.[13] Public transportation thus seems increasingly confined to a few specialized markets that, for the most part, have been declining in importance: trips in larger, denser metropolitan areas; commuting trips; and travel to or from downtown areas.

TABLE 2.4. Postwar trends in travel to and from downtown commercial zones in eight metropolitan areas.

Metropolitan area	Years of travel data	All metropolitan trips			Trips to or from downtown commercial zones			Downtown trips as a percentage of all trips
		Number (thousands)	Absolute change (thousands)	Percent change	Number (thousands)	Absolute change (thousands)	Percent change	
Chicago	1956	9,931	8,685	87.5	1,165	−293	−25.2	11.7
	1970	18,616			872			4.7
Detroit	1953	6,392	3,440	53.8	389	−84	−21.6	6.1
	1965	9,832			305			3.1
Dallas/Ft. Worth	1950–51	1,232	4,474	363.1	234	12	5.1	19.0
	1964	5,706			246			4.3
Minneapolis/ St. Paul	1949	1,633	1,734	106.2	313	−1	−0.3	19.2
	1958	3,367	1,610	47.8	312	−42	−13.5	9.3
	1970	4,977			270			5.4
Denver	1959	1,819	1,284	70.6	189	−34	−18.0	10.4
	1971	3,103			155			5.0

	Year							
Kansas City	1957	1,870 ⎫						11.6
	1963	2,504 ⎬	634	33.9	216 ⎫			*
	1970	3,797 ⎭	1,293	51.6	102 ⎭	−114	−52.8	2.7
Phoenix	1947	576 ⎫	435	75.5	* ⎫			*
	1957	1,011 ⎭			* ⎭	*	*	
Wichita	1951	638 ⎫	237	37.1	203 ⎫			31.8
	1960	875 ⎭			149 ⎭	−54	−26.6	

Source: Figures compiled by the authors from various origin-destination studies.
* Not available.

TABLE 2.5.   Revenue passengers carried on urban mass transit, 1940–1977 (millions).

Year	Rail transit			Trolley bus	Motor bus	Total transit
	Light rail	Heavy rail	Total rail			
1940	4,182	2,282	6,464	419	3,620	10,503
1945	7,081	2,551	9,632	1,001	8,335	18,968
1950	2,790	2,113	4,903	1,261	7,681	13,845
1955	845	1,741	2,586	869	5,734	9,189
1960	335	1,670	2,005	447	5,069	7,521
1965	204	1,678	1,882	182	4,730	6,794
1970	172	1,574	1,746	128	4,058	5,932
1971	155	1,494	1,649	113	3,735	5,497
1972	147	1,446	1,593	100	3,561	5,254
1973	144	1,424	1,568	74	3,653	5,295
1974	114	1,435	1,549	60	3,998	5,607
1975	94	1,388	1,482	56	4,095	5,633
1976	86	1,353	1,439	54	4,168	5,661
1977	79	1,335	1,414	51	4,246	5,711
1978	80	1,415	1,495	51	4,406	5,952

Percent change:

1950–72	−94.7	−31.6	−67.5	−92.1	−53.6	−62.1
1972–78	−45.6	−2.1	−6.2	−49.0	23.7	13.3

Average annual percent change:[a]

1950–72	−12.5	−1.7	−5.0	−10.9	−3.4	−4.3
1972–78	− 9.6	−0.4	−0.9	−10.6	3.6	2.1

Source: American Public Transit Association, Transit Fact Book '78–'79 (Washington, D.C.: American Public Transit Association, 1980), p. 27.
[a] Calculated by fitting an exponential curve.

Urban congestion and highway performance. The key determinants of urban highway performance are the level and growth of traffic during peak commuter hours at central locations where highway use nears (or sometimes exceeds) capacity. Approaches to central business districts are typically the locations where travel volume is highest, and therefore potential highway congestion problems most serious.[14] But the growth in automobile traffic to downtown areas has usually not kept pace with

TABLE 2.6. Postwar trends in urban public transportation use in eight metropolitan areas.

Metropolitan area	Years of travel data	All trips in the metropolitan area		Worktrips		Nonworktrips		Trips to or from the downtown area	
		Number by public transport (thousands)	Percent by public transport	Number by public transport (thousands)	Percent by public transport	Number by public transport (thousands)	Percent by public transport	Number by public transport (thousands)	Percent by public transport
Chicago	1956	2,414	24.3	664	32.7	1,750	22.2	640	54.9
	1970	1,711	9.2	529	19.1	1,182	7.5	452	51.8
Detroit	1953	879	13.8	460	26.5	419	9.0	174	44.7
	1965	452	4.6	174	8.2	278	3.6	87	28.5
Dallas/	1950–51	206	16.7	115	35.3	91	10.0	100	42.7
Ft. Worth	1964	198	3.5	67	7.0	131	2.8	40	16.3
Minneapolis/	1949	432	26.5	124	33.5	308	24.4	123	39.3
St. Paul	1958	252	7.5	70	12.2	182	6.5	81	26.0
	1970	162	3.3	45	5.4	117	2.8	45	16.7
Denver	1959	83	4.6	*	*	*	*	38	20.1
	1971	58	1.9	*	*	*	*	28	18.1

TABLE 2.6. (Cont.)

Metropolitan area	Years of travel data	All trips in the metropolitan area		Worktrips		Nonworktrips		Trips to or from the downtown area	
		Number by public transport (thousands)	Percent by public transport	Number by public transport (thousands)	Percent by public transport	Number by public transport (thousands)	Percent by public transport	Number by public transport (thousands)	Percent by public transport
Kansas City	1957	161	8.6	*	*	*	*	64	29.6
	1963	*	*	*	*	*	*	*	*
	1970	64	1.7	*	*	*	*	13	12.7
Phoenix	1947	71	12.3	*	*	*	*	*	*
	1957	*	*	*	*	*	*	*	*
Wichita	1951	199	31.2	29	*	*	*	40	19.7
	1960	297	33.9	8	*	*	*	11	7.4

Source: Figures compiled by the authors from various origin-destination surveys.
* Not available.

TABLE 2.7 Postwar trends in vehicles entering the downtown district in five U.S. metropolitan areas (weekdays).

Metropolitan area	Year	Vehicles entering the down-town district			Weekday person-trips by automobile in metropolitan area
		Auto-mobiles	Trucks and buses	Total	
Chicago	1956	108,793	66,397	175,190	7,515,000
	1960	139,275	70,734	210,009	*
	1965	159,965	55,702	215,667	*
	1970	146,582	61,933	208,515	*
	1976	138,846	47,397	186,243	16,905,000
Percent change	1956–76	27.6	−28.6	6.3	124.9
Detroit	1952–53	122,000	34,494	156,494	5,513,000
	1964–65	126,873	22,258	149,131	9,380,000
	1970	125,123	21,118	146,241	*
	1976	112,076	18,801	130,877	*
Percent change	1952–53/1976	−8.1	−45.5	−16.4	70.1
Boston	1954	*	*	260,329	*
	1964	*	*	362,620	*
	1974	*	*	429,276	*
Percent change	1954–74	*	*	64.9	*
Dallas	1946	82,274	30,017	112,291	*
	1958	139,632	30,615	170,247	*
					*
Percent change	1946–58	69.7	2.0	51.6	*
Denver	1962	*	*	191,656	*
	1977	*	*	281,769	*
Percent change	1962–77	*	*	47.0	*

Source: Compiled by the authors from various origin-destination surveys.
* Not available.

the growth in automobile traffic throughout metropolitan areas (see Table 2.7). In Chicago, for example, the number of automobiles entering the heart of the metropolis increased by 28 percent between 1956 and 1976, while automobile persontrips in the metropolitan area as a whole increased by 125 percent.

Slow relative growth in downtown automobile traffic, combined with a considerable expansion in urban highway capacity, has kept perform-

TABLE 2.8.   Trends in postwar urban traffic speeds.

Metropolitan area	Trends in travel speeds	Years of study	Average recorded speed (mph)	Time of day	Location of route
Detroit	Improved	1949	18.2	P.M. peak	Urban but not in CBD[a]
		1961–68	21.2		
Phoenix	Mixed	1947	24.7	Peak	Urban
		1957	29.6		
		1962	28.8		
		1966	26.3		
Phoenix	Degraded	1970	57.9	Peak	Urban
		1976	49.1		
Baltimore	Improved	1961	31.0	Off-peak	Urban
		1968	32.0		
Philadelphia	Degraded	1960	30.5	Off-peak	Suburbs to CBD
		1971	29.1		
Los Angeles	Improved	1957	24.8	Peak	Suburbs to CBD
		1963	30.7		
Washington, D.C.	Improved	1959	16.0	P.M. peak	CBD to ring 25 minutes distant
		1966	18.1		
		1969	19.4		
Milwaukee	Mixed	1946	18.4	7:00 A.M.	CBD to ring 30 minutes distant
		1960	15.3	to	
		1963	20.0	6:00 P.M.	
		1967	24.6		
San Diego	Improved	1955	18.2	Peak	Not given
		1959	26.2		
		1964	39.0		
St. Louis	Improved	1957	23.5	Off-peak	CBD to ring 30 minutes distant
		1965	26.5		
Portland	Improved	1946	20.5	Off-peak	CBD to ring 20 minutes distant
		1960	24.0		
Nashville	Improved	1959	21.0	Peak	Routes serving CBD
		1968	22.0		
Omaha	Degraded	1948	20.0	P.M. peak	CBD to points 3.5–6.5 miles distant
		1969	19.5		

TABLE 2.8.   (*Cont.*)

Metropolitan area	Trends in travel speeds	Years of study	Average recorded speed (mph)	Time of day	Location of route
Akron	Improved	1955 1969	11.3 14.1	4 peak and 1 off-peak routes	Not given
Tucson	Improved	1948 1960	10.5 16.0	P.M. peak	CBD
Madison	Degraded	1949 1962	20.0 19.2	Not given	CBD to 9 points 3 miles distant
Knoxville	Improved	1962 1968	28.1 28.3	P.M. peak	CBD to 9 suburban points
Erie	Degraded	1962 1967	20.0 15.0	Not given	CBD to point 10 minutes distant

Source: Peter G. Koltnow, *Changes in Mobility in American Cities* (Washington, D.C.: Highway Users Federation for Safety and Mobility, 1970), and speed studies compiled by the authors.
[a] CBD = central business district.

ance speeds on centrally located urban highways at reasonably high levels in the postwar years. The only documented case of reduced off-peak highway performance occurred in Philadelphia (see Table 2.8); even then the deterioration was minor, perhaps the result of a measurement or control error. Peak-period performance improved substantially in many cases (San Diego, Tucson, and Los Angeles), although some reduction is evident in others (Erie and Phoenix).[15] While the record is mixed, speeds probably increased slightly (on average) in most U.S. cities during the postwar period.

SUMMARY

Cities around the world—in developed and developing countries, with and without widespread automobile ownership, almost without reference to demographics—have been decentralizing for a century or more (or as long as records have been kept). American cities are no exception, experiencing a particularly rapid decentralization of residences and employment during the post–World War II years. This decentralization, together with a steady rise in real household incomes, encouraged phenomenal growth in urban travel and a dramatic shift from public transportation to the private automobile. In many metropolitan areas the volume of urban travel doubled in fifteen years, and urban automobile use increased at even more rapid rates. Public transportation patronage fell in both absolute and relative terms so that even in the very largest metropolitan areas (with the exception of New York) it now carries 10 percent of all trips at most, and in the smaller metropolitan areas public transportation's share is even smaller, often only 3 or 4 percent.

These postwar trends in metropolitan development and travel, especially the growth in automobile use, are fundamental to most current urban transportation problems. Some of the problems, particularly traffic congestion, have long been recognized by public officials and have been mitigated to some extent by government actions. Traffic congestion, for example, was kept at relatively stable levels by greatly expanding the capacity of the urban highway system. But by moderating traffic congestion, new highways also encouraged growing automobile use, with all of its attendant problems.

PART II
PUBLIC TRANSPORTATION: RETROSPECT AND PROSPECT

3

Government Programs to Revitalize Urban Mass Transportation

POLICY OBJECTIVES

Achieving a "proper" balance between the automobile and public transportation was the central goal of urban transportation policy during the 1960s and early 1970s. With the support of the federal government, ambitious plans were undertaken to arrest, possibly even reverse, the precipitous postwar decline in transit patronage.

But a balance between mass transit and automobile use was not achieved. In 1975, approximately 84 percent of all workers in metropolitan areas commuted in private automobiles or trucks, while only about 8 percent traveled by mass transportation (see Table 3.1). Outside metropolitan areas, the dominance of the automobile was even more complete. Furthermore, the automobile continued to account for a higher percentage of trips for recreation, shopping, personal business, and so forth than for commuting, whether urban or rural.

Although extensive government assistance for urban public transportation in the 1960s and 1970s did not greatly increase transit rider-

TABLE 3.1. Means of commutation, 1975.[a]

| | Total workers in United States | | Workers residing in Standard Metropolitan Statistical Areas (SMSAs) | | | | | | | | Workers residing outside SMSAs | |
| | | | All SMSA residents | | Central city residents | | Suburban residents | | | | | |
	Thousands of workers	Per-cent	Thousands of workers	Per-cent	Thousands of workers	Per-cent	Thousands of workers	Per-cent			Thousands of workers	Per-cent
Private automobile or truck	67,869	84.7	46,498	83.9	17,557	77.2	28,941	88.6			21,371	86.5
Drive alone	52,294	65.3	36,378	65.6	13,622	59.9	22,756	69.7			15,916	64.4
Carpool	15,575	19.4	10,120	18.3	3,935	17.3	6,185	18.9			5,455	22.1
Mass transportation	4,684	5.9	4,525	8.2	3,117	13.7	1,408	4.3			160	0.6
Bus or streetcar	3,100	3.9	2,953	5.3	2,028	8.9	924	2.8			147	0.6
Subway or elevated	1,179	1.5	1,177	2.1	1,037	4.6	141	0.4			2	0.0
Railroad	405	0.5	395	0.7	52	0.2	343	1.1	—		11	0.0
Taxicab	141	0.2	100	0.2	72	0.3	29	0.1			41	0.2
Other means	1,067	1.3	734	1.3	289	1.3	446	1.4			332	1.3
Walked only	3,778	4.7	2,482	4.5	1,350	5.9	1,125	3.4			1,296	5.2
Worked at home	2,585	3.2	1,079	1.9	370	1.6	709	2.2			1,506	6.1
All modes	80,125	100.0	55,418	100.0	22,755	100.0	32,658	100.0			24,706	100.0

Source: U.S. Bureau of the Census, Statistical Abstract of the United States, 1978 (Washington, D.C.: U.S. Government Printing Office, 1978), p. 657.

[a] Excludes workers living in group quarters.

ship or reduce urban automobile use, complete disillusionment with urban public transportation would seem premature. Public transportation is clearly not a remedy for all of urban transportation's ills, but it is still capable of playing a significant role in solving some problems. In this and the next two chapters, an attempt is made to define that role more precisely.

URBAN PUBLIC TRANSPORTATION MODES AND TRENDS

The basic modes. Urban public transportation is usually divided into two categories: "mass transportation," which involves large vehicles, usually seating thirty people or more, and "paratransit," which offers more individualized service in smaller vehicles, such as taxis or vans.

Mass transportation includes "urban transit" and commuter railroads. Urban transit is service within metropolitan areas provided by motor buses, trolley buses, light rail vehicles (streetcars or trolley cars), and heavy rail vehicles (subways, elevated, and surface). Commuter trains provide service much like that of heavy rail transit lines, but are commonly operated by railroads over right-of-ways also used for freight or intercity rail passenger service; they are further distinguished from traditional transit by typically operating over quite long distances, nonstop while in or near the city center, with most residential origins or destinations concentrated in the outer periphery of a metropolitan area.

In 1978, buses carried 71 percent of urban mass transportation passengers and heavy rail vehicles 23 percent.[1] Trolley buses, light rail vehicles, and commuter railroads[2] carried only 0.8, 1.3, and 4.3 percent of mass transportation ridership, respectively.

The major paratransit forms are taxi, dial-a-ride, carpool, and vanpool. Like the taxi, dial-a-ride usually operates door to door and is available on telephone request, but unlike most taxis, a dial-a-ride vehicle will service several passengers simultaneously. In a carpool, two or more individuals travel together in an automobile driven by one of them, often with the passengers taking turns at driving their own automobiles. The term "vanpool" describes large-scale carpooling, as when several people destined for the same workplace commute together in a van with one of the commuters doing the driving.

In 1978, all the mass transportation modes taken together carried only about six billion passengers. By comparison, taxi industry spokesmen estimate that taxis alone carry as many as 2.4 billion passengers per year. Since taxi fares are higher than transit fares, the taxi industry probably collects slightly more in annual revenues than the mass trans-

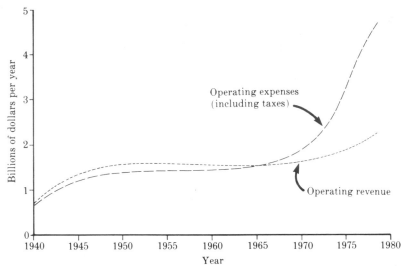

Figure 3.1. Transit industry operating expenses, revenues, and deficits, 1940–1978. (*Source:* American Public Transit Association, *Transit Fact Book, 1980* [Washington, D.C.: American Public Transit Association, 1980].)

portation industry.[3] Carpools and vanpools are also heavily used. In 1978, over 19 percent of all U.S. commuters used some form of carpool or vanpool for their journey to work, for a total of 7.8 billion trips per year.[4]

Patronage and finances. As noted in the last chapter, urban public transportation has suffered from declining patronage in the years since World War II. The decline in ridership actually began in the 1920s and 1930s, but was temporarily halted by wartime fuel rationing and limited automobile production. Transit patronage rose nationwide from 10.5 billion in 1940 to a wartime peak of about 15 billion in 1946, only to fall thereafter until the 1970s. The decline in annual transit ridership was finally halted at 5.3 billion passengers in 1972 and has increased slowly since, reaching 6 billion per year by the end of the decade.

But even as mass transportation ridership stabilized, operating deficits and subsidy requirements continued to rise. The urban transit industry as a whole did not begin to show an operating deficit until the early 1960s, but from the late 1960s on, this deficit grew at a rapid rate, often as much as 20 percent per year (see Figure 3.1). In 1978, transit industry operating revenues (mainly fare-box receipts) covered less than half the industry's operating expenses, and the operating deficit exceeded $2.5 billion per year. Accurate figures on capital investment in the transit industry are not available, but annual capital costs probably amount to at least $1 billion, and possibly more; thus, passenger revenues may have fallen short of total costs (both capital and operating) by at least $3.5 billion per year by the late 1970s.

Commuter railroads operated at a deficit at an earlier date than transit, even though the railroads experienced relatively less patronage decline in the postwar years than transit.[5] Commuter railroad deficits are difficult to measure precisely, since commuter trains share some facilities with freight and intercity passenger trains and cost allocations are necessarily somewhat arbitrary. In 1955, when mass transit as a whole was still profitable, the aggregate commuter railroad operating deficit was estimated at $118 million.[6] Commuter railroad deficits have grown less rapidly, however, than transit deficits. By 1978, the aggregate commuter railroad operating deficit was placed at $408 million.[7]

In terms of dollars per passenger, heavy rail transit and commuter railroads have much higher operating losses than light rail vehicles and motor buses (see Table 3.2). Although the fares are higher per passenger on heavy rail vehicles and commuter railroads, operating costs are higher as well (due partly to longer trip lengths). In 1976, on average, motor buses and light rail vehicles lost only 26 cents per passenger on operations, while heavy rail vehicles and commuter railroads lost 42 cents and $1.24, respectively.[8]

EARLY GOVERNMENT AID: FROM LOCAL SUBSIDIES AND OWNERSHIP TO FEDERAL CAPITAL GRANTS

Although public ownership and control of large transit systems were initiated as early as 1922,[9] local government assistance to urban mass transportation did not begin in earnest until the 1950s. Concern about mass transportation problems spread rapidly during the late 1950s, especially in the major metropolitan areas of the Northeast, which hoped to avoid or postpone construction of expensive new urban highways by stemming ridership declines on their mass transportation systems. Philadelphia, for example, experimented extensively with fare and service changes on its commuter railroad system. In several other cities, rail transit extensions or new systems were planned, often the first to be seriously considered since the 1920s. By far the most ambitious of these efforts was that of the San Francisco Bay area, which, in a 1962 bond referendum, committed itself to construction of a new 71-mile rail transit system.

Because local government financial resources were limited, demands for federal aid rapidly developed.[10] In response, the Housing

TABLE 3.2. Urban mass transportation operating results by mode, 1976.

Mode	Operating expense (thousands of dollars)	Operating revenue (thousands of dollars)	Operating deficit (thousands of dollars)	Ratio of operating revenue to operating expense	Passengers (millions)	Operating expense per passenger (dollars)	Average fare per passenger (dollars)	Operating deficit per passenger (dollars)
Motor bus, trolley bus, and light rail	2,651	1,528	1,123	.58	4,308	.62	.35	.26
Heavy rail	1,188	617	571	.52	1,353	.88	.46	.42
Subtotal, urban transit	3,839	2,145	1,694	.56	5,661	.68	.38	.30
Commuter railroad	657	334	323	.51	260	2.53	1.28	1.24
Total, urban mass transportation	4,496	2,479	2,017	.55	5,921	.76	.42	.34

Source: Transit statistics are from American Public Transit Association, *Transit Fact Book, 1977* (Washington, D.C.: American Public Transit Association, 1978). Commuter railroad statistics are from John Pucher, "Losses in the American Transit Industry: An Analysis of the Variation in Operating Expenses, Revenues, and Ridership Levels by Mode and Urban Area, 1973–1976," technical report no. 2, submitted to the U.S. Department of Transportation under contract no. DOT–05–50240 by the Massachusetts Institute of Technology, Center for Transportation Studies, 1978.

Act of 1961 authorized a $75 million program of mass transportation aid to be disbursed over three years. Two thirds of the funds were for loans to acquire capital equipment; the balance was for demonstration programs to assess possibilities for increasing the demand for public transportation. The capital loan program carried low interest rates, but the loans were small and were granted only when prospects for repayment were reasonable. As it turned out, the loans were so unattractive that the full $50 million authorization was never completely used.

In 1964, Congress passed an Urban Mass Transportation Act that authorized much more generous grants for transit capital outlays [11] This became the single most important government program to aid urban mass transportation; expenditures increased from about $100 million per year in 1964 and 1965 to about $1.3 billion per year by the end of the 1970s.[12] The capital grants could be used for equipment and right-of-way acquisition, for construction, and for the purchase of privately owned companies—but not for operating expenses. The federal government paid up to two thirds (after 1973, 80 percent) of the cost of an approved capital project; the balance came from local government sources. Capital grants were distributed at the discretion of the secretary of transportation, with the restriction that no more than one eighth of the funds go to cities in any one state.[13] The capital grant program and most subsequent programs of federal mass transportation assistance have been administered by the Urban Mass Transportation Administration (UMTA), an agency of the U.S. Department of Transportation.[14]

The original intention in restricting federal assistance to capital expenses was to limit the federal role. Mass transportation was regarded by most congressmen as a local problem, best solved by local initiative and resources. By restricting federal assistance to capital expenses, opponents of aid hoped to limit and distinguish the federal commitment from that of state and local governments. Some believed that capital assistance was less likely to be wasted than operating assistance, since operating subsidies might reduce incentives to control operating costs and could encourage transportation unions to demand higher wages. Many also thought that mass transportation desperately needed more modern, air-conditioned vehicles. Capital assistance thus was seen as providing the one-time shot in the arm that would allow the industry to break its "vicious cycle" of decline.[15]

In the 1960s, purchase of private transportation firms and replacement of existing vehicles absorbed most of the available capital grant funds. As time passed, however, funding levels increased, the number of private firms dwindled, and most vehicles had been replaced. Accordingly, a shift in policy took place: a larger proportion of federal funding was designated for the construction of new rail transit lines. By the mid-1970s, capital grants were split fifty-fifty between the rehabilitation of existing facilities and rolling stock (both bus and rail) and the construction of new rail transit extensions or systems.[16]

The Federal Highway Aid Act of 1970 broke new ground by allowing use of some federal highway moneys for transit purposes, such as constructing bus lanes or parking areas at mass transportation stops. As of 1973, however, only about $64 million in highway aid had been used for such purposes.[17] In 1973, amendments were made to the Federal Highway Aid Program providing that if state and local governments did not wish to construct an urban segment of the Interstate Highway System, and if the secretary of transportation agreed that the segment was not essential, the state could apply to the secretary to use available funds for mass transportation capital projects. The 1973 amendments also provided that, starting in fiscal 1975, state and local governments would have the option of diverting federal aid designated for noninterstate urban road systems to mass transportation projects.[18]

EVALUATION OF THE CAPITAL GRANT PROGRAM

Ridership and operating deficits. By the late 1960s, it was evident that new capital equipment and new transit lines had not attracted large numbers of new riders. Where new ridership did develop, moreover, only a small fraction were former automobile users; thus there was little reduction in highway congestion.

Despite the capital grant program, mass transportation operating deficits increased nationwide. In some cities, capital grants may have hindered rather than helped the financial situation by encouraging uneconomic expansion of mass transportation services. Local governments, for example, were saddled with new financial obligations when federal capital aid prompted them to buy out ailing, privately owned transit companies that could not cover their operating expenses out of the fare box.

It is unclear whether local officials realized the effects that additional services could have on their operating budgets. Some may have believed that the services, with a new infusion of capital, would break even; others may have anticipated operating losses, but considered them worthwhile in light of social or political benefits. Whatever the motivations, federal capital grants often meant additional local operating losses (and therefore pressures for further federal aid).

The shortcomings of capital grant programs designed to attract new ridership and to stem operating losses became especially apparent when new rail transit lines and systems opened for business. The Bay Area Rapid Transit (BART) system in San Francisco, part of which opened in 1972, with full operation in 1974, is a dramatic example.[19]

In the original BART plan, it was anticipated that fare-box revenues would cover all operating expenses and the capital costs of the rolling stock (the rest of the capital was to be paid through property taxes). In practice, fare-box revenues covered only a third of the operating expenses and made no contribution to capital costs. In 1976, the average fare on BART was 72 cents, while the operating cost per rider was about $1.95. It has been calculated that public subsidies to the BART system in 1976—including both operating aid and amortized capital assistance— amounted to $3.76 per rider. Since approximately 38 percent of the BART riders were former bus users, the cost in public subsidy per passenger attracted from private to public transportation averaged a staggering $6.08. And since only 35 percent of all BART riders in 1976 were former automobile users, the subsidy for attracting these passengers to BART amounted to $10.74.[20]

Extensions to existing rail transit systems in Cleveland, Chicago, and other cities produced similarly disappointing results. The federally funded extension of the Cleveland rail transit system to Hopkins Airport in 1968 added four route-miles to the original 15-mile system. This extension attracted an additional 400,000 to one million riders per year above the system's previous patronage of about 16 million. But only 8 percent of the new riders were former automobile users, most of the balance coming from other modes of public transportation (especially airport limousines and taxicabs). Not surprisingly, the reduction in traffic congestion on routes to the airport was estimated to be small.[21]

Another federally funded transit route that opened in the late 1960s was the 9.5-mile extension of a rail transit system down the median of the Dan Ryan Expressway in Chicago. This new line also diverted travelers from existing public transportation service; over 80 percent were former users of other transit lines, 6 percent had never made the trip before, and only 8 percent were former automobile users.[22]

Capital grants and inefficiency. The original restriction of federal aid to capital expenses created incentives for local operating authorities to use federally funded capital outlays to reduce operating expenses paid for locally. As a result, premature retirement has been made of mass transportation vehicles, particularly buses. It has been estimated that because of this about one fifth of the value of federal capital grants may have been wasted.[23] Similarly, and perhaps more significantly, when the federal government pays up to 80 percent of the capital expenses of new systems but none of the operating costs, local governments are encouraged to employ more highly capitalized rail systems in place of less capital-intensive buses, even if buses are cheaper overall.

Numerous studies have compared the costs of metropolitan rail and bus commuting. Such cost comparisons are meaningful, of course, only if the two transit modes are providing roughly equivalent service. While it is difficult to make all aspects of service identical, cost studies usually set the ratio of seated to standing passengers the same on both modes and establish bus system travel times comparable to those of rail (for example, by operating the buses on an exclusive busway or an expressway whose access ramps are controlled to ensure relatively free-flowing traffic).[24] These cost studies generally show that in a radial corridor with hourly transit volumes below 15,000 passengers in the weekday peak periods, bus is less expensive than rail. When a peak-hour corridor volume is more than 30,000 passengers, rail is usually less expensive than bus. For corridor volumes between 15,000 and 30,000, the costs of the two modes are often close, and their rank depends upon specific characteristics such as the cost of land, the prevailing wage rates for transit drivers, or the existence of controlled-access expressways that can be used by bus.[25] Radial corridor volumes above 15,000 persons per peak hour—the minimum necessary to consider rail transit economic—can be found in only a score of U.S. metropolitan areas, usually those areas with populations of several million or more, with high population densities, and with large employment concentrations in the metropolitan center.[26]

It is therefore significant and unfortunate that the availability of federal capital grants strongly encouraged the planning and construction of new rail systems and extensions to old ones. Between World War II and the start of the capital grant program in 1964, only five extensions were made to existing rail systems, and only two metropolitan areas—Cleveland and San Francisco—undertook entirely new systems. In contrast, during the first decade of the capital grant program, construction began on twelve extensions to existing rail systems and on three entirely new systems (in Washington, D.C., Atlanta, and Baltimore).[27] Since 1974, the federal government has made commitments to fund new rail systems in three other cities—Miami, Honolulu, and Buffalo. Several other metropolitan areas have applied for new, federally supported rail systems. But most of the new rail systems under construction or consideration are in metropolitan areas without sufficient population or density to support efficient rail service, or are systems that include lines extended to distances where travel volumes are too low for economic operations.[28]

In addition to its other disadvantages, the restriction of federal assistance to capital expenses did not limit the federal government's role in mass transportation aid, as some supporters had hoped. Applications for capital grants grew more rapidly than available funds, as more and more cities began to modernize their bus and rail fleets or planned new rail systems or extensions. The demand for federal capital aid seemed nearly inexhaustible, so long as only a small local matching contribution was required.[29]

THE 1970s: NEW EXPERIMENTS IN TRANSIT AID

Federal and local operating assistance. In 1974, mass transportation administrators and local government officials finally succeeded in persuading Congress to authorize and fund federal grants for operating as well as capital expenses. Political pressure for operating aid had come primarily from two groups of cities: those too small to consider rail mass transportation (who found that capital expenses were only a small portion of bus transit costs) and the larger, older cities whose rail systems predated federal aid and who felt that the restriction of aid to capital expenses penalized them for foresight in building their rail systems early. The new operating grant program[30] was initially authorized at a level of $3.5 billion over six years, with the annual rate of disbursement increasing from $300 million in fiscal 1975 to $900 million in fiscal 1980.[31]

Operating grants were to be distributed among metropolitan areas according to a formula specified in the authorizing legislation (unlike capital grants, which are distributed largely at the discretion of the secretary of transportation). The formula, designed by Congress to ensure that the grants are not monopolized by a few large metropolitan areas, is based on population and population density. It provides much higher operating assistance per passenger in small urban areas than in the larger and older urban areas where mass transportation ridership is concentrated. For example, the metropolitan area comprising New York City and northern New Jersey, which contains about 38 percent of the nation's mass transportation ridership, has received only 18 percent of this operating aid, while urban areas with populations between 50,000 and 100,000, which contain only 4 percent of mass transportation ridership, were allocated about 12 percent of the assistance.

Initially, the operating grants did little to alleviate the financial strain of operating deficits in larger and older metropolitan areas: local governments in these areas were still required to fund about 80 percent of their mass transportation operating deficits, while governments in small metropolitan areas paid only about half of theirs. In some small metropolitan areas, where service had been severely curtailed or abandoned altogether, the availability of federal operating assistance encouraged substantial expansion.[32] In 1978, Congress increased operating aid for large cities through two new, smaller grant programs that mainly provided operating funds for urban areas with populations over 750,000 or with rail systems. Under the 1978 legislation, the federal government was authorized to provide a total of roughly $1.4 billion per year in operating aid for mass transportation through fiscal 1982.[33]

Federal grants for operating expenses did not forestall increases in state and local operating aid. During the 1970s, state aid for operating expenses showed a particularly large growth. A number of states established their own grant programs to aid localities hard pressed by operating deficits. Local government assistance increased as well. In a few metropolitan areas, voters granted transit authorities powers to levy regional sales, gasoline, or property taxes to finance transit operations. In 1972, for example, voters in several Georgia counties created a transit agency, the Metropolitan Atlanta Regional Transit Authority (MARTA), with the power to levy up to a 1 percent regional sales tax.[34]

The results of all this aid were disappointing. In the case of urban transit, for which the data are most complete, nationwide ridership increased from about 5.3 billion trips per year in the early 1970s to only about 6.0 billion trips in 1978, even though operating aid grew from approximately $0.5 billion per year (or 10 cents per rider) to $2.5 billion (or 40 cents per rider) during that period.[35] Much of the aid was dissipated, though, by unusually rapid cost inflation in the mass transportation industry, so that the effects on fares and service offerings were smaller than expected. For example, during the 1970s, the cost of providing a vehicle-mile of transit service increased far more rapidly than the consumer price index—rising from a nationwide average of about $1.75 in 1970 to $2.32 in 1978, measured in constant 1978 dollars.[36] As a result, much of the massive increase in operating aid allowed nationwide average fares to decline only slightly in real terms, from about 44 to 38 cents in constant 1978 dollars.[37] Similarly, the number of vehicle-miles of service offered nationwide increased by only 7 percent.[38]

Many factors contributed to the unusually rapid rise in mass transportation costs, including a lengthening of trips (due to suburbanization) and the increased concentration of ridership during the morning and evening rush hours.[39] The availability of operating assistance itself probably contributed to cost inflation by weakening the incentives of mass transportation managers to control expenses, improve productivity, and resist union demands for higher wages. It is notable that while transportation employees' wages increased rather slowly in the 1950s and early 1960s, once substantial public aid was made available in the 1970s, the average wage rates of mass transportation employees increased more rapidly than those of other industrial workers.[40]

But even in those metropolitan areas where operating aid made significant fare reductions and service improvements possible, the resulting increases in ridership were often small.[41] The effects of fare and service improvements on ridership in Boston and Atlanta serve as typical examples.

In Boston, the operating subsidy for mass transportation increased from approximately $80 million in 1971 to $240 million in 1979, while revenue remained relatively constant at $50-$60 million per year. The operating aid was used to maintain existing service and to keep the transit fare at 25 cents, despite rapid inflation in operating costs. Since the consumer price index more than doubled between 1971 and 1979, retaining the 25-cent fare actually amounted to reducing the fare by half, in real dollars, over the course of the decade. Despite this substantial price discount, the ridership on the Boston lines remained stable or declined slightly.

In Atlanta, with its new sales tax to finance transit subsidies, MARTA reduced the transit fare from 40 to 15 cents and increased bus service by 30 percent. At most, these changes brought approximately 8.2 million new passengers per year to the Atlanta mass transportation system and, in the first year, increased the operating deficit by approximately $12 million for an average subsidy of $1.45 per new rider. Since 62 percent of the new riders had previously made their trips by car, the operating subsidy to attract these passengers amounted to $2.35 per rider. Furthermore, only 42 percent of these new riders had formerly made the trip as a driver (as opposed to an automobile passenger), so the cost in subsidy per automobile vehicle trip removed from the road amounted to $3.48 (in 1972 dollars).[42]

A few metropolitan areas were relatively successful, though, in attracting new patronage to mass transportation. Six cities[43] increased ridership by 40 percent or more in the 1970s, at a cost of not much more than 30 to 50 cents per passenger.[44] These successes were partly attributable, however, to unusual circumstances or to other policies besides service expansion; a few of these cities, for example, had allowed transit service to deteriorate to unusually low levels before operating aid was provided. In some cases, ridership gains were partly due to policies restraining automobile use, such as parking regulations and bus priority over automobiles in traffic, rather than vehicle improvements or fare reductions. Nevertheless, these positive experiences suggest that operating aid can be successful in certain situations.

Encouraging more efficient use of aid. The 1970s also saw the introduction of regulations and other measures designed to reduce inefficiency in the use of federal grants and, particularly, to encourage low-cost options to rail systems. The first such proposals were advanced in 1972 and required that every application for a rail transit grant include a comparison of the costs of alternative modes.[45] In 1975, UMTA and the Federal Highway Administration jointly promulgated regulations requiring that before urban areas receive capital grants they must submit a Transportation System Management (TSM) plan showing that they are using their existing highway and transit facilities effectively.[46] These regulations were further tightened in 1978, when UMTA specified that any new rail systems must be approved and built only in stages, with preference given to the sections serving the most densely populated central portions of metropolitan areas.[47]

During the 1970s UMTA's research, development, and demonstration (RD&D) program was also reoriented so as to place greater emphasis on the investigation of low-cost techniques to improve mass transportation service. Hardware and technology development still absorbed the majority of UMTA's annual RD&D budget,[48] but a large share of the funds was shifted to developing and demonstrating the potential of fare and service innovations on conventional transit service, paratransit services (particularly dial-a-ride), and improved transit management and planning.[49]

The overall impact of these changes is difficult to determine. The regulations were not popular with UMTA's traditional supporters and constituents—the mass transportation industry and big cities. Some observers argue that UMTA altered its regulations only because applications for assistance grew more rapidly than available funding, so that the agency was forced to develop criteria in order to select the most deserving pending applications.[50] Even if there were enthusiastic acceptance of the regulations, effective enforcement would be difficult to bring about because noncompliance is hard to detect and to demonstrate.

Mobility for the poor, the elderly, and the handicapped. During the 1970s, special programs and regulations also were introduced to ensure that mass transportation be made accessible to persons with mobility problems—particularly the elderly, the poor, and the physically handicapped. The essence of these special programs, decribed in detail in

Chapter 12, was that UMTA would require all new transit buses purchased with federal aid to have low floors and an ability to "kneel" at stops for easy boarding, as well as ramps or hydraulic lifts to accommodate wheelchairs. UMTA also considered regulations—again as a condition for federal aid—that all new and many existing rail transit and commuter rail vehicles and stations be equipped with elevators, lifts, and other facilities for the handicapped. Meeting these requirements could be extremely costly, calling for either additional aid for mass transportation or diverting aid from existing services (and thereby decreasing ridership). Furthermore, as explained in Chapter 12, these proposals would improve the mobility of disadvantaged groups only to a limited extent, especially compared with other alternatives.

PROSPECTS FOR MASS TRANSPORTATION RIDERSHIP

A major public policy lesson of the 1960s and 1970s was that government aid, whether in the form of capital or operating grants, failed to bring about a significant increase in urban mass transportation ridership. The growth in government aid during these decades was spectacular: from negligible levels in the 1950s to amounts equal to more than half of all industry operating expenses and almost all capital expenses by 1980. The decline in mass transportation ridership was arrested by the 1970s, but only in congruence with the pressures created by the oil embargo of 1973.[51]

Mass transportation apparently remains competitive with the automobile in only two major markets. The first of these is radial commuting trips to the centers of large and dense metropolitan areas, especially those with limited or old highway networks. In these circumstances, the quality of automobile service is relatively low because highways are congested, and the out-of-pocket costs of an automobile trip can be high (say, because parking is expensive). In contrast, the large number of commuters in these radial corridors of larger and denser metropolitan areas allows mass transportation vehicles to operate at convenient intervals while achieving the economies of relatively full passenger loads. Mass transportation's advantages in this type of market can often be further enhanced if bus speeds are increased by providing express service or by adopting inexpensive traffic management and bus priority schemes.[52]

It is difficult to determine a priori how large or congested a metropolitan area must be for mass transportation to capture a significant share of the ridership market. A number of studies have concluded, however, that mass transportation can achieve service and costs roughly comparable to those of a private automobile (including highway costs) when there are as few as 3,000 to 7,000 travelers per peak hour bound for the central business district (CBD). Estimates citing 3,000 travelers are for situations in which there are long commuting trip lengths, dense residential areas, and compact downtown areas, while estimates of 7,000 travelers are for comparatively short trips and dispersed residential and downtown areas.[53] Table 3.3 shows that volumes of 3,000 and 7,000 travelers per peak hour can be found in urban areas with populations as low as 250,000 to 550,000, if the downtown area is vital.

The second major market where mass transportation has a competi-

TABLE 3.3. Peak-hour travel demand in typical urban areas with a vital (strong) CBD during the 1950s and 1960s.

	Population of the urban area			
	250,000	500,000	1,000,000	2,000,000
Weekday trips to CBD	40,000	80,000	135,000	225,000
Peak-hour (P.M.) *trips from CBD:*				
Total	16,000	32,000	54,000	100,000
In heaviest-traveled route	4,000–5,600	8,000–11,000	13,500–19,000	25,000–33,000
Number by transit in heaviest-traveled route	400–800	2,000–3,300	5,400–8,500	12,500–21,300
Percent by transit in heaviest-traveled route	10–14	25–30	40–45	50–65

Source: Adapted from Herbert S. Levinson, Crosby L. Adams, and William F. Hoey, *Bus Use of Highways: Planning and Design Guidelines*, National Cooperative Highway Research Report No. 155 (Washington, D.C.: Transportation Research Board, 1975), p. 25; F. Houston Wynn and Herbert S. Levinson, "Some Considerations in Appraising Bus Transit Potentials," *Highway Research Record 197*, Highway Research Board, Washington, D.C., 1967, p. 4 (used with permission of the Transportation Research Board, Washington, D.C.); Wilbur Smith Associates, *Transportation and Parking for Tomorrow's Cities*, report for the Automobile Manufacturers Association (Detroit: Automobile Manufacturers Association, 1966), p. 294; and John R. Meyer, John F. Kain, and Martin Wohl, *The Urban Transportation Problem* (Cambridge, Mass.: Harvard University Press, 1965), esp. p. 86.

tive edge is in neighborhoods that have extremely high population densities and many low-income residents—neighborhoods such as those found near the centers of many large metropolitan areas.[54] High population density and low incomes often ensure sufficient transit demand so that mass transportation vehicles can operate on conveniently frequent schedules and still maintain full loads. High density is also associated with high levels of street congestion and parking costs, which make the automobile less attractive. Commuter trips in these situations also tend to be short, so that mass transportation service discomforts may be more tolerable and speed disadvantages less significant.

As mass transportation ridership has declined over the postwar period, the passenger (and financial) losses have tended to be smallest in these traditional big-city and downtown-oriented markets. Table 3.4 shows the operating ratios—the ratio of operating expenses to operating revenue (mostly from fares)—for different types of bus routes in a typical large northeastern metropolitan area in the early 1970s. Not only do inner-city and express radial routes have by far the best operating ratios, but in this particular city they actually generate operating profits. On the other hand, crosstown routes (which usually do not pass through the CBD) and suburban routes incur substantial operating deficits.

Among the various forms of mass transportation, the urban bus is most likely to earn an operating profit, whereas suburban bus, rail transit, and commuter railroad are the least likely to do so. Table 3.5 shows the operating expenses, fares, and operating deficits (operating expenses minus fares), for different mass transportation modes in eight

TABLE 3.4. Operating ratios[a] on different types of bus transit routes in a typical large metropolitan area, early 1970s.[b]

Type of route	Operating ratio	Percent of total operating expenses incurred on route
Inner-city and short radial	.75	53
Express radial	.98	19
Crosstown[c]	1.37	21
Suburban[d]	1.52	7
All routes	.91	100

[a] Ratio of operating expenses to operating revenues.
[b] These data were supplied under the condition that the name of the metropolitan area not be given. The metropolitan area contains a population of over one million.
[c] Crosstown routes cross major radial routes at right angles.
[d] Routes entirely within the suburbs.

TABLE 3.5.   Mass transportation operating expenses, fares, and operating deficits by mode in eight major metropolitan areas, 1976.

	Urban bus (dollars)	Suburban bus (dollars)	Subway or elevated (dollars)	Commuter rail (dollars)	All modes[a] (dollars)
Operating expense per passenger:					
New York	.58	.88	.83	3.09	.91
Chicago	.38	.71	.78	1.38	.50
Boston		1.09	1.37	3.25	1.31
Philadelphia	.61	.73	.68	2.22	.80
Cleveland		.46	.88	—	.53
San Francisco/Oakland	.66	.86	1.79	3.07	.93
Detroit	.82	1.33	—	2.69	.87
Washington, D.C.		.91	[b]	2.22	.93
Average fare per passenger:					
New York	.45	.71	.46	1.56	.56
Chicago	.25	.42	.35	.96	.33
Boston		.34	.44	.88	.41
Philadelphia	.30	.35	.40	.83	.38
Cleveland		.17	.19	—	.19
San Francisco/Oakland	.21	.37	.73	.98	.34
Detroit	.42	.65	—	.95	.44
Washington, D.C.		.52	[b]	.95	.53
Operating deficit per passenger:					
New York	.13	.17	.37	1.53	.35
Chicago	.13	.29	.43	.42	.17
Boston		.75	.93	2.37	.90
Philadelphia	.31	.38	.28	1.39	.42
Cleveland		.29	.69	—	.34
San Francisco/Oakland	.45	.49	1.06	2.09	.59
Detroit	.40	.68	—	1.74	.43
Washington, D.C.		.39	[b]	1.27	.40

Source: John Pucher, "Losses in the American Transit Industry: An Analysis of the Variation in Operating Expenses, Revenues, and Ridership Levels by Mode and Urban Area, 1973–1976," technical report no. 2 under U.S. Department of Transportation contract no. DOT–05–50240 to the Center for Transportation Studies of the Massachusetts Institute of Technology, January 1978.

[a] Weighted average.
[b] The Washington, D.C., subway system was not open for service in 1976.

major metropolitan areas in 1976. Operating expenses per passenger are higher on rail transit, commuter rail, and suburban bus than on urban bus, partly because of longer average trip lengths and (especially in the cases of many suburban bus and commuter rail lines) low traffic volumes. Although average fares are also often higher on rail and suburban buses, they are usually not high enough to offset the additional expense; thus the operating deficit per passenger is typically greater on suburban bus or rail than on urban bus.

Mass transportation costs have been increased, even in the best markets, moreover, by a steady rise in the proportion of trips made during the peak weekday morning and evening rush hours. During the off-peak hours, automobile travel becomes more attractive because highways are less congested. The personal business, shopping, and recreational trips that are typical of travel in the off-peak hours are also often made in family groups, so that the automobile cost per passenger is relatively low. The result has been a concentration of transit trips in the peak period such that mass transportation systems are increasingly undcrused for all but a few hours each weekday. When mass transportation right-of-ways, equipment, and employees are idle during the off-peak period, this increases the costs borne by peak-period travelers.

The situations in which mass transportation tends to be most competitive—radial commuting and inner-city trips in large metropolitan areas— are also precisely those in which increased automobile use can create the most serious problems. Traffic congestion is almost always much more serious in larger and older metropolitan areas than in smaller and newer ones. Certain automobile-related problems, such as air pollution, tend to be most severe during the rush hours and close to the downtown area. Substituting conventional mass transportation for automobile trips during the peak hours can therefore make an important contribution.

It is ironic that the mass transportation trips that make the largest contribution to resolving urban transportation problems are also the trips that least need special subsidies. Efforts to spread conventional mass transportation patronage far beyond its traditional and most advantageous markets are, thus, not only costly and difficult to implement but may also contribute little to dealing with the problems associated with urban automobile use.

The need for public assistance might also be reduced if the productivity of mass transportation could be improved and if other forms of public or quasi-public transportation, such as carpooling and vanpooling, were selectively encouraged. These and other possibilities for improving the capabilities of public transportation, conventional and unconventional, are investigated in the next two chapters.

4

*Improving
Conventional
Mass
Transportation*

PRODUCTIVITY: THE RECORD

Productivity is normally deemed to have improved in an industry if outputs increase more rapidly than inputs. When output is measured in terms of the amount of transportation services provided to passengers (for example, passengers carried or passenger-miles), the productivity of urban mass transportation has decreased at an average rate of about 1 percent a year since the end of World War II.[1] Much of this decline in productivity can be attributed, however, to the insistence of public officials that extensive route networks and schedules be maintained despite sharp declines in patronage.[2] Abstracting from these considerations, mass transportation productivity may have actually increased in the postwar period, perhaps by as much as 1 percent a year.[3]

But even using this generous estimate, the rate of productivity improvement in mass transportation has fallen far short of that for the economy as a whole, which was experiencing productivity gains averaging about 2.5 percent per year in recent decades.[4] Mass transportation also makes a poor showing compared to other roughly comparable transportation sectors, such as trucking and intercity buses. In the postwar years, the truckers have had a productivity growth record of close to 2.5 percent per year, the average for the entire economy. The intercity bus lines have done about half as well.[5]

Mass transportation's poor productivity record helps explain the general decline in the industry's fortunes and, to some extent, the limited ability of public policies to reverse the trend toward other forms of urban travel. All else being equal, low productivity growth raises costs and prices, which makes an industry less attractive to consumers. Productivity improvement may not by itself assure the prosperity and growth of an industry, but it is almost always helpful.[6]

This chapter will identify possibilities for improving the productivity of the mass transportation industry with existing technology and services. In the next chapter, more unconventional possibilities will be explored.

ALLEVIATING THE PEAKING PROBLEM

The peaking of travel demand in the morning and evening rush hours creates serious problems for the transit industry by causing underutilization of labor and equipment for all but a few hours per day. Moreover, the share of mass transportation trips made during the peak hours has increased over the postwar period and is likely to continue to do so.

Peaking problems are exacerbated by work rules and labor practices limiting the use of part-time or split-shift drivers.[7] One transit operator in San Diego, using computerized scheduling techniques, estimated that an increase in the maximum length of split shifts from 11.0 to 12.5 hours would decrease total operating labor costs by 21.5 percent.[8] In Toronto, it was forecast that the same work-rule change would decrease labor costs by 17 percent.[9]

The exact gains to be made from work-rule changes vary among transit operations and can only be estimated by detailed schedule simulations. Until recently, so many specialized skills and repetitive calculations were required to do this that estimating the gain from a work-rule change was often regarded as prohibitively expensive. With the development of computerized scheduling techniques, work-rule changes can now be costed to a reasonable degree of accuracy relatively cheaply. Nevertheless, widespread implementation of computer scheduling is still impeded by the financial and managerial limitations of the industry.

The financial burden of peaking could also be alleviated by finding other tasks for mass transportation drivers to do during the off-peak hours. In implementing such a solution, there might be two groups of drivers: a cadre who drive during both peak and off-peak hours, and a group of part-time or peak-only drivers. The peak-only drivers might have full- or part-time jobs elsewhere, either in the mass transportation firm or outside. If the part-timers were employed outside, this arrangement would parallel certain existing arrangements for providing school bus and some other public services.[10] If the part-time drivers were full-time employees of the mass transportation operation, they might perform light maintenance or bookkeeping, or drive jitneys or taxis in the off-peak hours.[11]

A taxi-driving option would be particularly efficient where taxi ridership does not peak during the hours of highest transit use.[12] Mass transportation drivers could also staff the special transportation services for the elderly, handicapped, and poor that their firms are under increasing public pressure to provide. These services can be very labor intensive (often involving door-to-door transportation) and, unlike regular transit, are generally used for nonworktrips, so that they often experience peak demand during the midday hours.

Another approach to alleviating peaking problems would be to reduce the number of vehicles used during the peak hours. Such a reduction might be made, for example, by using buses larger than the industry's standard 40-foot, 45-passenger model during peak periods. Double-deckers or articulated vehicles could provide the same number of passengers with service, making fewer trips and using fewer drivers. Labor savings, moreover, would offset the higher capital costs in most situations.[13] Seat-for-seat replacement of conventional buses by larger vehicles would cause an increase in "headways" (the waiting time between buses). But if the oversized vehicles were confined to busy routes for which headways are already quite short, or to lightly traveled routes where headways are already so long that passengers are accustomed to meeting specific schedules, there would be little reduction in perceived service quality.

Use of smaller buses during the off-peak periods might also improve productivity. During these hours, on lightly patronized routes, conventional 40-foot buses operate with relatively small loads. In these circumstances, the frequency of service is determined more by the need to offer passengers convenient schedules than by the capacity of the vehicles. It should cost substantially less to purchase, fuel, and, perhaps, maintain smaller vehicles than the standard bus.[14] Should a mass transportation company provide jitney or taxi service to make better use of the off-peak time of regular drivers, a fleet of small vehicles would also be appropriate.[15]

Another means of reducing peak-period labor and vehicle requirements would be to increase average vehicle speeds by using more peak-hour express buses,[16] establishing priority bus lanes on highways and streets during rush hours, and improving traffic management.[17] By reducing running times, these changes decrease the number of drivers and vehicles required to make a given number of trips.[18]

Peak-period labor and vehicle needs might also be reduced by discouraging peak-hour travel. This might be done by charging a higher fare during peak hours than off-peak hours.[19] Since mass transportation usage is generally not overly responsive to fare changes, the reduction in peak demand might be small. But even a small decline in peak use could be helpful in cutting mass transportation expenses, since peak-hour use determines the number of vehicles needed and, under current labor practices, much of labor expense as well. Higher peak fares may also be justifiable because the higher labor and vehicle costs associated with peak service mean that a peak-hour passenger usually costs more to carry.[20]

ADAPTING TO NEW MARKETS AND DISCONTINUING LESS PRODUCTIVE SERVICES

A key determinant of the productivity of any industry or firm is the degree to which it successfully identifies and serves markets where it has a comparative advantage. Unfortunately, public officials have not encouraged, or allowed, the mass transportation industry to concentrate on the two markets where it best competes with the automobile: (1) rush hour commuting to the centers of large, high-density, and congested metropolitan areas; and (2) trips from inner-city, low-income neighborhoods to central business districts. Governments often insist that new and different service be provided—such as off-peak, cross-town, and suburban service—as a condition for subsidy.

These "extended" services have been motivated by public officials' desire to broaden the political base for mass transportation subsidies (at both the federal and metropolitan levels) and a sincere belief in their social benefits. But fare-box revenues seldom come near to paying for these services, and officials have seldom been willing to subsidize them fully. As a consequence, mass transportation firms often have been forced to cross-subsidize publicly mandated services with revenues generated from their few profitable activities.

Cross-subsidies hurt the mass transportation industry's ability to compete in its most advantageous markets since they force either higher fares or a lower quality of service than otherwise might be the case. Inner-city routes have been especially burdened by the demands of cross-subsidization, although other short radial commuting lines are often adversely affected as well.

Cross-subsidy is also linked to overreliance on uniform fares[21] and service offerings, weaknesses common to many mass transportation operations. Uniformity stands in sharp contrast to the diverse needs of travelers in different markets. In particular, the relative importance of fares and service quality would appear to be significantly different in mass transportation's two major markets: radial commuting and inner-city travel. Passengers commuting between the suburbs and the downtown area are usually more sensitive to service quality than to fares because their trips are long and because they generally have high incomes. On the other hand, inner-city passengers are less willing to pay for higher-quality service since they usually travel for short distances, have lower average incomes, and have a variety of feasible options, such as walking or taxi.

Uniform fares also ignore differences in the costs of providing service. Commuting trips between the downtown area and the suburbs are almost invariably more expensive to service than inner-city trips; not only are the suburban trips longer, but they are more heavily concentrated in peak hours (when the real cost of adding operating labor and vehicles is highest). By contrast, inner-city trips are shorter, and a sizable proportion take place during the off-peak hours (for shopping or recreational purposes).

Using the same fares and offering the same quality of service for radial commuting as for inner-city markets may thus reduce patronage unnecessarily. For example, in longer-distance radial markets, uniform fares may discourage desired premium service. Some suburban commuters may not only find a flat low fare a small attraction, but would be more than willing to pay for better services such as express operation, assurance of a seat, more comfortable seating, or air conditioning.

The merits of increasing service and fares on radial commuting routes are borne out by the fact that the few remaining private transit firms in large cities that have survived have done so largely because they adopted such policies. For example, in Boston and New York, several small private operators provide express service from outer suburban communities to the central business district using comfortable buses and assured seating. These companies are able to charge fares high enough to cover costs, usually more than double or triple the fares charged by the local public transportation authority on parallel routes that offer competing but lower-quality service.

Uniform fares and service may discourage inner-city transit patronage as well. Although inner-city trips are generally less expensive to service than suburban trips, and therefore are relatively profitable when a flat fare is charged (see Tables 3.4 and 3.5), the higher markup on short trips implicit in a flat-fare structure will encourage the use of alternatives, such as walking or taxis. Inner-city riders also tend to be more price conscious since they usually have lower incomes. Because the trips are shorter, moreover, certain commonly provided service amenities, such as air conditioning, may not be worth their added cost.

Mass transportation in both radial commuting and inner-city markets might also be aided by changes in routes and timetables. In virtually every metropolitan area, new residential, shopping, and employment areas have developed, while others have declined. New freeways or arterials have often opened that permit higher traffic speeds and alter the attractiveness of mass transportation routings. Where such changes have occurred, passenger satisfaction can be greatly enhanced at little cost by extending routes slightly or shifting them a street or two so as to improve access, coordinating schedules so that transfers require less waiting, or combining routes to eliminate transfers altogether.

Identifying improvements of this kind often requires careful analysis, of a kind greatly facilitated by computerized scheduling. A change in service on one route can affect costs and service on almost all routes, since vehicles and drivers are commonly "interlined" among routes to improve productivity.[22] And again, a change in service at one hour of the day can also affect the costs of services at other hours because of the complex work rules governing the use of split shifts.

In summary, mass transportation could do more to tailor the quality of its service, fare, route, and schedule offerings to the different needs of its markets. In longer-distance radial commuting, quality might be upgraded through greater use of high-speed express bus services, greater availability of seats, and air conditioning. In addition, fares might be raised, in some cases substantially, to reflect the costs of these amenities, longer distances, and higher concentrations of peak-hour traveling. In inner-city markets, on the other hand, quality improvements may be less important and the value attached to certain amenities, such as air conditioning, might be questioned. Fares, in contrast, may be quite significant in these markets. Finally, routes and schedules should be adjusted to reflect the changes constantly occurring in cities as new centers of activity emerge, others decline, and still others relocate.

SPECIALIZATION AND CONTRACTING OUT

Greater specialization has long been suggested as a means of improving the transit industry's productivity. The obvious way to do this would be to contract out routine tasks—such as maintenance, administration, and bookkeeping—to others.[23] A competitive contracting procedure (for example, through sealed bids) might provide strong incentives for the suppliers to perform tasks efficiently, possibly by adopting productivity improvements that have eluded the transit industry.

A number of municipal services have, in fact, achieved significant savings by contracting with outsiders. Such savings are best documented in the case of refuse collection.[24] In many of the nation's largest metropolitan areas—including New York, San Francisco, and Boston—publicly operated refuse collection is supplemented with private carting that is either contracted by the relevant public agency or operates in competition with it. In New York City, the cost per ton of garbage collected by private carting companies is less than half the cost per ton of refuse collected by public carters.[25] Similarly, in Douglaston (a New York City suburb with large, single-family residences), twice-a-week public collection of garbage at the curbside costs $207 per dwelling per year, while in Bellerose (a similar municipality four miles away), a private carting firm under contract to the city collects refuse three times a week from behind the house for only $72 per year. Comparable savings have also been experienced in Boston and San Francisco.[26]

Many other municipal services have been provided under contract. Contracting for school bus services and snow removal is routine. Street cleaning, road repair, and the towing of abandoned or illegally parked cars are other common examples. In a few municipalities, even public safety services are contracted out. Firefighting is done by private firms in Scottsdale, Arizona, and private emergency ambulance services are provided under contract in sections of New York City, Los Angeles, and in many smaller cities. Even police services are sometimes put out to bid. For example, some New York City housing projects are patrolled by private guards.[27] The large variation in the costs of performing certain tasks among mass transportation firms (such as engine rebuilding) suggests the potential gain in contracting out mass transportation activities.[28] Some of the cost variation is undoubtedly due to differences in local operating conditions and the types of service provided, but a large part is probably attributable to managerial and labor differences.

Some moderate-sized, publicly owned mass transportation firms now do contract with private companies for management services. In general, only the top executives are supplied by the private management firm, and all other managers, supervisors, and workers remain employees of the public authority. The management company is usually given limited discretion over marketing and operating decisions and labor negotiations. The majority of these management contracts are held by four companies that in the 1930s and 1940s, when the industry was more profitable, had been holding companies owning numerous mass transportation firms. Competition among these four companies is reportedly keen, and in 1972 they managed or owned fifty-nine properties, including major operations in such large cities as Seattle, Minneapolis, Richmond, Houston, and Providence.[29]

Unfortunately, the typical transit management contract establishes only weak incentives for productivity improvement. In most contracts, management firms do not pay expenses or retain passenger revenues, but instead receive a percentage of gross fare-box revenues, normally about 5 percent for a small operation and 2 percent for a larger one. The management company thus has little direct motivation to control expenses, since expenses do not affect its fee. In addition, the company is encouraged to increase ridership regardless of cost, since the management fee is solely a function of gross fare-box revenues.

A more direct and innovative approach to enlisting outside talent to improve mass transportation productivity would be to contract out the entire transportation function. A public transportation agency might entertain bids, for example, for specific bus routes, subject to a stipulation of minimum standards of service (such as location of stops and length of headways) and maximum fares.[30] Negative bids, or requests for subsidies, could be allowed if needed. Potential bidders might include operators of school buses, sightseeing or taxi services, or small privately owned transit companies.

If bidding for transportation contracts were on a competitive, fixed-price basis and contracts were enforced effectively, contracting would establish strong incentives for productivity improvement. The firms with the lowest costs would earn the largest profits and would be in the best competitive position for bidding on renewals or new contracts. Suppliers would also have incentives to meet the particular demands of the passengers served: the more attractive their services, the higher their revenues and, all else being equal, the higher their profits. Marketing efforts could be constrained somewhat, of course, by the service and fare levels specified in the contracts, but the inhibiting effect of these constraints would likely be attenuated as the public agencies and the private vendors acquired experience with the contracting procedures.

The firms bidding for transportation contracts might also have more flexibility and, with competition, more incentive than local mass transportation authorities to cope with peaking problems.[31] For example, the contracting firms might be involved in other, nontransit businesses that could productively employ peak-hour drivers during off-peak periods. Taxi or limousine operators and school, sightseeing, or charter bus companies often have peak-period labor and vehicle needs that do not occur at the same time as those of mass transportation. Other potential bidders might include light manufacturing or service firms, such as custodial, guard, or carting companies that might effectively also employ part-time transit workers.

If urban transportation services were put out to bid, it might be more advisable to award many separate, small contracts in each metropolitan area—perhaps one for each bus route—than to award a single service contract for an entire area. The principal benefit of route-by-route bidding and contracting is to increase the number of firms that can compete for contracts, which would strengthen the incentives of these firms to control costs and market services effectively.[32] If the service for an entire metropolitan area is let as a single contract, then only a few firms may have sufficient resources and experience to bid on the contract. Competition then might be limited to the largest taxi, charter, school, or inner-city bus firms. Route-by-route bidding will also make it easier for local transit authorities to maintain service standards because the default of a single firm will not be so disruptive. The contract can be quickly rebid among the remaining firms with little, if any, interruption. The local transit authority might even operate a few routes itself so that it can readily take over in the event of a default by one contractor. With smaller contracts rebid every few years, firms can also increase or reduce their involvement in manageable stages rather than in large and infrequent jumps. On the other hand, the advantages of route-by-route bidding would be offset to some extent by higher administrative costs for the contracting agency. Some economies of scale in the provision of the transportation service might also be lost if there is too much fragmentation.

A major potential obstacle to contracting out is the concern of mass transportation employees that they will lose their jobs or that compensation and working conditions will worsen. In the management contracts currently used by industry, this concern is alleviated by the requirement that contractors hire all the current employees (with the exception of a few top managers) and use the existing labor agreement as the basis for future negotiations. Another possibility, which might provide the contractors with more flexibility for making productivity improvements, is to allow the contractors to hire their own labor forces but to contract out transportation services only at the rate at which the existing mass transportation labor force declines through attrition. Transit unions might object to this gradual approach if the labor force of the contractor were not unionized or were organized by a different (say, a nontransit) union. Even then, local mass transportation authorities might avoid political and labor union objections by contracting out only those peak-period transportation needs that are in excess of off-peak requirements and by providing all other services with their own full-time staffs.[33]

APPRAISAL AND CONCLUSIONS

Though many possibilities exist for improving productivity in urban mass transportation, probably only enough improvement (say, 1–3 percent per year) will occur to keep the industry in line with general productivity growth in the economy as a whole. Although this achievement may be modest by the standards of many other industries, it would be a substantial improvement over the industry's record of the recent past. If achieved, pressures on costs, rates, and subsidies would be diminished.

If the transit industry's decline can be slowed or arrested, further productivity improvement may be easier to accomplish. There is a strong positive empirical relationship between an industry's growth and its productivity record: faster-growing industries tend to have higher rates of productivity improvement.[34] Similarly, retrenchment impedes productivity improvement. Most firms are reluctant or incapable of quickly laying off workers, and thus, during periods in which output declines (as in a general economic recession) productivity usually declines as well. By the same token, when output expands, the number of workers is not usually increased proportionately, and productivity improves.

Clearly, the mass transportation industry's postwar decline in profitability and ridership cannot be ascribed to low productivity growth alone. Rising family incomes, suburbanization, and other adverse market trends have played a significant role in the industry's declining fortunes. Therefore, as helpful as productivity improvement might be, public transportation cannot hope to challenge the automobile's market without a more radical change in its operations. In the next chapter, some of these possibilities will be explored.

5

Dial-a-Ride,
Pooling, Taxis,
and Futuristic
Public
Transportation

MARKETS AND POSSIBILITIES

If conventional mass transportation can do little more than keep pace with the automobile, would unconventional approaches do better? Evaluating unconventional public transportation technologies is conjectural. It means forecasting the performance of unproven operating techniques in markets that have yet to be fully established or even defined. The gap, though, between fact and conjecture has been reduced in recent years by various experiments and demonstrations, mainly funded by the Urban Mass Transportation Administration.

What separates the profitable from the unprofitable in mass transportation operations is primarily population density, which affects the volume of traffic available to a particular route. Rising labor costs are also a serious handicap to mass transportation. Between 60 and 80 percent of mass transportation operating costs are typically for labor. The automobile, in contrast, is a "do-it-yourself" mode, and thus rising wage rates are not so much of a handicap.

A variety of unconventional forms of public transportation have been proposed to meet the needs of low-density markets, to conserve on labor costs, or both. A major evaluation of urban transportation technologies and modes, completed by the federal government in 1968, suggested several possibilities that have since undergone extensive research and testing; these included various forms of automated rapid transit and dial-a-ride (a hybrid between conventional bus and taxi service).[1] More recently, interest has also developed in carpooling and vanpooling as alternatives or supplements to conventional mass transportation. These and other possibilities are reviewed below.

AUTOMATIC TRAIN CONTROL

Technologies that use automation to save on labor and other costs were the major subject of the 1968 government report on future transportation systems. The possibilities for labor-saving automation are greatest with rail transit (or fixed-guideway) modes. An underlying premise of the 1968 report therefore was that automation could greatly enhance the attractiveness of rail transit compared to bus or other modes if labor costs rose in the years to come.

The most significant practical application of automation is automatic train control (ATC). There are three major categories of automated operating functions: automatic train protection (ATP), automatic train operation (ATO), and automatic train supervision (ATS). ATP is the most widespread and well proven of the three and mainly deals with those operating functions controlling safety: train speed and separation.[2] The simplest form of ATP is the use of wayside signals and "tripstops." Under this system, the track is divided into segments or "blocks" that are insulated from each other and carry an electric current that controls red, yellow, and green wayside signals. The presence of a train on a block short-circuits the current, causing the appropriate signals to light up on blocks behind the train. At the beginning of each block, there is also a mechanical arm, or tripstop, which is raised by a passing train and does not drop until that train has made contact with a similar device on the next segment of track. While the tripstop is in the raised position, it will engage a brake-activating "triplock" on any train entering the track segment in violation of the wayside signal, thus automatically controlling train separation. Timing devices are often incorporated with the tripstops to provide a simple method of speed control.

Car-borne train protection, or "cab signaling," is a slightly more sophisticated type of ATP. This involves using current in the track circuit, which pulsates at different rates according to track conditions. Such protection is superior to wayside signals: message transmission is not obscured by bad lighting or weather and a greater variety of messages can be sent, allowing trains to operate at the highest safe speed.

All rail transit systems in the United States have wayside signals and tripstops. Cab signaling is generally considered the minimum level of automation for new transit systems, and most older systems have been at least partially if not totally converted to this type of train protection. Accidents still occasionally occur on systems equipped with these basic types of ATP, but usually because the system was overridden or ignored by the trains' operators.

In comparison to ATP, ATO and ATS are relatively new and unproven technologies. ATO controls all aspects of train movement: speed regulation, acceleration, stopping position at stations, door operation, and so on. ATS is the *centralized* control of system operations, including dispatching, routing, communications, and performance monitoring. The only entirely new transit system that opened in the 1960s—the Port Authority Transit Corporation (PATCO) line, which links Philadelphia to communities in southern New Jersey—is equipped with ATO. All of the new transit systems that opened since are equipped with both ATO and ATS.

Automatic train control has high initial capital costs, which can run well over $100 million (in 1975 dollars) on a new rail transit system. In 1975, capital cost estimates for an ATC system equipped with only cab-signaling protection were $9,000–$11,000 per vehicle and $500,000–$650,000 per single-track mile. If the system also incorporated automatic operation and supervision, capital costs would increase to $18,000–$25,000 per vehicle and $750,000–$900,000 per single-track mile.[3] The cost per route-mile for ATC capability has also tended to rise significantly over time, reflecting both increased complexity and inflation.

There is little question that some minimal automatic protection equipment is a virtual necessity for all rail transit systems. Although the capital costs of an ATP system can be high, the equipment is well proven and dependable and substantially improves the safety of train operations. It is doubtful, however, whether ATO or ATS is worth the added capital costs, given the state of technology in the late 1970s, because any savings made from reducing the size of the train crews would probably be offset by increased outlays for additional and specially trained personnel to maintain the equipment. The percentage of maintenance employees involved in ATC-related repairs increases sharply with greater levels of automation; for example, it is 5 percent in the Chicago Transit Authority (CTA) system with only ATP, and 15 percent in PATCO with both ATP and ATO, and 33 percent in BART with ATP, ATO, and ATS.[4] Similarly, the percentage of all equipment failures that are ATC-related increases with the level of automation, from 4 percent in the New York City Transit Authority system (NYCTA) with only ATP, to 6–10 percent in PATCO with ATO and ATP, to 20 percent in BART with ATP, ATO, and ATS. Some of these increases in equipment failures and maintenance requirements may recede as experience is gained with the newer equipment. But the complexity of automation equipment will probably prevent the complete disappearance of additional costs and personnel.

Of course, as an offset to their greater maintenance requirements, the newer and more automated transit systems employ fewer persons on a per-car basis. The relatively automated PATCO and BART systems employ between 2.6 and 2.9 employees per vehicle, while the less automated New York and Boston systems employ 3 or a bit more per vehicle.[5] But these savings are probably not solely attributable to ATC technology. Many of the newer systems do not offer as extensive off-peak midday, weekend, and evening service as the older rail systems, and thus require fewer operator shifts per car. In addition, part of the labor savings on some of the newer systems may be due to changes in work rules governing train crew size.

The potential for train crew reductions is also limited by other considerations. Persistent reliability problems with automatic operations and supervision equipment and the lack of backup equipment have made continued on-board crew supervision necessary on many new installations. Furthermore, even if fully automated operation becomes reliable (as it probably will), on-board employees may still be necessary to ensure passenger safety from crime and other hazards. Thus, while automatic train control beyond ATP has some benefits, currently they do not seem sufficient to justify the expense of sophisticated ATP and ATS technologies.[6] Such advanced systems will be worthwhile only when the technology advances to the point where capital and maintenance costs are both greatly reduced.

Many proponents of ATO and ATS argue that, beyond possible labor savings, these systems can also improve the riding quality and safety of rail transit. In theory, moreover, ATO and ATS should permit a closer spacing of trains (a shortening of headways) to increase capacity over a given amount of track.

But the safety and riding-quality benefits of ATO and ATS are at best small, since they can contribute little more than smoother acceleration and deceleration to the considerable operating safety provided by ATP equipment. In most newer systems, moreover, a smoother ride will as likely be the result of new propulsion, suspension, and roadbed construction methods as of ATO or ATS. Finally, at least during its initial tryouts, ATO has been known to detract from passenger safety: doors have opened while vehicles were in motion, and in at least one instance a BART train failed to stop at the end of a track.

The claimed gains of shortened headways have also not yet been supported by experience. In some early ATO installations, such as BART, trains have been constrained to operate with one-station separation, which is considerably worse than the headways possible with more conventional technologies. It is questionable, in any event, whether any U.S. city, with the possible exception of New York, has sufficient demand to benefit from the shorter headways eventually achievable with ATO and ATS.

AUTOMATED GUIDEWAYS

Automated guideways are a natural extension of automatic train control, in which fully automated vehicles operate on a network of fixed guideways. The vehicles have either rubber or steel wheels, are typically smaller than conventional rail transit cars, and are not operated in trains. The mass transportation industry has little experience with automated guideways other than some simple versions at several U.S. airports and amusement parks, in which the automated vehicles are operated in shuttle or loop routes.

Three major variations of automated guideway transit have been proposed. The simplest is to use small-capacity vehicles of a fixed guideway to perform line-haul service, much the way conventional rail transit does not (with residential feeder and downtown distribution segments of trips largely left to buses or automobiles). A second, more ambitious version would use small automated vehicles to provide complete automobile-like, door-to-door service, using a much more extensive fixed guideway system. A third proposal is for a "dual-mode" automated guideway system, providing door-to-door service with small, automobile-like vehicles that operate under automated control when on a guideway and under driver control when on regular streets.

The line-haul guideway system would function like a horizontal, long-distance elevator. Passengers boarding the vehicles would press buttons to signal the stations at which they wished to disembark. Proponents of the system argue that it would be an improvement over conventional mass transportation because line-haul speeds would be increased by the elimination of some or all of the intermediate stops. Small vehicles would also shorten headways and could reduce passenger waiting time at stations (although any such reduction might be limited, as with elevators, if insufficient vehicle capacity were provided, since full vehicles would probably stop at intermediate stations).

But even a substantial increase in line-haul speeds may translate into only a modest improvement in overall travel time, since much of a mass transportation passenger's time is spent walking to stations, waiting at stations, and in the residential collection and downtown distribution segments of the journey. Gains in line-haul speed through skipping intermediate stops are also feasible, of course, with conventional mass transportation modes (although perhaps not to the extent possible with an automated guideway system because of the larger vehicles used).

Advocates of the line-haul guideway system also claim that it should cost only slightly more, and possibly less, than conventional mass transportation. In the near future, though, automated guideway systems will almost surely increase rather than reduce costs compared with conventional mass transportation. As with automatic train control, the high capital and maintenance costs of automated equipment are likely to offset savings in operating labor. While future automated systems may be inexpensive to build and maintain, the costs and performance of the most advanced automated guideway systems built to date—in Morgantown, West Virginia, and at the Dallas/Ft. Worth airport—suggest that inexpensive and reliable equipment of this type is not easily brought on-stream.[7]

An automated system may also not reduce guideway costs below those of conventional mass transportation, even ignoring outlays required for control equipment. The bus, for example, usually has a substantial advantage in guideway costs over any exclusive guideway system, especially at low passenger volumes, since it usually can share the costs of its "guideway"—a street or freeway—with nontransit users. An automated system using small, light vehicles might have lower guideway costs per track-mile than those of conventional heavy rail transit, but at the same passenger volume an automated system with small vehicles could also require more tracks than a rail line, especially if the safe headways permissible under automated systems are not substantially reduced.

Automated guideway systems might be made sufficiently extensive to provide door-to-door service. Small vehicles and complex switching and branching might be used to ensure privacy and eliminate transfers by permitting express and personalized vehicle routings. Such systems are often described as "personal rapid transit" (PRT), since the quality of service would be more like that of a private automobile than any conventional transit mode.[8] Proponents of PRT argue that such systems would compare favorably with the automobile in terms of costs. Since automated operation should permit closer vehicle spacing (assuming trouble-free operation) than is safe with automobiles, the PRT system would require less land for right-of-way. Furthermore, the automated vehicles could be "recycled" to different users and thus be used more intensively than private automobiles; this could also reduce the need for parking facilities in congested downtown areas. Finally, the automated system would be less dependent on oil for power, making long-run import savings possible.

A key difficulty with PRT systems is the high cost of the guideway network. Automobile-like service would require the construction not only of line-haul facilities but of extensive residential and downtown collection and distribution systems as well. This would essentially duplicate the enormous investment that has been sunk over many decades into the existing street system, and at a much higher cost per mile because of the automated equipment required. Compared to these capital costs, any savings in land use or fuel made possible by automation are likely to be trivial. The complexity and expense of a PRT system would also increase geometrically with urban decentralization. And probable improvements in automotive fuel economy could offset some of the savings and other advantages of substituting electricity for petroleum.

Supporters of the dual-mode automatic guideway concept, which uses small vehicles that can operate under either driver or automatic control, argue that it avoids the prohibitive cost of an extensive automatic guideway system while exploiting most of its principal advantages. Dual mode provides door-to-door service with no transfers, just like the private automobile. It also has some of the do-it-yourself cost advantages of the automobile. Since the automated guideways would allow closer vehicle spacing than is safely possible with automobiles, the line-haul facilities would also conserve on land use. But although dual mode is probably the most attractive automatic guideway technology proposed, implementation would also be the most complicated, since dual mode has all the technological complexities of the other automation devices discussed, plus the added difficulty of "dualing" or transferring from one mode to another. Accordingly, dual mode can be logically viewed as an extension of line-haul automatic guideways once that technology is established.[9]

DIAL-A-RIDE

While most of the 1968 federal report on new urban transportation technologies was devoted to various types of automated systems, dial-a-ride was listed as first among the recommended new future transportation systems, and its potential for serving low-density markets was particularly emphasized. Dial-a-ride, also known as demand-responsive transit, offers service similar to that of a conventional taxi, except that it reputedly achieves economies of scale by exploiting ridesharing—that is, simultaneously serving two or more unrelated passengers in a single vehicle by deviating slightly from direct routes. Taxi operators, in contrast, are prohibited by public ordinances in most large cities from engaging in ridesharing. While the quality of dial-a-ride service is below that of conventional taxis (because the time passengers spend waiting or traveling will increase), dial-a-ride advocates suggest that in many situations the added delay will be small, especially if computer programs can be employed efficiently to assign passengers to specific vehicles or trips. The 1968 report optimistically projects that "door-to-door transit can serve its passengers almost as fast as a private taxi but at one-quarter to one-half the price, indeed, at only slightly more than the fare for a conventional bus."[10]

The federal government, and especially the Urban Mass Transportation Administration, has played a major role in testing dial-a-ride since 1968. In the early 1970s, UMTA sponsored several major dial-a-ride demonstration projects. In 1973, the UMTA capital grant program was modified to allow up to 2 percent of the funds to be used to support special services for the elderly and handicapped, most of which were dial-a-ride systems. In 1974, UMTA mass transportation operating grants were also made available for dial-a-ride.[11] During this same period, several states also established grant programs to support local dial-a-ride services.

The quality of service provided by dial-a-ride proved in many cases to be significantly less than expected (see Table 5.1). In dial-a-ride demonstration projects, average waiting times of 15–30 minutes were typical. And the circuitous routing necessary for picking up and dropping off passengers usually increased the distance a passenger traveled by 50 percent so that average transit times for dial-a-ride passengers were undoubtedly longer than in a taxi.

The hoped-for economies of dial-a-ride also proved elusive. In a majority of the demonstrations for which cost data are available, the average cost per passenger was higher on dial-a-ride than fares on conventional taxis operating in the same locality.[12] In the minority of cases

TABLE 5.1.   Service characteristics of dial-a-ride demonstration projects.

Location	Wait time (avg. min.)	Ride time (avg. min.)	Trip time (avg. min.)	Actual trip length (avg. miles)	Direct-route trip length (avg. miles)[a]	Circuity (actual miles ÷ direct-route miles)
Ann Arbor	23	27	50	6.6	2.9	2.3
Benton Harbor/St. Joseph	27	15	42	4.8	1.7	2.8
Beverly/Fairfax	24	9	33	1.9	1.8	1.1
Columbus	27	19	46	3.3	1.2	2.8
El Cajon	12	12	24	3.5	2.7	1.3
Harper Woods	25	8	33	1.9	1.3	1.5
La Habra	28	14	42	2.7	2.1	1.3
Levittown	5	10	15	2.3	2.1	1.1
Ludington	8	10	18	1.9	1.8	1.1
Merced	25	16	41	4.3	1.7	2.5
Midland	13	18	31	4.6	3.3	1.4
Niles	30	15	45	2.5	1.6	1.6
Oneonta	20	18	38	3.5	2.8	1.3
Rochester	28	17	45	3.1	3.0	1.0
Santa Clara County	39	13	52	3.3	2.8	1.2
Xenia	8	9	17	1.9	1.9	1.0

Source: Ried H. Ewing, "Demand Responsive Transit: Problems and Possibilities" (diss., Massachusetts Institute of Technology, September 1977), p. 104.
a With the exception of Ludington, Merced, Midland, and Niles, direct-route trip-length figures are based on the computing formula: direct-route trip length = 0.78 × (service area)$^{1/2}$. The formula was derived from known direct-route trip lengths in Ludington, Merced, Midland, Niles, Holland, and Mt. Pleasant. There were assumed to be no interzonal trips in Benton Harbor/St. Joseph and Santa Clara County. (Interzonal trips constituted only 8 percent of total trips in Santa Clara County.)

where dial-a-ride costs were lower, they were usually only slightly so. Moreover, the dial-a-ride systems with lower costs often offered only limited service: for example, traveling only between residences and a major shopping center, a train or transit station, a social service agency, or a hospital.[13]

Early optimism about dial-a-ride was based on simple simulation models that indicated that a combination of high-quality service and high levels of ridesharing would be possible in a wide variety of situations.[14] But the dial-a-ride demonstrations suggest that favorable ridesharing conditions are much more specialized. Furthermore, although computerized passenger assignment has only been used in a few locations, thus far it has not been shown to have much advantage over the manual dispatching systems used by taxi companies that offer shared-ride service.[15] In fact, if the ordinances in the communities that prohibit taxis from offering shared-ride services were repealed, taxis might well dominate the field completely and eliminate the advantages of dial-a-ride service.

Totally negative conclusions about the potentialities of dial a ride are, though, perhaps premature. To start, dial-a-ride cost disadvantages relative to taxis are often due to paying transit wages to dial-a-ride operators while taxi wages, which are lower, are used for taxi operations. These wage disparities might or might not persist if dial-a-ride became more universal. In the same vein, taxi fares usually do not include an allowance for tips, which may be a customary part of the taxi driver's compensation.

Furthermore, much depends on the particular application and what it is that dial-a-ride replaces. The real choice in many instances might not be between dial-a-ride and taxis, but rather between dial-a-ride and conventional mass transportation. For example, dial-a-ride might be used as a substitute for conventional mass transportation on low-density routes or on other routes at times of day when volume is very low. On chronically low-density routes, dial-a-ride would simply substitute a small vehicle for a large vehicle, and therefore dial-a-ride should be cheaper than conventional mass transportation. Furthermore, if and when there is attrition in the mass transportation labor force, a number of conventional transit buses *might* be replaced in low-density sectors by a smaller fleet of dial-a-ride vehicles because of dial-a-ride's greater versatility and adaptability.

In off-peak-only applications, the trade-off between dial-a-ride and conventional mass transportation would be more complicated, since the capital outlays for purchasing a dial-a-ride vehicle (approximately $12,000–$15,000 at 1979 prices) would represent an additional expense over and beyond the cost (approximately $90,000 in 1979 prices) of the conventional buses serving the route during peak periods. The question, then, is whether these extra capital costs are offset by savings (for example, on fuel) from using the smaller vehicle during the off-peak hours and from any additional life achieved for the conventional bus by operating it fewer hours per day.[16]

TAXIS

Where there is low-density travel, the costs of providing taxi service may be only slightly higher, or perhaps no higher, than the costs of mass transportation. In 1975, the average operating cost to the transit industry per revenue passenger was about 65 cents. It seems plausible that in a medium-sized city, costs per passenger on some of the least-traveled routes might have been two, three, or four times that average, or close to the typical 1975 taxi fare (between two and three dollars).[17]

Taxis, of course, offer a higher quality of service than mass transportation, in that they provide door-to-door transport on short notice. Many of those for whom the availability of some form of public transportation is thought to be most important (the elderly and physically handicapped, for example) are likely to find these service features attractive.

If the regulations that limit entry into the taxi business in many cities were changed, the economics of taxi operation might be substantially improved. In some large cities (for example, New York and Boston), the number of taxi licenses (or medallions) that can be issued is limited by statute or by a public regulatory authority. In other large cities (for example, Los Angeles and Chicago), public regulatory authorities have given a single taxi firm an exclusive service franchise. Limiting the number of medallions or firms has the effect of granting monopoly privileges, the artificial scarcity often reflected in the high prices that medallions or firms with exclusive franchises sometimes command. If controls on entry were reduced or eliminated, fares should drop and availability of cabs would increase. However, the potential economies should not be overestimated. There are cities where demand for taxis will not support the maximum number of medallions allowed or where a monopoly franchise has already limited fare increases for fear of provoking public regulators into granting franchises to additional firms.[18]

The mass transportation industry might also encourage taxi firms to assume responsibility for service where transit is costly or not competitive. To keep fares low for the poor and for others who might be disadvantaged by such a substitution, some of the public aid now received by mass transportation for operating underutilized routes might be transferred to taxi companies, in exchange for their accepting responsibility for maintaining these services. Even if the subsidies were not sufficient to make taxi fares comparable to mass transportation fares, some of the automobileless individuals for whom this service is being preserved might find the superior quality afforded by taxis worth an additional outlay. This public assistance might be made even more effective by distributing it directly to the elderly, handicapped, or other recipients (say, in the form of transportation vouchers) so that intended beneficiaries had a more direct say in how their needs were met.

CARPOOLS AND VANPOOLS

Carpooling and vanpooling have only recently been recognized as major forms of public transportation, though they appear to have greater potential than automated modes or even dial-a-ride or taxis. Carpooling and vanpooling are both forms of ridesharing, the main difference between them being a matter of scale. In carpooling, two to six people travel together in one vehicle. In vanpooling, there are normally at least eight and often as many as twelve or fourteen commuters in a vehicle. Vanpooling vehicles are often owned by employers, who then lease them—sometimes at less than cost—to groups of employees.[19]

The major advantage of carpools and vanpools over conventional mass transportation is that, like the automobile, the driving is on a do-it-yourself rather than paid-labor basis. Carpools and vanpools, also like the automobile, do not require empty return trips or backhauls to be positioned for further use. On the other hand, parking must be provided for the pooling vehicle during the day at the place of work, although the amount of space required for parking is diminished if commuters previously driving automobiles are induced to travel to work in pools.

Increased carpooling became a major objective of federal transportation policy shortly after the imposition of the Arab oil embargo in 1973. The Emergency Highway Energy Conservation Act, signed into law in January 1974, authorized the Federal Highway Administration (FHWA) to use highway aid funds to finance 90 percent of the costs of projects that would demonstrate the potential of carpooling.[20] At about the same time, the Federal Energy Administration began a nationwide promotional campaign to encourage carpooling.

The first efforts to promote vanpooling predate the oil embargo and were made by employers concerned about the costs of providing employee parking. These employers were contemplating facility growth and were confronted with the need to either provide a great deal more parking (often at quite a high cost per space) or find some alternative to private automobile commuting. The most typical initial response, particularly when the company was located in a relatively high-density area, was the express bus. But even before the 1973 embargo, some employers, most notably the Minnesota Mining and Manufacturing Company (3M) in St. Paul and the Tennessee Valley Authority (TVA) in Knoxville, found that the express bus did not meet all of their needs and undertook vanpool experiments as well.

An essential "trick" in making carpooling and vanpooling effective is to match the participants properly. Successful carpools or vanpools are almost invariably composed of people who work with one another and whose hours of work closely correspond. Obviously, people who work irregular hours, starting very early or working very late, are poor candidates for pools. Another prerequisite for successful pooling is that those participating reside either close to one another or along a fairly straight line connecting the farthest participant's residence with the place of work. Finally, experience suggests that carpools, and to a lesser extent vanpools, tend to work best when the participants are of relatively homogeneous backgrounds, incomes, and tastes. Some specialists in organizing pools therefore recommend that carpools at the residential end are best organized through local community groups, such as churches and social clubs.[21]

If potential pool members do not have roughly the same origins and destinations or do not live along a straight-line route to the workplace, then the decision to pool involves a trade-off between the extra cost of circuity and the savings achieved by sharing costs over several riders. Of course, even without circuities, costs generally rise with pooling because of the time and resources involved in making stops to pick up additional rides and the increased probability of delay the larger the number of participants. To those with high incomes, the time lost through delay often seems worth more than the savings available through shared costs. Thus, in a survey of commuters on the Hollywood Freeway, 67 percent of those with family incomes above $25,000 reported no interest at all in joining a carpool, while only 39 percent of the commuters with incomes below $10,000 were not interested.[22]

Carpools of three or more persons and large-scale vanpools can be especially difficult to form because the direct cost savings realized from pooling do not increase in proportion to the number of participants. For example, when two people who previously drove by themselves consolidate into a two-person carpool, they cut their costs by about one-half (always assuming that not too much circuity is introduced by pooling). However, if they were to add a third participant to their pool, the two original poolers would reduce their costs by only 17 percent of their original, separate (unpooled) driving costs. Proceeding along with this arithmetic, if a tenth person is added to a nine-person pool, the reduction in costs as compared to driving alone is roughly 1 percent.

Pooling is most effective when long commuter trips are involved.[23] This is because the longer the trip, the more commuting expenses the participants can save by joining a pool, and the more the "fixed" costs of time delay in picking up other poolers can be averaged out over additional units of travel. Furthermore, commutes over very long distances are less likely to be well served by mass transportation.

These various complications (for example, of finding people whose personal and residential characteristics match reasonably well and who have sufficient cost incentives) suggest some inherent limits in promoting carpooling and vanpooling as an alternative to either the automobile or more conventional forms of public transportation. Also, pooling is largely used for worktrips, and although worktrips contribute disproportionately to some urban transportation problems (such as congestion and air pollution), they constitute only about one fifth to one quarter of all trips in a typical metropolitan area.

Furthermore, an increase in carpool and vanpool commuting may not proportionately reduce vehicle-miles traveled (VMT). In the first place, the vehicle-miles saved by consolidating trips into a pool can be partly offset by added mileage necessitated by *trip circuity* to pick up pool members. Moreover, several studies suggest that approximately 40 percent of the potential savings in VMT through pooling is offset by increased use by other family members of the automobiles that poolers leave at home. Finally, the number of vehicle-miles saved will be small if some of the new poolers are attracted from express buses or other high-occupancy modes rather than from private automobiles.[24] Many of the circumstances that make pooling feasible or attractive—such as large employment or residential concentrations—are also advantageous for mass transportation, and thus a certain amount of competition between the modes is likely. It is therefore at least conceivable that a ridesharing program implemented in a dense, central area might drain patronage from transit and thereby increase vehicle-miles of travel, fuel consumption, and costs.[25]

A simulation of the effects of pooling on travel in Washington, D.C., however, suggests that a reasonably well-designed ridesharing promotion by major employers might reduce automobile use by several percentage points in that city.[26] Four promotion policies were tested in this simulation: (1) publicizing and assisting employees in organizing carpools; (2) providing preferential parking spaces for carpooling employees; (3) charging more for parking spaces used by commuters who drove alone; and (4) reserving special traffic lanes for carpools and transit vehicles in order to reduce their travel time. The results of the simulation suggest that the percentage of commuters using carpools could be increased by 3–4 percent if assistance in forming carpools is provided and if reserved lanes are made available; it might be increased by as much as 8–17 percent with parking incentives. The estimated changes in automobile VMT are much more modest—usually less than 1 percent—since drivers using automobiles for nonwork purposes do not usually enter pools, cars left at home are used by others, and a portion of the new poolers are attracted from mass transportation.[27]

The results of actual experiments with ridesharing promotion are roughly consistent with those of the Washington, D.C., simulation. Federally funded carpool demonstration projects indicate that publicity efforts and assistance in organizing carpools alone will decrease VMT by 1–1.5 percent at most. Because carpooling is more likely where employment is concentrated, most demonstration programs have focused on firms with several hundred employees or more, with promotional material on carpooling distributed and the employees offered assistance in matching prospective poolers. In a few cases, the employers have also offered inducements for carpooling, usually preferential parking for poolers in company-owned lots. In a sample of sixteen federally funded demonstration programs (see Table 5.2), only 0.7 percent of the workforce became new carpoolers, and the resulting reductions in VMT on worktrips and all trips averaged only 0.35 and 0.16 percent, respectively. A reduction in VMT, however, may be a less legitimate objective for pooling than reducing the number of vehicles driven to central workplaces at the rush hours. And if the results of the demonstration projects were modest, so too were the costs, averaging 4.4 cents per vehicle-mile reduced and $58 per year for each new carpooler.

Experience with vanpool promotion is more recent and limited and therefore difficult to assess. As late as 1976 there were only about thirty major vanpool operations in the entire country, although by the 1980s the number had grown to perhaps a thousand.[28] Most of the operations were sponsored by employers, who purchased or leased the vans and rented them to pooling employees, sometimes below cost. With one or two exceptions,[29] the vanpools attracted at most 5–10 percent of the employees. As might be expected, participants tended to travel long distances, since the delay of the circuitous routing necessary to pick up eight to ten poolers is less significant over a longer commute.

Several ridesharing programs have been relatively successful, however, specifically those at the headquarters of TVA in Knoxville, the 3M Center in St. Paul, and the Greyhound headquarters in Phoenix. TVA's pooling program began in 1973 as a counterproposal to employee requests that the utility provide free parking next to its Knoxville headquarters. TVA encouraged ridesharing by subsidizing the operation of express buses, by paying for carpoolers' parking spaces, and

TABLE 5.2. Results of sixteen federally funded carpool matching and promotion demonstration projects.

Location	Participating employers		New carpoolers		Reductions in vehicle-miles traveled		Annual cost of carpool promotion and matching	
	Number	Percentage of metropolitan workforce	Thousands	Percentage of metropolitan workforce	As percentage of work trips	As percentage of all trips	In cents per vehicle-mile reduced	In dollars per new carpoolers
Los Angeles	490	16	8.10	0.2	0.20	0.70	1.30	62
Sacramento	61	54	2.70	1.0	0.70	0.23	0.95	30
San Diego	67	30	2.20	0.5	0.30	0.11	1.90	62
Boise	20	34	0.12	0.3	0.14	0.05	17.50	207
Louisville	247	*	3.00	0.9	0.20	0.07	2.50	24
Omaha	100	*	1.20	0.5	0.26	0.09	15.00	88
Salem	73	43	0.28	0.4	0.14	0.05	14.00	125
Portland	177	26	7.70	2.0	1.00	0.36	1.60	32
Raleigh	73	*	0.75	0.8	0.30	0.10	1.80	27
Rhode Island	79	17	1.50	0.4	*	*	1.60	46
Dallas	52	*	1.60	0.2	0.11	0.04	2.40	39
Fort Worth	152	25	2.10	0.7	0.30	0.10	0.70	15
Houston	75	*	2.10	0.3	0.23	0.08	1.80	58
San Antonio	60	*	5.00	1.8	0.80	0.28	1.60	32
Seattle	200	18	3.20	0.6	0.20	0.07	4.40	67
Washington, D.C.	850	36	10.80	0.6	0.37	0.13	0.70	13
Average	173.5	30	3.30	0.7	0.35	0.16	4.40	58

Source: Data from Frederick A. Wagner, "Evaluation of Carpool Demonstration Projects," paper presented at the annual meeting of the Federally Coordinated Program of Research and Development in Highway Transportation, Columbus, Ohio November 8, 1977. The data is also reprinted in Alan M. Voorhees, Inc., *Transportation Systems Management: An Assessment of Impacts*, report prepared for the U.S. Department of Transportation and the U.S. Environmental Protection Agency (Washington, D.C.: U.S. Department of Transportation, 1978), pp. 56–68.

* Not available.

by providing each vanpooler with the equivalent of $9.50 per month in subsidies. Between late 1973 and early 1977 (see Table 5.3), the number of commuters' automobiles arriving at TVA (including private cars, carpools, and vanpools) declined by more than one half (from 2,195 to 1,066), despite a 15 percent increase in employment (from 2,950 to 3,400). This achievement is all the more remarkable because almost 12 percent of the TVA vanpoolers previously commuted by bus, and almost 37 percent previously commuted by carpool. The annual benefits to TVA of the pooling and express bus incentive programs in savings on parking spaces alone has been estimated to be $337,820 per year against a direct cost to TVA of $125,000 per year.[30]

At the 3M Center in St. Paul, the results were almost as successful as at TVA. 3M began by subsidizing express bus service and later organized vanpools, renting the vans to the pools at cost. Between 1970 and 1974, 3M cut the number of employees driving alone by close to 2 percent (see Table 5.4) despite a 23 percent increase in employment.

A less ambitious effort, emphasizing carpooling only, was undertaken by Greyhound at its headquarters in downtown Phoenix, and it did about as well as the more comprehensive 3M experiment in reducing the number of automobiles driven to work. Between November 1973 and May 1975, the number of carpools increased almost sixfold, and the percentage of employees in carpools increased from 10 to 47 percent.[31]

Another way of evaluating carpooling programs is to measure the occupancy of automobiles used for commuting. Nationally, about 1.2 persons (plus or minus a bit, depending on circumstances) typically occupy each commuter automobile. Before the carpooling experiment was launched at TVA, its employees commuted to and from work in automobiles filled to about this usual occupancy level; by 1977, however, the occupancy level had been raised by over 50 percent to 1.90 (excluding vanpools). At 3M, vehicle occupancy in 1970 before the pooling experiments was 1.24 (including private automobile, transit, carpool, and vanpool), and rose by 25 percent to 1.55 by 1974. Although precise data are not available, the Greyhound experience seems to have been roughly analogous to that at 3M: carpooling raised the typical automobile occupancy level by 15–20 percent, starting at a level below the national average and ending at a level somewhat above.

The successful TVA, 3M, and Greyhound programs were, though, all at large employment centers not well served by mass transit. Moreover, the companies engaged in extensive promotional efforts and subsidies, mainly to avoid the costs of providing additional parking. Furthermore, the oil embargoes and large gasoline price increases during the mid-1970s provided additional incentives for ridesharing.

Nevertheless, it seems possible that well-implemented pooling

TABLE 5.3. Results of ridesharing at TVA's Knoxville headquarters.

	Before ridesharing program: November 1973	During ridesharing program: January 1977
Percentage of worktrips by mode:		
Drive alone	65.0	18.0
Regular bus	3.5	3.0
Express bus	0.0	28.0
Carpool	30.0	41.0
Vanpool	0.0	7.0
Bicycle, walk, etc.	1.5	3.0
Total	100.0	100.0
Number of workers by mode.		
Drive alone	1,918	612
Regular bus	103	102
Express bus	0	952
Carpool	885	1,394
Vanpool	0	238
Bicycle, walk, etc.	44	102
Total	2,950	3,400
Number of express buses	0	23
Number of automobiles:		
Carpool	277	436
Drive alone	1,918	612
Total	2,195	1,048
Number of vans	0	18
Total automobiles and vans	2,195	1,066

Source: Frederick J. Wegmann, Arun J. Chatterjee, and Stanley R. Stokey, "Evaluation of an Employer-Based Commuter Rideshare Program," photocopied manuscript, Department of Civil Engineering, University of Tennessee, Knoxville, July 1977, pp. 4 and 6. Published in *Urban Transportation Innovations, Special Report 184* (Washington, D.C.: Transportation Research Board, 1979), pp. 43–49.

programs, augmented by improved transit and express bus services where appropriate, might substantially lower the number of private automobiles driven to work. Specifically, instead of 70 or so automobiles arriving at work each day for every 100 employees (the U.S. average in the late 1970s), only 50–60 vehicles might do so. Pooling programs are also relatively inexpensive to implement, so that even if they do not attract large numbers of employees, they are likely to be cost effective. Finally, pooling programs provide many benefits not easily quantified but nevertheless appreciated by the parties involved.[32]

TABLE 5.4.   Results of ridesharing promotion at the 3M Center in St. Paul.

	Before ridesharing program: 1970	During ridesharing program: 1974	Percent change 1970–74
Number of workers by commuting mode:			
Drive alone	6,224	6,126	− 1.6
Transit	43	118	174.4
Carpool	1,002	1,908	90.4
Vanpool	0	567	—
Total	7,269	8,719	19.9
Average vehicle occupancy	1.24	1.55	25

Source: Robert D. Owens and Helen L. Sever, *The 3M Commute-a-Van Program, Status Report II*, prepared and distributed by the 3M Company, 3M Center, St. Paul, Minnesota, January 1977.

TRANSIT'S FUTURE

The productivity and marketing improvements discussed in the last chapter, taken together with some of the possibilities for developing unconventional or more advanced transit systems described in this chapter, suggest at least a possibility that public transit can hold its present market share. Indeed, some unconventional transit, such as dial-a-ride and taxi and, more importantly, various forms of carpooling and vanpooling, might make substantial inroads on the percentage of workers actually driving a car or similar vehicle to work. Specifically, all else equal, if conventional transit's productivity improvement can be brought up to national averages, and if express buses, vanpools, and carpools can be instituted on a broad scale, as much as a one-quarter reduction might be made in the number of cars now used for commuting.

Although not a "definite solution" to all urban transportation problems, this would represent a major contribution. But it will not be easy to achieve. Design and implementation of new transit systems, changes in commutation habits, and productivity improvements all take time, so that their beneficial effects will only be slowly realized.

PART III
ISSUES AND POLICIES

6

Automobile Futures: Some Speculations on Ownership and Fleet Composition

DINOSAUR OR EVOLVING SPECIES?

Given the limitations on improving the productivity of public transit and paratransit, a major urban transportation policy goal almost surely has to be making the automobile a more acceptable participant in urban society.

The only circumstance that could alter this conclusion would be if a combination of improved transit and changes in the environment "did the automobile in." Rising energy prices, for example, may significantly diminish the role of the automobile, since gasoline is a major operating cost. The price of petroleum increased by nearly 58 percent between 1973 and 1979.[1] If oil prices continue to increase, as many expect, the cost of operating an automobile may also rise, thus reducing future automobile ownership and use.

Government regulations to reduce automobile air pollution and improve safety may also increase future costs and lead to further reductions in the use of the automobile. Federally mandated controls on new car emissions, for example, contributed to a reduction in overall fuel economy of new cars produced and sold in the United States in the early 1970s—from just over 15 miles per gallon in 1970 to under 14 in 1974. Since that time, the adoption of catalytic mufflers and other devices has lessened this impact, and the average mileage per gallon rose to a level of 15.6 in 1975, 17.6 in 1976, and 18.6 in 1977. The Ford Motor Company contends, in addition, that government-stipulated safety and pollution equipment added approximately $700 to the basic cost of its cars by the model year 1978. It also claims that these safety and pollution installations have reduced fuel economy by approximately 30 percent. Similarly, General Motors insists that prospective improvements in gas mileage (from weight reduction, changes in design, better transmissions, and so on) could easily be canceled out by emission controls and safety equipment increasing the weight of future cars. Even the National Highway Traffic Safety Administration concedes that an airbag would cost approximately $220 per car, including contingency and lifetime operating costs, while automobile companies estimate these costs at over $300 per vehicle (in mid- to late-1970s prices).

There is, nevertheless, a strong possibility that the automobile will adapt to these changes and retain its dominant role in urban transportation. But the typical car that evolves almost surely will be very different from the one previously on the American scene. In particular, it may be smaller.

Any demise or adaptation of the automobile will not occur in an economic vacuum. The basic forces that will determine the future size and character of the American automobile fleet are the same as those at work in any market: the number, income, and demographic characteristics of consumers and the cost of automobiles relative to other goods and services—especially the major competition, public transportation.[2]

DEMOGRAPHIC AND INCOME CHANGES

The most significant demographic factor affecting automobile ownership is the number of households. In the 1950s, the 1960s, and the first half of the 1970s, the average annual rate of growth in the number of households was 2.1, 1.8, and 2.8 percent, respectively. The U.S. Census projects that between the late 1970s and 1990 the number of households will increase at about 2 percent per year, despite a slowdown in population growth.[3] This continued increase in the number of households should result in an approximately proportionate increase in the number of automobiles owned, provided the average number of automobiles per household does not fluctuate greatly.

The number of automobiles per household is primarily determined by the level of household income. Until high income levels are reached, studies consistently show an increase in automobile ownership with rises in household income. At income levels above $40,000 per year (in 1980 dollars) households seemingly become "saturated" with automobiles, and additional income results in little change in the number of cars owned.[4] If past experience is a reliable guide, real household income will probably increase at an average and fairly steady rate of about 2 to 3 percent per year, and this should translate into some—though less than a proportionate—increase in automobile ownership.

Other demographic trends will also influence levels of automobile ownership per household. Many of these trends will lead to a reduction in the number of automobiles per household, such as a likely decline in the average size of households (due to declining fertility, later marriages, and more frequent divorces) and an increase in the average age of household heads (due to increasing longevity and the aging of those born during the postwar baby boom). Other demographic trends will lead to increased car ownership per household. For example, the growing number of workers per household (due largely to greater participation of women in the labor force) should create more demand for automobiles to be used for commuting. Also, the decline of population and jobs in central cities and the growth of population in the suburbs, smaller metropolitan areas, and the Sunbelt states with lower densities and more extensive and higher-performance highway systems should also increase automobile ownership per household.

Research on the effects of demographic and income changes on levels of automobile ownership for the 125 largest U.S. metropolitan areas indicates that if real household income grows at a rate of 3 percent per year the number of cars per household will increase by 0.57 percent per year between 1980 and 1990.[5] When other demographic trends—such as smaller family size, older family heads, increasing numbers of workers, and migration to the suburbs and the Sunbelt—are considered in addition to income, the forecast annual rate of increase in automobile ownership per household rises to 0.61 percent per year. In either case, a marked reduction occurs in the proportion of total households that own no car or only one car, while a substantial increase is observable in the proportion of households that own two or more cars.

The combination of a 2 percent annual increase in the number of households with a 0.6 percent annual increase in the number of cars per household would generate a 2.6 percent annual increase in the total number of cars owned in large metropolitan areas. With a total U.S.

fleet of approximately 120 million cars in 1980, and a 2–3 percent annual growth rate in automobile ownership, the 1990 U.S. automobile
fleet would be between 145 million and 160 million cars.[6]

THE COSTS OF AUTOMOBILE USE

American automobile ownership has been encouraged in the past by the
stable or declining costs of automobile use as compared to the costs of
other goods and services. Table 6.1 shows automobile ownership and
operating costs from 1950 to 1979 as estimated by the U.S. Federal
Highway Administration. The cost of owning and operating a standard-sized, four-door American sedan was about 17 cents per mile (in
1975 dollars) for much of the postwar period, increasing to 19 cents per
mile only in the late 1970s. Cost estimates for compact and subcompact
cars are only available starting in 1972, but they show a similar stability at 14 and 12 cents per mile, respectively, until they each increased
by approximately 2 cents per mile in the late 1970s.

Furthermore, while automobile ownership and operating costs have
remained relatively stable, the quality of the automobile has improved
over the postwar period—it is safer, has less need for repairs and routine maintenance, and offers a wider variety of options, such as automatic transmissions and air conditioning. The cost estimates also do not
incorporate all of the savings made possible by the postwar improvements in highway systems, especially increased traffic speeds and con-
sequent reductions in automobile travel times.

It is difficult to forecast whether these trends encouraging automobile use will continue. Much depends upon such unknowns as future
energy prices and how closely government will regulate the environmental, safety, and other aspects of automobile design and use. Equally
important and uncertain are future technological advances to improve
fuel economy or meet government standards at reasonable cost.

The relative stability of automobile costs in the past, however,
strongly suggests that even substantial fuel prices or government standards might not affect automobile costs greatly. Especially impressive
is the record of automobile costs from the late 1960s through the late
1970s. This was a period of rapidly rising energy prices and increasingly stringent automobile safety and air pollution regulations, and yet
the real cost of owning and operating a new automobile remained constant from 1960 through 1976 (see Table 6.1). Automobile ownership
and operating costs did increase in 1979, after the revolution in Iran
brought about the second big increase in real gasoline prices of the
1970s. Even then the real costs of automobile use grew by only 12 per-

TABLE 6.1.   Costs of owning and operating an automobile in constant (1975) cents per mile, 1950–1979.

Size of car and model year of cost estimate	Depreciation	Maintenance, parts, and tires	Gas and oil (excluding taxes)	Garage parking and tolls	Insurance	State and federal taxes	Total costs[a]
Standard:							
1950	3.1	2.9	3.1	2.0	2.0	1.6	14.8
1960	4.5	3.6	2.9	2.0	2.4	2.2	17.8
1968	4.3	3.3	2.6	2.8	2.2	1.9	17.0
1970	4.4	2.6	2.6	2.5	2.4	1.9	16.5
1972	5.7	3.3	2.7	2.3	1.8	1.7	17.5
1974	4.6	3.7	3.5	2.2	1.8	1.6	17.4
1976	4.7	4.0	3.1	2.1	1.6	1.5	17.0
1979	4.9	4.3	4.3	2.5	1.9	1.2	19.0
Compact:							
1972	3.5	2.8	2.3	2.3	1.7	1.3	13.9
1974	3.2	3.0	2.8	2.2	1.6	1.3	14.1
1976	3.6	3.2	2.4	2.0	1.5	1.1	13.9
1979	4.0	3.7	3.8	2.5	1.8	1.0	16.8
Subcompact:							
1972	2.7	2.7	1.8	2.3	1.5	1.0	12.1
1974	2.5	2.7	2.2	2.2	1.6	1.0	12.2
1976	3.0	3.0	1.7	2.0	1.4	0.9	12.0
1979	2.9	3.2	3.2	2.5	1.7	0.8	14.3

Source: Figures for 1950–1976 from U.S. Federal Highway Administration, Costs of Owning and Operating an Automobile, various years (Washington, D.C.: Federal Highway Administration, various years) as reported in U.S. Congress, Office of Technology Assessment, Changes in the Future Use and Characteristics of the Automobile Transportation System: Summary and Findings (Washington, D.C.: U.S. Government Printing Office, 1979), p. 30. Figures for 1979 based on preliminary and unpublished data supplied by the Vehicles, Drivers, and Fuels Branch, Office of Highway Planning, Federal Highway Administration, U.S. Department of Transportation.
[a] Figures may not add up exactly because of rounding of omitted digits.

cent for standard-sized cars, 22 percent for compacts, and 19 percent for subcompacts; these costs may also recede to former levels as automobile manufacturers have more time to adapt designs to higher fuel costs.

The Federal Task Force on Motor Vehicle Goals Beyond 1980 predicted in 1976 that steady improvements in new-car fuel economy—stimulated by consumer demand and the new-car mileage standards legislated in the Energy Policy Conservation Act of 1975—would slightly reduce the costs of owning and operating automobiles in the 1980s, especially for standard- (six-passenger) and intermediate-sized vehicles.[7] The task force estimates indicate that, with more weight-conscious design and more widespread use of the most efficient engines already in mass production in 1975, the costs of owning and operating small cars (subcompacts and compacts) could be reduced by 5.2 percent, while the costs of owning and operating larger cars could be reduced by between 9.7 and 12.0 percent, depending upon the size of the car (see Table 6.2).

The task force estimates anticipated neither the real fuel price increases of 1979 nor all aspects of federal regulations governing new-car air pollution emissions and safety devices promulgated in the late 1970s. Table 6.3 provides rough estimates of lifetime automobile costs that incorporate allowances for emissions and safety regulations (but not increases in gas price). These estimates suggest that tighter federal regulations will largely offset any drop in automobile costs that might occur in the absence of gasoline price increases.

Even allowing for further increases in gasoline prices, a good guess would be that total costs of automobile ownership and use will not change much in relation to other goods and services in the next decade, because the various forces at work will simply offset one another.[8] The estimates in Tables 6.2 and 6.3 assumed only the adoption of technologies and designs already in production in the mid-1970s. Increases in gasoline prices should stimulate an even more ambitious search for fuel efficiency. On balance, prospective operating cost and price changes

TABLE 6.2.   Cost of current and more fuel-efficient automobiles as estimated by the Federal Task Force on Motor Vehicle Goals Beyond 1980.[a]

	1975 cost in cents per vehicle-mile		
	4-passenger car (subcompact and compact)	*5-passenger car (intermediate)*	*6-passenger car (standard)*
1975 models	13.5	15.5	18.4
"Weight-conscious design" with top 1975 engine and improved drivetrain	12.8	14.0	16.2
Percent change	−5.2	−9.7	−12.0

Source: Report by the Federal Task Force on Motor Vehicle Goals Beyond 1980, September 1976, p. 13–7.
[a] Costs include depreciation as well as operating expenses.

TABLE 6.3. Estimates of lifetime purchase and operating costs of 1977 and 1985 model automobiles allowing for government pollution and safety regulations.[a]

	Lifetime discounted costs in 1977 dollars		
	Subcompact	*Compact*	*Standard/ intermediate*
1977 model:			
Purchase	3,100	3,600	5,000
Operating	4,294	5,234	6,710
Total	7,394	8,834	11,710
1985 model:			
Purchase	3,500	4,000	5,400
Operating	3,825	4,496	5,569
Total	7,325	8,496	10,969
Percent change (1977–85)	−0.9	−3.8	−6.3

Source: Estimated by the authors from various public sources.
[a] Estimates assume a discount value of 8 percent, a lifetime of ten years and 100,000 miles, and gasoline prices that increase no faster than the rate of general inflation.

would not seem of sufficient scope to give the automobile an advantage or disadvantage in the competition for consumer dollars.

FUTURE MARKETS FOR LARGE AND SMALL CARS

Even if the real costs of automobile use increased, consumers might mitigate much of the impact by switching from standard-sized vehicles to compacts and subcompacts. Compacts and subcompacts respectively cost about 20 and 35 percent less to own and operate per mile than standard-sized vehicles (see Tables 6.1, 6.2, and 6.3). Small cars are less affected by fuel price increases, as they have a large advantage in fuel economy due to their lower weight. The average standard-sized car sold in the United States in 1979 achieved an estimated 18–22 miles per gallon, for example, while the smallest subcompacts (under 2,250 pounds) were rated at 32 miles per gallon that same year.[9]

A key issue is whether small cars are acceptable to American automobile users. The future mix of small (compact and subcompact), intermediate, and standard cars in the automobile fleet will be determined largely by the same price changes and income and demographic trends that govern overall levels of automobile ownership. But the size mix is more difficult to predict than overall ownership levels; small-car sales were extremely volatile in the 1970s, and the predicted price, income, and demographic trends of the 1980s establish conflicting incentives for the sales of small over large cars.

Two trends in particular may discourage the sale of small cars in the near future. First, government fuel economy programs, stricter air quality standards (particularly for nitrogen oxides, as explained in Chapter 9), and the requirement of airbags could all act to raise the *relative* costs of small cars. The cost of meeting environmental and safety standards will not be dissimilar for large and small cars so that, when these roughly equivalent numbers are added on to the smaller base prices of the smaller cars, the addition will represent a larger percentage of the initial purchase price for the small cars. Percentage improvements in mileage per gallon may also be easier for a big car, which starts from a somewhat inefficient base, than for a more tightly engineered small car. Improvements of 30–40 percent in the gas mileage of so-called standard American cars are more easily achieved than 10–20 percent improvements, which often require substantial sacrifices in performance, in the gas mileage of American subcompacts. Put somewhat crudely, it may be fairly easy to improve the efficiency of a gas-guzzling dinosaur, but difficult to improve the efficiency of a reasonably well-engineered and trim smaller vehicle.

This supposition is supported by the changes in automobile costs that occurred at the end of the 1970s and that are forecast for the 1980s. When the cost of automobile use and ownership finally increased in 1979, subcompact and compact costs increased by 19 and 22 percent respectively, while standard-sized vehicle costs grew by only 12 percent. Similarly, the rough estimates of 1985 car costs shown in Table 6.3 indicate that standard-sized car costs might drop by 6.3 percent while subcompact and compact car costs might fall by only 0.9 and 3.8 percent respectively. Even this slight change in relative prices might precipitate a detectable shift in new-car sales, since empirical analyses suggest that small-car sales are sensitive to relative price changes.[10]

A second trend that may dampen small-car sales is the expected steady increase in real income per household. As incomes increase, households are better able to afford the comfort, the convenient large-load capacity, and the other amenities usually associated with larger vehicles.[11]

Any trends adverse to small cars are likely to be at least partially offset, however, by several other developments. One is the decline in average family size expected in the next decade, which will increase the share of small households for whom the added passenger-carrying capacity of a standard- or full-sized car offers little advantage.

The fact that, to a considerable extent, the future increase in automobile ownership will occur in households with two or more cars may also lead to a greater purchase of small automobiles. Households with two or more cars have an opportunity to buy cars for different purposes. For example, a common practice is to have one newer and more reliable car, which is used more intensively, and a second, older and less reliable but less costly car, which is used less frequently and for shorter trips. Another tendency in multiple-car households, which again encourages small car sales, is to have a larger car for vacation and other trips, when the entire family travels, and a smaller car that is used exclusively for commuting or for trips when only a few passengers are carried. Even in 1969, when small-car ownership was far less common than it later became, 33.5 percent of two-car families owned both a compact car and a larger automobile.[12]

Any rise in real fuel prices would also favor a shift to small cars. Future petroleum prices are uncertain, but many energy experts argue that prices will probably increase by as much as 50–100 percent in real terms (that is, relative to increases in the prices for other goods and services) between 1980 and 1990. While the fuel-economy advantages of small over large cars may also shrink over this decade, small cars will still undoubtedly remain more fuel efficient.

Finally, the shift to smaller vehicles may be encouraged by including in small cars the luxury features traditionally associated with large cars. Research on the reasons why consumers choose cars of different sizes suggests that size per se, measured in passenger-carrying capacity or weight, accounts for only part of the attraction of large cars.[13] Interior noise levels, ride quality, power options, air conditioning, and other luxury features contribute significantly to sales of larger automobiles. Most of these luxury features can be provided in smaller vehicles, although probably at some increase in their purchase prices and at some cost in fuel economy. Manufacturers began to offer a wider variety of small cars with luxury features in the 1970s, and this trend should reduce consumer resistance to smaller automobiles.

While it is difficult to predict the net effect of these various conflicting forces on the future large- and small-car mix, the record of car sales in the 1970s strongly suggests that consumers will readily substitute small for large vehicles when confronted with an economic incentive to do so. Table 6.4 shows that consumers responded quickly to increases in

TABLE 6.4.   Market shares of seasonally adjusted sales of new cars by size class, April 1970–March 1980.

	Percent of new car sales by size			Total sales (millions)	Gasoline prices in 1980 dollars
	Small	Intermediate	Full		
April 1970–September 1970	36.8	22.5	40.7	4.40	0.722
October 1970–March 1971	41.3	19.7	39.0	4.33	0.709
April 1971–September 1971	40.2	19.1	40.7	5.03	0.683
October 1971–March 1972	38.2	21.5	40.3	5.33	0.683
April 1972–September 1972	38.5	21.6	39.8	5.38	0.670
October 1972–March 1973	39.6	22.2	38.1	6.10	0.687
April 1973–September 1973	42.2	22.5	35.3	5.71	0.688
October 1973–March 1974	48.5	22.7	28.8	4.91	0.765
April 1974–September 1974	47.7	25.2	27.0	4.65	0.850
October 1974–March 1975	54.3	22.0	23.8	4.00	0.786
April 1975–September 1975	52.5	24.5	23.0	4.19	0.814
October 1975–March 1976	48.4	25.9	25.7	4.94	0.809
April 1976–September 1976	49.0	26.1	24.9	4.96	0.799
October 1976–March 1977	45.3	29.6	25.2	5.42	0.804
April 1977–September 1977	47.7	26.8	25.5	5.57	0.801
October 1977–March 1978	48.7	27.2	24.1	5.52	0.785
April 1978–September 1978	47.5	28.6	23.9	5.77	0.770
October 1978–March 1979	51.5	24.9	23.6	5.82	0.803
April 1979–September 1979	57.1	23.0	19.9	5.28	0.971
October 1979–March 1980	60.6	21.4	18.0	4.93	1.140

Source: Unpublished data from the U.S. Department of Commerce, Bureau of Economic Analysis, as reported in U.S. Congressional Budget Office, *Fuel Economy Standards for New Passenger Cars after 1985* (Washington, D.C., U.S. Government Printing Office, 1980), p. 32.

gasoline prices over the course of the decade. From the spring of 1970 through the spring of 1973, when gasoline prices were stable, small-car sales were a relatively constant 37–40 percent of all sales. But when the real price of gasoline jumped in 1973 and 1974, small-car sales also jumped, reaching over 50 percent of total sales in late 1974 and 1975. Small-car sales declined slightly during the period of stable or declining real gas prices from early 1976 through 1978 (though they were still almost 10 percentage points higher than they had been in 1970–73). When gasoline prices increased rapidly again in 1979, after the Iranian revolution, small cars gained another 10 percentage points of total sales. Obviously, many consumers may well be willing to substitute small for large cars to offset increasing real petroleum prices or other costs of automobile use.

TRANSIT AVAILABILITY AND COST

While the cost of automobile use may remain stable in relation to the overall consumer price index, it may not remain stable compared to the cost of public transportation, the automobile's principal competitor. Although significant fare decreases and major improvements in the availability of conventional public transportation are unlikely, at least without substantial public subsidies, some improvements are possible. Furthermore, less conventional public modes, particularly some forms of paratransit, might expand considerably. These developments could have implications for automobile ownership and use.

Among the many considerations that enter into a decision on whether or not to buy an automobile are the availability of public transportation and choice of residential location. These considerations all interact with one another, and it is difficult to determine which has the most significance. Thus, whether one owns an automobile will depend to some extent upon whether one lives in an apartment or a single-family dwelling, and whether one decides to live in an apartment or a single-family dwelling will depend to some extent on whether one owns an automobile; both, in turn, will depend to a degree upon the availability and quality of public transit, and to some extent the availability of transit will depend on housing choices, particularly the density at which people have chosen to live.[14]

Some progress has been made in recent years in empirically sorting out the relative strengths of these considerations. In one of the earliest and most important of these efforts,[15] the sensitivity of expected or average automobile ownership choices to various influences was derived using sophisticated statistical demand models to analyze 1968 data for the Washington, D.C., metropolitan area. These results can be converted into probabilities (shown in Table 6.5) concerning automobile ownership and transit usage for a "prototypical urban household" residing in the suburbs and working downtown.

The column at the far left in Table 6.5 indicates various combinations of autmobile ownership and transit use for the commuter worktrip. The other columns of the table indicate the extent to which these various al-

TABLE 6.5. Choice probabilities for a prototypical household[a] residing in the Washington, D.C., suburbs and working downtown—four transit scenarios.[b]

Alternative transportation choices available to household	Base Case No transit available	Case 1 Transit available at typical current levels	Case 2 Transit as good as auto for worktrips but shopping unchanged	Case 3 Transit better than auto for worktrips and equal to auto for shopping
Own no auto; commute by transit	*	.0004	.0008	.0011
Own 1 auto; commute by auto	.175 } .17	.207 } .29	.186 } .34	.170 } .38
Own 1 auto; commute by transit	*	.082	.152	.206
Own 2 autos; commute by auto	.825 } .83	.687 } .71	.617 } .66	.564 } .62
Own 2 autos; commute by transit	*	.024	.044	.059
Expected auto ownership	1.83	1.71	1.66	1.62
Reduction in expected auto ownership from a Base Case (percent)	—	-6.3	-9.0	-11.3

Source: Steven R. Lerman, "Neighborhood Choice and Transportation Services," in The Economics of Neighborhood, ed. David Segal (New York: Academic Press, 1979).

[a] Household characteristics: (1) income of $13,500; (2) resides in single-family dwelling; (3) white-collar head of household with license; (4) two children; (5) spouse has driver's license; (6) head of household works in downtown Washington, D.C.; (7) suburban residential location (Montgomery County) five miles from workplace.

[b] Scenarios: description of Base Case and Case 1 as in headings; Case 2—good line-haul service level of transit service is as good as automobile for worktrips, but shopping service at the same level as Case 1; Case 3—level of transit service as good as or better than automobile for worktrips, in-vehicle transit time 50 percent of car, out-of-vehicle transit time 66 percent of car, and shopping service equal to that of car. (Case 3 would correspond, for example, to an extensive personalized rapid transit or dual-mode system, as described in Chapter 5.)

* Not applicable.

ternatives might be expected to be chosen by the prototypical household, considering the availability and effectiveness of transit. The most salient finding is that only an 11 percent reduction in automobile ownership is projected when the situation changes from one in which there is no transit (the Base Case) to one (Case 3) in which transit is provided at a very high level (perhaps exceeding present technological capabilities). Similarly, despite exceedingly good transit (Case 3), the study projects a 73 percent use of automobiles for worktrips (0.56 + 0.17), or about 60 cars driven to work for every 100 employees at the current average of 1.2 people in every commuter automobile. It should be emphasized, however, that these projections extend the analysis well beyond the range of historical experience and observation and therefore should be interpreted with some caution.

In a later and more detailed study extending these analyses,[16] a combination of transit improvements and automobile restraint schemes is found to be moderately more effective in reducing automobile ownership than the transit-improvement-only schemes investigated in the earlier study. Specifically, as shown in Tables 6.6 and 6.7, a policy combining major transit improvements with strong automobile-use disincentives could reduce automobile ownership on average in high-income white households by as much as 43 percent. The most dramatic reductions in automobile ownership are shown to be in high- and middle-income white households and high-income black households because these households are more likely to own more than one car.

From a policy standpoint, the obvious question is whether a program of strong automobile-use disincentives and major transit improvements is at all realistic. For example, the strong automobile-use disincentives outlined under Policy 2 in Table 6.6 might well be politically unpopular and not possible to implement. If only moderate automobile-use disincentives and transit improvements are possible, as outlined under Policy 5 in Table 6.6, then only about a 5 percent (or less) reduction in automobile ownership might be expected.

Another attempt to disentangle the effects that transit availability, automobile ownership, and urban structure have on one another has been made by John F. Kain, Gary R. Fauth, and Jeffrey Zax,[17] and is summarized in Tables 6.8 and 6.9. They found that approximately one fifth of the difference (0.35) in the proportion of carless households in Phoenix and Boston (two rather dissimilar cities) could be explained by differences in their mass transportation capabilities.[18] Of course, to the extent that urban structure (for example, development density) is also a function of transit, more of the difference in automobile ownership patterns between the two cities could be attributed to transit differences, since approximately another third of the difference in the

TABLE 6.6. Expected auto ownership for prototypical households under different policy scenarios (households with licenses).

		Base Case	Policy 1[a]	Policy 2[b]	Policy 3[c]	Policy 4[d]	Policy 5[e]	Policy 6[f]
Income	Race	Current auto and transit service	Moderate auto disincentives	Strong auto disincentives	Moderate transit improvements	Major transit improvements	Moderate joint incentives	Major joint incentives
Low	White	1.02	0.97	0.89	1.00	0.93	0.95	0.88
Middle	White	1.50	1.46	1.40	1.49	1.01	1.45	0.99
High	White	1.69	1.69	1.68	1.69	0.97	1.68	0.96
Low	Black	0.97	0.95	0.91	0.97	0.95	0.94	0.90
Middle	Black	1.18	1.13	1.09	1.15	1.05	1.12	1.04
High	Black	1.59	1.58	1.54	1.57	1.03	1.56	1.02

Source: Steven R. Lerman, "Neighborhood Choice and Transportation Services," in The Economics of Neighborhood, ed. David Segal (New York: Academic Press, 1979).

[a] Impose a $1 parking charge downtown, increase automobile operating costs by 50 percent via a fuel tax, increase automobile out-of-vehicle time by five minutes per trip by regulating on-street parking.

[b] Take all actions in Policy 1 as well as a 25 percent automobile ownership tax ($200 per year) and increase car in-vehicle time 25 percent by banning traffic in certain downtown areas.

[c] Improve transit routing and scheduling to decrease in-vehicle time by 20 percent and out-of-vehicle time by 50 percent, halve all fares.

[d] Install a new rapid transit system serving the entire urban area (including fringe) at speeds equal to that of the automobile in noncentral business district zones and 2 minutes faster in the central business district. System has wait time 50 percent less than Base Case with a 15-minute maximum, and should have fares that are 50 percent of the Base Case with a 25-cent maximum. Prices for nonworktrips should be comparably improved.

[e] Policies 1 and 3 combined.

[f] Policies 2 and 4 combined.

TABLE 6.7. Percent change in expected auto ownership over Base Case for prototypical households under different policy scenarios[a] (households with licenses).

Income	Race	Base Case[a] Expected auto ownership	Policy 1[a] (percent)	Policy 2[a] (percent)	Policy 3[a] (percent)	Policy 4[a] (percent)	Policy 5[a] (percent)	Policy 6[a] (percent)
Low	White	1.02	−4.9	−12.7	−2.0	−8.8	−6.9	−13.7
Middle	White	1.50	−2.7	−6.7	−0.7	−32.7	−3.3	−34.0
High	White	1.69	0	−0.6	0	−42.6	−0.6	−43.2
Low	Black	0.97	−2.1	−6.2	0	−2.1	−3.1	−7.2
Middle	Black	1.18	−4.2	−7.6	−2.5	−11.0	−5.1	−11.9
High	Black	1.59	−0.6	−3.1	−1.3	−35.2	−1.9	−35.8

Source: Steven R. Lerman, "Neighborhood Choice and Transportation Services," in *The Economics of Neighborhood,* ed. David Segal (New York: Academic Press, 1979).
[a] See Table 6.6 for definitions of Base Case and Policies 1–6.

TABLE 6.8. Proportions of households owning zero, one, or two or more cars in Phoenix Standard Metropolitan Statistical Area (SMSA) and 125 largest SMSAs under various hypothesized circumstances.

		Probability of owning:		
Household description		Zero cars	One car	Two or more cars
A.	Average of 125 largest SMSAs	0.14	0.46	0.39
B.	A with Phoenix transport	0.13	0.47	0.41
C.	A and B with Phoenix urban structure	0.11	0.45	0.45
D.	A–C with Phoenix residences	0.08	0.44	0.48
E.	A–D with Phoenix workplaces	0.08	0.44	0.48
F.	A–E with Phoenix demography (predicted Phoenix)	0.07	0.46	0.46
G.	Actual Phoenix	0.07	0.47	0.46

Source: John F. Kain, Gary R. Fauth, and Jeffrey Zax, *Forecasting Auto Ownership and Mode Choice for U.S. Metropolitan Areas,* research report no. R77-4, Program in City and Regional Planning, Harvard University, Cambridge, Mass., December 1977.

TABLE 6.9. Proportions of households owning zero, one, or two or more cars in Boston SMSA and 125 SMSAs under various hypothesized circumstances.

		Probability of owning:		
Household description		Zero cars	One car	Two or more cars
A.	Average of 125 largest SMSAs	0.14	0.46	0.39
B.	A with Boston transport	0.20	0.45	0.35
C.	A and B with Boston urban structure	0.29	0.48	0.22
D.	A–C with Boston residences	0.36	0.49	0.15
E.	A–D with Boston workplaces	0.37	0.48	0.14
F.	A–E with Boston demography (predicted Boston)	0.40	0.49	0.12
G.	Actual Boston	0.42	0.47	0.11

Source: John F. Kain, Gary R. Fauth, and Jeffrey Zax, *Forecasting Auto Ownership and Mode Choice for U.S. Metropolitan Areas,* research report no. R77-4, Program in City and Regional Planning, Harvard University, Cambridge, Mass., December 1977.

proportion of carless households in the two cities is explained by urban structure.

If the Phoenix and Boston comparisons reported in Tables 6.8 and 6.9 are reasonably representative, transportation improvements might effectuate a 5-6 percent reduction in automobile ownership levels in urban areas. Such a figure is *remarkably* consistent with results reported in Tables 6.5, 6.6, and 6.7 from other studies; specifically, for a moderate but realistic improvement in transit (which would seem to correspond with the difference between Phoenix's and Boston's transportation capabilities), about a 5 percent reduction in automobile ownership could be projected. This would suggest that if 70 percent of the 131–143 million cars expected to exist in the United States in 1985 "resided" in urban areas (as the population will), approximately 4.5–5.0 million automobiles might be "eliminated" from the American urban scene by transit improvements attainable in the near future. Any such reduction in automobile ownership would clearly be helpful in alleviating automobile-related urban problems but would hardly be a complete solution, as the total car fleet would still be substantial and would continue to grow.

PUBLIC POLICY AND THE AMERICAN AUTOMOBILE: 1980 AND BEYOND

In summary, the prospect is that American cities will have as many or more—if slightly smaller—cars operating in them in the 1980s as in the past. The automobile is a remarkably adaptable species, whose costs can be controlled in myriad ways (not the least of which is adjusting size and performance characteristics). Until that potential for adaptability has been fully exhausted, it is premature to anticipate the automobile's demise.

Since the automobile is the dominant form of transportation in all but a handful of the very largest American cities, continued growth in automobile ownership implies that the problems created by automobiles in cities will also continue to loom large. Smaller cars will help alleviate these problems but will hardly solve them all. These problems will be analyzed in the following chapters.

7

Land Use

THE ISSUES IN HISTORICAL CONTEXT

Planners and policy makers have long viewed transportation policy as a potential tool to control broad patterns of urban land use and metropolitan development, particularly the rate of suburbanization of households and employment in large metropolitan areas. Federal aid for highway construction, for example, is often criticized for contributing to the redistribution of population and jobs from central cities to the suburbs.[1] Conversely (and in spite of the fact that any transportation improvement increases mobility), expanded or improved mass transit in cities is often alleged to lead to more compact residential and commercial development, which would permit savings in transportation, home heating, and other energy-related costs.[2] As might be expected, recent concerns about energy consumption in the United States and other Western industrialized countries have led to a resurgence of such claims.[3]

The hope that urban transportation policies can alter land use seems well based on historical observation and personal intuition. Innovations in urban transportation technology have played a significant role in shaping urban land use in the past. Development and spread of the horse-drawn and electric street railways between 1870 and 1910, for example, are widely credited with stimulating early suburbanization.[4]

Street railways were faster than walking and cheaper than horse-drawn omnibuses, and thereby increased the land area within commuting distance of the metropolitan center. Introduction of the automobile encouraged additional suburbanization of residences by further increasing the areas within commuting range. More recently, the introduction of high-performance urban highways has had an impact on the form and development of American cities.

History, though, may be a misleading guide to the present and to the future. The dramatic urban transportation innovations that greatly modified urban development patterns—for example, the electric streetcar and the first urban freeways—were those that brought new lands into development. In contrast, most public transit improvements proposed since 1960, particularly new rail transit systems, have largely been for the benefit of established urban areas. Even most proposed extensions to established rail transit systems have usually involved only expanding the system into well-populated suburbs, often substituting rail for bus transit. Similarly, many central artery and inner-loop, high-performance urban highways improve at the inner rather than at the outer margin of development.

While many past innovations in urban transportation technology made significant changes in transportation speeds and costs, these are not likely to be matched by future improvements. In large part, this is because the level of urban transportation services in most U.S. metropolitan areas is extremely high today. The average worktrip takes only 30 minutes or less in virtually every U.S. city.[5] And there is growing evidence from time-valuation studies and consumer surveys that most U.S. commuters do not "resent" commuter trips as long as they are less than about 30 minutes in length.[6] This suggests a considerable degree of satisfaction in most cities with existing urban transportation capabilities (in spite of the understandable grumbling whenever actual traffic congestion is encountered).

The impact of transportation on urban development is also slowed or limited in the short run by the durability of existing houses or commercial structures and the value of the investments they represent. The enormous expense of moving, demolishing, or abandoning an existing structure is reflected by the fact that most standing buildings in U.S. cities are the first and only structures that ever stood on their sites. Thus, even if transportation policies provided powerful incentives for households or businesses to relocate, the cost of moving or replacing the present stock of buildings is such that it might take many years before substantial changes in location were observable.

The potential for influencing urban development patterns through transportation improvements at the inner margin is further limited by the likelihood that new, dense development may be considered incompatible with established land uses—especially in residential areas— and therefore restricted by zoning or other public policies. In contrast, when prior urban transportation improvements opened up development at the outer margin, the restraining influence of neighborhood preferences (and accompanying zoning controls) was far less inhibiting.

Moreover, the role of past transportation improvements in shaping metropolitan development may very well have been exaggerated by some observers. Changing transportation techniques were not the only wellsprings of suburbanization during the past century or first three quarters of this century. Rising incomes played a critical part by allowing for the purchase of larger and better-quality housing, which tended to be more readily available and at lower prices in the suburbs. Changes in production technology, such as those favoring the one-story factory layout, also encouraged suburbanization. While it is impossible to determine the precise contribution of each of these factors to business and residential location changes, transportation improvements are clearly not responsible for all observed changes in urban development patterns. As shown in Chapter 2 and the Appendix, over the past century, cities around the world have decentralized almost without regard to the transportation facilities available.

Any attempt to use transportation policy to modify urban form thus runs the danger of being undermined by other factors that govern location choices. Understanding the potential impact of transportation improvements requires not only an analysis of past trends but also a comprehension of the various theoretical linkages between transportation improvements and land-use development, and of the relative empirical strengths of these linkages.

TRANSPORTATION IN RELATION TO LAND USE: THE THEORY

Location theory. The theoretical models that constitute "location theory" provide a conceptual basis for examining the linkages between transportation and land use.[7] Location-theory models usually focus on either residential-location decisions or workplace-location decisions, but seldom consider both simultaneously. The models also tend to analyze the effects of changes on only one transportation mode (such as freight or passenger) and only one type of trip (such as shopping or commuting) at a time. The models are theoretical in the sense that they are rarely calibrated with empirical data, and thus at best predict only the direction, not the magnitude or rate, of land-use change. A model might be able to predict, for example, whether a particular transportation change will create incentives for firms or households to move away from or closer to the metropolitan center but not what portion of the households would move, how far, or when. One important insight that location-theory models do provide, however, is that most transportation changes establish complex and conflicting incentives for the relocation of households and businesses, and thus for altered land use and development.

Residential-location decisions. The traditional "monocentric" model of residential location postulates that everyone is employed at a central location and that the number of employees is predetermined or fixed. The residential-location decision then reduces to a worker deciding how far from the center to live. Generally, it is presumed in these models that the farther one lives from the center, the higher the costs of commuting (both in time and out-of-pocket) and the lower the price of a housing unit of a given type.[8] The total cost, or "gross price," of choosing a particular residential location and housing type is the sum of the commuting costs and the rent for that type of housing at that location.[9] It is hypothesized that households reside at locations that minimize the gross price of the particular type of housing desired.

Within such a model, an increase in income is likely to encourage households to move farther from the central city, although it affects the trade-off between housing prices and commuting costs in conflicting ways. On the one hand, higher incomes allow households to spend more on housing services and thus encourage moves to the suburbs where the price of a housing unit of any particular size or quality is generally lower. On the other hand, increased incomes generally raise the value placed on time spent traveling, thus increasing commuting costs and encouraging moves closer to the metropolitan center. Most analysts argue that when incomes increase, the desire of the average U.S. household to use income gains for better housing is strong enough to overcome the increased time costs of transport; higher incomes will therefore cause households to move farther from the central city.[10]

The impact of any reduction in commuting costs, in contrast, will have an unmistakable, decentralizing effect on residential-location decisions. In essence, a reduction in commuting costs will effectively increase the real incomes of households, since they can purchase more transport capability for a given sum or, alternatively, spend less to consume the same capability. Moreover, if the reduction in commuting costs lowers the marginal cost of commuting an additional mile (as opposed to lowering commuting costs by the same amount for all workers, no matter how far they travel), then households will have an additional incentive to move farther out, all else being equal. A reduction in commuting costs will thus encourage households to move farther from the central city because of its indirect effect on income as well as its direct effect on price; this, in turn, will decrease residential density near the metropolitan center and in the metropolitan area as a whole. Conversely, increased commuting costs will reduce real incomes and housing consumption and cause households to move closer in, thereby increasing residential density near the metropolitan center and in the metropolitan area as a whole.

Some transportation improvements may have different cost impacts on different income groups. In particular, if higher-income groups place more value on their time (as widely believed), then the introduction of faster forms of urban transportation (such as commuter trains, express buses, express highways) could lower their total commuting costs, even if the higher-performance facilities had greater out-of-pocket costs (that is, for the higher-income groups, time savings would outweigh the direct travel cost increases). Clearly, then, if incomes are increasing, if better-quality housing is cheaper and more available in outlying locations, and if urban transportation improvements emphasize time-saving rather than direct-cost reductions, location theory would unequivocally predict that residences would decentralize.

Transportation changes will not only influence residential location decisions but will also influence land prices. The exact extent of such influence will depend on the elasticities of the relevant supply and demand curves. Thus, at least part of any change in transportation costs is likely to be absorbed by landowners in the form of altered rents. The monocentric model just outlined would predict that when commuting costs decrease, all else being equal, the price of residential land close to the center will decrease relative to the price of land farther out (because of the shifts in demand indicated above).[11] These price changes, in turn, can be expected to influence business-location decisions by changing the relative costs of doing business at central and less central locations.

Business-location decisions. The standard business-location model, in contrast with the residential model just described, starts with the supposition that the number and location of jobs are not fixed and that the firms located in a metropolitan center compete for sales and profits with firms located in the suburbs and other metropolitan areas. A change in the cost of commuting to a metropolitan center may affect the competitive advantage of firms located there and thus, ultimately, the number of workers they employ.[12]

Specifically, a change in commuting costs is hypothesized to affect the competitive advantage of central-area firms in two ways. First, by altering the amount of time or money workers must spend commuting, a transportation change should affect the real incomes of those employed in the metropolitan center and thus the wages that centrally located employers must pay in order to attract a given number of workers. A commuting cost decrease, for example, should allow employers (all else being equal) to reduce wages, thereby improving their firms' position relative to competitors located in other areas; a commuting cost increase would force them to increase wages, degrading their competitive position.

The second (and probably more important) way in which commuting costs may affect the competitive position of a centrally located firm is through changes in residential and land rents. As noted, a commuting cost decrease is likely to reduce rents for residential land adjoining a central business area and thus make workplace location or expansion there less expensive. On the other hand, a commuting cost increase will increase central rents and therefore the site costs of central workplace locations or expansion.[13]

A change in commuting costs, then, should influence not only the residential choices of workers employed in the metropolitan center but also the number of workers who have jobs there. Lower commuting costs will increase employment in the central area relative to other areas by increasing central-area workers' real incomes and decreasing rents on adjoining residential land. A commuting cost increase will decrease central-area employment by reducing workers' real incomes and raising rents on adjoining land. Thus, in theory, a commuting cost decrease tends to decentralize residences while it centralizes job locations (which, in turn, should help centralize residences, all else being equal); an increase in commuting costs will work in just the opposite fashion, centralizing residences and decentralizing jobs.[14]

Residence and workplace interactions. Locations of residences and workplaces are, obviously, closely tied because workers must be able to commute to their jobs. The residential- and workplace-location models reviewed above reflect this tie in their predictions that a change in commuting costs can affect both the distance between a worker's residence and his workplace and employment levels at different workplaces. There is, however, one additional significant interaction between residences and workplaces that is not captured by the models just described. This interaction is caused by the tendency of firms in certain "population-serving" industries to locate close to residences. Population-serving industries (in contrast to nonpopulation-serving or "basic" industries, which export their goods and services to other areas) sell frequently purchased goods and services—such as food, toiletries, drugs, clothing, gasoline, and dry cleaning—to households. Locations convenient to major residential neighborhoods are therefore attractive to firms in these industries.[15]

To the extent that population-serving firms locate close to residences,[16] the effect of any transportation change on residential location will be reinforced by a corresponding effect on population-serving employment. In particular, if a transportation change decentralized residences, then it would also decentralize employment in population-serving firms and the residences of the workers employed in those firms. The link between residential location and the location of population-serving firms will be strengthened or weakened by changes in shoppingtrip costs as well. A general reduction in shoppingtrip costs, for example, can decrease the tendency of population-serving employment to locate close to residences and increase the relative size of larger retail centers.[17] Or if a transport cost reduction applies to a single shopping center, employment at that center should grow (partly at the expense of neighboring centers).[18]

The net effect. A commuting cost change clearly establishes conflicting incentives for location changes. A commuting cost reduction, for example, tends to lower residential densities because it encourages workers employed in the central production area to buy or rent larger or better-quality housing and, consequently, to relocate farther from the center, and because population-serving firms probably will move to be close to the relocated residences. But the same commuting cost reduction also tends to raise central densities because centrally located employers *may* be able to pay less, all else being equal, for centrally located land and centrally employed labor; employment levels would thus increase in the metropolitan center, as would the number of workers living within commuting range.

Using location theory alone, it is therefore extremely difficult, if not impossible, to predict with any certainty what a transportation policy or improvement will do to urban form. It is at least conceivable, for example, that construction of urban expressways in the post–World War II decades did not greatly alter the overall distribution of population between central cities and the suburbs. By decreasing commuting time within a metropolitan area, central-city radial expressways probably induced downtown workers to move farther out. They also increased the competitive advantage of centrally located firms, however, by lowering land rents and wages, thus increasing downtown employment. If the expressways had not been built, central-area workers might have lived closer to the downtown, but employment would also have been less concentrated in the central city; this combination of less downtown employment and more suburban jobs might well have produced distributions of residential populations within metropolitan areas not too dissimilar from those that exist today. The impact, if any, was probably to increase the intensity of daytime activities in central business districts and to reduce nighttime activities there—giving rise to what has been characterized as the "empty doughnut" effect in urban development patterns.

Simulation models. In recent years, several attempts have been made to simulate the impact of transportation changes on urban development patterns. In these efforts, empirical data are used to calibrate the important relationships identified in the location-theory models: for example, how consumer demand for housing services and other products responds to changes in prices and real incomes, and how business production decisions are affected by changes in land and wage costs. In addition, these simulation models usually attempt to reveal some of the "disequilibria" created by the longevity of many urban investments; thus, these models often will describe the characteristics of the current stock of housing and commercial buildings and the expense and delay that would be involved if the location, quantity, and types of housing and buildings were altered to accommodate changes in household and business demands.

Calibration with empirical data enables the simulation models, unlike location theory, to make specific—and, it is hoped, realistic—predictions about the direction, magnitude, and rate of land-use change; thus, these models can be used to isolate the impact of transportation changes by simulating metropolitan or regional land-use development patterns with and without the specified change.

Two of the earliest and best-known simulation efforts are the Lowry model[19] and the EMPIRIC model.[20] The Lowry model (circa 1964) is named after its developer, Ira S. Lowry, and has been used by other researchers in analyzing data from a large number of U.S. and British cities. The Lowry model predicts the location of residences and population-serving employment within a metropolis, given an outside (exogenous) forecast of basic employment locations. The number of residences within each zone in the metropolis is assumed to be a function of the distance between the zone and important workplaces (both for basic and population-serving industries) and the amount of developable land in the zone. The level of population-serving employment in a zone is assumed to be a function of the level of population in and near the zone. The Lowry model thus assumes that the location of basic employment is fixed but that the locations of both residences and population-serving employment may change. Consequently, its forecasts of transportation's impact on metropolitan development have the drawback that movements of residences and population-serving employment may be offset by conflicting shifts in basic employment that are not part of the model.[21]

EMPIRIC, in contrast, allows for movement of residences and all types of employment. The model was developed by Daniel Brand, Brian Barber, and Michael Jacobs (circa 1967) and has been widely used in many U.S. cities as part of local land-use and transportation planning efforts. EMPIRIC uses extremely simple versions of conventional residential and workplace location-theory models to predict future distribution of employment and population among different zones within a metropolitan area. EMPIRIC does not forecast the total population and employment in a metropolitan area; rather, given such a forecast, it predicts the level of population and employment in each zone. Employment is classified into five types (manufacturing, retail, service, financial/insurance/real estate, and other). The future employment level of each type in each zone is assumed to be a function of the zone's future population levels, an index of its future "accessibility" by automobile and transit, its current employment levels, and its current quantity of vacant land. Future population is assumed to be a function of past population, future accessibility between the zone and major workplaces by automobile and transit, and a few other variables. These EMPIRIC employment and population functions are fitted by choosing equation forms and empirical values that enable the model to replicate past land-use changes as closely as possible. Even though the EMPIRIC model replicates past changes reasonably well, it remains an open question as to whether these highly simplified representations of complex location decisions[22] will predict future location patterns accurately.

More recent attempts to develop urban land-use simulation models have been undertaken by a group of researchers at the National Bureau of Economic Research (NBER)[23] and by Edwin S. Mills[24] (both published in 1972). The NBER and Mills simulation models were constructed primarily to explore the theory of residential-location choice and to pioneer or extend the art of calibrating location models with empirical data. While both models were eventually used to simulate the effects of opening new expressways and other transportation changes, the researchers recognized that these simulations were not very accurate, because their forecasts of residential-location changes would be at least partially offset by workplace-location changes that were omitted from both models.

An even more recent attempt to use simulation analysis to explore the impact of transportation on land use has been made by Kenneth A. Small.[25] Small investigates changes in both workplace and residential locations and, more than any predecessor, focuses on the impact of prospective transportation improvements on land use. He also places much greater emphasis on the direct employment effects of constructing and operating a new transportation facility, and he estimates the secondary jobs created by an increase in primary employment. Small also investigates how different kinds of transportation improvements—say, transit versus highway—will affect city versus suburban residents and employers.[26]

In spite of Small's somewhat different interests and focus, his results (derived from an application of his model to Cleveland) are not unlike those of previous experiments with simulation models or, for that matter, the broad conclusions derivable from location theory as outlined above. He concludes as follows: "The results . . . show the total effect [of a transit improvement] to be pro-city for jobs, and practically neutral for households and population . . . Given the potential for error, however, the most important finding may well be that the opposing effects of improved accessibility to CBD and suburbs are indeed of comparable magnitude, and are therefore substantially offsetting . . . The relatively stronger positive impact on jobs suggests that improving transit on radial corridors provides further impetus to the tendency of large cities to become daytime centers of activity."

In sum, while simulation models hold potential for more accurate forecasts of transportation effects on land use, to date this promise has not been fully realized. All of the simulation models are dependent to a greater or lesser extent upon the reliability—not yet well established—of the underlying theory and empirical estimates of relevant parameters. An important contribution of these simulation models, however, may be to provide keener insights about where the theoretical and empirical underpinnings are particularly weak and sensitive.

TRANSPORTATION IN RELATION TO LAND USE: THE EMPIRICAL EVIDENCE

Empirical studies of the effects of transportation changes on land use are of two major types: (1) intercity comparisons that contrast land-use development patterns in metropolitan areas with different types of transportation facilities (for example, areas with and without rail transit systems or with and without circumferential expressways); and (2) intracity studies that compare patterns of land use before and after the opening of a major new transportation facility (such as an expressway, rail transit line, or airport) and also compare patterns of land use near a new facility with patterns in control areas in the same city presumably not affected by the transportation improvement under investigation.

A major difficulty of all these empirical studies is controlling for the multiplicity of factors besides transportation that can influence land-use choices. These control problems, as noted below, tend to be different for the different types of studies and always make firm conclusions difficult to establish.

Intercity comparative studies. Perhaps the earliest attempt to use intercity comparisons as a means of estimating the impact of transportation on land-use patterns was that undertaken by John R. Meyer, John F. Kain, and Martin Wohl as part of their study of U.S. urban transportation problems.[27] They did not find any strong evidence that the availability or extensive use of public transit in a city led to greater centralization of the city's economic activity. Their evidence suggested that cities with widely used transit were decentralizing at least as quickly, if not more quickly, than those without much of a transit tradition. This pattern of decentralization even seemed to apply to employment in corporate headquarters, financial institutions, and other central-office functions that might be expected to benefit most from the availability of transit.[28] Recognizing that these observed patterns of development in transit-oriented and nontransit-oriented cities might be explained by other factors, Meyer, Kain, and Wohl concluded only that the availability of transit did not appear to be a sufficient condition to guarantee continued growth and prosperity of an older CBD.

More recently, an Urban Institute study has compared patterns of retail sales in six metropolitan areas: three where beltways opened in the 1960s and three without beltways.[29] The data shown in Table 7.1 are taken from that study and indicate that, between 1963 and 1972, CBD retail sales declined by 7 percent in the metropolitan areas with beltways but grew by 18 percent in the metropolitan areas without beltways. From this, the Urban Institute researchers concluded that beltways probably depressed retail sales and employment in metropolitan centers. But their analysis did not control for all nontransportation influences that could have contributed to differing patterns of retail sales, and thus their interpretation of the results must be qualified.

This "failure" was not for want of trying: the Urban Institute researchers were careful to select metropolitan areas with similar popula-

TABLE 7.1. Comparisons of three SMSAs with and three SMSAs without beltways.

	Three SMSAs without beltways[a]	Three SMSAs with beltways[b]
Retail sales:		
Average 1977 retail sales (in millions of dollars):		
SMSA as a whole	6,412	6,881
CBD only	790	585
Percent change in retail sales, 1963–72:		
SMSA as a whole	106	111
CBD only	18	−7
CBD sales as percent of SMSA sales:		
In 1963	21.4	19.4
In 1972	12.3	8.5
Percent change, 1963–72	−43	−56
Other characteristics:		
Average 1970 SMSA land area in square miles	1,733	2,178
Average household income:		
In 1970 (dollars)	10,146	9,729
Percent change, 1960–70	66.4	65.3
Average SMSA population:		
In 1970	918,000	963,000
Percent change, 1960–70	28.4	39.6

Source: Data from Tom Muller et al., *Economic Impact of I–295 on Richmond Central Business District* (Washington, D.C.: Urban Institute, 1977), pp. 32–38.
[a] New Orleans, La.; Louisville, Ky.; and Rochester, N.Y.
[b] San Antonio, Tex.; Columbus, Ohio; and Indianapolis, Ind.

tions, land areas, income levels, and rates of growth in metropolitan retail sales. During the 1960s, however, the three metropolitan areas with beltways were experiencing much higher rates of population growth than the areas without beltways; this could have made the number of new housing starts, and thus suburbanization, much larger and faster in the metropolitan areas with beltways even if the beltways had not existed. The Urban Institute also did not investigate differences in the industrial composition of the different metropolitan areas, which might have been important if, for example, the metropolitan areas with beltways had relatively high concentrations of industries that were suburbanizing particularly rapidly in the 1960s.

Intracity comparative studies. Attempts to determine the impact of urban transportation improvements on land use from intracity comparisons are generally made by contrasting what happens in land areas close to a new facility before and after the facility's installation with changes that occur in similar areas in the same metropolitan area not adjacent to the new facility (and therefore presumed not to be affected by the new transportation installation). But as location theory indicates, transportation system changes can affect land use in distant as well as neighboring areas. For example, a reduction in transportation costs to a particular workplace may increase employment at that site at the expense of other workplaces in the metropolitan areas (or even in other metropolitan areas for that matter); similarly, a reduction in commuting costs in one radial corridor of a metropolitan area may increase residential density in that corridor while decreasing residential density in other corridors. Use of other workplaces or residential areas as controls is thus likely to exaggerate the land-use effects of a transportation change, even if the control areas are distant from the improvement under analysis.

Still another problem common to intracity analyses[30] is the difficulty distinguishing whether a transportation improvement or a shift in population and employment is the cause of change. For example, it is not always obvious whether the construction of a new expressway caused or was caused by growth in nearby population and employment. These relationships are especially difficult to disentangle because developers, politicians, and transportation planners may anticipate one another's decisions. For example, developers' expectation of a new transportation facility may cause them to build new housing developments or industrial parks prior to the opening, construction, or even planning of the new facility. A clear identification of causal relationships therefore requires not only geographically detailed data over many years but also a sophisticated understanding of the expectation and lags of developers and policy makers.

In spite of these limitations, intracity comparisons have been popular as a means of understanding the impact of transportation improvements on land use. Particularly interesting for present purposes are the investigations of four all-new, large-scale rail transit systems installed in Toronto, Montreal, San Francisco, and Washington, D.C.[31]

The Toronto subway system has been the subject of numerous investigations, three using sophisticated econometric analyses[32] and others using a less rigorously quantitative, historical, case-study approach.[33] The historical studies have generally affirmed transit development impact on land use. But these studies suffer acutely from the control problems outlined above. Specifically, many case studies do not clearly delineate between land-use changes that might have occurred anyway (say, because of general growth in the Toronto or Canadian economies) and land-use changes clearly attributable to the subway.

The three econometric studies are split in their conclusions. One of the three studies[34] concludes that the Toronto subway had no impact on property values once controls were established for other influences. A second study,[35] focusing on population density changes rather than on real estate values, found little population density effect in the first few years after the subway was partially completed and opened, but significant density effects after the subway was fully opened (in 1955) in areas close to the transit system. The third study,[36] focusing primarily on rent gradients at various distances and angles to the Bloor-Danforth line of the Toronto system, concluded that residential values for properties nearest the subway line increased more rapidly between 1961 and 1971 than property values farther away (while controlling for other influences).

An intensive review of all these studies and related evidence concluded that the Toronto subway system did have a major impact on the distribution and intensity of development, though not as much as many proponents claimed.[37] The impact appears to have largely taken the form of shifting development from one radial corridor to another; there was less evidence, by contrast, of a shift in employment or population between the suburbs and the center. The Toronto subway system's influence on land use was apparently greatly enhanced by the local government's coordination of the subway system's development with zoning and other land-use policies in a way unique to North American experience.[38] The evidence also demonstrated that the transit system was not the "single cause" of the observed land-use effects but that a "variety of economic and social factors combined to create a heavy and continuing demand for new central-city office space and apartments" in Toronto. Furthermore, "recent historical forces such as European immigration" helped ensure a strong orientation toward transit usage, again unique for North America.

There is less evidence that San Francisco's BART had major land-use impact,[39] although BART may have been responsible for some redirection of office building activity within downtown San Francisco south of Market Street. Before BART, there was little new office development in this area; since the inception of BART's operation, 88 percent of the major new downtown office development has been south of Market Street. BART also seems to have accelerated residential development in certain outlying areas previously perceived as beyond commuting distance to San Francisco. Although it has proven impossible to determine exactly what land developments would have occurred without BART, the most careful analysis yet undertaken suggests that BART's overall impact was relatively slight in its first few years of operation.[40]

The BART experience illustrates the uphill nature of any attempt to use transportation improvements to modify land-use patterns. In the BART service area, worktrips to the major employment centers, on average, take about 40 minutes on BART. The bus transit that BART supplanted served such trips, on average, in about 54 minutes. Thus, BART effectuated a 14-minute average improvement per trip over previously available public transit. But automobile trips to these same employment centers average about 26 minutes during peak periods so that commuting by automobile is faster than BART by a fairly substantial margin.[41]

A typical "modal split" curve, shown in Figure 7.1, illustrates how such changes in travel time might influence the choice between public transit and the private automobile in San Francisco. A modal split curve is often used by transportation planners to summarize estimates of the relationship between the shares of travelers carried by transit and auto and the relative travel times or costs of the two modes. Modal split curves typically have the shape shown in Figure 7.1. In essence, BART moved the average ratio of transit to automobile travel times in San Francisco from 2.15 (56 minutes divided by 26) to 1.54 (40 minutes divided by 26). Since such a change is located on the right-hand flat section of the curve in Figure 7.1, BART should have little impact on the modes used by San Francisco travelers. If the change in travel times brought about by BART is not sufficient to affect travelers' choices of mode, it is also unlikely to be sufficient to affect the choices of residential or business location, especially in the short run.[42]

These travel-time figures are overall averages, though, which may disguise a great deal of diversity and change in particular areas. For example, if BART created several areas (perhaps around important transit stations) where the transit-to-automobile time ratio moved close to unity, choice of mode and land usage could well change. The potential number of areas with such favorable transit-time ratios would be greater if the overall reduction in the average transit-to-automobile

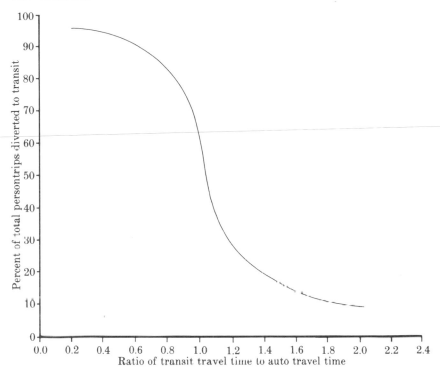

Figure 7.1. Typical modal split curve.

time ratio had been more dramatic. For example, if BART had brought the overall transit-to-automobile time ratio down to 1.00 rather than 1.54, transit would likely have been preferred to the automobile for commuter worktrips in large sectors of the BART service area.

Without a dramatic lowering in the overall transit-to-automobile trip time, however, the potential for a major transit improvement like BART to influence land use would depend on a considerable independent boom in the demand for high-density housing or workplaces. BART might then serve to concentrate the resulting high-density developments around major stations. This apparently did not occur, however, especially in residential areas. Where there was a demand for high-density development near a BART station, local community opposition often prevented such development through zoning or other policy constraints, and in neighborhoods where such opposition was not manifested, there was often insufficient demand.[43] Prior existence of structures of some value in many locations also often precluded development to higher densities.

What little evidence there is on the land-use impacts of the new Montreal and Washington, D.C., systems is not inconsistent with the findings on the Toronto and San Francisco systems. The general view seems to be that Montreal's Metro made the downtown business area more accessible and perhaps strengthened its development potential but that it did not alter the size or the structure of the downtown area to any appreciable degree.[44] The lack of much open space for development around most of Montreal's Metro stations and the fact that there are no special zoning provisions for higher-density developments, such as those provided in Toronto, also seem to have minimized the Metro's land-use impacts in Montreal.

The Washington system is too new to provide much evidence one way or another about the land-use impacts of public transit. What evidence there is would suggest little impact. The following "progress" report has been made on the Washington Metro: "It is apparent that Metro has had little effect on actual development around its stations at [an] early stage in the system's own life . . . Many Metro stations tend to be either in fully-developed commercial areas (where the costs of redevelopment are high), in deteriorated areas (where demand is low), or in low-density residential areas (where resistance is strong). So far, the advantages of Metro, coupled with the effects of public agencies to encourage development, have not been strong enough to overcome these obstacles."[45]

Several analyses have also been made of the impact of various extensions made to existing transit systems. The Lindenwold line, extending from Philadelphia to Camden, New Jersey, and environs, has received particularly intense scrutiny.[46] Studies of the impact of extensions to existing systems generally arrive at much the same conclusions as those found for entirely new systems: not much impact is observable except where development or redevelopment is supported by other forces, such as a strong underlying demand for higher-density development and public policies favoring special zoning or other redevelopment incentives. This conclusion appears to be particularly sustainable for heavy rail and commuter rail extensions, with even less impact discernible for other transit improvements such as busways, new express bus services, or extensions of light rail systems.[47]

SUMMARY AND IMPLICATIONS

In sum, there are several reasons why transportation policy is unlikely to be a major force in molding large-scale changes in metropolitan land use, and particularly unlikely to shape the relative growth rates of central cities and suburbs in the United States. Prospective investments in urban transportation facilities generally will make only small changes in overall metropolitan travel times or in the amount of readily accessible and developable land. Any possible effect of transit improvements on land use will be dampened by the fact that changes in transportation costs or accessibility generally establish conflicting, and thus at least partially offsetting, incentives for the locations of households and businesses. Land-use changes are also influenced by a variety of other factors, such as income growth or changes in production technologies, which can overwhelm the impact of altered transportation.

Even when transportation does influence land development, its impact tends to be on a limited or local scale and most effective when coordinated, as in Toronto, with other public policies (such as zoning incentives and urban renewal) favoring higher-density development at relevant locations (such as transit stations). Furthermore, if there is no underlying demand for higher-density development, then almost no combination of public policies will elicit a more compact urban structure in a modern market economy such as that of the United States.

The fact that transportation's impact on metropolitan development is probably small, and certainly poorly understood, has clear policy implications. Above all, the conflicting incentives established by transportation changes make it extremely difficult to design a transportation policy that is certain to achieve any particular desired effect on metropolitan development.

If a significant change in the rate of suburbanization or other large-scale development patterns is desired, moreover, current transportation policies would probably have to be drastically altered. Such policy changes are likely to impose substantial inconveniences on travelers or involve the expenditure of large amounts of public and private funds in the abandonment of some existing transportation facilities or the construction of new ones. Transportation policies designed to control metropolitan development could also conflict, perhaps seriously, with policies that advance other objectives, such as reducing transportation energy consumption or air pollution or improving the mobility of the handicapped.

Such expense and conflict may be unnecessary, moreover, since more effective alternatives to control metropolitan development—such as zoning controls or housing policy—may be available. Wage subsidies for low-income persons trapped in central-city residential areas, or increased federal revenue sharing for central cities, may also provide more direct means of alleviating any social or economic problems caused by the suburbanization of residences and employment.

As a policy tool for shaping urban growth and development, transportation thus seems best restricted to very localized or small-scale applications where the transportation change is conceived as a complement to other public policies more directly serving the specified goals.[48] Transportation in and of itself is not likely to be a panacea for correcting perceived deficiencies in urban form, though it can sometimes play a helpful but limited role when linked to other public policy initiatives.

8

Energy

THE U.S. ENERGY SITUATION: AN OVERVIEW

The United States accounts for roughly one half of the world's total consumption of energy and produces substantially less than it consumes. U.S. consumption of energy is also very high on a per capita basis, or even relative to gross national product, though this high national average may be explained to a considerable extent by climate, industrial mix, and transcontinental distances.[1] As a consequence, the United States ran a very large trade deficit on its energy accounts in the 1970s, and many observers in the United States and elsewhere expressed the belief that the U.S. government should take steps to reduce consumption of energy in general and of imported oil in particular.

An even more urgent reason for energy conservation is that available supplies may prove inadequate, especially in the long run. Viewed from the standpoint of U.S. energy consumption alone, this seems highly probable—even though in the mid-1970s the announced national policy was to achieve energy independence or self-sufficiency. A commonly used metric for determining the future supply and demand of a particular resource is "index years of availability," defined as the estimated time required to exhaust the economically retrievable reserves or resources of a given raw material.[2] This definition, as used here, will be refined to restrict a resource's use to its most productive applications, since many energy sources are specialized, some adapting better to particular functions than others.[3]

To estimate the index years of availability, the major functional uses of energy must be identified. In the United States, roughly one quarter of energy use is consumed by transportation, one third is consumed in generating electricity, another third is consumed by (nonelectrical) space heating, and the remainder (about 10 percent) goes to a variety of miscellaneous purposes, the most important of which are direct inputs to industry.[4]

Another essential step in estimating index years of availability is to make some inferences about how energy resources might be optimally deployed—say, under circumstances in which the market mechanism was not too inhibited and prices determined the most logical or economically efficient use of fuels. Technological limitations on substitutability must also be taken into account. For instance, transportation is heavily dependent on the use of oil derivatives or liquid hydrocarbons as an energy source. In contrast, a variety of energy sources can generate electricity. A rational allocation of energy resources, therefore, might be to limit the use of liquid hydrocarbons in electric power generation and place major reliance instead on coal and uranium, augmented by hydroelectric and solar energy. Concerns about air pollution might fortify the case for this reallocation, since cleaning up the air is characterized by substantial economies of scale; accordingly, dirty fuels, such as coal, might be used for electric power generation, an industry in which plants are large and relatively few, while clean fuels, such as natural gas, might be used almost exclusively in small-scale but widespread applications, such as residential space heating.

Thus, in a society in which environment concerns loom large and markets are permitted to determine the allocation of resources, it might be expected that: (1) transportation energy requirements would be mainly, although not exclusively, satisfied by petroleum (as long as it was available); (2) space heating would be primarily achieved by natural gas and electricity (to the extent that heating requirements continue to be satisfied from nonrenewable energy sources);[5] and (3) the generation of electricity would be primarily performed by the burning of coal or the development of nuclear energy, augmented wherever possible by hydroelectric or other renewable (for example, solar) power sources.

The impact of such specialization on the consumption of major energy sources at 1976–77 levels is shown in Table 8.1. Without specialization and without imports, domestic consumption of crude oil and natural gas would exhaust U.S. reserves recoverable at 1976–77 energy prices in 5–12 years and exhaust U.S. reserves at "high" energy prices

TABLE 8.1. U.S. energy reserves at 1976–77 consumption levels with and without specialization by sources and uses.

| | Annual consumption in quads[a] per year | | Index years of availability | | | |
| | | | Without specialization | | With specialization | |
	Mid-1970s use without specialization	With use specialization	Recoverable resources[b] at 1976–77 prices	Recoverable resources[c] at "high" prices	Recoverable resources[b] at 1976–77 prices	Recoverable resources[c] at "high" prices
Crude oil:						
Exclusive of tar sands and oil shale	35	18	5–6	25–55	10–12	50–115
Inclusive of tar sands and oil shale	*	*	*	190–360	*	370–725
Natural gas	21	15	11–12	26–62	16	36–87
Coal	14	24	445	1,600–3,000	260	950–1,740
Uranium	2	14	168–10,500	700–56,000	24–1,500	100–8,000
Hydroelectric	3	4	*	*	*	*

Source: Alternatives for Growth, copyright 1977, National Bureau of Economic Research, Inc., reprinted with permission from Ballinger Publishing Company; Energy: The Next Twenty Years, copyright 1979, the Ford Foundation, reprinted with permission from Ballinger Publishing Company.

[a] One quad equals 10^15 British thermal units.
[b] Generally defined to be "material on the ground that can be produced and sold with currently available technology at current prices," roughly equivalent to "proven reserves."
[c] An estimate (sometimes characterized as "hypothetical" or "speculative") of that portion of the earth's crust to be found in a raw material and that can be recovered without "overwhelming technological difficulties" or unduly "high costs of ultimate recovery."
* Not applicable.

in 25–62 years (but longer if oil from tar sands or oil shale is counted). Domestic reserves of coal, uranium, and hydroelectric power would be depleted over a much longer period. With specialization, in contrast, U.S. crude oil and natural gas reserves recoverable at 1976–77 prices would last perhaps twice as long, and reserves recoverable at "high" prices would last some 50–115 years (longer if oil from tar sands and oil shale is counted).

Whether specialization and, specifically, the consumption levels in column 2 of Table 8.1 represent sensible targets for U.S. energy policy is debatable.[6] For example, if national self-reliance or independence in energy sources is rejected as public policy, specialization may be less valuable and more petroleum might be used (for example, for purposes of generating electricity) on the premise that oil can be imported from abroad for a reasonable price (reasonable being defined as cheaper than alternative and equivalent sources, allowing for all social, environmental, and national security costs, and so on). Another argument against specialization is that it may involve substantial transitional problems; it would be impossible to move quickly from the 13–15 quads of coal produced in the United States per year in the late 1970s to 24 or so without encountering significant difficulties. Finally, the numbers in Table 8.1 are based on mid-1970s energy-use statistics; any growth in energy use—as might be expected with population and income increases—would reduce the availability estimates for most reserves and resources.[7] On the other hand, conservation efforts that switched energy use from nonrenewable to renewable sources would have an offsetting effect.

Presuming some need for energy self-sufficiency and specialization, however, the numbers in Table 8.1 clearly indicate that any U.S. energy problem is primarily one of oil, or, more generally, liquid hydrocarbons. There are three policy options for dealing with this liquid hydrocarbon problem, all of which might be pursued simultaneously. One possibility is to make a major shift from oil and gas to coal and nuclear energy. Another is to greatly reduce total consumption of liquid hydrocarbons through conservation programs. A third is to greatly expand supplies of liquid hydrocarbons or their substitutes, most probably by accelerating the rate at which "synthetic" oil can be produced from tar sands, oil shale, or coal.[8]

Urban transportation policy would be affected in a major way by the substitution option only if electric or steam automobiles reappeared in substantial numbers. Replacing petroleum with coal or nuclear energy seems most likely in electric utilities (but is greatly complicated by environmental concerns). Finding a substitute for natural gas involves coal gasification and, possibly, using more solar energy or electricity, each more applicable to space heating than to transportation.

When it comes to the conservation option, however, urban transportation comes very much to the fore. Indeed, the real possibilities for major conservation in U.S. energy use would seem to be in space heating and automobiles.[9] Certainly, conservation in these areas has an obvious priority, since both involve considerable use of liquid hydrocarbons. Electricity conservation, in contrast, assumes urgency only in the short term, presuming that nuclear energy, coal, or renewable sources (such as solar energy or wind) *can* and will be eventually substituted for petroleum in electricity generation.[10]

Three basic alternatives have been suggested to achieve automobile fuel conservation: (1) promote public transportation as an alternative to the automobile and as a means of encouraging more compact land use; (2) mandate improvements in the mileage per gallon achieved by the automobile fleet; and (3) increase the price of gasoline and automobile use. In addition, as noted, there is always some possibility of substituting other, more abundant fuels for gasoline in automobiles. And if a synthetic-fuel program were successful enough, it might totally eliminate energy as a concern.

Of these various policies, which are not mutually exclusive, the last two conservation options have by far the greatest possibility for success, largely because it is easier to conserve energy by improving the fuel economy of the automobile—through the stimuli of higher gasoline prices or direct regulations—than it is to promote use of substitute fuels in automobiles, or to reduce the volume of automobile travel by encouraging substitute modes or alternative development patterns. Nevertheless, all options merit consideration.

THE SUBSTITUTION OPTION: POWERING AUTOMOBILES WITH ALTERNATIVE FUELS

A variety of alternative power sources have been suggested for automobiles, including hydrogen and the use of external combustion engines (such as the steam engine), which are extremely flexible in fuel use. The most realistic alternatives, however, appear to be automobiles powered by either electricity or some form of synthetic liquid fuel.

Electric vehicles, powered by rechargeable storage batteries, use approximately the same amount of energy per vehicle-mile as comparable gasoline-powered vehicles.[11] But since electricity can be generated from a variety of nonpetroleum sources, the electric vehicle holds the potential of lessening petroleum consumption.

The key limitation on the electric vehicle is the technology of the storage battery, and particularly the ability to store large amounts of energy in a battery of reasonable weight and price. The energy density of current batteries is so low that the battery typically accounts for one third or more of the vehicle weight and imposes severe limitations on vehicle range and performance. Prototype electric vehicles can carry only two passengers for not much more than 50 miles before requiring overnight recharging, and at average speeds of only 25–40 miles per hour and with relatively slow acceleration.[12]

Expected advances in battery technology are likely to increase the payload capacity of electric vehicles and extend their range to perhaps 100–150 miles. But the purchase price and operating costs of such longer-range and larger vehicles are likely to be significantly higher than those of conventionally powered automobiles, even considering substantial real increases in the price of gasoline.[13] Hybrid vehicles have been proposed, which combine electric propulsion with a small gasoline engine to extend the range. The expense of providing both electric and gasoline propulsion systems in the same vehicle reduces their potential market, however.[14]

Technological constraints will thus likely restrict electric vehicles to specialized uses where short range, small payload capacity, poor acceleration, and low top speeds are not a handicap. Small urban delivery vehicles offer the most immediate possibility, especially for postal services, utilities, or other companies that have large fleets and thus can more easily cope with the problems of servicing and recharging these unfamiliar vehicles. Electric urban delivery trucks have been successfully tested in the United States and, especially, England.[15]

By far the largest, but as yet untested, potential application of electric vehicles, however, is a two-passenger "city car" to be used primarily for commuting and short shoppingtrips. The key uncertainty is whether the American public will buy a vehicle with severely limited range and performance in significant numbers. Although only around 10 percent of all automobile travel involves long-distance intercity trips, households may be willing to pay a substantial premium to have that flexibility in at least one of their family cars. Small size and poor acceleration would also reduce the electric vehicle's utility for family outings and raise concerns about safety.

But even if there is a market for a small, low-powered city car, gasoline engine designs may well dominate electric over the next decade or two. Very small and fuel-efficient three-cyclinder gasoline-powered "mini" cars are currently used in Japan and other countries, and in the near future their costs may be comparable to or only slightly higher than those of electric vehicles. Since the gasoline-powered vehicles would not be subject to the same range limitations, moreover, car buyers might be willing to pay a small premium over electric models.

Several studies of the market for an electric city car suggest that by the year 2000 only 2–8 percent at most of U.S. vehicles would be electric powered, and then only under optimistic assumptions about the rate of improvement in battery technology.[16] These studies generally assume that electric vehicles would be restricted to two- or three-car households and that some type of gasoline- or diesel-powered automobile would be chosen as the first car. The range, payload, and acceleration of the electric vehicle are so different from those of vehicles that have been traditionally offered, however, that firm predictions about the ultimate size of the market are impossible. Test marketing, perhaps initially of very small gasoline-powered city cars, will be necessary before the full potential of electric vehicles can be established.

Synthetic liquid fuels made from coal, biomass, or other materials offer more potential for weaning the automobile from petroleum, if only because the conventional internal-combustion engine can be readily modified to accept them so that the automobile's characteristics (and motorists' driving habits) are not so severely affected. Most synthetic fuels significantly increase the energy required per vehicle-mile over that for gasoline-powered vehicles, since energy must be expended in producing the synthetic fuel, especially from coal.[17] As with the electric vehicle, however, the potential advantage is that the energy source need not be petroleum.

The critical limitation is the cost of developing synthetic liquid fuels in appreciable quantities. Synthetic fuels are being produced currently in small amounts on a commercial basis, but the real price of petroleum would probably have to double or more than double before it would be profitable to produce large quantities. As petroleum prices approached these higher levels, moreover, they might encourage the development of additional petroleum resources from heavy oils, tar sands, oil shale, and other sources, thereby forestalling synthetic oil development. Finally, even if petroleum prices increased sufficiently to make large-scale synthetic fuel production profitable, it would take many years for the industry to develop to the size where it would displace significant quantities of petroleum. Thus, while synthetic liquid fuels probably hold potential for the distant future, over the next decade or two the greatest possibilities for reducing energy consumption in urban transportation probably lie elsewhere.

PROMOTING PUBLIC TRANSPORTATION

To conserve on energy, new public transportation systems or routes must above all attract a significant number of patrons who previously *drove* a car. If a sizable portion of any new transit ridership came from relatively fuel-efficient modes (such as buses or carpools), or if some new riders were taking altogether new trips, the potential energy savings could be small, or even negative. Even if all the new riders came from automobiles, moreover, the potential energy gains would be reduced if and when new cars meet high mileage-per-gallon standards.

Most of the possibilities for attracting automobile users to mass transportation, as discussed in Chapter 3, are limited to rush hour or commuting trips in larger metropolitan areas. Commuting accounts for only one quarter to one fifth of all the automobile miles of travel in urban areas, so that at best only a small proportion of urban automobile travel would be affected. Moreover, most mass transit systems operate at or near capacity in the rush hours, so that any substantial influx of new riders would require added service with attendant increases in mass transit energy consumption.

These limitations can be illustrated with a simple example. If mass transportation's share of worktrips in U.S. metropolitan areas could be doubled over mid-1970s levels, which would be quite an impressive achievement, then 16 percent of all workers would commute by mass transportation instead of 8 percent.[18] If all the new transit riders were former automobile drivers, the number of automobile commuters would decline by approximately 10 percent (from 84 to 76 percent of all metropolitan area workers) and the number of cars driven to work would decline from about 70 per 100 commuters to 62 per 100 commuters. Given that worktrips account for only one quarter or less of all trips, total urban automobile travel and, presumably, automobile energy consumption might decline by as much as 3 percent.

The actual reduction in urban transportation energy consumption would likely be far less. A significant portion of the new riders would come from carpools and other more fuel-efficient modes rather than from single-occupant automobiles. Moreover, the cars formerly driven to work by commuters would be left at home for other family members to use. Finally, energy would be required to build and operate the new transit services, which should be counted against automobile fuel savings. The net change in energy consumption from even a doubling in transit use would therefore clearly be small, and there might even be an increase.

The exact trade-off between the energy requirements of the automobile and alternative urban commuting modes was the subject of a detailed study by the U.S. Congressional Budget Office (CBO).[19] Table 8.2 shows CBO estimates of the energy needed to provide a vehicle-mile of service for various urban transportation modes. These figures include not only the energy used for vehicle propulsion but also the energy needed to build and maintain the right-of-way, stations, and vehi-

TABLE 8.2. Estimates of energy required per vehicle-mile for various urban transportation modes.

Mode	Propulsion energy	Station and maintenance energy	Construction energy	Vehicle manufacturing energy	Total (line-haul) energy
Mid-1970s automobile (12 mpg)	11,000	2,000	125	1,100	14,225
Future automobile* (27–28 mpg)	4,800	2,000	125	1,000	7,925
Carpool	11,000	2,000	125	1,100	14,225
Future carpool* (27–28 mpg)	4,800	2,000	125	1,000	7,925
Vanpool	14,000	2,000	200	2,000	18,200
Dial-a-ride	15,500	2,000	200	2,000	19,700
Heavy rail (old)	61,000	9,000	3,000	1,500	74,500
Heavy rail (new)	75,000	15,000	4,000	1,500	95,500
Commuter rail	105,000	7,000	1,200	2,500	115,700
Light rail	75,000	7,000	1,700	2,000	85,700
Bus	30,000	900	370	1,200	32,470
Personal rapid transit	11,000	5,000	300	1,000	17,300
Group rapid transit	20,000	6,000	600	1,000	27,600
Shuttle loop transit	23,000	7,000	600	1,000	31,600

Source: All estimates except those marked with an asterisk are from U.S. Congressional Budget Office, Urban Transportation and Energy: The Potential Savings of Different Modes, report prepared for the Senate Committee on Environment and Public Works, serial no. 95–8 (Washington, D.C.: U.S. Government Printing Office, 1977).

* Estimates made by the authors using the same methodology and assumptions as the CBO. The "future" (27–28 mpg) automobile estimates were not in the CBO report but have been added here for purposes of comparison. The CBO assumption of 12 miles per gallon for automobiles and the assumption of 27–28 miles per gallon for "future" automobiles added for purposes of the present analysis should represent the feasible range of alternatives for the next decade or more. Specifically, with new U.S. cars averaging approximately 18 miles per gallon in the late 1970s, the overall fleet average for both new and old cars had crept upward to approximately 15 miles per gallon by 1976. On the other hand, even though new cars may meet the legislative mandate of 27–28 miles per gallon by 1985, the overall average for the entire U.S. automobile fleet might not reach this average until older, less-efficient automobiles in the stock had been scrapped or otherwise replaced by the newer, higher-mileage-per-gallon vehicles.

cles, which in some modes account for as much as one third of the total energy requirement.

The energy efficiency of the automobile and mass transportation also depends on the average passenger load that each vehicle carries. Mass transportation vehicles carry much larger average loads per vehicle-mile than the automobile, although not nearly so large as their vehicle capacity might suggest, since the imbalanced flows of urban commuting frequently force transit systems to operate as much as half of their vehicle mileage "deadheading," or empty. Automobiles do not deadhead, but their average loads are commonly well below their maximum capacity, with the exception of carpools.

The energy effectiveness of mass transportation modes is further affected by how riders reach the stations where they board the transit vehicle; among the possibilities are driving, walking, or being driven to the station. The circuity of different public transportation modes also affects their energy needs as compared with those of the automobile; normally, transit use will increase the circuity and mileage of the typical commute, as will vanpools, carpools, or most other forms of paratransit. Energy comparisons will also be affected by how the new patrons of a mode commuted previously. The CBO reports several estimates of these various effects. Their "middle" (that is, most typical) estimates of average passenger loads, access, circuity, and patronage source for different urban transportation modes are shown in Table 8.3.

Table 8.4 combines the CBO "middle" or most typical estimates of energy needed per vehicle-mile, passenger load, circuity, and access into total energy requirements per passenger-mile for various transportation modes. Also shown in Table 8.4 are some estimates for more efficient automobiles; these were not developed by the CBO but were added here for purposes of comparison. The first column in Table 8.4 represents the propulsion energy per vehicle-mile, divided by load factor or average number of occupants. The line-haul energy requirements shown in the second column represent the estimated sum of the propulsion, maintenance, construction, and vehicle manufacturing energy per vehicle-mile, again divided by average number of occupants. The third column—modal energy—incorporates an estimate of the additional energy required because of extra access or circuity requirements, developed from the figures in Table 8.3. The final two columns in Table 8.4 represent the extra energy that would be required or saved as a result of implementing new programs associated with the different modes; these figures are based on the CBO's estimates of the typical sources of new riders (as shown in Table 8.3) and assume that previous automobile commuters came from vehicles with either the 11–12 miles per gallon average fuel economy common in the early 1970s (see column 4), or the 27–28 miles per gallon more likely in the 1980s (see column 5).

The only significant data omitted from the CBO calculations are allowances for the use of cars left behind by a former driver who now goes to work by carpool, vanpool, or public transit, thereby releasing a car for possible use during the day by other members of the household.[20] Without more information, it is difficult to estimate how important this offset might be to the energy savings reported in the right-hand column of Table 8.4. The numbers in the far right-hand column of Table 8.3 do, though, provide some clues. Specifically, the energy loss or offset from use of vehicles left behind would be largest for those programs whose patrons previously commuted by automobile. Therefore, the range of savings shown in columns 4 and 5 of Table 8.4 would almost certainly be smaller if this offset were incorporated into the calculations, since the largest energy savings are recorded by those modes that find more of their patrons among former automobile commuters.

The program savings figures also assume that the development of new transit will not have a significant impact on residential-location decisions. For reasons explained in Chapter 7, this assumption seems reasonable, especially in the medium to short term. But a few commuters should alter their residential location decision so as to achieve better access to any new offering of express bus or rail transit systems. Allowance for possible locational shifts induced by availability of new transit systems would therefore tend to increase the potential program savings reported in Table 8.4, all else being equal.

The numbers shown in Table 8.4 are broad generalizations that may or may not apply to specific situations or programs. Load factors achieved by different modes are particularly significant in determining their effectiveness in reducing energy consumption. A new rail transit system placed in a high-density corridor, properly scheduled and routed so as to achieve a high load factor, could record energy savings well in excess of that suggested by the figures in columns 4 and 5 of Table 8.4. Similarly, and even more probably, a bus transit innovation, because of buses' flexibility and small unit of operation, might well be positioned so as to achieve higher load factors than the average of about 20 percent (or an occupancy of 11) hypothesized in Table 8.3. A properly designed bus operation is also more likely to make it possible for people to walk to and from the system and therefore requires less energy for access.

While the figures in Table 8.4 are sensitive to changes in the underlying assumptions, as well as to offsetting biases, they are nevertheless suggestive of the total energy efficiency of different urban transportation modes and of the likelihood, on average, that new programs will achieve energy savings. As for the specific possibility of achieving energy conservation through the introduction of new rail systems, the

TABLE 8.3. Middle or typical estimates of passenger loads, access, circuity, and source of patronage by urban transportation modes.

Mode	Average number of occupants per vehicle-mile	Mode of access (percent)	Percent of trip devoted to access	Circuity (relative to trip by automobile)	Percent of new patrons by former mode
Single-occupant automobile (mid-1970s or future)	1.0	[a]	0	1.0	[a]
Average-occupancy automobile (mid-1970s or future)	1.4	[a]	0	1.0	[a]
Carpool (mid 1970s)	3.0	[a]	0	1.15	15 bus 25 carpool 60 single-occupant automobile
Future carpool*	2.5[b]	[a]	0	1.15	15 bus 25 carpool 60 single-occupant automobile
Vanpool	9.0	[a]	0	1.2	5 bus 40 carpool 55 single-occupant automobile
Dial-a-ride	1.6	[a]	0	1.4	10 bus 25 walk 45 automobile (15 taxi) 20 new trip[c]

Heavy rail (old)	24	20 bus 40 automobile 40 walk	15	1.2	[a]
Heavy rail (new)	21	10 bus 70 automobile 20 walk	18	1.3	45 bus 35 automobile 10 new trip[c] 10 other[d]
Commuter rail	40	5 bus 15 walk 80 automobile	18	1.3	30 bus 40 automobile 10 new trip[c] 20 other[d]
Light rail	20	20 bus 50 walk 30 automobile	10	1.2	50 bus 30 automobile 10 new trip[c] 10 other[d]
Bus (express)	11	25 automobile 75 walk	10	1.1	25 bus 55 automobile 10 new trip[c] 10 other[d]

Source: All estimates except those marked with an asterisk are from U.S. Congressional Budget Office, *Urban Transportation and Energy: The Potential Savings of Different Modes*, report prepared for the Senate Committee on Environment and Public Works, serial no. 95–8 (Washington, D.C.: U.S. Government Printing Office, 1977).

[a] Not applicable.

[b] Future carpools are assumed to average fewer occupants because of the smaller size of the vehicle.

[c] There is no diversion from a former mode; a person who previously did not use a mode of urban transportation is using the new mode.

[d] Taxi, walking, and so on.

* Estimates made by the authors using the same methodology and assumptions as the CBO.

promise would not appear great. The figures for the program efficiency of new rail systems are either quite small or even negative. When the estimates assume that previous commuters drove automobiles that achieved 27–28 miles per gallon, then all new rail systems are actually energy losers.

The figures in Table 8.4 do suggest, though, that energy savings are possible with express buses and some paratransit modes. Of all the public modes, with the exception of the rail modes, only dial-a-ride is a net energy loser, while carpools, vanpools, and buses offer substantial energy savings, depending upon assumptions about the average fuel efficiency of the automobile fleet.

Somewhat surprisingly, moreover, carpools and vanpools do better than express buses in potential program savings. This appears to be largely due to the fact that buses must deadhead or be returned partially empty. If buses could achieve higher load factors, say by 50 percent or so (implying an *average* occupancy of about 25 passengers), their potential for energy savings would be greatly enhanced.

Carpools using fuel-efficient automobiles would achieve energy savings almost comparable to those of vanpools. This conclusion even allows for the fact that future carpools in smaller automobiles might be expected to have a lower average occupancy (2.5 people rather than the 3.0 assumed to be characteristic of carpools in less fuel-efficient automobiles).

TABLE 8.4.   Estimates of energy required per passenger-mile for various urban transportation modes (in British thermal units).

Mode	Propulsion energy	Line-haul energy	Modal energy	Net program energy savings (or losses)[f]	
				Assuming 11–12 mpg for prior autos	Assuming 27–28 mpg* for prior autos
Single-occupant automobile (11–12 mpg)	11,000	14,225	14,225[b]	[a]	[a]
Average-occupancy automobile (11–12 mpg)	7,860	10,160	10,160[b]	[a]	[a]
Single-occupant future automobile (27–28 mpg)	4,800	8,025	8,025[b]	[a]	[a]

TABLE 8.4. (*Cont.*)

Mode	Propulsion energy	Line-haul energy	Modal energy	Net program energy savings (or losses)[f]	
				Assuming 11–12 mpg for prior autos	Assuming 27–28 mpg* for prior autos
Average-occu- pancy future automobile (27–28 mpg)	3,430	5,730	5,730[b]	[a]	[a]
Carpool	3,670	4,740	5,450	4,890	[a]
Future carpool au- tomobile (27–28 mpg)	1,920	3,210	3,690	8,400	2,500
Vanpool	1,560	2,020	2,420	7,720	3,620
Dial-a-ride	9,690	12,310	17,230	(12,350)[c]	(13,920)[c]
Heavy rail (old)	2,540	3,100	3,990	[a]	[a]
Heavy rail (new)	3,570	4,550	6,580	(980)[c]	(2,440)[c]
Commuter rail	2,620	2,890	5,020	970	(690)[c]
Light rail	3,750	4,280	5,060	30	(1,220)[c]
Bus	2,610	2,820	3,070	3,590[d]	1,300
Personal rapid transit	5,500	8,650	[e]	[e]	[e]
Group rapid tran- sit	3,300	4,600	[e]	[e]	[e]
Shuttle loop transit	2,300	3,160	[e]	[e]	[e]

Source: All estimates except those marked with an asterisk are from U.S. Congressional Budget Office, *Urban Transportataion and Energy: The Potential Savings of Different Modes,* report prepared for the Senate Committee on Environment and Public Works, serial no. 95–8 (Washington, D.C.: U.S. Government Printing Office, 1977).

[a] Not applicable.

[b] By definition, there are no access energy requirements for automobiles, so modal energy equals line-haul energy.

[c] Energy loss.

[d] For new express bus service. Conventional bus service would show smaller savings.

[e] Data not available for access modes and source of patronage, since these modes are still largely under development.

[f] The figures shown for program savings in columns 4 and 5 are almost surely overestimates of the actual savings that would be achieved even in the next few years, since these numbers are constructed on the assumption that all previous automobile commuters were using 11- to 12-miles-per-gallon vehicles; on the other hand, the program savings estimated if 27- to 28-miles-per-gallon vehicles were used almost surely represent an understatement of the potential program savings over the next decade or so.

* Estimates made by the authors using the same methodology and assumptions as the CBO.

MANDATING IMPROVED AUTOMOBILE MILEAGE
PER GALLON

Several government initiatives have been undertaken to reduce the amount of energy used per automobile-mile. By far the most important of these is a provision in the Energy Policy and Conservation Act of 1975 requiring that each U.S. automobile company's fleet of new cars average 18 miles per gallon by model year 1978 and 27.5 miles per gallon by model year 1985.[21] These standards represent a dramatic change from the 15.8-miles-per-gallon national average for new cars sold in model year 1975, when the legislation was passed. Failure to meet the prescribed fleetwide averages would result in penalties such that for every tenth of a mile that the fleet average fell below the standard, the manufacturer would be fined five dollars against every car produced during the year. Manufacturers who exceeded the target would be assigned credits that could be applied to past or future fines. In 1977, legislation was passed to enforce similar fuel economy standards for new light-duty trucks, such as pickups or vans.[22] Congress has also been considering tougher standards for the post-1985 period, particularly the possibility of requiring a 40-miles-per-gallon average for new cars sold by model year 1995.

Although there are many doubts about the feasibility of industry compliance with these federally mandated standards, at least through the 1970s the standards did not impose much of a constraint on automobile manufacturers. As Table 8.5 shows, in model years 1978–1980, the average fuel economy of new cars exceeded the federal standards by 1–2 miles per gallon, mainly because consumers demanded more fuel-efficient automobiles in response to rising fuel prices. By model year 1981, new cars averaged 25.0 miles per gallon according to government tests, which amounted to more than a 60 percent improvement over new cars sold in the first half of the decade.

The new-car fuel economy figures used by the government and reported in Table 8.5 overestimate actual fuel economy by as much as 30 percent, depending upon the model, because the federal test procedures do not accurately reflect actual driving conditions.[23] The upward bias in the federal test is larger for more fuel-efficient than less fuel-efficient models, moreover, so that reported percentage improvements in new-car fuel economy during the 1970s are also somewhat exaggerated. Future changes in the federal test procedures may correct these difficulties. But in any event, the average new-car fuel economy gain was still substantial during the 1970s, amounting to perhaps 40 or 50 percent rather than the reported 60 percent or more.

Many of the fuel economy improvements of the late 1970s were

TABLE 8.5.   Mandated and actual average new-car fuel economy, 1968–1985.

Model year	Actual average fuel economy	Federally mandated average fuel economy	Average test weight
Pre-emissions controls	14.9	a	3,812
1968	14.7	a	3,863
1969	14.7	a	3,942
1970	14.8	a	3,877
1971	14.4	a	3,887
1972	14.5	a	3,942
1973	14.2	a	3,969
1974	14.2	a	3,968
1975	15.8	a	4,058
1976	17.5	a	4,059
1977	18.3	a	3,944
1978	19.9	18.0	3,587
1979	20.1	19.0	3,507
1980	22.4	20.0	3,283
1981	25.0[b]	22.0	3,099[b]
1982	c	24.0	c
1983	c	26.0	c
1984	c	27.0	c
1985	c	27.5	c

Source: J. D. Murrell, J. A. Foster, and D. M. Bristor, "Passenger Car and Light Truck Fuel Economy Trends through 1980," Society of Automotive Engineers, technical paper no. 800853, 1980, p. 5.
[a] Not applicable.
[b] Preliminary estimates.
[c] Not available.

achieved by reducing the weight of the average vehicle through either (1) "downsizing" (shifting to cars of smaller size with less passenger and trunk capacity), or (2) using more weight-conscious designs and lighter-weight materials (while holding passenger and trunk capacity constant). In 1975, the year in which the original federal fuel economy legislation was passed, the average mileage performance of new compacts and subcompacts was approximately 22.8 miles per gallon, while intermediate- and standard-sized cars achieved averages of only 18.3 and 14.7 miles per gallon, respectively. Thus, the shift from larger to smaller cars that occurred through the 1970s offered significant opportunities for fuel economy gains.

Estimates made during the 1970s of the improved fuel economy possible from weight-conscious design (holding vehicle size constant), ranged from 2 percent to 20 percent: automobile manufacturers estimated an improvement of 2–9 percent, while a Rand Corporation study[24] and an analysis by the Federal Task Force on Motor Vehicle Goals Beyond 1980[25] cited savings of 16–20 percent as within reach. Estimates by Rand and the federal task force also suggested that a further substitution of plastic and aluminum materials could lead to further weight improvements that would be reflected in additional fuel economy improvements of some 8–20 percent.

Downsizing and weight-conscious design will probably continue to play a significant role in fuel economy improvements through the 1980s and beyond, but the opportunities for gains in these areas may be more limited than they have been in the past. Consumers shifted rapidly to small cars during the 1970s, particularly after the gasoline price increases of 1974 and 1979, but further inroads into the large-car market share may well be more limited for reasons explained in Chapter 6. Similarly, many of the least expensive opportunities for weight-conscious design and materials substitution were exploited in the 1970s, and additional weight reductions will probably prove more difficult and costly.

Sources of fuel economies throughout the 1980s and 1990s should include performance reductions and, what is more important, engine, transmission, and drivetrain modifications. These were not ignored in the 1970s; one study suggests that only about 2.6 miles per gallon of the 5.9 miles per gallon improvement in the average fuel economy of new cars between the 1974 and 1979 model years was due to reduced weights, while the remaining 3.3 miles per gallon was gained as the result of other changes.[26] The potential importance of these other sources of fuel savings is suggested by the wide variance in the fuel economy of different 1979 makes with the same weight. As Table 8.6 shows, in model year 1979 the cars with the best fuel economy were often 10 miles per gallon more fuel efficient than the average new car in their weight class. If the technological and other improvements embodied in those fuel-efficient cars are incorporated in most vehicles, the average fuel economy would be greatly improved, even without further downsizing or weight-conscious design.[27]

One particularly interesting and controversial source of fuel economy is reduced performance, particularly lower acceleration power. A government-sponsored study estimated that reductions in the acceleration capabilities of full-sized automobiles to levels comparable with a subcompact would result in fuel savings of 5 to 10 percent.[28] Automobile manufacturers generally agree that reductions in performance

TABLE 8.6.   Range of fuel economies, 1979 model passenger cars.

	Weight class (in pounds)									
	2,000	2,250	2,500	2,750	3,000	3,500	4,000	4,500	5,000	5,500
Highest miles per gallon (diesel)	*	46.0	40.2	*	*	31.6	29.2	23.9	23.1	*
Highest miles per gallon (gasoline)	38.9	39.5	33.4	30.4	28.4	24.0	21.5	17.3	13.6	11.4
Sales-weighted average (all)	32.7	32.9	27.7	24.0	21.5	20.0	17.9	16.3	14.2	10.7
Lowest miles per gallon (gasoline)	25.3	24.5	23.4	18.5	15.2	13.8	13.9	9.2	12.1	10.0

Source: J. D. Murrell, "Light Duty Automotive Fuel Economy Trends through 1979," Society of Automotive Engineers, technical paper no. 790225, 1979, p. 7.
* No diesel cars of this weight.

standards will result in greater fuel economy and decreased costs, but they question whether consumers would buy models with significantly less acceleration power and therefore have been reluctant to exploit this possibility.

Drivetrain and transmission modifications also offer opportunities for future improvements.[29] In the 1970s, manufacturers began to offer some models with front-wheel drive and transverse-mounted engines, in which power is transmitted directly to the front axle from the engine, mounted parallel to and above the axle. Fuel economies of 12–15 percent are gained through improved power transmission and reduced weight due to the elimination of the drive shaft and rear differential as well as the shortening of the engine compartment.

Other state-of-the-art improvements in transmissions include the lock-up torque converter and the four-speed automatic transmission, both of which have long been offered and provide fuel savings of about 5 percent each. The lock-up torque converter improves fuel economy by mechanically linking the engine and the drivetrain during cruise conditions, thereby eliminating slippage, while the four-speed automatic transmission offers an additional gear ratio to reduce engine speeds. A longer-term possibility is the continuously variable transmission, still in the research and development stage, which may offer fuel economies in the 10–15 percent range.

A variety of possibilities exists for improving the fuel economy of conventional, internal-combustion engines. Turbocharging, for example, may offer about a 10 percent fuel economy by boosting the performance of smaller and more fuel-efficient engines so that they can be substituted for larger engines. Electronic control systems also are being introduced in many models; these achieve better fuel economy without sacrificing polllution control by closely monitoring engine performance and adjusting air/fuel intake, ignition timing, and even the number of pistons in use. The stratified-charge engine holds the promise of burning fuel more completely by providing a rich air/fuel mixture near the spark plug and a lean mixture elsewhere, although the practicality and fuel savings of this technology are still uncertain.[30]

Diesel engines also promise fuel economies in the 15–20 percent range, but command slightly lower horsepower and exhibit poorer performance.[31] Although the use of diesel engines in automobiles has been increasing, their application ultimately may be limited by air pollution regulations.[32]

Longer-term technological innovations include the Stirling, the Rankin, and the gas-turbine engines. It is premature, though, to estimate their fuel economy, emission levels, cost, and practicality.[33]

One recent assessment by the CBO suggests that between 1985 and 1995 average new-car fuel economy can readily be increased from 27.5 miles per gallon to 34.9 miles per gallon without downsizing or further technological innovations. The prospective fuel economy improvements would come from more widespread application of innovations that are currently available, such as the four-speed automatic transmission and diesel engines. Moreover, these improvements, listed in Table 8.7, are estimated to increase the new-car price and maintenance costs by an average of only $600–654 (in late 1970s dollars), an amount small enough to be offset by the anticipated savings in fuel expenses over the life of the car.

Achievement of the 27.5-mile 1985 standard or tougher post-1985 standards would result in significant reductions in total automotive fuel consumption, despite rapidly growing automobile use. According to government predictions, shown in Table 8.8, average new-car fuel economy (as measured by government tests) will exceed the mandated standard in 1985, representing an improvement of 83 percent over 1975 levels; total fleet fuel economy (again, as measured by government tests) will grow by 59 percent in the same period. *Actual* in-use fuel economy will improve only slightly less, by 66 percent for new cars and 43 percent for the fleet as a whole.

Since these estimates assume that total automobile ownership and use increase at an average annual rate of 3.3 percent, total automotive fuel consumption is forecast to drop by only 3 percent between 1975 and 1985. If automobile ownership and use increase by a more modest 2–2.5 percent per year, as suggested in Chapter 6, savings of 8–10 percent over 1975 levels are possible. Furthermore, if a new-car standard

TABLE 8.7. Possible fuel economy improvements between 1985 and 1995 using twelve existing technologies.

| Technology | Market penetration | | | Fuel economy improvement | | Consumer cost increase[a] | | | | |
| | | | | | | Purchase price of automobiles | | Maintenance cost of automobiles[b] | | |
	1985 (percent)	1995 (percent)	Changes in market penetration between 1985 and 1995 (percent)	Per car (percent)	Average for new-car fleet (percent)	Base cost per unit (dollars)	Average increase per car (dollars)	Base cost per unit (dollars)	Average increase per car (dollars)	Total for average vehicle lifetime (dollars)
Weight reduction:[c]										
Material substitution	50	100	50	4	2.0	131	66	0	0	66
Front-wheel drive	80	100	20	12	2.4	166	33	0	0	33
Downsizing	60	80	20	10	2.0	146	29	0	0	29
Four-speed automatic transmission	27	54	27	6	1.6	198	53	36	10	63
Electronic controls	5	25	20	15	3.0	179	36	0	0	36
Diesel engine	7	30	23	15	3.5	679	156	0	0	156
Stratified-charge engine	0	12	12	15	1.8	679	81	0	0	81
Turbocharger	7	30	23	10	2.3	332	76	112	26	102
Lubricants	20	70	50	3	1.5	1–5	1–8	9–103	5–52	6–60
Aerodynamics	60	100	40	5	2.0	17	7	0	0	7
Accessories	50	100	50	2	1.0	16	8	0	0	8
Rolling resistance	50	100	50	2	1.0	26	13	0	0	13
Total					26.9[d]		559–566		41–88	600–654

Source: U.S. Congressional Budget Office, *Fuel Economy Standards for New Passenger Cars after 1985* (Washington, D.C.: U.S. Government Printing Office, 1980), pp. 30–31.

[a] 1980 dollars.
[b] Maintenance costs are discounted at a 10 percent annual rate.
[c] Second round of weight reduction.
[d] Percentages are compounded (multiplied) to total 26.9 percent.

TABLE 8.8. Estimates of future automobile fuel economy and consumption.

	Actual 1975	1985		2000, with existing standards		2000, with post-1985 standards[a]	
		Amount	Percent change from 1975	Amount	Percent change from 1975	Amount	Percent change from 1975
Vehicle-miles of travel by automobile (trillions per year)	1.03	1.40	36	1.80	75	1.74	69
New-car fuel economy (mpg):							
Required standard	none	27.50	*	27.50	*	40.00	*
Federal test estimate	15.60	28.50	83	29.40	88	40.00	156
Actual in-use economy	14.00	23.20	66	25.00	79	34.00	143
Fleet fuel economy (mpg):							
Federal test estimate	15.10	24.00	59	28.50	89	37.60	149
Actual in-use economy	13.60	19.40	43	24.60	81	32.10	136
Annual automobile fuel consumption (billions of gallons)	76.00	73.90	−3	73.30	−4	51.70	−32

Source: U.S. Congress, Office of Technology Assessment, *Changes in the Future Use and Characteristics of the Automobile Transportation System*, vol. 1 (Washington, D.C.: U.S. Government Printing Office, 1979), p. 122.
[a]Post-1985 standards are assumed to be set at 40 mpg by 1995.
* Not applicable.

of 40 miles per gallon is adopted in the 1980s, total automotive fuel consumption might decrease by as much as 32 percent over 1975 levels by the year 2000, despite continued and rapid growth in automobile ownership and use. On the other hand, if standards are not raised or if the market price of gasoline does not rise so as to impose higher standards, automobile fuel consumption could stabilize after 1985.

RAISING ENERGY PRICES TO REDUCE CONSUMPTION

Many observers feel that it is uncertain whether Americans can be induced to drive more fuel-efficient automobiles, particularly if this requires a continued shift to smaller vehicles. Skepticism on this point has motivated proposals to impose "gas guzzler" taxes on automobiles with high energy consumption and to increase the price of energy in general and gasoline in particular.

Policies to increase fuel prices were adopted in the late 1970s, at which time the federal government began the process of gradually decontrolling prices for domestic crude oil. But there was little enthusiasm for price increases, in part because it was thought that the demand for gasoline might be insensitive to higher prices. Higher prices thus might not induce much conservation but rather only impose a serious financial burden on low- and moderate-income families. In economists' terms, the issue at question is the size of the price elasticity of demand for gasoline—defined as the percentage reduction in gasoline consumption that results from a percentage increase in price. The higher the elasticity, the greater the impact higher prices will have on conservation (and the smaller the impact on family budgets).

The available evidence suggests that in the short run—say, one to five years—the price elasticity of gasoline will be relatively small. Most estimates cluster around .2 (meaning a 1 percent price increase brings only a .2 percent decline in consumption, resulting from a reduction in vehicle travel and a shift to smaller, more fuel-efficient cars).[34] These estimates are at least consistent with the pattern of U.S. gasoline consumption, vehicle mileage, and car sales shown after the increases in gasoline price in 1974–75 and 1979. For example, each of the two price increases appeared to stimulate at least a 10 percent rise in the small cars' share of total new-car sales.[35] After the 1974–75 price increase, the number of miles traveled per automobile also declined by about 5 percent. Even by 1977, before the next major round of real price increases in 1979, the number of miles traveled per automobile had not recovered to pre-1974 levels.[36] Fuel shortages and the imposition of a nationwide speed limit of 55 miles per hour were accountable for some of this shift to smaller cars and reduced travel, but higher fuel prices almost surely were a major cause.

The elasticity of demand is estimated to be much higher in the long run than in the short run. In the long run, consumers and automobile manufacturers have more opportunities to avoid increased energy prices by, for example, redesigning cars of all sizes to be more fuel efficient or, conceivably, changing residential or workplace locations. Long-run price elasticities are difficult to estimate from domestic data, since U.S. gasoline prices were fairly stable until the early 1970s. But comparisons between the United States and other developed countries provide some indications of long-run price elasticities, since many of the other developed countries long have had higher gasoline prices (mainly as a matter of public policy) than the United States. Three such comparisons completed in the 1970s estimate long-run price elasticities of around 1.0 or greater, although they disagree as to whether the larger source of long-run economies is a reduction in automobile driving and ownership or an improvement in the average vehicle-mileage per gallon.[37]

A high long-run elasticity of gasoline demand suggests that high prices should be effective in inducing conservation. Higher prices provide incentives to conserve through less automobile ownership and use as well as through more fuel-efficient cars, in contrast with mandatory standards that provide only the latter incentives. In fact, a mandatory fuel economy program that was not accompanied by fuel price increases might well reduce the marginal cost of driving (since higher fuel costs would not offset the savings of better fuel economy).[38] A high long-run elasticity of gasoline demand also suggests that any financial problems caused for low- and middle-income groups by high energy prices will diminish over time. A long-run elasticity of 1.0, for example, means that most households will eventually hold total expenditures for gasoline roughly constant despite rising fuel prices, although perhaps not without some sacrifices associated with conservation measures.

Mandatory fuel economy standards also entail their own costs. One study estimated that if the 27.5-miles-per-gallon target for 1985 could be met *only* by forcing many consumers to buy small cars with poor performance and few luxury features (much like the compacts and subcompacts of the mid-1970s), the dissatisfaction would amount to as much as $20 billion per year in 1977 dollars.[39] Actual losses would probably be much smaller, though, since manufacturers now offer small, fuel-efficient automobiles with many of the luxury features that were available only on larger vehicles in the past.

Higher fuel prices and mandatory standards are not mutually exclusive policies, of course, and might be best pursued in some combination. Higher fuel prices would provide the economic incentive for consumers to buy more fuel-efficient vehicles and to exploit other appropriate conservation measures. Mandatory standards, even though seldom binding, might also provide manufacturers with a useful target for corporate planning and give policy makers a margin of safety in case higher prices and other market forces failed to induce the desired conservation efforts.

The appropriate mix of mandatory standards and higher prices will be less critical if the technological opportunities for improving automotive fuel economy allow the production of inexpensive, fuel-efficient vehicles with most of the performance and other features desired by consumers. In such a situation mandatory standards are unlikely to be binding, and modest fuel price increases will stimulate significant conservation with little effect on family budgets. This possibility seems likely, given the range of fuel economy improvements that can be incorporated into American automobiles.

SUMMARY

The main hope for conserving energy in urban transportation is in reducing the energy consumed by automobiles. The most promising possibility for doing this is by improving the fuel efficiency of the automobile fleet through mandatory standards for new-car fuel economy, fuel price increases, or both. A second possibility is the substitution of vanpools, carpools, or express buses for automobile travel, although the applicability of this measure is limited largely to commuting trips. The substitution of rail transit for automobile use is at least as likely to cause a net increase in energy consumption as a decrease.

The potential impact of each of these possibilities is difficult to forecast with any precision. A best guess would be that because automobile ownership and use will continue to increase—say, at an annual rate of 2.5 percent or so—actual reductions in *total* gasoline consumed will be difficult to achieve. On average, over the next few decades, a 1–2 percent per year reduction in total gasoline consumed by U.S. cars would appear to be an achievable, but difficult, goal. If exceptionally high retail gas price increases occur, or if express buses or pools prove unexpectedly effective in attracting automobile commuters, then slightly more substantial reductions would be possible.

The striking thing about all these calculations is how difficult the task of energy conservation is likely to be. Returning to the overall policy goal of a better balance between U.S. energy consumption and production, all these efforts might save a quad or two or even three, or roughly 2–4 percent of total U.S. energy consumption at mid-1970 levels. Obviously, that is a start, but hardly a program in and of itself for achieving U.S. energy self-sufficiency. Unfortunately, as will be discussed in later chapters, conserving energy becomes even more complex and difficult when pursued simultaneously with public policy goals such as improving air quality or automobile safety.

9

Air Pollution

THE PROBLEM AND POLICY DEVELOPMENTS

The problem of controlling air pollution generated by urban transportation is part of a much larger public policy concern with improving air quality. Five kinds of harmful effluents have been targeted for control: (1) carbon monoxide (CO); (2) volatile organic compounds (VOC), including hydrocarbons (HC); (3) nitrogen oxides (NO_x); (4) various sulfuric emissions, particularly sulfur oxides (SO_x); and (5) total suspended particulate matter (TSP)—that is, actual solids dispersed in the air.

Of these five air pollutants, only three are generated in significant amounts by urban transportation, or so-called mobile sources, while the balance are more strongly associated with stationary sources.[1] On a nationwide, aggregate basis, carbon monoxide originates primarily from mobile sources (particularly automobiles), and hydrocarbons and nitrogen oxides originate about equally from mobile and stationary sources (see Table 9.1). In contrast, sulfuric and particulate emissions come almost exclusively from stationary sources, although mobile sources may become more important generators of particulates if the use of diesel-powered automobiles spreads.

While air pollutants cause damage to crops and to materials, their effects on human health have been the primary concern. Unfortunately,

TABLE 9.1.   1977 estimates of nationwide emissions from man-made sources (millions of metric tons per year).

Source	TSP	SO_x	NO_x	VOC^a	CO
Transportation	1.1	0.8	9.2	11.5	85.7
Fuel combustion in stationary sources	4.8	22.4	13.0	1.5	1.2
Industrial processes	5.4	4.2	0.7	10.1	8.3
Solid-waste disposal	0.4	0	0.1	0.7	2.6
Miscellaneous	0.7	0	0.1	4.5	4.9
Total	12.4	27.4	23.1	28.3	102.7

Source: U.S. Environmental Protection Agency, Office of Air Quality Planning and Standards, National Air Quality, Monitoring, and Emissions Trends Report, 1977, report no. EPA–450/2–78–052 (Research Triangle Park, N.C.: Environmental Protection Agency, 1978), pp. 5–11.
a Includes volatile hydrocarbons (HC).

the impact of air pollution on health is incompletely understood and the subject of substantial controversy. Little is known about what levels of pollutant concentration bring about health problems, or even whether a pollutant affects health at all.

It is known, though, that exposure to high concentrations of carbon monoxide can reduce the maximum exercise capacity and the alertness of otherwise healthy individuals and may cause pain (angina) for persons with cardiovascular disease. Similarly, hydrocarbons react with other airborne pollutants to create ozone (smog), which at high concentrations can cause physical discomfort, coughing, and nausea among healthy persons and can have far more serious complications, including death, for persons with severe respiratory problems such as emphysema. Nitrogen oxides are known to contribute to the formation of ozone. Some researchers suspect that high concentrations of nitrogen oxides can also cause acute respiratory illnesses; others argue that they have little or no health effects. Particulates can cause respiratory problems and some, including those from diesel engines, are suspected of causing cancer, although the evidence is far from conclusive. High levels of sulfur oxides also exacerbate respiratory problems, particularly when combined with high levels of particulates.

The federal government has defined threshold concentrations of pollutants in the air above which air pollution is regarded as unhealthful, particularly for persons with preexisting heart or respiratory conditions. These air standards are exceeded primarily in the centers of urban areas, where there is a high enough concentration of human activity to create this level of pollution. Since urban areas have higher population densities, "persondays" of exposure to air pollution also will be greater in urban settings.

The severity and cause of air pollution problems vary greatly from city to city because of differences in densities, topographies, prevailing winds, and mixes of industries. Among the 41 largest metropolitan areas for which data are readily available, the number of days during 1977 in which air pollution exceeded federal standards ranged from 273 (in New York City) to 2 (in Grand Rapids, Michigan). Only 7 cities violated air standards for more than 100 days, however, and the frequency of violations was well below 50 days for the majority of cities. CO is the leading cause of violations in almost half of the largest metropolitan areas; ozone (formed by HC and NO_x) is the leading cause of violations in most of the remainder. The extent to which the violations are attributable to emissions from mobile or stationary sources also differs substantially from city to city, particularly for ozone; for example, in Chicago, the NO_x emissions contributing to ozone formation come primarily from stationary sources, whereas in Los Angeles they come primarily from mobile sources.[2]

Public concerns about automotive air pollution date back to the 1950s. The State of California led the nation in such concerns—largely because of the smog problem in Los Angeles—and made exhaust-control equipment mandatory for new cars beginning with the 1966 model year. Although the federal government sponsored research and data collection on air pollution problems even earlier, the major federal effort to control air pollution did not begin until the Clean Air Act of 1970, when Congress required that the U.S. Environmental Protection Agency (EPA) establish standards for concentrations of air pollutants that would not adversely affect human health. The act empowered the EPA to enforce these standards and, in the automotive area, legislated that within a decade new-car HC, NO_x, and CO emissions per vehicle-mile be reduced, in stages, to 10 percent or less of the precontrol levels—although the statue also made provisions for waivers that could delay enforcement of the standards for several years.

The original 1970 schedule of new-car emission standards has been modified several times, as evidence of the cost or technological difficulty of meeting these standards developed. There have been 96 percent reductions in new-car HC and CO emissions per mile, but these came several years late (see Table 9.2). NO_x reduction has proved more difficult; the original objective (0.4 grams of NO_x per mile) has been postponed indefinitely and a target of one gram per mile has been established, with possible waivers for diesel and other innovative engines. In 1980, the EPA added particulate emissions to the list of motor vehicle

TABLE 9.2. New-car air pollution standards (in grams per vehicle-mile).

Model year	Original standards under the 1970 Clean Air Act (without waivers)			Actual and currently scheduled standards			
	HC	CO	NO_x	HC	CO	NO_x	Particulates
Emissions of pre-control (1968) cars	*	*	*	8.70	87	4.0	.02–2.0[a]
1970–71	3.90	33.3	*	3.90	33.3	*	*
1972	3.00	28.0	*	3.00	28.0	*	*
1973–74	3.00	28.0	3.1	2.00	28.0	3.1	*
1975	0.41	3.4	2.0	1.50	15.0	3.1	*
1976	0.41	3.4	0.4	1.50	15.0	3.1	*
1977–79				1.50	15.0	2.0	*
1980				0.41	7.0	2.0	*
1981				0.41	3.4[b]	1.0[c]	*
1982–84				0.41	3.4	1.0	0.6
1985 and beyond				0.41	3.4	1.0	0.2

Source: Section 202 of the Clean Air Act of 1977; Edwin S. Mills and Lawrence White, "Government Policies toward Automotive Emissions Control," in Approaches to Controlling Air Pollution, ed. Ann F. Friedlaender (Cambridge, Mass.: MIT Press, 1978); National Academy of Sciences and National Academy of Engineering, Air Quality and Automobile Emission Control, vol. 4, The Cost and Benefits of Automobile Emission Control, prepared for the Senate Committee on Public Works (Washington, D.C.: U.S. Government Printing Office, 1974).

[a] The .02 figure is for vehicles using gasoline; the 2.0 figure is for large vehicles with diesel engines.

[b] The EPA may waive the 3.4 gpm CO standard for 1981–82 based on technical feasibility. So far, waivers have been granted for 1981 and 1982 to various engine families produced by British Leyland, Chrysler, General Motors, and Toyota. Toyo Kogyo has received a waiver for certain 1981 engine families.

[c] The EPA may change the 1.0 gpm NO_x standard to 1.5 for 1981–84 model years for diesel vehicles and those equipped with innovative control technologies. All other vehicles must meet the 1.0 gpm NO_x standard in 1981. American Motors, General Motors, Daimler-Benz, and Volvo have all received waivers for certain 1981 and 1982 engine families.

* Not applicable.

air pollutants to be regulated—largely because of the growing use of diesel-powered automobiles—and mandated reductions for the 1982 and 1985 model years.

In the early 1970s, in metropolitan areas where air standards cannot be met by reduced new-car emissions rates or stationary-source controls alone, the EPA attempted to force adoption of Transportation Control Plans (TCPs), which met air standards by reducing or relocating travel. These TCPs often required draconian measures such as outright prohibitions on downtown driving, strict controls on downtown parking, enforced carpooling, or various schemes compelling drivers not to use their cars one day a week. The measures were unpopular with local officials, and in most cases only the mildest of them were implemented. The need for TCPs has lessened somewhat as progress has been made on new-car emissions and stationary-source controls, but there are still a number of areas (such as Los Angeles, Chicago, and Salt Lake City) where reduced or relocated travel might be necessary to meet federal air standards.

In the 1970s, there was also growing concern about the possible conflict between automotive air pollution and automotive energy conservation goals. All else being equal, programs to reduce vehicle-miles of travel and to reduce the amount of energy consumed per mile of travel should help reduce air pollution as well as energy consumption. But unfortunately, reducing energy consumption and the amount of effluent produced per unit of energy consumed can often be very much in conflict. For example, the very earliest measures taken to reduce automobile effluents in the early 1970s increased total gasoline consumption by American automobiles, since the quickest way to reduce effluent per vehicle-mile of travel was simply to detune engines, thereby reducing mileage per gallon.

The conflict between automobile energy conservation and reduced pollution lessened somewhat in the mid-1970s, when automobile manufacturers began to shift to catalytic converters as their primary means of pollution control. The catalytic converter, placed between the engine and the muffler, removed pollutants from the exhaust stream. The catalytic converter permitted an improvement in gasoline mileages over early-1970s levels, since it was no longer necessary to reduce the formation of pollutants during combustion by detuning the engine. But the catalytic converter also added weight to the vehicle and, in the long run, produced additional problems that contributed to energy consumption (as compared with a base case in which there are no controls over automotive emissions).[3] Catalytic converters also cost between $100 and $300 each to manufacture, thus increasing automobile purchase prices, and required the use of more expensive unleaded fuel.

Fortunately, other options exist for reducing harmful automobile emissions. Certain modifications in carburetors used with internal-combustion engines and totally different engine concepts could improve both mileage per gallon and emissions (although possibly with some increase in manufacturing costs). Some of these technologies are known (such as the diesel engine); others involve an extension in the state of the art (such as the stratified-charge engine, which thus far has been applied only to very small cars) or new engineering (such as electronic fuel injection); still others involve basic changes in automobile design (such as continuously variable transmissions).

Each of the alternatives to the standard internal-combustion engine has different limitations and capabilities. The diesel, for example, can easily meet all the established goals for reducing automotive emissions with the possible exception of the rollback of nitrogen oxide to 1.0 grams per mile. Unfortunately diesels also can produce 10–100 times more particulates per mile than a gasoline-powered vehicle. But even with a considerable expansion of diesel-powered cars, diesel emissions would still account for only a very small percentage of *total* particulates in the air, say, between 5 and 10 percent. Dust, brake linings, power plants, and space heating would still be predominant sources of particulate matter. However, diesel particulates, like other combustion particulates, may be more carcinogenic than most. Therefore, experiments with various devices for removing particulates from diesel systems have been conducted—thus far with only limited success. Accordingly, *if* diesel particulates are established as being especially harmful to human health, and *if* no efficient means is found for removing them, diesels may be foreclosed as a means of conserving on automobile energy consumption. If so, the larger U.S. car will be an even more endangered species, since dieselization is one of the more attractive ways to make large cars compatible with government miles-per-gallon targets.

There are, then, many ways in which automobile air pollution might be reduced, some conflicting and some complementary, not only with each other but with other public policy goals. Essentially, though, reducing harmful automobile air pollution involves two basic strategies: (1) reducing vehicle travel or redistributing it in such a way that the harm done by automobile emissions is attenuated; and (2) reducing the amount of effluent produced per unit of travel by automobiles. There are many ways of pursuing these basic strategies—each with different limitations, trade-offs with other public policy goals, benefits, and costs.

REDUCING OR REDISTRIBUTING AUTOMOBILE TRAVEL

Transportation controls and other "indirect" programs for reducing harmful automobile air pollution take many forms, but for the most part are much like policies advocated for meeting other goals, such as energy conservation. Typical are suggestions for achieving cleaner air through greater use of mass transportation. These suggestions include: (1) expanding or creating rail transit systems to wean people from commuting by automobile; (2) making mass transportation more attractive by, say, instituting express bus services that would operate on specially reserved, uncongested highway lanes; (3) lowering transit fares to provide an economic incentive to shift from automobiles to transit; or (4) creating more private or paratransit services in the form of jitneys, carpools, or vanpools to increase automobile occupancy in urban travel.

Among the traffic-restriction schemes also frequently suggested as a means of reducing air pollution are: (1) surcharges for central parking—particularly all-day commuter parking—to provide an incentive for people to switch from automobile to transit; (2) special license fees for access to central business areas; (3) outright prohibition of automobile access to central urban areas; (4) restrictions on automobile speeds in urban areas to reduce gas consumption and make transit more attractive; or (5) metered access to urban expressways or freeways to reduce traffic congestion on such facilities during the rush hours and thereby reduce pollution-creating stop-and-go travel.[4]

Land-use policies have been advanced as another means of improving the air quality in urban areas. Here, too, there is striking variety and contradiction among the proposals. Some suggestions call for centralizing employment and residences in urban areas to encourage more transit use and walking, thus reducing the pollutants emitted from automobiles. Others call for decentralizing employment and residences to reduce pollution concentration in urban areas to levels below thresholds considered unsafe.

Analyzing the effectiveness of these policies is not easy. Among the many complications is the fact that the very same automobile will produce effluents differently under different operating circumstances; for example, operating stop-and-go or from a cold start, the automobile will produce more effluent than it will under most other operating conditions. Similarly, parking bans or other restrictions on automobiles in central business districts could give rise to cruising, which would be counterproductive to reducing vehicle-miles of travel and air pollution; such bans could also simply relocate pollution from a very central area to a nearby central location, say, the ring just around the central busi-

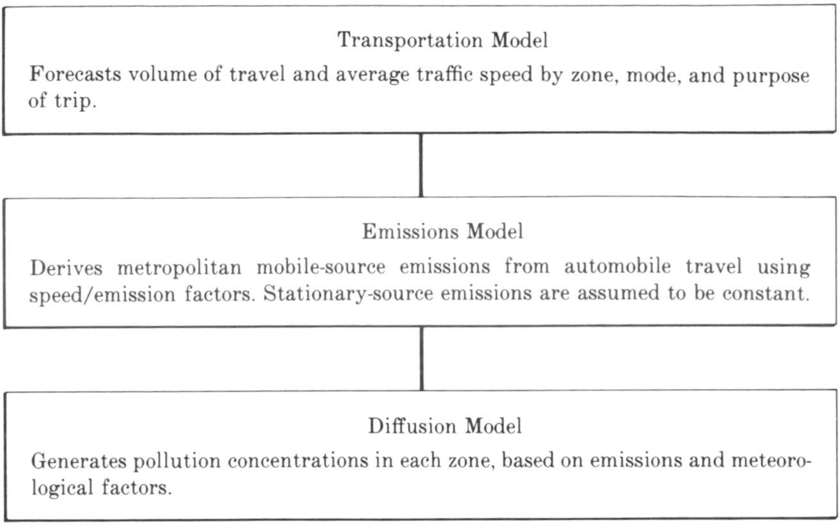

Transportation Model

Forecasts volume of travel and average traffic speed by zone, mode, and purpose of trip.

Emissions Model

Derives metropolitan mobile-source emissions from automobile travel using speed/emission factors. Stationary-source emissions are assumed to be constant.

Diffusion Model

Generates pollution concentrations in each zone, based on emissions and meteorological factors.

Figure 9.1. Major components of a transport and air shed simulation model. (*Source:* Gregory K. Ingram, Gary R. Fauth, and Eugene Kroch, "Cost and Effectiveness of Emission Reduction and Transportation Control Policies," *Rivista Internationale di Economia dei Transporti,* April 1975, p. 18.)

ness district,[5] with little positive benefit in reducing exposure to air pollution.

A reasonably adequate analysis of these various control policies requires a systems analytical capability of some complexity and scale. In the present state of the art, the best way to provide such a capability is to link together various models, generally developed for other purposes, as shown in Figure 9.1. The key component is a standard urban transportation planning model that simulates and forecasts urban travel patterns, including a reasonably adequate treatment of transit mode choice. An automobile emissions model is also needed that incorporates speed-emission relations, emission rates, and emissions deterioration. Finally, an atmospheric diffusion model is required (generally the best that can be done is a synthesis of simple diffusion models developed by meteorologists).[6]

Several transportation-control policies aimed at improving air quality have been evaluated by applying a systems analysis, of the type just outlined, to Boston and Los Angeles, two metropolitan areas that probably span much of the range in American urban experience.[7] Two measures of the effectiveness of air quality controls were established for this analysis, one local and one regional. The local measure of effectiveness was the predicted percentage reduction in carbon monoxide concentrations in central business districts. The regional measure was millions of persondays of exposure to pollution levels exceeding minimal health standards summed across an entire metropolitan region.

The results of this analysis of air quality control policies for Los Angeles and Boston are summarized in Table 9.3. As benchmarks for comparison, the table also incorporates (on the top two lines) estimates of the cost, local effectiveness, and regional effectiveness of policies that directly control automobile emissions—that is, policies meant to reduce the effluent produced per mile of automobile travel. The cost estimates shown in Table 9.3 are first approximations at best, but they are probably correct hierarchically if not in absolute terms. The costs of direct automobile emissions controls are high (and increase rapidly with the later and more stringent controls), but their effectiveness in reducing emissions is also comparably great.

Based on the results for Los Angeles and Boston, the only control policy that can be universally recommended without much equivocation is carpooling. Not only does the policy save money by reducing vehicle-miles of travel and expenditures for automobile operation, but it also contributes to improving air quality. In Los Angeles, carpooling is one of the more effective control policies for improving air quality; in Boston, while it is not as effective as it is in Los Angeles, it still makes a positive contribution.

Table 9.3 also shows that identical policies may have different effects in Los Angeles and Boston. A program to raise traffic speeds throughout the Los Angeles Basin would not only save money (at least exclusive of capital costs) but would also contribute substantially to improving air quality. Such a policy in Boston, while still saving money, would adversely effect air quality. Raising CBD traffic speeds is helpful in Los Angeles, whereas it is detrimental in Boston; conversely, lowering all automobile speeds hurts in Los Angeles, whereas it helps in Boston. Apparently, the automobile and transit modes are more closely competitive in Boston than in Los Angeles because Boston's transit system is better developed and more convenient, while its highway system is older and more congested. Thus, when automobile traffic speeds worsen in Boston, travelers will more readily change their travel mode, while in Los Angeles, transit service is so inconvenient compared with automobile travel that changes in automobile speeds do not greatly affect travel choices.

The various transit policies examined also have quite a mixed record. Extension of the rail transit network in Boston, for example, not only would be costly, but would actually be harmful in terms of air quality. On the other hand, transit-fare reductions are relatively inexpensive in both cities, especially in Los Angeles, and make a small positive contri-

TABLE 9.3. Costs and effectiveness for several air quality policies in Los Angeles and Boston.

Policy	Los Angeles			Boston		
	Total annual estimated cost (thousands of dollars)	Local effective-ness[a]	Regional effective-ness[b]	Total annual estimated cost (thousands of dollars)	Local effective-ness[a]	Regional effective-ness[b]
Moderate auto emission controls[c]	197,000	54	1,480	43,000	48	300
Stringent auto emission controls[c]	334,000	80	1,650	71,000	63	810
CBD parking surcharge	63,933	12	175	11,792	19	225
Special CBD license fee	83,271	44	225	16,909	30	200
CBD auto prohibition[d]	117,783	45	225	14,734	35	250
Transit fare reduction	3,417	6	2	8,829	2	25
Improved transit performance	82,986	11	180	63,690	20	100
Rail transit extension	f	f	f	95,642	0	-300
Raise CBD auto speeds	-13,865	0	100	104	-9	-400
Lower CBD auto speeds	14,304	4	0	239	10	50
Raise all auto speeds	-617,744[e]	12	600	-50,819[e]	-4	-400
Lower all auto speeds	336,648[e]	-20	-500	50,315[e]	6	50
Increased auto occupancy (carpooling)	-273,312	9	500	-21,000	3	50

Decentralization	f	f	8,549[e]	19	475
Centralization	f	f	1,449[e]	−10	−700

Source: Gregory I. Ingram, Gary R. Fauth, Eugene Kroch, "Cost and Effectiveness of Emission Reduction and Transportation Control Policies," *Rivista Internazionale di Economia dei Transporti*, April 1975, pp 17–47.

[a] Percent CO reduction in CBD.

[b] Reduction of persontimes of exposure to harmful pollutants in thousands for the entire region.

[c] The moderate automobile emission control standards are the same as those shown in Table 9.2 for 1977–79 model years (1.5 gpm HC, 15.0 gpm CO, and 2.0 gpm NO$_x$). The stringent controls are the most restrictive contemplated in the original 1970 Clean Air Act (0.41 gpm HC, 3.4 gpm CO, and 0.4 NO$_x$).

[d] Allowing for extra congestion just outside the CBD created by traffic diverted from CBD by prohibition.

[e] These costs are exclusive of many or all capital, operating, and administrative costs, which are either difficult to estimate or are not applicable in these cases.

[f] Not applicable.

bution to reducing harmful exposure to air pollutants. Improving transit performance in the two cities (mainly through more express bus services) seems more attractive in Los Angeles than in Boston: in Los Angeles, such a policy would cost approximately one fourth as much as the 1980 automobile emissions controls and would make substantial contributions to reducing harmful exposure to air pollution; in Boston, such a policy would be almost as expensive as the 1980 automobile emissions controls and would not be as effective overall as in Los Angeles. In large part, this may simply reflect the fact that Boston already has extensive, high-performance transit service, while Los Angeles does not.

The two land-use proposals—decentralization and centralization—tested only for Boston,[8] are not particularly expensive (at least in direct costs and as measured). However, using these measures of effectiveness, only decentralization reduces exposure to harmful air pollutants. Decentralization is effective in Boston, especially on a regional basis, because it lowers the concentration of harmful pollutants in dense areas where many people are likely to be exposed. It must be stressed, though, that NO_x and HC pollutants were *not* included in this analysis, and these create concentrations of photochemical oxidents that might be expected to increase with decentralization.

Modifying land-use patterns to reduce mobile emissions would thus appear to be a limited possibility at best. Some land-use policies might even have surprisingly perverse results. As a policy, decentralization does have the advantage, though, of requiring little in the way of incentives or promotional programs. As documented in Chapter 2, decentralization of urban activities seems to be occurring naturally, and, as shown in Chapter 7, reversing such a trend is likely to be difficult.

The policies restricting automobile activities in central business districts seem, in both cities, to be costly relative to their effectiveness. The costs of such policies are more modest in Boston, while their effectiveness is roughly the same as or (in some cases) greater than it is in Los Angeles. Prohibition on CBD automobile use and licenses for use of automobiles in the CBD may, moreover, be politically difficult to implement.

In sum, transportation controls and other indirect policies for reducing exposure to harmful air pollutants are not cost-effective when compared with directly cleaning up automotive emissions. While it has been widely suggested that mobile emissions might be decreased by reducing the amount, the speed, or the stop-and-go characteristics of urban travel in lieu of directly reducing emission rates themselves, changing the basic urban transportation habits or choices of Americans is a difficult enterprise at best. Even worse, some plausible possibilities for reducing emissions through transportation policies may work perversely, increasing rather than reducing emissions. Nevertheless, not all of these policies should be dismissed out of hand. Carpooling seems to have merit in almost all circumstances. Traffic engineering to speed traffic flow could save money and, in some circumstances, such as newer and lower-density western cities like Los Angeles, could be effective in improving air quality.

REDUCING AUTOMOBILE EMISSIONS PER VEHICLE-MILE

Apparently, if *major* improvements are to be made in urban air quality, automobile effluents must be cleaned up. Various transportation control policies and other indirect programs, as just outlined, can make a marginal contribution—say a 10–20 percent rollback in harmful effluents—but not much more. Reductions in automobile use and fuel consumption, as indicated in Chapter 8, might contribute as much as 10–15 additional percentage points toward achieving the rollbacks of 90 percent or so targeted by public policy. Nevertheless, automobile pollution per vehicle-mile of travel also must be reduced if government-mandated goals for improving air quality are to be met.

Unfortunately, reducing automobile emissions can be quite expensive. On a national basis, the annual cost required to meet the strictest standards of the Clean Air Act Amendments of 1970 could range as high as $11.0 billion in 1973 dollars.[9]

The question is whether this potentially very expensive effort to control automotive emissions is really worth it. Making any such calculation is hazardous and uncertain at best. However, in a heroic effort to bracket the range of possibilities, a joint committee of the National Academy of Sciences (NAS) and the National Academy of Engineering (NAE) extrapolated what they considered to be low, median, and high estimates of both the costs and benefits of automobile emission controls. Studies of residential property values were used to estimate the annoyance and damage done by air pollution. These figures were supplemented with estimates of the effects of air pollution on human health, on vegetation (particularly commercial crops), and on materials (on the premise that these impacts may not be fully reflected in residential property values).[10] Combining the indirect effects on property value and directly measurable effects on health, vegetation, and materials may involve some double counting of costs, but the magnitude of this error is probably small relative to other uncertainties surrounding the calculations.[11] The committee's projections, to the year 2010,[12] are shown in Table 9.4. The benefits and costs of cleaner air will change

TABLE 9.4. Various estimates of national benefits and costs of automobile emission controls, 1975–2010 (in billions of dollars).

Year	Costs			Benefits		
	Low	Median	High	Low	Median	High
1975	2.8	2.8	2.8	1.000	1.50	3.00
1976	2.9	2.9	2.9	1.258	2.07	4.13
1977	3.3	3.2	3.5	1.516	2.63	5.26
1978	3.2	3.4	4.2	1.774	3.20	6.39
1979	3.2	3.6	4.8	2.032	3.76	7.52
1980	3.1	3.9	5.4	2.290	4.33	8.65
1981	3.1	4.2	6.0	2.540	4.89	9.78
1982	3.1	4.5	6.6	2.806	5.46	10.91
1983	3.1	4.8	7.2	3.064	6.02	12.04
1984	3.1	4.9	7.8	3.332	6.59	13.17
1985	3.1	4.8	7.9	3.580	7.15	14.30
1986	3.0	4.8	7.9	3.690	7.36	14.73
1987	3.0	4.8	7.9	3.800	7.59	15.17
1988	3.0	4.8	7.9	3.910	7.81	16.63
1989	2.9	4.8	7.9	4.030	8.05	16.09
1990	2.7	4.8	7.9	4.150	8.29	16.58
1991	2.5	4.8	7.9	4.270	8.54	17.07
1992	2.3	4.8	7.9	4.400	8.80	17.59
1993	2.0	4.8	7.9	4.540	9.06	18.11
1994	1.7	4.8	7.9	4.670	9.33	18.66
1995	1.4	4.8	7.9	4.810	9.61	19.22
1996	1.1	4.8	7.9	4.960	9.90	19.79
1997	0.8	4.8	7.9	5.100	10.20	20.39
1998	0.5	4.8	7.9	5.260	10.50	21.00
1999	0.2	4.8	7.9	5.420	10.82	21.63
2000	0.0	4.8	7.9	5.580	11.14	22.28
2001	0.0	4.8	7.9	5.690	11.36	22.73
2002	0.0	4.8	7.9	5.810	11.59	23.18
2003	0.0	4.8	7.9	5.920	11.82	23.64
2004	0.0	4.8	7.9	6.040	12.06	24.12
2005	0.0	4.8	7.9	6.160	12.30	24.60
2006	0.0	4.8	7.9	6.280	12.55	25.09

TABLE 9.4.   (*Cont.*)

	Costs			Benefits		
Year	Low	Median	High	Low	Median	High
2007	0.0	4.8	7.9	6.410	12.80	25.59
2008	0.0	4.8	7.9	6.540	13.05	26.10
2009	0.0	4.8	7.9	6.670	13.31	26.63
2010	0.0	4.8	7.9	6.800	13.58	27.16

Source: National Academy of Sciences and National Academy of Engineering, *Air Quality and Automobile Emission Control,* vol. 4, *The Costs and Benefits of Automobile Emission Control,* prepared for the Senate Committee on Public Works (Washington, D.C.: U.S. Government Printing Office, 1974).

with the passage of time. They will also be sensitive to public acceptance of less polluting cars and to the achievement and enforcement of emissions standards.[13] For example, a relaxation of the schedule of federal new-car emissions standards could reduce both costs and benefits. Similarly, different efforts by state and local governments to ensure that cars in use continue to meet the new-car standards could lead to different rates of maintenance on devices for meeting air standards, thereby modifying costs and benefits in the process.

Benefits will also vary with growth in urban population and personal income levels. Even with sharply reduced birth rates, the U.S. population will almost certainly grow from its 1980 level of about 223 million people to 260 million or 270 million before achieving stability. On the basis of previous trends, the urban "air polluted" population of the United States should grow a little more rapidly than the total population (although possibly in decentralized ways that *might* reduce exposure to harmful pollutants). Furthermore, if real income per capita continues to increase at its traditional growth rate of about 2 percent per year in the United States, this will make cleaner air more important, as people place a higher value on their health.

Manufacturers should also become more sophisticated and efficient in producing hardware for cleaning up automobile emissions as time goes by and as experience with such production processes increases. Time is needed as well for the development of and increased investment in new technologies and control devices. Thus, over time, technological and productivity improvements should partially offset costs created by the stiffening of standards, growing size of the automobile fleet, and increased percentages of cars brought under controls.

Putting all these considerations together, the NAS/NAE committee projected (see Table 9.4) that the costs of implementing automobile emission standards would probably peak in the early 1980s, after the institution of the strictest standards, and then decrease over time because of learning-curve effects, the development of better technologies, and increased investment in equipment for producing control devices, and so on.[14] They expected benefits to grow rapidly, as the present automobile fleet, much of which does not meet the emission standards, is replaced by a fleet that does. When all the cars in the fleet meet the strict emission standards, benefits are projected as growing more or less in step with the combined growth in incomes and urban population, or about 3 percent a year. Once the total U.S. population stabilizes, however, the benefit growth rate is projected to drop to about 2 percent a year (in line with growth in per capita incomes). Thus, even though annual costs may exceed benefits in these projections for the first few years after implementation of the strictest emission standards, benefits will then begin to exceed costs, with the excess of benefits over costs rising steadily over time.

For a benefit/cost analysis, these different cost and benefit streams must be discounted back to present value equivalents. The results of doing this under various assumptions about interest rates, benefit and cost estimates (taken from Table 9.4), and time horizons are shown in Table 9.5. The 4 and 5 percent interest rates used in these calculations are assumed to be representative of the true cost of capital, *exclusive* of any inflation or special risk considerations that would not normally apply to government or social investments.

These different net present values for costs and benefits can be used in different combinations to estimate benefit/cost ratios, as shown in Table 9.6. However, not all of these ratios are equally valid or meaningful. The lower-cost strategies, for example, will likely never achieve maximum benefits, since these probably sacrifice some emission reductions in the process of reducing costs. It is interesting to note that with the high-cost estimates, which provide the most pessimistic view of the control programs, the benefit/cost ratio moves well above unity only if the upper range of benefit estimates is accepted, whereas if a low-cost approach is adopted, the benefit/cost ratio is consistently above unity even if low- or median-benefit estimates are used.

This conclusion, moreover, is not too sensitive to the number of years over which the benefits and costs are discounted. For example, if cut off at the year 2000 instead of 2010 and using a conservative 5 percent discount rate, the benefit/cost ratio relating the lowest benefit estimate to highest costs falls from 0.6 to 0.5 while the central estimate, relating "median" benefits and costs, falls from 1.7 to 1.5 and all the low-cost ratios still remain above unity.

TABLE 9.5.   Total discounted national benefits and costs of automotive emissions controls, 1975–2010 (in billions of dollars).

	Costs	Benefits
At a 4 percent discount rate until the year 2010:		
Low	41	71
Median	82	137
High	126	273
At a 4 percent discount rate until the year 2000:		
Low	41	52
Median	68	101
High	102	201
At a 5 percent discount rate until the year 2000:		
Low	38	45
Median	60	88
High	90	175

Source: Table 9.4 discounted and cumulated as shown and taken from National Academy of Sciences and National Academy of Engineering, *Air Quality and Automobile Emission Control*, vol. 4, *The Costs and Benefits of Automobile Emission Control*, prepared for the Senate Committee on Public Works (Washington, D.C.: U.S. Government Printing Office, 1974), p. 419.

In sum, when one compares plausible benefit and cost streams for automotive emission controls, a benefit/cost ratio greater than unity seems likely only if low-cost automobile emission-control strategies are pursued.[15] It is therefore important that several methods exist for reducing the costs of cleaning up automobile emissions. In the main, these involve modifying the standards in one way or another (for example, by allowing cars used in rural areas and less polluted cities to meet less stringent standards or by accepting more NO_x emissions).[16]

Independent of any change in pollution standards, moreover, greater use of smaller cars in the United States should help reduce the costs of compliance with air quality controls. Smaller cars not only consume less gasoline but they also reduce the costs of achieving specified emissions standards. It has been estimated that reducing the average new-car size from an intermediate to a compact by 1985 would save $2.97 billion in pollution control costs over the decade from 1975 to 1985.[17]

The most obvious strategy for keeping the cost of automotive emis-

TABLE 9.6.   Various estimates of benefit/cost ratios for automotive emissions controls.

Benefits	Costs		
	Low	Median	High
At a 4 percent discount rate until the year 2010:			
Low	1.7	.9	.6
Median	3.3	1.7	1.1
High	6.7	3.3	2.2
At a 4 percent discount rate until the year 2000:			
Low	1.3	.8	.5
Median	2.5	1.5	1.0
High	4.9	3.0	2.0
At a 5 percent discount rate until the year 2000:			
Low	1.2	.8	.5
Median	2.3	1.5	1.0
High	4.6	2.9	1.9

Source: Table 9.5 rearranged in ratio form as taken from National Academy of Sciences and National Academy of Engineering, *Air Quality and Automobile Emission Control*, vol. 4, *The Costs and Benefits of Automobile Emission Control*, prepared for the Senate Committee on Public Works (Washington, D.C.: U.S. Government Printing Office, 1974), p. 420.

sions controls low would be to relax the NO_x standards. Requiring a low level of NO_x emissions may prevent or make difficult the use of diesels, stratified-charge, and similar engines that can readily meet strict HC and CO standards, but cannot easily meet NO_x targets much below 2.0 grams per mile. With a 2.0 gpm NO_x standard, these "other" engine technologies might make meeting the emissions standards almost costless by the latter part of this century. Stratified-charge engines alone (which might be available for most automobiles by the early 1980s) could reduce the costs of meeting strict emission standards by more than two thirds. Similar or even larger cost reductions might be achieved by greater use of diesel engines, although at some loss in performance and possibly with a serious increase in offensive odors and particulate emissions.

More concretely, if the original 1970 Clean Air Amendments requiring 0.4 gpm of NO_x emissions by 1978 had been retained, vehicles meeting that standard would have cost as much as $850 more over their lifetime than vehicles meeting pre-1970 standards, and total national automobile pollution-control expenditures could have reached almost $8 billion per year by 1985 (in 1974 dollars).[18] On the other hand, if the most stringent standard required only 2.0 gpm of NO_x instead of 0.4 gpm, vehicles meeting the standards would probably cost only about $475 more (in 1974 dollars) over their lifetime than vehicles meeting pre-1970 standards.[19] Total national automobile pollution-control expenditures would then be about $4.7 billion per year.[20] Thus, adoption of a 2.0 gpm NO_x standard in place of 0.4 gpm NO_x standard might save over $3 billion per year by 1985.

A question arises, though, of how much any relaxation in NO_x standards might sacrifice in benefits. The best guess from currently available data is that the cost savings gained from easing the NO_x emission standard probably exceed any loss in benefits.[21] Only a few urban areas, principally Chicago and Los Angeles, had NO_x levels above established thresholds in the late 1970s. Most of the benefits of the strict automobile NO_x standards might be achieved by adopting strict standards for those areas only. Again, in most cities about half of NO_x emissions originate from nonautomotive sources, and an attack on these other sources might be more cost effective than cleaning up automobile NO_x.[22] Although the need to clean up automotive NO_x in cities such as Los Angeles may be undeniable, elimination of nonautomotive NO_x probably deserves more attention than it now receives.

The irregular incidence of NO_x problems, uncertainties about their importance, and varying contributions of mobile and stationary sources in different cities also suggest the possible use of a so-called mixed or two-car strategy, long advocated by many analysts. No doubt, building vehicles to two standards can achieve substantial cost savings. For example, if 0.4 gpm of NO_x is required only for the 37 percent of vehicles in the most seriously polluted areas rather than in the entire country, and a 2.0 gpm standard is used elsewhere, nearly $2 billion per year could be saved.[23]

The potential cost savings from these various strategies for relaxing standards are, of course, not independent. In essence, with the two-car strategy alone the annual costs can be brought down to an annual level of $6 billion or even less; with total relaxation of the NO_x standards, the annual costs would be even lower and might eventually become negligible (because of other savings potentially derivable from greater use and production of diesel, stratified charge, and similar engines). However, until more is known about the actual health effects of NO_x and the costs of reducing NO_x emissions from other sources, some caution seems advisable about relaxing NO_x standards.

Still another way to reduce the costs of automotive emission controls would be to change the means of implementing them. Specifically, instead of setting standards, fees or fines might be assessed against those who pollute—those polluting most having to pay the most. A common and economically naïve objection made to this alternative is that it condones pollution for a price. However, even simple economic theory would indicate that this is merely a matter of establishing the "correct price" (that is, a fee or fine high enough so that it lowers emissions to a level considered socially satisfactory).

The main advantage of using fees rather than standards to reduce harmful emissions is that the fee approach provides continuing incentives for producers and consumers[24] alike to find cheaper and more effective methods of abatement. As Mills and White, ardent advocates of effluent fees, put it:

> Effluent fees would induce manufacturers to build those cars for which abatement was cheapest; it would equate marginal abatement costs among sources . . . Furthermore, if a similar fee schedule were applied to other mobile and stationary sources the program would equalize marginal abatement costs among all sources, mobile or stationary . . . Present programs do not come close to achieving this. [With effluent fees] consumers would have an incentive to seek, buy, and maintain clean cars. They would also become interested in additional retrofit devices if they found the devices cost effective.[25]

Several practical objections to effluent fees are commonly made. In particular, administrative costs are often projected to be unduly large. But this depends on how the program is administered. A reasonably good case can be made that costs could be kept within bounds, so as not to exceed the added efficiency benefits.[26]

Other administrative approaches to effluent control have been suggested that might achieve many of the advantages of effluent fees at somewhat lower cost. For example, fleet-average emissions standards for newly produced cars have been proposed similar to those employed for fuel efficiency (see Chapter 8). Fleet-average standards, as contrasted with specific standards for each and every car produced, would permit manufacturers to make trade-offs between different technologies for different car sizes and models, as market demands or production economies dictated. A difficulty with the fleet-average approach could occur, though, if there were a tendency for the high polluters to collect in a few sensitive locations—that is, already polluted cities. However, there is no reason to believe that this should occur. It seems more likely that small cars, which are generally the cheapest to clean up, will appear in greater numbers in urban areas, while vehicles that are costly to clean up (such as large cars and utility vehicles) will find a market in rural areas.

In general, it seems highly probable, indeed almost certain, that techniques for achieving emissions reductions can be found that will be more imaginative and flexible than a program of highly specific standards set for virtually every new vehicle entering the fleet. Flexibility has value because it permits cost savings through marginal adjustments of many types. When combined with suggestions for a two-car strategy or some relaxation of standards, an emissions-control program that has benefits well in excess of costs is almost guaranteed. But the question remains open as to whether the established program, as set by government legislation and administrative procedures, meets this benefit/cost test.

SUMMARY

While carpooling, transit enhancement, traffic restriction schemes, and other indirect transportation-control programs *might* help attenuate air pollution in some instances, substantial improvements in urban air quality will almost certainly require a significant reduction in the amount of effluent dispersed by automobiles for every mile they travel. Unfortunately, the benefits derivable from meeting very strict automobile emission standards may not immediately exceed the expected costs of those standards. A desirable (greater than unity) benefit/cost ratio can be achieved only if: (1) some form of two-car strategy is adopted, wherein only a minority of the U.S. fleet would be required to meet the strictest standards; (2) some relaxation is accepted in the target for NO_x emissions—say, a 1.5–2.0 gpm standard; or (3) a more flexible approach to administering the program, such as effluent fees or fleet-average standards, is substituted for individual vehicle standards. All of these strategies should effect substantial cost savings and thereby greatly enhance the prospects of benefits exceeding costs.

In the final analysis, the benefit/cost ratio of the automotive emission-control program will depend on a number of subjective evaluations, such as judgments about the aesthetic value of less air pollution and perception of risks. A highly favorable omen is that demographic, income, and technological trends strongly favor an increase in the ratio of annual benefits to annual costs for automotive emission controls. But even if the benefit/cost ratio of reducing automobile emissions is, or eventually becomes, favorable, an economically prudent person would not necessarily advocate these controls as a good investment of public or private moneys. That would depend on what the person believes will be the availability of investment funds over the relevant time horizon and whether other, more desirable, projects may be rationed out of the market by possible limits on available capital. Much will also depend on whether lower-cost alternatives might be identified for achieving the same goals.[27]

10

*Aesthetics and
Other
Community
Concerns*

THE PROBLEM OF TRANSPORTATION BLIGHT

While city dwellers have long sought improved mobility, they have also recognized that most modes of transportation create unsightliness and environmental blight. Air pollution is probably the most obvious such harm. It is not surprising, therefore, that the belching steam locomotive was of concern almost from its introduction, in Victorian times. Also of concern have been the grime and environmental damage associated with elevated structures used for urban transportation: projects to dismantle the rail loop around Chicago's central business district were discussed almost as soon as the loop was finished, while the urban renewal and development that followed the dismantling of the Third Avenue El on the East Side of Manhattan exceeded all but the most optimistic expectations. In addition, transportation modes have almost always been noisy, to the point of being seriously disturbing to those who live nearby; steel wheels on steel rails, for example, create a whine not totally unlike that of rubber wheels on smooth concrete.

New technologies have changed the details but not the substance of these anxieties. Substitution of the automobile for horses replaced pollution under foot with pollution in the air. The use of diesel and internal-combustion engines instead of steam locomotives may have accentuated rather than alleviated noise problems. Elevated highways, because they are so massive, may be more aesthetically objectionable than the elevated railroads that preceded them. Furthermore, the open cut to accommodate an express highway must often be wider than that needed for a railway, and as such is often at least as disruptive of community relationships: in many cities, the other side of the expressway may be as far away physically and socially today as the other side of the tracks once was.

Another long-standing concern has been the simple fact that transportation lanes and corridors take up space. Though there is widespread intuitive, if not formal, recognition that property access requires transportation lanes and corridors, the allocation of space to such facilities is often begrudged. In the automobile/internal-combustion era, this concern has often taken the form of bewailing the excessive amount of land devoted to the automobile and its use, particularly in central business districts. "Scare statistics," to the effect that some very high percentage—60–80 or so—of some downtown areas are now allocated to highways, are used to make this point. Similarly, discussions of noise and other aesthetic problems created by transportation operations in cities have been marked by at least as much emotion as facts or analysis.

This chapter seeks some redress in that balance. An attempt will be made to estimate the costs imposed on society by traffic noise, as well as the aesthetic damage associated with the building of high-performance modern highways. An investigation will also be made of what effects substitution of the automobile and truck for horse and steam power have had on the percentage of land allocated to transportation functions under different density and urban configurations.

NOISE POLLUTION

The most striking single fact about traffic noise pollution is the very large percentage produced by trucks and motorcycles. The essential statistics are shown in Table 10.1. The typical passenger automobile generates only 69–75 decibels (on the A-weighted scale or dBA) at 50 feet, while the typical heavy truck, highway bus, or motorcycle emits 82–85 dBA at the same distance. The dBA index is a logarithmic scale, weighted to reflect people's perceptions about the annoyance of noises of different loudness and pitch; thus, this approximate 10 dBA differ-

TABLE 10.1.   Noise emissions levels by motor vehicles.

Motor vehicle type	Typical sound level (dBA at 50 feet)	Estimated total sound energy (kwh/day)
Passenger automobiles:		
Sports and compact	75	1,150
Intermediate- and full-sized	69	800
Subtotal		1,950
Other motor vehicles:		
Trucks (medium and heavy)	84	5,800
Trucks (light and pickup)	72	570
Motorcycles (highway)	82	325
Motorcycles (off-road)	85	160
Buses (highway)	82	12
Buses (city and school)	73	20
Snowmobiles	85	500
Subtotal		7,387
All motor vehicles		9,337

Source: From U.S. Environmental Protection Agency, "Identification of Products as Major Sources of Noise," *Federal Register*, vol. 39 (June 21, 1974), p. 22,298, as cited in Jon P. Nelson, *Economic Analysis of Transportation Noise Abatement* (Cambridge, Mass.: Ballinger, 1978), p. 19.

ence in sound levels implies that the typical automobile is perceived as being only one tenth as noisy as the typical truck or motorcycle. Although passenger automobiles account for about three quarters of the traffic in the nation as a whole, the typical car is so quiet relative to the typical truck that the total sound energy produced by passenger automobiles in the United States amounts to substantially less than one half of the total sound energy produced by all types of motor vehicles.[1]

Traffic noise seldom reaches levels thought to damage human health or materials; thus, in contrast with air pollution, noise is more of an aesthetic than a medical or physical problem. The primary cost imposed by traffic noise is annoyance, or disturbance of sleeping or other activities. In recognition of this, a special day/night sound-level scale (commonly designated as Ldn) is usually employed when measuring exposure to traffic noise. This Ldn index is based on the dBA measure for single events, but weights the various sounds heard during a 24-hour period according to the duration and time of day as well as loudness and pitch.[2]

The normal background noise level for an urban neighborhood is generally placed at about 55 on the Ldn index. The Environmental Protection Agency (EPA) estimated in 1972 that approximately 79 million urban residents were exposed to noise levels above 55 Ldn because of motor vehicle traffic. Most of these residents were exposed to noise levels only in the 55–65 Ldn range, a level at which, the EPA believes, most people are not sufficiently annoyed to consider themselves "significantly impacted." The agency estimated that only about 17 million urban residents were exposed to traffic noise levels above a 65 Ldn threshold.[3]

The impact of traffic noise is likely to be exerted in much more complicated ways than might be expressed by a simple threshold level. For example, the severity of traffic noise depends on such specific characteristics of a road as the presence of shielding objects (such as trees), the average speed of the traffic, whether the road itself is level and how it is situated relative to its surroundings, and traffic volumes.[4] Noise pollution may also depend to a considerable extent on perceptions. For example, the annoyance imposed by the noise from the passage of an additional automobile may be higher on lightly traveled suburban roads and in the off-peak hours than on downtown expressways in the peak period. (Again, this is in contrast to air pollution.) Therefore, the noise cost imposed by the marginal user on lightly traveled roads might often be much higher than the noise cost of the marginal expressway user in the rush hour.[5]

In order to estimate the cost of noise pollution, it is necessary to determine how the market will react to the presence of different types and levels of noise. A general assumption in making such cost estimates is that discomfort or annoyance with noise will be reflected in variations in property values, particularly in the value of residential property. Despite differing data sets and varied (and sometimes controversial) statistical techniques, the half dozen existing studies relating noise to residential property values generally concur that a one-unit increase on the Ldn scale reduces housing values by 0.2–0.6 percent, or $50–150 for the average house measured in 1975 prices.[6] Amortizing these housing-value changes over the lifetime of the house at a 5 percent discount rate, assuming an average of three persons per household and that only "significantly annoyed" (over 65 Ldn) households suffer, the total cost of noise from all types of traffic in 1972 can be placed at somewhere between $600 million and $1.9 billion (in 1975 dollars).[7]

While these estimates of noise pollution costs are only about one fifth as high as those generally attributed to air pollution, they are nevertheless quite substantial. Of the total, however, traffic noise pollution is attributable more to trucks and motorcycles than to automobiles. Even if allowance is made for the much greater volume of automobile than truck or motorcycle traffic, automobiles still seem responsible for only about one quarter to one third of the sound energy emitted by motor vehicles in urban areas, or $200–600 million of costs (in 1975 dollars). Dividing that sum by the approximately 650 billion vehicle-miles of automobile travel that takes place each year in urban areas, the average cost of automobile noise pollution in the 1970s probably amounted to less than one tenth of a cent per vehicle-mile.

One solution to the traffic noise problem that is currently being pursued is a legal requirement that motor vehicles be less noisy. State and local governments have long sought to reduce motor vehicle noise through changes in designs and operation (for example, requirements for mufflers). In 1972, partly to preempt an increasing number of conflicting state and local noise regulations, Congress passed a Noise Control Act that gave the EPA the power to establish uniform, nationwide noise-emission standards for products distributed or operated in interstate commerce.

In its rulings on motor vehicles, the EPA has concentrated on standards for medium- and heavy-weight trucks (trucks over 10,000 pounds), since they are the greatest source of urban traffic noise and have been a target of noise regulations in an increasing number of states. In 1975, the EPA issued standards for existing heavy- and medium-weight trucks of 90 dBA at 50 feet at speeds over 35 miles per hour, 86 dBA at 50 feet for speeds of 35 miles per hours or less, and 88 dBA at 50 feet for stationary vehicles. It also prohibited the use of certain types of retread truck tires that are particularly noisy.[8] In 1976, the EPA promulgated stricter lifetime standards of 83 dBA at 50 feet at the speed of 35 miles per hour for heavy- and medium-weight trucks produced after January 1, 1978, and 80 dBA for trucks produced after January 1, 1982.[9] The standards for new vehicles are enforced by vehicles certification tests and selective assembly-line audits administered by the EPA, while enforcement of in-use standards is the responsibility of the Bureau of Motor Carrier Safety within the Federal Highway Administration (FHWA). The EPA estimates that the 80 dBA new-truck noise standards will reduce the number of persons adversely affected by urban street and freeway noise by about 25 percent by the 1990s.[10]

Another solution to the traffic noise problem that is being pursued increasingly is better design and shielding of highways. Recent federal policies to encourage noise-sensitive highway design have potential influence because the federal government is the largest supplier of highway construction funds.[11] In 1970, partly in response to local pressure, Congress required that the FHWA develop noise standards for new highways constructed with federal aid. In 1973, Congress authorized the FHWA to issue noise standards for previously constructed segments of highway systems built with federal aid and to provide aid for projects to abate noise on these highways, under the condition that the minimum local share of such project costs be the same as for construction projects on the same type of highway.

The standards established by the FHWA prohibit mean-energy sound levels of more than 57 Ldn outdoors in areas such as historic places or parks where serenity is of "extraordinary significance," 67 Ldn outdoors in residential or recreational areas, and 52 Ldn indoors in residences, schools, churches, and hospitals. The regulations also established a maximum-energy sound level of 72 Ldn outdoors for other developed lands and a sound level that cannot be exceeded 90 percent of the time for each of these types of land.[12] When the standards are violated, noise abatement procedures—for which federal aid may be available—include the acquisition of adjacent property to create a buffer, the creation of noise barriers such as vegetation- or earth-banks, and the construction of depressed highways (highways placed in open cuts or tunnels). The noise standards may be waived by the FHWA, however, if nonhighway sources in the area generate noise levels in excess of the standards or if the costs of noise abatement would exceed the benefits to be gained. The ultimate impact of these highway noise standards is uncertain, partly because it is unclear how the FHWA will measure and interpret the benefits and costs of abatement. Nevertheless, increasing federal and local efforts to "shrub up" and otherwise redesign highways hold the potential for greatly reducing noise problems on at least some (generally the most offensive) highways.

UNSIGHTLINESS

In spite of widespread concern about the aesthetic disruption caused by urban transportation facilities—particularly elevated highways and railways—only one systematic effort has been made to estimate its social costs.[13] This one effort was a study of Boston's Fitzgerald Expressway, considered by many observers as one of the most aesthetically damaging highways in the United States.

The Fitzgerald Expressway, opened in 1959, passes between the eastern edge of Boston's central business district and Boston Harbor. The highway separates one of the older and more historic parts of Boston, the Faneuil Hall Market area, from the harbor. Many of the structures near the Fitzgerald Expressway are handsome examples of commercial architecture from the mid-nineteenth century. The Faneuil Hall neighborhood has been slowly redeveloping,[14] despite the blighting effect of the elevated highway, but city officials and developers agree that the area would be significantly more attractive and valuable if the view to the harbor could be restored by removing the highway. In 1978, therefore, the City of Boston and the Commonwealth of Massachusetts proposed that a three-quarter-mile section of the Fitzgerald Expressway be rebuilt as a depressed highway at a cost estimated (in 1978 dollars) to be approximately $1 billion.[15] The expense was partly justified on the grounds that the deck of the existing highway would have to be replaced anyway due to corrosion and other problems.

The aesthetic benefits of rebuilding the expressway were estimated by analyzing variations in property values from 1955, a year before the original construction plans were announced, to 1978, nineteen years after the expressway was opened; the objective was to assess changes in property values that might have occurred either in anticipation of construction or after the full impact of highway traffic was apparent. The presence of the elevated highway was estimated to have reduced property values on the three-quarter-mile stretch where the depressed expressway has been proposed by approximately $300 million in 1979 dollars. Because of unavoidable methodological difficulties, this figure should be regarded as an upper-bound estimate of the lost property value due to the unsightliness of the elevated highway.[16]

Amortizing these property-value losses over a 40-year life for the buildings on the property, the annual aesthetic cost of the highway can be placed at $17.4 million at a 5 percent interest rate or $30.6 million at a 10 percent interest rate.[17] Since approximately 35 million vehicles use this section of the expressway each year, the cost amounts to 66 cents per vehicle-mile at a 5 percent discount rate or $1.16 per vehicle-mile at a 10 percent discount rate (all in 1979 dollars). While aesthetic damage by itself is apparently not enough to justify a $1 billion expenditure to rebuild the road as a depressed highway, the damage per vehicle-mile is extremely high relative to noise pollution and other social costs that motorists generate[18] and is of sufficient scale to suggest that these costs should have been considered when the decision was made to build this highway in elevated form.

The Fitzgerald Expressway is hardly the only high-performance urban facility that has drawn objections in recent years. San Franciscans prevented the completion of the Embarcadero Freeway, which was to have connected the Golden Gate and Bay bridges, largely because of aesthetic considerations. New Orleans redirected the building of an expressway that would have been disruptive to its French Quarter. New York's Westway (a proposed highway along the West Side of Manhattan) has been delayed for many years and considerably modified because of aesthetic objections.[19] Similar delays, modifications, or outright rejections of urban highway construction have occurred in several other cities in recent years.

Responding to concerns about the aesthetic and community disruptions of urban highway construction, Congress has gradually amended the federal highway aid program to make the highway planning process more sensitive to a wide variety of social and environmental issues. The 1962 Federal Highway Aid Act, for example, for the first time provided funds for relocation assistance to persons and businesses displaced by highway construction. The 1962 act also instituted the first of many increasingly stringent planning requirements by mandating that before any urban area with a population greater than 50,000 can receive additional federal highway aid, it must demonstrate that its highway plans were developed as part of a metropolitan planning process that was "continuing" (in the sense that every project is consistent with a frequently updated master plan), "comprehensive" (in that public transportation is considered as well as highways), and "cooperative" (in that all concerned agencies and governments were involved in the plan's development).[20]

Congress subsequently acted to reduce the environmental damage of highways by making federal highway projects subject to the National Environment Policy Act of 1969 (NEPA). Under NEPA, the Department of Transportation must prepare, for EPA review, an "Environmental Impact Statement" on each federally aided highway project. These statements must outline not only the environmental consequences of the proposed highway project itself, but also the impacts of alternatives to highway construction, such as mass transit or not building any new facility. Congress was even more specific in Section 4(f) of the Department of Transportation Act of 1970, which prohibited the secretary of transportation from approving the use of publicly owned parkland, open spaces, or historical sites for federal highway or mass transit projects unless "no feasible and prudent alternative is available."[21]

In general, federal transportation planning requirements have become much more specific and extensive, so that by the late 1970s every metropolitan area had to file several different types of plans each year—each requiring public hearings or other opportunities for public comment and dissent—in order to maintain eligibility for federal highways and transit grants.[22] Some observers fear that these regulations may have made it too easy for small but intensively motivated interest groups to protest and delay projects and that it will be impossible to construct new highway segments in urban areas in the future, regardless of merit. Nevertheless, if the Fitzgerald Expressway cost calculations are at all characteristic (as the intense opposition to more construction in several cities would suggest), then the need for some evaluation process would seem well founded.

The difficult issue is how to balance these proceedings so as not to inhibit the building of facilities that are truly needed while still protecting urban aesthetic values of importance. One compromise in particularly sensitive areas might be the construction of tunnels or the adoption of circuitous routings. To finance these, which could sometimes be very expensive alternatives, funds might be made available by, for example, setting aside a portion of federal highway trust funds for such purposes and having these funds allocated by a process very different from that otherwise used. Mayors or community groups, for instance, might apply for the use of such funds to alleviate what they deem to be aesthetically objectionable features in highways proposed (or built) in their areas, and the decision to make such allocations might be shared by the Departments of Transportation and Housing and Urban Development (rather than being the exclusive responsibility of the FHWA, as is now the case). Alternatively, special tolls might be charged to use these facilities on the grounds that they are not only expensive but that it is necessary to establish their indispensability (by establishing that demand is sufficient to finance their costs). One clear advantage in these approaches is that they do not necessarily involve a reduction in spending on construction (and may actually increase such spending) so that building trades unions and their employers may therefore be less opposed—an opposition that has often blocked change in the past. Furthermore, under such schemes, highway trust funds are not diverted from highway purposes, a diversion to which automobile associations and other highway groups tend to object; rather, the trust funds are used more creatively to meet highway needs.

TRANSPORTATION LAND REQUIREMENTS

Anxieties that expanding transportation facilities will take up excessive amounts of scarce urban land generally are expressed by the assertion that reliance on the automobile will increase the amount of urban land used for transportation purposes. Since any functioning city must allocate some land to transportation, the question of "excessive" land requirements for transportation must be considered in relation to some measure of scale. In popular discussions, this matter of scale is often expressed in the notion that exceptional reliance on the automobile will result in the "paving over" of important segments of the city landscape.

The truth, though, is that automobile use does *not* result in an exceptional *percentage* of land being given to transportation purposes. Rather, the automobile seems to create exceptional demands for transportation land relative to the number of people in an urban area. Specifically, cities more dependent on the automobile tend to have more street acreage per person but a smaller percentage of total land in streets, as shown in Table 10.2.

Despite a few individual exceptions (such as Miami and St. Louis), the relationships between automobile dependence and land usage are remarkably stable and strong. For the 15 large cities shown in Table 10.2, the percent of workers using automobiles for worktrips is correlated at about a 0.7 level *negatively* with the percent of land in streets and *positively* with the acres of streets per 10,000 of population. If these same correlations are calculated for the entire sample of 93 cities with populations greater than 100,000 in 1968 (included in a study of land use done by the National Commission on Urban Problems),[23] the relationships are not quite so strong but are still quite suggestive: specifically, the percent of workers using automobiles for worktrips is negatively correlated at a 0.31 level with the percent of land in streets and positively correlated at a 0.59 level with acres of street per 10,000 of population. A possible explanation for the weaker correlations in the larger sample might be that this sample includes many more small cities for which special considerations (such as development histories or social patterns) may condition transportation land requirements.[24]

These findings are not significantly modified when space for parking is taken into consideration. In some cities, much of the parking is on the street, so that little land in addition to that reflected in the space statistics of Table 10.2 will be required. Off-street parking can also be provided in garages as well as in parking lots; to the extent that such space is in multistory structures, land use per vehicle will be further reduced, although the capital costs will normally be greater because of the expenditures required to erect such structures.

Automobile ownership rates will also affect parking space requirements. Cities more dependent on the automobile, and therefore with higher rates of automobile ownership, clearly will need more parking spaces than cities not so dependent. To illustrate, it might be hypothesized that in an automobile-dominated city, one automobile is in use for every two persons in the population. Furthermore, it might be assumed that each automobile requires two off-street parking spaces and that

TABLE 10.2. Population, automobile use, and transportation land use in fifteen large U.S. cities.

	1960 population (in thousands)	Using auto for worktrip		Population density		Land in streets		Street space per 10,000 of population	
		Percent	Rank	Population per square mile	Rank	Percent	Rank	Acres	Rank
New York	7,782	20.2	15	24,697	1	30.1	1	79.1	14
Chicago	3,550	45.0	12	15,836	4	24.3	4	97.3	11
Los Angeles	2,479	75.8	3	5,451	12	14.2	12	170.0	5
Philadelphia	2,003	41.6	14	15,743	5	19.3	7	83.9	13
Houston	938	77.2	1	2,860	14	12.6	15	363.9	1
Cleveland	876	57.5	7.5	10,789	8	17.1	9	95.4	12
St. Louis	750	56.0	9	12,296	6	25.2	3	139.9	7
Milwaukee	741	57.5	7.5	8,137	10	20.4	6	166.3	6
San Francisco	740	42.2	13	16,599	3	25.6	2	101.2	10
Dallas	680	76.4	2	2,428	15	13.2	13.5	361.6	2
Pittsburgh	604	48.6	10	11,171	7	17.8	8	104.3	9
Cincinnati	503	62.7	5	6,501	11	13.2	13.5	131.5	8
Atlanta	487	60.0	6	3,802	13	15.3	11	257.2	3
Newark	405	46.2	11	17,170	2	15.8	10	59.0	15
Miami	292	62.8	4	8,529	9	24.1	5	178.7	4

Source: Allen D. Manvel, "Land Use in 106 Large Cities," paper prepared for the consideration of the National Commission on Urban Problems, research report no. 12 (Washington, D.C.: U.S. Government Printing Office, 1968). The 15 cities in this table are the 15 largest of the 106 investigated by Manvel for which all data are available.

neither of these spaces is in a garage. If each of these parking spaces took up approximately 250 square feet of land, then for each 10,000 of population about 50 acres of land would be required for parking. These 50 acres could be compared with the 200–300 acres of street space per 10,000 of population seemingly needed in automobile-dependent cities (see Table 10.2). Similar calculations for less automobile-dependent communities would result in lower land requirements for parking, since automobile ownership rates would be lower; but such cities would probably need more off-street parking, particularly in garages, because of their higher density and their lower amounts of street space per 10,000 of population.[25] Overall, then, it seems highly probable that parking would add approximately 15–25 percent to the land requirements for street space, for both automobile-dependent and transit-oriented cities.

An explanation of why automobile-dependent cities require a low percentage of land in streets but a relatively large amount of street space per person is that the availability of the automobile in recent years has allowed the development of larger blocks. When people were more dependent on walking, blocks were smaller to make foot travel more efficient. When property access for goods delivery or emergency purposes was dependent on horse-drawn vehicles, smaller and squarer blocks were also more sensible. But now that virtually all vehicles are powered by the internal-combustion engine, and most urban travel is by automobile, blocks can be longer without making trips any more time-consuming. Furthermore, when people want to have more land attached to each individual domicile, as in the typical American suburb, long rectangular blocks create an offsetting economy by giving less land to street space. Because more and more areas have been developed since the advent of the car, the net result over the years has been a declining percentage of urban land in streets in many American cities. Of course, cities developed before the internal-combustion engine came into dominance still retain many older and higher-density areas with higher percentages of land devoted to streets but less street space per unit of population.[26]

Freeways built in recent years also conserve on street space by moving more traffic in a given amount of time for a specified allotment of space than previously existing surface avenues or boulevards. Furthermore, freeways account for a very small percentage of street space, as access streets are the predominant consumer of urban land for transportation purposes.

The charge that reliance on the automobile leads to an excessive amount of urban land being used for transportation purposes would thus seem to require very careful interpretation. Specifically, if the allegation is that an excessively high *percentage* of land must be used for transportation purposes when the automobile becomes the dominant mode of urban transportation, then the charge seems fallacious. On the other hand, if the charge is that an exceptional amount of land *per person* must be devoted to transportation purposes when reliance is placed on the automobile, then there is substance to the indictment. In this latter form, however, the complaint reduces to the long-standing charge that the automobile promotes sprawl. As discussed in Chapters 2 and 7, placing the responsibility for urban sprawl mainly on the automobile is a bit simplistic. The automobile is only one of many factors creating decentralization, which has been observable in virtually all cities around the world over the past 100 years (see the Appendix). It is therefore difficult to believe that a substantial change in the automobile's role as an urban transportation mode would greatly change these underlying land-use trends.

CONCLUSION

It has often been said that "beauty is in the eye of the beholder"; judgments about aesthetics are therefore likely to be subjective. Nevertheless, some agreement on at least a few basic points seems achievable.

There seems little doubt that traffic noise can be a problem in many circumstances and can create some nontrivial economic losses. Traffic noise is not as severe an economic or health problem as air pollution, but at an annual cost of $1 billion (plus or minus $0.5 billion), it should not be ignored. It is also understandable that most cities do not take kindly to historical districts, park facilities, or natural scenic attractions being visually blocked or otherwise blighted by transportation developments.

Although much remains to be done, substantial progress has been made in alleviating the aesthetic problems created by urban transportation. Federal regulations designed to quiet trucks hold significant potential for alleviating noise pollution, since these vehicles produce a substantial portion of highway noise. Noise standards for federally funded highways should also help, as will the availability of federal aid to redesign high-performance highway facilities to contain their traffic noise. More generally, federal restrictions on the use of parks or historic sites for highway purposes and the requirement of public hearings, analysis of environmental impacts, and consideration of transit alternatives or not building at all should make aesthetically or environmentally damaging transportation facilities less likely.

The key question is how far these policies should be carried. Some of the aesthetic problems associated with transportation land use in urban areas may be mainly those of perception and must be balanced against other needs. Cities tend to be tightly knit, highly interdependent economic and social systems. Introducing new facilities or otherwise modifying established behavior patterns is unavoidably disruptive. Tearing down old buildings and replacing them with a highway or a mass transit system upsets established ways of doing things and, what is more important, neighborhood relationships. The problem is how to effectuate change while accommodating or preserving what is best in the existing order. The planning, public hearings, and environmental statements that have now been mandated by law as a formal prerequisite to transportation construction in U.S. cities would certainly seem to be useful steps toward hearing out and establishing perceptions before the fact.

The great danger in all these processes, though, is that they may become not so much a means of surfacing legitimate objections but rather a way of totally blocking *all* change. As in almost all political processes, the difficulty is juggling highly divergent interests so as to achieve a reasonable balance or consensus. Early experiences with the planning, public hearings, and environmental statements mandated by Congress suggest that the pendulum may have swung too far in the direction of impeding change. But given that some substantial costs and problems are involved, the proper next step in public policy would not appear to be total repeal of what has already been attempted but rather to fine-tune so as to achieve better balance. One of the means for achieving better balance would be to involve more market or pseudomarket mechanisms in the process. If the transportation need to be met by a new facility is great enough, then prospective users should be willing to pay the costs of making the transportation facility acceptable. The simplest way to establish this fact is to levy more tolls or charges for the use and financing of such facilities. In general, for reasons explained in much greater detail in the next chapter, greater use of the pricing mechanism, or greater refinement of the taxation techniques used to finance transportation developments, would help establish which particular facilities are truly needed and which are not. Establishing such need, or its lack, could be helpful in solving many other public policy problems as well.

11

Traffic
Congestion

BASIC PRINCIPLES

Concern over congestion, viewed as *the* principal urban transportation problem in much of the 1950s and 1960s, was a primary justification for the massive highway construction that took place in U.S. urban areas during the postwar decades. Largely because automobile ownership and use have continued to grow, traffic congestion remains a problem today.

Congestion also affects other urban transportation problems. Reduced congestion and increased traffic speeds, for example, may encourage additional automobile use, which, in turn, intensifies automobile pollution, energy consumption, and safety problems. These adverse effects may be at least partially offset, however, by the fact that reduced congestion lowers emissions, energy consumption, and accident rates per vehicle-mile.

Traffic congestion is normally defined by reference to a speed/volume curve. This curve relates the volume of traffic passing a point on a road (usually expressed in passenger-car-equivalent units per lane-hour, that is, one lane for one hour)[1] to average traffic speed. Highway engineers estimate these speed/volume curves for different types of high-

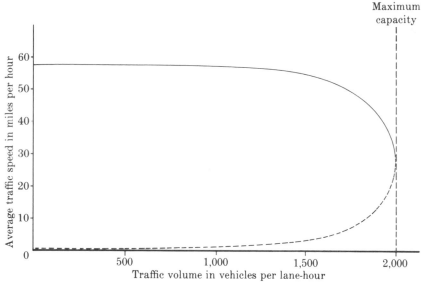

Figure 11.1. Hypothetical speed/volume relationship for an urban expressway.

ways or streets through statistical analyses of observed traffic speeds and volumes.[2]

The speed/volume curve shown in Figure 11.1 is typical of limited-access highways. The solid line shows the relationship between speed and volume when vehicles are entering a highway at rates lower than maximum capacity. The average traffic speed falls slowly as traffic volume increases until the volume approaches maximum capacity, whereafter average speeds drop rapidly. The dashed line illustrates supersaturated conditions, which can occur if automobiles enter the highway in excess of maximum capacity for even a brief period of time. With supersaturation, both volumes and speeds decrease sharply and can fall to zero if the entering volume of traffic does not decrease quickly.

By way of calibration, maximum capacity on an urban freeway can be as high as 2,000 vehicles per lane-hour (though most have capacities in the range of 1,700 to 1,900 vehicles per lane-hour due to less than ideal alignments, grades, curves, or frequent entering and exiting of traffic). The average traffic speed on a freely flowing urban expressway can exceed 50–60 miles per hour, while speeds at maximum capacity are in the range of 25–35 miles per hour.

Supersaturation is clearly to be avoided, since a highway can carry the *same* volume at far higher speeds by avoiding such a condition.

Even operating near capacity is deemed undesirable because small increases in traffic volumes greatly reduce speeds and enhance the danger of supersaturation.

Normally, though, no attempt is made to design or operate highways so as to eliminate congestion altogether. Highway construction and every other means of reducing highway congestion involve at least some costs, and the costs of further reducing congestion by most means usually exceed the benefits of faster travel long before congestion is eliminated entirely. The choice of how many lanes wide to build a highway, for example, involves trading off increased highway construction and maintenance costs against decreases in travel time and operating costs for motorists. The number of lanes is economically optimal if the costs of constructing one more lane are equaled or barely exceeded by the gains to motorists from that lane. A highway large enough to allow freely flowing traffic during the height of the rush hours in the centers of large metropolitan areas is seldom optimal, because building such highway capacity is very expensive and the benefits in time savings and operating costs accruing to only a small group of rush hour users will be comparatively small. In short, highway engineers and planners understand that some traffic congestion is almost always advisable in a well-designed highway system.

It should also be noted that to a certain degree highway congestion is self-limiting, since highway users are unwilling to tolerate infinite delays. Future congestion levels are therefore not likely to deteriorate quite as much as some naïve extrapolations of traffic growth would suggest, because as congestion worsens, motorists will adopt strategies to avoid highly congested situations. The most obvious such strategy is to travel by less congested alternative routes. Commuters, for example, often know a variety of routes to travel to work and are alert to any changes that might give one route a slight advantage over another. Traffic will tend to distribute over a highway network so that travel times on alternative routes become roughly equivalent. Drivers can also avoid congestion by changing the time of day or the day of the week they travel. They can also change destinations or forgo a trip altogether, although these strategies are probably only employed in extreme cases.

Strategies used by motorists to avoid delays may slow or limit the growth of congestion, but they may not be by themselves a satisfactory solution to the congestion problem. Essentially, these strategies substitute one kind of expense and inconvenience for another; for example, they trade traffic delays for travel by more circuitous routes, at less convenient hours, by less comfortable modes, or to less desirable destinations.

As a corollary, highway construction or other policies to increase highway capacity should not necessarily be regarded as failing or self-defeating if they attract so much new traffic that peak-period traffic speeds remain unchanged. To start, off-peak speeds are nearly always improved even if peak speeds are not. Even more important, with augmented capacity, more motorists are able to travel during the peak period than could previously.

There are many ways of alleviating highway congestion. Since building bigger and better highways has been the principal public strategy to date, it will be analyzed first. Subsequently, a variety of means to either reduce highway demand or increase effective capacity will be evaluated; these range from greater use of sophisticated traffic engineering to charging fees for automobile use of congested streets.

THE BENEFITS AND COSTS OF URBAN HIGHWAY INVESTMENTS

In order to calculate the benefits of highway investments, it is necessary to estimate what traffic volumes and congestion levels would have been with and without the added highway segments. Traffic growth is usually the result of rising incomes, population gains, or changes in traffic speeds, but it is not easy to assess the strength of these different influences. Consequently, the amount of traffic growth and congestion that would have occurred in the absence of new highway investments is extremely difficult to predict, particularly for urban roads where traffic and congestion vary significantly by location and time of day.[3]

Although there have been some benefit/cost analyses of isolated highway segments, only one study has attempted an estimate of the benefits and costs of a substantial portion of the urban highway system.[4] This study, completed in 1965, compared the actual and projected government outlays for the federally funded Interstate Highway System with the savings in travel time and operating costs these highways offered to users and shippers. For the Interstate Highway System as a whole, the present value of savings to motorists, truckers, and shippers between 1956 and 1991 was estimated to exceed the present value of government construction and operating costs by $14,277 million at a discount rate of 5 percent, and $1,953 million at a discount rate of 10 percent (in 1961 dollars). Moreover, most of the net benefits were earned on the urban portions of the Interstate System, for which the present value of benefits less costs between 1956 and 1991 was estimated at $13,442 million at a 5 percent discount rate, and $4,029 million at a 10 percent rate (in 1961 dollars). In contrast, on rural parts of the Interstate Highways, the present value of benefits exceeded costs by only $835 million with a discount rate of 5 percent, and costs exceeded benefits by $2,076 million when a discount rate of 10 percent was employed.[5]

In this same study, the net benefits of the Interstate Highway System were compared with those of smaller alternative highway systems to see if more modest highway investments could have generated the same or higher net benefits. The comparisons, summarized in Table 11.1, suggest that the urban portions of the Interstate System were as good as or better than a smaller system of urban superhighways that were four lanes wide instead of the six or eight lanes common to urban Interstate System segments. The rural portions of the Interstate System generally had a higher present value than an alternative two-lane rural road system, but both systems produced only small positive net benefits or net losses.[6]

This early analysis strongly suggests that the urban portions of the Interstate Highway System are a desirable investment. But the results cannot be regarded as conclusive, because the estimates of highway costs do not include motor vehicle air pollution, noise pollution, or other more recently recognized social costs of highway use, and therefore may exaggerate the estimated gains from the Interstate System. In addition, a substantial portion of the Interstate System had not been completed by the early 1960s, when the analysis was performed, so forecasts of traffic volumes and construction costs—prepared by the Federal Highway Administration—had to be used instead of actual figures. These FHWA forecasts incorporated various, somewhat offsetting, errors. On the one hand, construction costs for the entire system proved to be about 46 percent higher (in constant dollars) than the FHWA expected;[7] on the other hand, urban Interstate System traffic volumes grew at almost twice the rate forecast by the FHWA.[8] Finally, rather arbitrary assumptions had to be made about the levels of traffic that would have occurred without the construction of the Interstate System, and the analysis is extremely sensitive to these assumptions.[9]

User tax payments as a measure of highway benefits. Among the special taxes that motorists pay for highway use are gasoline taxes, tolls, and vehicle registration fees. Since motorists are willing to pay at least this much for highway use (and maybe much more, if necessary), these user charges provide a minimum estimate of the benefits that motorists receive from highway investments. In theory, then, a particular segment of the highway system might be deemed worthwhile if users pay enough in "highway" taxes to cover the costs that the segment imposes on society.

TABLE 11.1. Friedlaender's estimates of the net benefits of the Interstate Highway System and more modest alternative highway systems.

Interstate system	Smaller alternative	Type of user	Net present value 1956–91 (in millions of 1961 dollars)			
			5 percent discount rate		10 percent discount rate	
			Interstate	Smaller alternative	Interstate	Smaller alternative
Rural portion of the Interstate System	Construction of new system of two-lane rural roads with high-speed standards but without access control or median strips	Passenger	−1,230	−4,302	−2,518	−2,955
		Freight[a]	2,065	730	442	80
		Total rural	835	−3,572	−2,076	−2,875
Urban portion of the Interstate System	Construction of a system of 4- rather than 6- or 8-lane urban superhighways that can accommodate all but peak commuting traffic	Passenger	7,772	6,289	1,809	1,732
		Freight	5,670	6,736	2,220	2,870
		Total urban	13,442	13,025	4,029	4,602
Entire Interstate System	As described above for rural and urban portions	Passenger	6,542	1,987	−709	−1,223
		Freight	7,735	7,466	2,662	2,950
		Total, entire system	14,227	9,453	1,953	1,727

Source: Ann F. Friedlaender, *The Interstate Highway System: A Study in Public Investment* (Amsterdam: North-Holland Publishing Company, 1965), p. 114.
[a] The rural freight estimates assume that government freight rate regulations do not cause a misallocation of freight traffic among rail and truck modes.

Much discussion of highway taxes and subsidies presumes that the revenues from special taxes on highway users should exactly equal government expenditures on highways. In fact, it may be desirable to set highway-user taxes above or below expenditures in order to compensate for other costs or benefits to society from highway use. For example, user taxes might be set higher than highway expenditures to reflect the social costs of increased air pollution, energy use, and noise that stem from highway use.

On the other hand, a reasonably compelling argument can be made for not requiring highway users to pay for all government highway expenditures on the grounds that some minimum network of narrow and unimproved roads is necessary for property development, emergency services (police, ambulances, and fire department), and other such access. Though property owners might be charged for this access in the form of highway-user fees, the irregular and infrequent nature of much of the demand may make it more practical to assess the costs through property taxes.[10] Since costs attributable to such a basic road system would be a significant portion of total highway expenditures only for lightly traveled local and rural roads, they can be ignored when doing aggregative assessments of heavily used urban arterials.

Economies or diseconomies of scale in the construction of highway capacity might be another reason for not setting highway-user receipts exactly equal to outlays. Economists often argue that users should pay the marginal cost of constructing and maintaining the increment to highway capacity that their use requires, so that individuals' decisions about whether or not to use the highway would accurately reflect the additional (marginal) capacity costs of such use. If there are economies to constructing large highway systems (that is, if the unit cost of capacity falls as more capacity is constructed), then the marginal cost of capacity will be less than the average cost, and total revenues generated from a uniform user charge set at marginal cost will be less than total costs. Conversely, if there are diseconomies of scale in constructing highway capacity so that unit costs increase with scale, the marginal cost of additional highway capacity will be higher than the average cost, and a marginal-cost user charge will yield revenues that exceed total costs.

Segments of the highway system almost certainly exhibit different economies or diseconomies of scale at different times and places.[11] Economies of scale may occur, for example, because the required right-of-way and grading do not increase proportionately with the number of lanes, due to allowances for shoulders and buffer zones.[12] Economies may also occur because adding a second or third lane in each direction may increase effective highway capacity more than proportionately (by allowing faster-moving vehicles more opportunities to pass slower traffic). On the other hand, the available evidence suggests that beyond three lanes in each direction, additional lanes do *not* increase capacity proportionately, because of interweaving to gain access and egress. On balance, economies and diseconomies of scale are probably roughly offsetting and therefore, like the costs of achieving basic property access, can be ignored when doing broad assessments of highway benefits and costs.

Government highway expenditures, shown in Table 11.2, are divided approximately equally between capital expenses and operating expenses. Capital outlays include all expenditures for the purchase of right-of-way (including relocation assistance),[13] grading and drainage costs, construction of bridges and tunnels, and pavement base and paving costs. Operating expenses include routine maintenance, snow removal, mowing, painting, and other similar activities as well as high-

TABLE 11.2.   U.S. highway capital and operating expenditures, 1956–1975 (in millions of dollars).

Year	Capital	Maintenance and traffic services	Administration, research, and traffic police	Other policy, judicial, prosecution, and correctional	Total
1956	3,986	2,088	521	528	7,123
1957	4,600	2,204	628	582	8,014
1958	5,660	2,371	724	625	9,380
1959	6,263	2,482	760	673	10,178
1960	5,900	2,640	811	722	10,073
1961	6,349	2,728	872	777	10,726
1962	6,738	2,839	921	813	11,311
1963	7,191	2,917	1,009	844	11,961
1964	7,670	3,059	1,159	892	12,780
1965	7,948	3,233	1,261	959	13,401
1966	8,722	3,515	1,485	1,016	14,738
1967	9,026	3,719	1,637	1,107	15,489
1968	9,715	3,910	1,874	1,212	16,711
1969	9,745	4,245	2,164	1,375	17,529
1970	10,993	4,792	2,441	1,574	19,800
1971	11,564	5,099	2,930	1,814	21,407
1972	11,385	5,421	3,205	2,041	22,052
1973	11,050	5,899	3,648	2,332	22,929
1974	11,218	6,399	3,937	2,657	24,211
1975	11,909	6,925	4,314	3,028	26,176

Source: Kiran Bhatt, Michael Beesley, and Kevin Neels, *An Analysis of Road Expenditures and Payments by Vehicle Class, 1956–1974* (Washington, D.C.: Urban Institute, 1977), pp. 95, 98, 101, 110.

way administration, research (on pavement durability, lane markings, sign design, and so on), safety, and law enforcement. Outlays for all police assigned to traffic and highway safety duties, as well as correctional expenses attributable to enforcing traffic laws and curtailing automobile theft, are included as highway law enforcement costs. Major resurfacing and reconstruction expenditures are counted as capital outlays when they can be distinguished from normal maintenance.

Estimating the user component in highway taxes involves differentiating between special charges made for highway use and general taxes levied on consumption, income, or personal property. One commonly used rule for making such separations is to regard a tax as a highway-user charge if collected from highway users or on motor vehicles but not on most other comparable goods or services.[14] By this rule, highway-user charges clearly include federal gasoline, vehicle, spare parts, and excise taxes; state motor vehicle and driver registration fees; and special highway-user taxes on trucks. State gasoline and motor vehicle sales and property taxes are not necessarily included, since many states or localities levy sales or personal property taxes on a variety of other goods, although typically at lower rates.[15] Estimates of U.S. highway-user charge receipts derived by following this separation principle (including state gasoline taxes in excess of state sales taxes) are shown in Table 11.3 in current dollars for the years 1956 through 1975.

When the entire road system in the United States is considered in the aggregate, the question of whether highway-user taxes exceed or fall short of highway capital and operating costs depends upon whether comparisons are made on a pay-as-you-go or amortized capital basis, as shown in Table 11.4. On a pay-as-you-go basis, user revenues approximately covered costs in the 1950s, fell to about 95 percent of costs in the 1960s, and by 1975 covered only 80 percent of costs. On an amortized capital basis, employing a conservative 10 percent discount rate,[16] user revenues exceeded costs by 20–30 percent in the 1950s and 1960s, but by 1975 had fallen short of costs by about 25 percent. If capital is amortized at a 5 percent discount rate, the results lie somewhere in between, with revenues exceeding costs by 50–178 percent in the 1950s and 1960s and falling to parity with costs by 1975. The deterioration in all cases of the ratio of revenues to expenses develops because total highway expenses have increased in real terms (although current capital investment has declined), while user revenues have not kept pace with inflation (mainly because most fuel taxes are fixed in cents per gallon).

Highway expenses and user revenues can be attributed in the main to either urban or rural parts of the national highway system. But some costs and revenues are not assignable—notably administrative and policy expenses or user charges that are collected on an annual or one-time

TABLE 11.3. U.S. highway-user charge receipts (in millions of dollars).

Year	Federal				State			Local	All government
	Fuel tax	Auto excise tax	Other vehicle and parts excise tax	Total	Fuel tax	Vehicle and driver registration fees	Total		
1956	1,254	1,152	549	2,955	2,775	1,582	4,357	208	7,520
1957	1,521	1,274	703	3,498	2,899	1,662	4,561	215	8,274
1958	1,604	924	633	3,161	3,017	1,702	4,719	244	8,124
1959	1,726	1,305	785	3,816	3,265	1,828	5,093	244	9,153
1960	1,738	1,327	798	3,863	3,435	1,926	5,361	272	9,496
1961	2,369	1,138	780	4,287	3,618	1,961	5,579	277	10,143
1962	2,467	1,445	956	4,868	3,812	2,060	5,872	283	11,023
1963	2,578	1,642	1,072	5,292	4,015	2,191	6,206	299	11,797
1964	2,716	1,822	1,155	5,693	4,284	2,364	6,648	306	12,647
1965	2,841	1,782	1,219	5,842	4,559	2,512	7,071	357	13,270
1966	2,984	1,383	1,186	5,553	4,806	2,761	7,567	423	13,543
1967	3,110	1,450	1,135	5,695	5,057	2,894	7,951	452	14,098
1968	3,317	1,708	1,245	6,270	5,524	3,161	8,658	484	15,439
1969	3,522	1,877	1,512	6,911	6,094	3,508	9,602	562	17,075
1970	3,694	1,697	1,497	6,888	6,510	3,800	10,310	482	17,680

Year								
1971	3,904	1,826	1,559	7,289	6,945	4,063	11,008	543	18,840
1972	4,202	0	1,312	5,514	7,74⊥	4,395	12,139	567	18,220
1973	4,418	0	1,680	6,098	8,35C	4,789	13,139	590	19,827
1974	4,242	0	1,786	6,028	8,23ε	5,060	13,298	640	19,966
1975	4,413	0	1,884	6,297	8,804	5,430	14,234	670	21,201

Source: Kiran Bhatt, Michael Beesley, and Kevin Neels, *An Analysis of Road Expenditures and Payments by Vehicle Class, 1956–1975* (Washington, D.C.: Urban Institute, 1977), pp. 125, 126 131, 132, 136, 139.

TABLE 11.4. Total highway expenditure and user revenues, 1956–1975 (in millions of dollars).

	1956		1960		1965		1970		1975	
	Expense	Revenue	Expense	Revenue	Expense	Revenue	Expense	Revenue	Expense	Revenue
Pay-as-you-go basis, using current prices:										
Interstate[a]	707	943	2,353	1,314	3,787	2,131	4,595	3,418	4,795	3,911
Federal primary[b]	2,160	2,356	2,477	2,997	2,936	4,176	4,714	5,439	6,294	6,830
Federal secondary[b]	1,517	1,190	1,754	1,496	2,336	2,100	3,636	2,918	5,212	3,704
Other	2,739	3,031	3,489	3,689	4,342	4,863	6,855	5,904	9,875	6,749
Total	7,123	7,520	10,073	9,496	13,401	13,270	19,800	17,679	26,176	21,194
Amortized capital basis, using 1975 prices and 5 percent discount rate:										
Interstate[a]	571	2,328	892	3,122	1,496	4,476	2,249	5,339	2,826	3,911
Federal primary[b]	3,576	5,817	3,864	7,121	4,032	8,772	4,503	8,496	5,081	6,830
Federal secondary[b]	2,140	2,938	2,515	3,555	3,032	4,411	3,864	4,560	4,704	3,704
Other	6,401	7,483	6,723	8,766	7,070	10,215	7,738	9,222	8,692	6,749
Total	12,688	18,566	13,994	22,564	15,630	27,874	18,354	27,617	21,303	21,194

Amortized capital basis, using 1975 prices and 10 percent discount rate:

Interstate[a]	586	2,328	1,120	3,122	2,155	4,476	3,364	5,339	4,255	3,911
Federal primary[b]	5,572	5,817	5,945	7,121	6,042	8,772	6,522	8,496	7,084	6,830
Federal secondary[b]	2,460	2,938	2,960	3,555	3,633	4,411	4,629	4,560	5,630	3,704
Other	8,316	7,453	8,577	8,766	8,860	10,215	9,404	9,222	10,309	6,749
Total	16,934	18,566	18,602	22,564	20,690	27,874	23,919	27,617	27,278	21,194

Source: Computed from data in Kiran Bhatt, Michael Beesley, and Kevin Neels, *An Analysis of Road Expenditures and Payments by Vehicle Class, 1956–1975* (Washington, D.C.: Urban Institute, 1977), pp. 115, 143, 195, 196.

[a] Highways that are part of the federally funded Interstate Highway System.

[b] In addition to grants for construction of the Interstate Highway System, the federal government also provides grants to states for the construction and maintenance of a "Federal-Aid Primary and Secondary Highway System." Each state, in consultation with the federal government, can designate only a small portion of its state highway system as part of the Federal-Aid Primary and Secondary Highway System to be eligible for federal aid. The designated highways tend to be the most heavily traveled in the state, other than those in the Interstate System.

basis (such as vehicle excise or registration fees). Fortunately, these unassignable costs and revenues only amount to about one quarter of the totals and are probably not unfairly, even if somewhat arbitrarily, allocated to the different types of highways by the vehicle mileage occurring on these highways.

Shortfalls between highway-user revenues and expenditures occur mostly in rural rather than urban areas (compare Tables 11.5 and 11.6). On a pay-as-you-go basis, aggregate payments from urban highway users exceeded urban highway expenditures by as much as 30 percent in some years (see Table 11.5), although by 1975 the margin of receipts over outlays had fallen to only 11.5 percent. On an amortized capital basis, urban payments were more than double highway expenditures in some years during the 1960s and, although revenues grew more slowly than outlays in the 1970s, by 1975 revenues still exceeded expenditures by 14 percent (using a 10 percent discount rate) or as much as 44 percent (using a 5 percent rate).

Government expenditures and revenues in 1975 for different portions of the highway system are shown in detail in Table 11.7. Urban highways are substantially more expensive to construct and operate per route-mile than their rural counterparts (partly because they tend to have more lanes but also because right-of-way, construction, and maintenance are more expensive in dense urban areas). The fact that government expenditure per vehicle-mile of travel in 1975 averaged only about 1.2 cents in urban areas as compared with almost 2.2 cents in rural areas mainly reflects the more intensive use of urban highways. Moreover, highway user revenues per vehicle-mile were slightly higher in urban than in rural areas (1.7 cents as opposed to 1.6 cents) apparently because of increased fuel consumption resulting from the more frequent acceleration and braking of urban driving.

Even though collectively urban highway users may pay their capital and operating costs, those using highways in the centers of large, dense metropolitan areas during the peak commuting hours may not. As shown in Table 11.8, highway costs per lane-mile (one lane of highway for one mile) average about 60–70 percent higher in metropolitan areas with a population above one million than in metropolitan areas with populations below 250,000. Costs per lane-mile are also about 50–60 percent more in the CBD of a metropolitan area than on the fringe.

The high cost of serving peak-period users can be illustrated with data from the Fitzgerald Expressway in downtown Boston. Approximately 39 percent of all daily traffic on the Fitzgerald Expressway travels between 6:00 A.M. and 9:00 A.M. and between 3:00 P.M. and 6:00 P.M.; the two top rush hours (7:00–8:00 A.M. and 5:00–6:00 P.M.) alone account for 15 percent of the daily volume.[17]

The Fitzgerald Expressway is three lanes wide in each direction. But the capacity of the third lane is required for only a small share of the daily traffic, the exact amount depending on the average traffic speeds desired and the effective capacity of the expressway at that speed. Average traffic speeds of 20–30 miles per hour are possible when the expressway is operating at maximum capacity, which the Massachusetts Department of Public Works estimates to be 5,300 vehicles per hour in each direction, or approximately 1,767 vehicles per lane-hour.[18] If speeds of 20–30 miles per hour are acceptable, the third lane is needed to serve only about 8,650 (7.4 percent) of the weekday average of 117,214 vehicles, and only during a few peak-travel hours of the day.

It might be desirable, however, to allow vehicles on the Fitzgerald Expressway to operate at higher speeds than those possible at maximum capacity, even during the peak hours. The merits of such a policy would depend upon the trade-off between the savings to motorists from faster transportation and the added capital and maintenance costs of the wider expressway that probably would be required. If speeds of 35–40 miles per hour were sought, for example, the capacity of the expressway might be only 1,600 vehicles per lane, and the number of vehicles requiring the third lane would increase to 13,478 per weekday (or 11.5 percent of the weekday total). For the two peak hours of the day, the third lane would probably operate very close to its capacity, so that a fourth lane might eventually be needed to maintain the desired traffic speeds.

In the early 1970s, the costs of a central-area highway like the Fitzgerald averaged $2–3 million per lane-mile for construction[19] plus an annual charge of $10,000 per lane-mile for maintenance[20] (all in mid-1970s dollars). Assuming a useful life of about 40 years and using interest rates of 5 percent (appropriate for constant dollars) and 10 percent (a more conservative rate), the total annual cost (capital plus maintenance) of a four-lane highway costing $2 million per lane-mile to construct would be either $522,000 or $874,000 per mile (at 5 and 10 percent, respectively), while the annual cost of a six-lane facility would be between $783,000 and $1.311 million per mile. The annual cost savings from constructing a four-lane instead of a six-lane facility could thus be estimated at either $261,000 or $437,000 per mile, depending on the choice of interest rates.

If traffic speeds as low as 20–30 miles per hour were tolerable, the costs attributable to the vehicles needing the third lane (8,650 on the Fitzgerald) would average about 12 cents (at 5 percent) or 20 cents (at 10 percent) per vehicle-mile. If speeds of 35–40 miles per hour were desired, the costs of accommodating the vehicles requiring a third lane (13,478 on the Fitzgerald) would average slightly less, about 8 or 13

TABLE 11.5. Urban highway expenditure and user revenues, 1956–1975 (in millions of dollars).

	1956		1960		1965		1970		1975	
	Expense	Revenue	Expense	Revenue	Expense	Revenue	Expense	Revenue	Expense	Revenue
Pay-as-you-go basis,										
using current prices:										
Interstate[a]	341	326	1,055	450	1,698	766	2,233	1,453	2,363	1,711
Federal primary[b]	688	706	809	943	1,002	1,442	1,668	2,357	2,412	3,337
Federal secondary[b]	206	230	230	296	290	464	464	916	796	1,357
Other	1,395	2,187	1,767	2,637	2,210	3,461	3,390	4,423	4,756	5,267
Total	2,630	3,449	3,861	4,326	5,200	6,133	7,755	9,149	10,327	11,672
Amortized capital										
basis, using 1975										
prices and 5 percent										
discount rate:										
Interstate[a]	315	805	457	1,069	725	1,609	1,092	2,270	1,378	1,711
Federal primary[b]	1,202	1,743	1,289	2,241	1,315	3,029	1,446	3,682	1,744	3,337
Federal secondary[b]	263	568	313	703	371	975	494	1,431	680	1,357
Other	3,403	5,399	3,526	6,266	3,573	7,270	3,777	6,909	4,308	5,267
Total	5,183	8,515	5,585	10,279	5,984	12,883	6,809	14,292	8,110	11,672

Amortized capital basis, using 1975 prices and 10 percent discount rate:

Interstate[a]	321	805	543	1,069	985	1,609	1,539	2,270	1,953	1,711
Federal primary[b]	1,929	1,743	2,019	2,241	1,989	3,029	2,096	3,682	2,372	3,337
Federal secondary[b]	331	558	400	703	478	975	622	1,431	836	1,357
Other	4,400	5,399	4,453	6,266	4,422	7,270	4,552	6,909	5,058	5,267
Total	6,981	8,515	7,415	10,279	7,874	12,883	8,809	14,292	10,219	11,672

Source: Computed from data in Kiran Bhatt, Michael Beesley, and Kevin Neels, *An Analysis of Road Expenditures and Payments by Vehicle Class, 1956–1975* (Washington, D.C.: Urban Institute, 1977), pp. 115 143 195, 196

a. Highways that are part of the federally funded Interstate Highway System.

b. In addition to grants for construction of the Interstate Highway System, the federal government also provides grants to states for the construction and maintenance of a "Federal-Aid Primary and Secondary Highway System." Each state, in consultation with the federal government, can designate only a small portion of its state highway system as part of the Federal-Aid Primary and Secondary Highway System to be eligible for federal aid. The designated highways tend to be the most heavily traveled in the state, other than those in the Interstate System.

TABLE 11.6. Rural highway expenditure and user revenues, 1956–1975 (in millions of dollars).

	1956		1960		1965		1970		1975	
	Expense	Revenue	Expense	Revenue	Expense	Revenue	Expense	Revenue	Expense	Revenue
Pay-as-you-go basis, using current prices:										
Interstate[a]	366	617	1,298	864	2,089	1,365	2,362	1,965	2,432	2,200
Federal primary[b]	1,472	1,650	1,668	2,055	1,934	2,734	3,046	3,082	3,882	3,493
Federal secondary[b]	1,311	960	1,524	1,200	2,046	1,636	3,172	2,002	4,416	2,347
Other	1,344	844	1,722	1,052	2,132	1,402	3,465	1,481	5,119	1,482
Total	4,493	4,071	6,212	5,170	8,201	7,137	12,045	8,530	15,849	9,522
Amortized capital basis, using 1975 prices and 5 percent discount rate:										
Interstate[a]	256	1,523	435	2,053	771	2,867	1,157	3,069	1,448	2,200
Federal primary[b]	2,374	4,074	2,575	4,880	2,717	5,743	3,057	4,814	3,337	3,493
Federal secondary[b]	1,877	2,370	2,202	2,852	2,611	3,436	3,370	3,129	4,024	2,347
Other	2,998	2,084	3,197	2,500	3,497	2,945	3,961	2,313	4,384	1,482
Total	7,505	10,051	8,409	12,285	9,646	14,991	11,545	13,325	13,193	9,522

prices and 10 per-
cent discount rate:

Interstate[a]	265	1,523	577	2,053	1,170	2,867	1,825	3,069	2,302	2,200
Federal primary[b]	3,643	4,074	3,926	4,880	4,053	5,743	4,426	4,814	4,712	3,493
Federal secondary[b]	2,129	2,370	2,560	2,852	3,155	3,436	4,007	3,129	4,794	2,347
Other	3,916	2,084	4,124	2,500	4,438	2,945	4,852	2,313	5,251	1,482
Total	9,953	10,051	11,187	12,285	12,816	14,991	15,110	-3,325	17,059	9,522

Source: Computed from data in Kiran Bhatt, Michael Beesley, and Kevin Neels, *An Analysis of Road Expenditures and Payments by Ve-hicle Class, 1956–1975* (Washington, D.C.: Urban Institute, 1977), pp. 115, 143, 195, 196.

a Highways that are part of the federally funded Interstate Highway System.

b In addition to grants for construction of the Interstate Highway System, the federal government also provides grants to states for the construction and maintenance of a "Federal-Aid Primary and Secondary Highway System." Each state, in consultation with the federal government, can designate only a small portion of its state highway system as part of the Federal-Aid Primary and Secondary Highway System to be eligible for federal aid. The designated highways tend to be the most heavily traveled in the state, other than those in the Interstate System.

TABLE 11.7. Government highway expenditures and highway-user receipts per vehicle-mile and per route-mile, 1975.

			1975 expenditures			1975 user receipts		
	Route-miles	Vehicle-miles	Total (millions of dollars)	Per route-mile (millions of dollars)	Per vehicle-mile (cents)	Total (millions of dollars)	Per route-mile (millions of dollars)	Per vehicle-mile (cents)
All roads:								
Interstate[a]	42,696	255,805	2,826	66,189	1.105	3,911	91,601	1.529
Federal primary[b]	214,756	395,445	5,081	23,652	1.285	6,830	31,794	1.729
Federal secondary[b]	639,906	237,426	4,704	7,351	1.981	3,704	5,788	1.560
Other	2,847,036	417,850	8,692	3,053	2.080	6,689	2,349	1.615
All roads	3,744,394	1,306,526	21,303	65,689	1.631	21,134	5,644	1.622
Urban roads only:								
Interstate[a]	8,828	129,292	1,378	156,094	1.066	1,711	193,815	1.323
Federal primary[b]	26,376	179,869	1,744	66,121	.970	3,337	126,517	1.855
Federal secondary[b]	31,351	76,219	680	21,689	.892	1,357	43,284	1.780
Other	533,310	310,348	4,308	8,077	1.388	5,207	9,764	1.697
All urban roads	599,865	695,728	8,110	13,520	1.166	11,612	19,358	1.678
Rural roads only:								
Interstate[a]	33,868	126,513	1,448	42,753	1.145	2,200	64,958	1.739
Federal primary[b]	188,380	215,576	3,337	17,714	1.548	3,493	18,542	1.620
Federal secondary[b]	608,555	161,207	4,024	6,612	2.496	2,347	3,857	1.456
Other	2,313,726	107,502	4,384	1,895	4.078	1,482	641	1.379
All rural roads	3,144,529	610,798	13,193	4,195	2.166	9,522	3,028	1.559

Source: Calculated from data in Kiran Bhatt, Michael Beesley, and Kevin Neels, *An Analysis of Road Expenditures and Payments by Vehicle Class, 1956–1975* (Washington, D.C.: Urban Institute, 1977), pp. 88, 115, 143, 195, 196; and U.S. Department of Transportation, Federal Highway Administration, *Highway Statistics, 1975* (Washington, D.C.: U.S. Government Printing Office, 1977), tables M–21 and M–12.

[a] Highways that are part of the federally funded Interstate Highway System.

[b] In addition to grants for construction of the Interstate Highway System, the federal government also provides grants to states for the construction and maintenance of a "Federal-Aid Primary and Secondary Highway System." Each state, in consultation with the federal government, can designate only a small portion of its state highway system as part of the Federal-Aid Primary and Secondary Highway System, to be eligible for federal aid. The designated highways tend to be the most heavily traveled in the state other than those in the Interstate System.

TABLE 11.8. Costs of constructing a new expressway by location in millions of 1973 dollars per lane-mile.

Type of cost	Location within area	Below 100,000	100,000– 250,000	250,000– 500,000	500,000– 1,000,000	Above 1,000,000
Land costs	CBD	0.36	0.43	0.54	0.72	1.11
	Fringe	0.36	0.39	0.43	0.54	0.72
	Residential	0.32	0.36	0.36	0.46	0.64
Construction costs	CBD	1.04	1.07	1.10	1.14	1.24
	Fringe	0.71	0.75	0.81	0.94	1.20
	Residential	0.62	0.62	0.65	0.71	0.84
Total costs	CBD	1.40	1.50	1.64	1.86	2.35
	Fringe	1.07	1.14	1.24	1.48	1.92
	Residential	0.94	0.98	1.01	1.17	1.48

Source: Kiran Bhatt and Marylou Olson, Capacity and Cost Inputs for Community Aggregate Planning Model (CAFM), working paper no. 5002-3 (Washington, D.C.: Urban Institute, 1973).

cents per vehicle-mile.[21] If the highway cost $3 million per lane-mile to construct, and maintenance costs rose accordingly, these vehicle-mile costs would rise by roughly 50 percent, thus approaching a possible high-end estimate of 30 cents per vehicle-mile.

Thus, the construction and maintenance costs of accommodating the marginal, peak-period motorists on an urban expressway might be as much, on average, as 10 times the costs of serving the remaining users, which average 2–3 cents per vehicle-mile.[22] These rough estimates of the costs of marginal, peak-period users on urban expressways are also 20–30 times larger than the average government capital and operating expenses of 1.3 cents per vehicle-mile on all urban interstates in 1975, reflecting the high costs of both peak-period use and downtown location.

While the capital and operating expenses attributable to peak-period and downtown motorists are much higher than average, the highway-user taxes paid by these motorists are only moderately higher. In 1975, tax receipts from all urban highway users—mainly in the form of the gasoline tax—averaged about 1.7 cents per vehicle-mile (see Table 11.7). Because of congestion, peak-period and downtown users probably consumed a bit more fuel and therefore paid somewhat higher taxes per mile than average. But the differential between peak and off-peak highway-user tax payments is generally estimated to be only about

10–20 percent, far smaller than the differential between peak and off-peak highway capital and operating costs.

Thus, in evaluating whether motorists pay as much in highway taxes as the government expends for highways (and, therefore, whether motorists are subsidized through government highway construction and operating expenditures), the answer will depend upon which group of highway users is being considered. If all U.S. highway users are considered collectively, user tax receipts probably fell just short of government expenditures in the mid to late 1970s—the exact margin depending upon how government expenditures are calculated and the year in question. These aggregate statistics, however, disguise substantial differences between urban and rural users; urban-user receipts as a whole exceed urban highway expenditures, while rural receipts fall short. There are also important variances among urban users, for while urban users as a whole may pay their way, the same cannot be said of downtown peak-hour commuters who are responsible for some of the most expensive segments of the urban highway system.

Since user taxes actually paid may be viewed as a lower-bound estimate of benefits (because many highway users might well be willing to pay more rather than do without), it seems highly probable that the benefit/cost ratio for most urban highways exceeds unity (still ignoring any externalities for the moment). Even high-cost, multilane, centrally located urban expressways might be able to generate receipts in excess of costs if special tolls were charged, but this is conjectural, since little direct evidence is available.[23]

External costs. An excess of aggregate urban highway-user taxes over government highway expenditures, if it were to exist, might be at least partly justified by the "external" costs (such as air and noise pollution) that highway construction and use impose on the public at large. Furthermore, the fuel prices paid by motorists may not reflect the full costs of energy use (such as the dependence on foreign sources of petroleum) to society.[24] Although these external costs are difficult to measure exactly, some estimates may be made, as indicated in Chapters 9 and 10, for air and noise pollution and aesthetic damage.

For example, if automobile air pollution emissions are reduced to 90 percent of 1970 levels (that is, prior to emissions controls), the annual savings in property, health, vegetation, and materials costs have been estimated (by the National Academies of Science and Engineering) to be between $2.5 billion and $10 billion (in 1973 dollars), with the most likely but highly tentative (even speculative) guess being $5 billion.[25] Dividing these total national costs by the estimated 650 billion urban vehicle-miles traveled per year, it can be estimated that in 1970, urban automobile users *on average* caused about 0.8 cents (in 1973 dollars) of air pollution damage per vehicle-mile—although the average damage could have been as low as 0.4 cents or as high as 1.7 cents per vehicle-mile, given the uncertainty of the cost figures.[26]

By comparison, a study of urban transportation in the San Francisco Bay area placed the cost of automobile air pollution emissions from the average car in the 1968 fleet at 1.29 cents per vehicle-mile (in 1973 dollars). Because of recent federally mandated reductions in new-car pollution-emissions rates (discussed in detail in Chapter 9), a new 1972 model automobile in San Francisco had estimated air pollution costs of only 0.48 cents per vehicle-mile (in 1973 dollars), while an automobile that achieved the full 90 percent reduction in emissions over 1970 levels was estimated as generating air pollution costs of only 0.08 cents per vehicle-mile when new and 0.17 cents per vehicle-mile after five years of use.[27]

In metropolitan areas with topographies and climates that impede the removal and dispersal of automobile emissions (such as Los Angeles), air pollution emissions costs per vehicle-mile are probably higher than the urban averages computed in the NAS/NAE and San Francisco studies. Air pollution emissions costs per vehicle-mile may also be higher than average around heavily traveled downtown roads, since carbon monoxide does not disperse readily and can cause discomfort and health problems in locally high concentrations. Nevertheless, the average costs computed by the NAS/NAE and San Francisco studies are probably representative and suggest that air pollution damage amounted to about 1 cent per vehicle-mile in 1970, and has been declining, to about 0.5 cents or less, as federal regulations governing emissions have become more stringent.

In 1972 (as shown in Chapter 10), the total cost of noise from all types of traffic may have amounted to between $600 million and $1.900 billion (in 1975 dollars). Automobiles contribute approximately one quarter to one third of the sound energy emitted by all urban motor vehicles; therefore, urban automobiles might be responsible for about $200–600 million of urban traffic noise costs (in 1975 dollars). Dividing again by the 650 billion vehicle-miles of automobile travel estimated as taking place each year in urban areas, the average cost of urban automobile noise pollution in the 1970s probably averaged less than one tenth of a cent per vehicle-mile.

The only systematic effort to date to estimate the social costs imposed by unattractive or visually disruptive highways (again reported in Chapter 10) is for Boston's Fitzgerald Expressway.[28] The costs in this case were placed between 66 cents and $1.18 per vehicle-mile (in 1979 dollars). The aesthetic costs of the Fitzgerald Expressway, however, are not representative, as most urban highways do not both pass by a major historic neighborhood and disrupt a particularly scenic view. Although in any metropolitan area there may be at least one highway segment as aesthetically damaging as the Fitzgerald, the vast majority of highways are not as visually disruptive.

Overall, urban air and noise pollution and aesthetic costs probably averaged somewhere between .5 and 1 cent per vehicle-mile in the mid-1970s, although the costs were surely higher on some poorly situated or badly designed highways. When these social costs of highway use are considered together with government outlays on highway construction, operations, and maintenance, urban highway users *on average* probably slightly underpaid their costs in the mid-1970s. Highway-user charges averaged approximately 1.7 cents per vehicle-mile in urban areas during 1975, while government expenditures averaged 1.2 cents and social costs probably slightly more than .5 cents.

The approximate parity of average urban highway costs with average highway-user payments strongly suggests that many of the urban highways constructed in the postwar period can be justified in terms of benefits to motorists—especially when it is remembered that highway-user fees represent a minimal estimate of benefits. Unnecessary highway building is not likely to be as serious a problem in the future, moreover, because changes made in the federal highway laws during the 1970s have removed restrictions that made it almost impossible to spend federal highway-user tax receipts on anything but highway construction.[29] As federal highway funds are used to a greater extent for maintenance, fewer distortions in state or local highway decisions should occur. Federal highway aid is also increasingly applied to correct aesthetic and pollution problems—for example, by depressing or shielding new highways that pass through residential neighborhoods or scenic areas.[30]

Another policy that might be employed to help assure an appropriate level of future highway construction would be to charge highway users directly for the full costs of the highways they use, including any social and environmental damage as well as costs for highway construction and operation. Given that gasoline and other highway-user taxes approximately cover costs for most urban highways, this policy would involve charging extra tolls or highway-user fees for only a small fraction of metropolitan highway use, generally in the downtown areas and during the peak hours.[31] Charging tolls for use of certain highway segments can, however, create difficult administrative and political problems; the merits and demerits of this proposal will be examined in more detail in the next section.

ALTERNATIVES TO HIGHWAY INVESTMENT AND CONSTRUCTION

The expense and disruption of urban highway investment and construction, especially in densely populated areas, have stimulated increasing interest in alternative means of alleviating traffic congestion. None of these alternatives is a panacea for congestion problems; almost every one is effective only in a few limited circumstances and can actually intensify rather than reduce congestion if not applied carefully. Nevertheless, these alternatives can alleviate congestion and are used increasingly, if not always successfully.

Sophisticated traffic engineering and management. Highway engineers and planners have long sought, through better traffic management, to augment highway capacity without greatly expanding roadspace or investment. The timing and control of traffic signals was one of the first of these capacity-enhancing techniques to be developed and is the subject of continuing research and refinement. Delays at an intersection can sometimes be reduced, for example, by altering the proportion of signal green time allotted to main and cross streets, by installing devices to vary the signal cycle according to the differing requirements of rush hour and midday traffic, or by adjusting the overall length of the traffic-signal cycle. At a modest additional cost, traffic signals at different intersections can be coordinated to improve traffic flow by allowing traffic moving at the proper speed to avoid red lights and by preventing the buildup of traffic queues longer than the capacity of a single-signal cycle. Computerized traffic-control systems can even adjust traffic signals in response to changes in traffic conditions (by, for example, using information from electronic sensors placed at strategic points).[32]

The cost of traffic-signal optimization is usually modest compared with the gains. Most of the benefits are generated by adjusting only a small portion of a metropolitan traffic-signal system, since traffic usually is concentrated on a few major arterials and streets. Even with computerized systems, the capital outlay is normally small; most of the expense is for traffic engineers or computer operators to monitor, repair, and adjust the system.[33] Experience with previous signal-optimization projects suggests that in the mid-1970s, the total annual expense for a city of one million might average about $250,000 per year without computerization and $800,000 with computerization. Given the projected traffic-flow improvements, these costs typically amount to only 25 cents per vehicle-hour of travel time saved with computerized systems, and as little as 2 cents per vehicle-hour without computerization.[34]

Another technique to increase street capacity is to reduce the space devoted to on-street parking. Significant improvements in street capacity were made in many cities during the 1940s and 1950s simply by replacing angle parking with parallel parking. Further useful gains may be made in some cases by eliminating on-street parking during rush hours (or even altogether). The roadway lost by on-street parking may be much larger than the physical space occupied by the parked cars; it has been estimated that "the cautious reactions of passing drivers, who fear sudden maneuvers by parked vehicles or doors opening into their paths, result in an effective loss of some 12 to 14 feet of roadway width, on average."[35] Thus, the elimination of on-street parking on congested arterials that have parking on both sides may add a lane or more of traffic in each direction.

The primary impediments to eliminating on-street parking are the cost of replacing the lost parking with off-street facilities[36] and merchants' fears that customers would find off-street spaces much less convenient. One compromise would be to ban on-street parking only during the rush hours, when added roadway capacity is most needed, and to allow on-street parking during the midday and evening hours. This would require unusually strict traffic law enforcement, however, since a single illegally parked car would eliminate the peak-hour curbside traffic lane. Where effective enforcement of rush hour parking bans is not possible, an outright ban on on-street parking for a few critical roadways may well be worth the additional cost of off-street facilities.[37]

Roadway capacity can also be increased by channeling traffic flows to reduce vehicular conflicts through such techniques as traffic islands, clearer and more effective lane markings, special turning lanes, or one-way streets.[38] For example, converting a pair of parallel two-way streets to one-way streets going in opposite directions often increases the combined capacity of the streets by eliminating left turns made against traffic flows. Signal-optimization is also more easily obtained with one-way streets, and reductions in accidents can be achieved due to fewer conflicting vehicle movements.

One-way streets do have disadvantages,[39] however, because they increase the distance that motorists must travel, sometimes enough to offset any gains in speeds. Channelization and one-way streets may also cause congestion problems at other nearby points in the street network and may reduce pedestrian safety and access to businesses. Transit riders may be inconvenienced by bus routes that operate on different streets inbound and outbound; by speeding general traffic flow, channelization may also reduce transit speeds by making it more difficult for buses to pull out of curbside stops.

Peak-period capacity can sometimes also be increased by using reversible or contra-flow lanes during the morning and evening rush hours. Reversible lanes have proved successful on arterial streets, expressways, and bridges in many metropolitan areas, including New York, Washington, Los Angeles, Seattle, Dallas, Chicago, and Milwaukee. Speed improvements of 20 percent and higher traffic volumes in the peak direction are not uncommon, at a cost of only small speed reductions in the off-peak direction. Expenses for signs, signals, and traffic law enforcement can be relatively small, and experience has shown that accident rates are no worse, and possibly even a little lower than before reversible lanes were established.[40] Reversible lanes, however, are only effective where the traffic flow is heavily imbalanced during the rush hours, which is not often the case on downtown and circumferential streets or expressways. Moreover, the segment with reversible lanes must be long enough to bypass the major traffic bottlenecks and should be sufficiently wide to provide more than one lane of capacity in the off-peak direction (to prevent long delays behind disabled or turning vehicles).[41]

A most successful and widely applied capacity-improving technique is to control or meter traffic volumes entering congested expressways with traffic lights or gates on entrance ramps. The basic purpose of expressway-ramp metering is to prevent the development of supersaturated conditions by ensuring that the highway's maximum capacity is never exceeded (even momentarily). In simple applications, the ramp signals are controlled by clocks, and rush hour traffic is metered at preset rates. More elaborate metering systems use vehicle-detectors to monitor actual expressway flows and computers to adjust ramp signals accordingly.

Metering has been shown to greatly increase expressway traffic speeds. For example, on the Harbor Freeway in Los Angeles, peak-period speeds increased from 15–20 miles per hour before metering to about 40 miles per hour after metering; peak-period traffic speeds in Dallas increased from 14 miles per hour before metering to 30 miles per hour after metering.[42] Delays at the ramps or from diversion to parallel streets may partially offset the time savings on the expressways, but if the expressway was operating at supersaturated conditions before metering, overall travel times almost always improve. The costs of installing and operating metering devices vary significantly, depending on the sophistication of the control system and the particular characteristics of the expressway, but they are usually relatively modest (typically an initial investment of $100,000 per freeway mile plus $10,000 per mile in annual operating expenses).[43] However, space must be available on expressway ramps for delayed vehicles, and parallel streets must have sufficient capacity to handle diverted expressway users. The technique yields the greatest benefits only for roads operating at or near sueprsaturation.

Sophisticated traffic management, although extremely promising, also has its limitations, as illustrated by a study of traffic capacity in Central London. In 1961, the London Traffic Management Unit (LTMU) was established. It rapidly implemented numerous traffic-management projects, including on-street parking bans, improved signal timing, turning restrictions, and one-way streets. An independent assessment in 1968 of traffic capacity in Central London concluded that, after correcting for growing traffic volumes, in the years from 1952 to 1960 (prior to the LTMU) average traffic speeds increased by 1.85 percent annually,[44] but in the years from 1961 to 1966 (after the LTMU) they increased by only 1.1 percent per year. Moreover, new turning restrictions and one-way streets increased the average Central London journey length by 5 percent, thereby nullifying the small improvement in average traffic speeds. Thus, traffic management may have reduced rather than increased the effective capacity of Central London streets.

Some of the traffic-management schemes used in London were probably wrongly assessed or implemented, which is understandable given the difficulties of forecasting travel behavior and performance in a city with as irregular a street layout as London. More significantly, traffic-management projects may have concentrated on local areas, ignoring impacts throughout the Central London traffic network; thus, some projects may have been frustrated or offset by others.[45]

Encouraging the use of public transportation, carpooling, and small cars. Increased use of mass transit and carpools (described in earlier chapters) may also alleviate highway congestion. The standard automobile takes up the same amount of roadway capacity whether it has only one occupant or as many as six. Similarly, a standard 40-foot transit bus operating on a freeway requires only about 1.5 times as much highway space as a standard-sized passenger car, while a bus operating on an arterial requires as little as 1.3 times the highway space occupied by a car.[46] If a bus is fully loaded with 50 passengers, the road space occupied per passenger is only 3–8 percent of that occupied by the sole occupant of an automobile.

The capacity of a freeway lane used by only single-occupant automobiles is about 2,000 persons per hour. If average automobile occupancy is increased to 1.2 persons per vehicle, as is currently typical during the rush hours in U.S. metropolitan areas, the person-carrying capacity of the freeway lane increases to 2,400 persons per hour (see Table 11.9). If only 10 percent of the freeway users are persuaded to use buses and average automobile occupancy remains at 1.2 persons, freeway capacity is increased by an additional 11 percent to 2,657 persons per hour. Further increases in carpool or bus use—while potentially difficult to implement—can bring comparable gains in effective highway capacity (see Table 11.9).

A shift from standard-sized cars to subcompacts may also modestly increase highway capacity. The dimensions of the average standard-sized car are slightly over six feet wide by seventeen feet long, or about 100–110 square feet, while the dimensions of a subcompact are typically a foot narrower and as much as four feet shorter, covering a much smaller area of about 60–80 square feet. Since most of the road capacity used by a car in traffic is for spacing between vehicles, however, rather than for the vehicle itself, the smaller dimensions of subcompact automobiles will only slightly reduce their use of road space.[47] The small car may have an advantage, however, in higher power to-weight ratios, better visibility, and better maneuverability, all of which could provide some reduction in needed headways.[48] Moreover, smaller cars use 30 percent less parking space, which might also help relieve congestion by increasing the capacity of on-street parking.

Traffic priority for high-occupancy vehicles. One relatively inexpensive policy to encourage carpooling and bus use, and thus increase effective highway capacity, is to give buses and carpools priority in highway traffic. This could be done by reserving lanes for the exclusive use of these vehicles or by permitting priority passage of these vehicles through traffic signals. The primary benefit of such traffic-priority schemes to passengers in high-occupancy vehicles is reduced travel times. Priority schemes can also reduce transit costs by increasing the average speeds at which transit vehicles travel.[49]

There are many priority schemes for high-occupancy vehicles, each with its own advantages and drawbacks, costs and benefits.[50] Perhaps the most promising calls for giving high-occupancy vehicles precedence at the ramps of metered expressways. As discussed earlier, the benefits to all highway users more than justify the modest cost of metering on many congested urban freeways. Once a metering system is established, it is often simple and inexpensive to provide high-occupancy vehicles a priority ramp or ramp access around the metering device, so that these vehicles have a slight advantage over single-occupant vehicles in avoiding any ramp delays. Although the margin of advantage from the prior-

TABLE 11.9. Passenger-carrying capacity of a freeway lane under alternative assumptions about carpool and transit use.

| | Percentage of freeway users | | | | Capacity of freeway | | |
| | | Carpool | | | | | |
Alternative	Auto, drive alone	Two-person	Three-person	Bus, transit	Persons per lane-hour	Vehicles per lane-hour	Average automobile occupancy
Single-occupant auto traffic	100	0	0	0	2,000	2,000	1.0
Typical urban freeway traffic	67	33	0	0	2,400	2,000	1.2
	60	30	0	10	2,657	1,998	1.2
Increasing carpooling	40	40	20	0	3,600	2,000	1.8
	30	40	30	0	4,000	2,000	2.0
	0	0	100	0	6,000	2,000	3.0
Increasing transit use	50	0	0	50	3,883	1,981	1.0
	0	0	0	100	66,650	1,333	*

Source: Authors' calculations.
a Estimates assume a basic capacity of 2,000 passenger cars per lane-hour and that one 50-passenger bus uses about 1.5 times as much capacity as a passenger car.
* Not applicable.

ity ramp is often modest (usually only a few seconds or minutes on each trip), the delay imposed on single-occupant vehicles and the costs of the priority device are typically small as well. Enforcement has not been a major problem either, even for priority ramps that expedite carpools as well as buses.[51]

The most frequently applied traffic-priority scheme is to reserve one existing lane for the exclusive use of buses and carpools. Unlike priority at ramp meters, however, reserving a lane for the exclusive use of high-occupancy vehicles can significantly reduce capacity available for other motorists, often by as much as one third or one quarter. Unless a large proportion of travelers already use buses or carpools, or can easily be induced to do so, some of the highway capacity in the reserved lane may be wasted, and the savings in travel times for passengers in high-occupancy vehicles may be more than offset by larger losses in travel times for single-occupant automobile users. If the innermost lane is designated for high-occupancy vehicles (as is often the case), the time saved by high-occupancy vehicles using the priority lane can also be reduced by their having to move across several lanes of extremely congested freeway traffic in order to enter or exit.

One way to minimize these problems is to establish a contra-flow bus lane. Contra-flow lanes on the innermost side of the highway, separated from oncoming cars by temporary marking cones, have been employed on several expressways, including the approaches to New York's Lincoln and Queens-Midtown tunnels. The safety problems anticipated, such as head-on accidents or buses weaving across the dominant-direction lanes to enter or leave the contra-flow lane, have proven minimal (although safety concerns have generally led highway planners to limit access to contra-flow lanes to buses and to exclude carpools). The initial capital costs of converting the lanes is usually small, unless special ramps must be constructed to give buses access to the contra-flow lane. Operating costs—largely the placement of lane markers—are also low.[52]

A key advantage of the contra-flow lane is that if rush hour traffic in the off-peak direction is much lower than that in the peak direction, motorists are little inconvenienced by the removal of the lane for exclusive bus use. On six-lane expressways where the traffic flow in the off-peak direction is only 50–60 percent as heavy as the dominant flow (and access to the contra-flow lane is not difficult), a mere 20–40 buses, each carrying 50 passengers, will ensure that transit-passenger time savings from the peak-hour contra-flow lane exceed automobile-traveler time losses.[53]

Experience with concurrent-flow freeway lane priority schemes, in contrast to the contra-flow, has been disappointing. The only concurrent-flow experiment generally regarded as an unqualified success was that on the approaches to the San Francisco Bay Bridge. But bridge approaches usually have many more lanes than the typical freeway, so reserving ramp lanes (three in the San Francisco case) for exclusive use of high-occupancy vehicles does not hurt other highway-user times by much, or at least not too obviously. Enforcement problems are also simple, since the bridge approach lanes are short and end at tollgates.

In Los Angeles and Boston, where concurrent-flow schemes have been applied to more typical expressway situations, the result has been well-publicized failure. In Los Angeles, one lane in each direction of the Santa Monica Freeway was reserved for the exclusive use of buses and carpools of three occupants or more. The exclusive lanes were nick-named "diamond lanes" after the large white diamonds that traffic engineers painted on the pavement so that the lanes could be quickly identified by motorists. Both the number of persons and vehicles carried on the freeway dropped after the implementation of these lanes. While average peak-period freeway travel times of buses and three-member carpools decreased from 15.7 to 14.7 minutes (see Table 11.10), the average travel time for all other motorists rose to 20.5 minutes. The diamond lane appeared underutilized to the majority of motorists stalled in the other lanes so that enforcement problems increased until, after six months, a judge ordered the project stopped on environmental grounds.

In Boston, the Southeast Expressway diamond lane experiment was launched when expressway use was restricted to three lanes (one way) from its normal four for several months of resurfacing; to encourage high-occupancy vehicle use during the repair period, one of the remaining three lanes was designated for the exclusive use of three-person carpools and buses. Initially, travel times in both the priority and regular lanes dropped, partly because of seasonal traffic declines but also because no effort was made to enforce the diamond lane experiment (even in the face of significant violations). As soon as the priority-lane policy was enforced, however, travel times increased from 28 to 40 minutes in the regular lanes (compared to a reduction to 18 minutes in the reserved lane) and within two weeks public objections forced cancellation of the experiment.[54]

The Los Angeles and Boston experiences are by no means definitive. In the final seven weeks of the Los Angeles experiment, travelers were adjusting to the scheme and travel volumes had almost recovered to former levels without degrading travel times in either the regular or priority lanes (see Table 11.10). Moreover, transit services were not significantly improved in either city, which contributed to poor performance by limiting the alternatives.[55] But the exclusion of two-person carpools from the reserved lanes in both Boston and Los Angeles may

TABLE 11.10. Results from the Los Angeles and Boston concurrent-flow priority-lane projects.

Location	Time of measurement	Average travel time in minutes		Peak-period expressway volume		Daily number of carpools	Average auto occupancy	Daily express bus ridership
		Regular lane	Priority lane	Vehicles	Persons			
Santa Monica Freeway, Los Angeles	Before designation of priority lanes	15.7	*	113,000	139,000	3,479	1.22	1,200
	First 7 weeks of lane operation	21.3	14.7	77,000	102,000	4,345	a	a
	Last 7 weeks of lane operation	20.5	14.7	102,000	136,000	5,749	1.31	3,800
Southeast Expressway, Boston	Before construction of priority lanes	28	*	15,200	23,600	680	1.31	6,800
	During construction and lane operation, no enforcement	23	18	14,800	22,400	900	a	7,000
	During construction and lane operation, with enforcement	40	18	13,900	21,600	1,170	1.38	7,200

Source: Howard J. Simkowitz, "A Comparative Analysis of Results from Three Recent Non-Separated Concurrent-Flow High Occupancy Freeway Lane Projects: Boston, Santa Monica and Miami," paper presented at the 57th annual meeting of the Transportation Research Board, Washington, D.C., January 1978, esp. pp. 20, 24, 27, 30, 32

* Not applicable.
a Not available.

have been the most significant adverse factor. Two-person carpools are much more readily formed than three-person pools, since the two-person pool provides almost as much commmuting cost savings per member without the difficulty of finding a third pool member with similar travel needs.[56] In both Boston and Los Angeles, inclusion of two-person carpools might have allowed for greater utilization of the reserved lane.

Experience with exclusive bus and carpool lanes on I-95 in Miami lends support to this hypothesis. In Miami, reserved lanes were newly constructed in the freeway median rather than sectioned off from existing lanes. The reserved lanes were initially opened to carpools of three or more persons and to buses but were later made available to two-person carpools as well. As shown in Table 11.11, travel times dropped in both the reserved and the regular lanes when the reserved lanes were initially opened. When the priority lane was made available to two-person carpools as well as three-person pools, travel times remained stable in the reserved lanes but dropped even further on the regular lanes, despite a 12 percent increase in the number of persons and a 14 percent increase in the number of vehicles using the facility.[57]

The construction of new lanes expressly for priority use can often overcome the disadvantages of reserved diamond lanes (as demonstrated not only by I-95 in Miami but also by the Shirley Highway in Washington, D.C., and the San Bernardino Freeway in Los Angeles). With additional capacity, priority schemes can be implemented so that travel times are improved for single-occupant automobiles as well as for carpools and buses. New lanes are usually very expensive, however, especially if right-of-way is not readily available on the median or the shoulder of the existing expressway. Nevertheless, it is obvious that the chances of successfully implementing a priority scheme are much better when total available highway capacity is expanded rather than contracted.

Priority lanes can be provided on urban arterials and city streets as well as on expressways, but the potential gain is generally smaller—mainly because the speed differences between congested and uncongested urban arterials or streets are relatively small, since the maximum speeds are limited at all times by intersections, on-street parking, driveways, and other traffic interruptions.

Congestion tolls and other roadway pricing systems. A congestion toll is a charge for highway use set equal to the costs that an additional highway user imposes on others by slowing average traffic speeds. Congestion tolls thus ensure that the level of highway use and congestion is not excessive by discouraging motorists who do not value highway use

TABLE 11.11. Results from the construction of new priority lanes on I-95 in Miami.

| Time of measurement | Peak-period travel time in minutes | | Peak-period expressway volumes | | Daily number of carpools | Average auto occupancy | Daily express bus ridership |
	Regular lane	Priority lane	Vehicles	Persons			
Before opening of priority lanes	13.5	*	15,200	18,600	390	1.23	1,400
During lane operations; lanes restricted to 3-or-more-person carpool and buses	11.3	8.0	15,900	21,200	630	a	1,600
During lane operations; lane opened to 2-person carpool	9.6	7.9	18,200	23,800	590	1.28	1,700

Source: Howard J. Simkowitz, "A Comparative Analysis of Results from Three Recent Non-Separated Concurrent-Flow High Occupancy Freeway Lane Projects: Boston, Santa Monica and Miami," paper presented at the 57th annual meeting of the Transportation Research Board, Washington, D.C., January 1978, esp. pp. 20, 24, 27, 30, 32, 37.
a Not available.
* Not applicable.

enough to pay the total marginal costs of their use, including the added congestion they create.

Congestion tolls can also signal whether to expand highway capacity. The optimal-sized highway system is one in which the congestion toll on every segment equals the marginal cost of expanding that segment to accommodate one more vehicle. If the congestion toll is larger than the marginal cost of expanding the highway so that one more vehicle can be accommodated (at some stipulated speed), additional highway investment is economically desirable. Conversely, a congestion toll smaller than the marginal cost of expanding the highway's capacity indicates that the highway has been overbuilt.[58]

Highway users should be charged either a congestion toll or the marginal cost of expanding the highway for one more vehicle, but not both, since both are essentially charges for the cost of providing capacity (in one case by delaying other motorists and in the other case by physically expanding the roadway). If the highway system is the optimal size, it does not matter which charge is collected, because they will be equal. If a highway system is not the optimal size, the choice between charging the congestion toll or the marginal cost of expanding the highway for one more vehicle will depend upon whether it is more important to use the existing facilities efficiently in the short run (in which case the congestion toll should be charged), or whether it is more important to provide potential highway users—who may be making long-term investment and location decisions based on transportation costs—with an estimate of the long-run costs of added highway capacity (in which case the marginal cost of expanding for one more vehicle should be appropriate).

The optimum congestion toll, at which the fee charged is equal to the marginal cost of expanding highway capacity, will vary greatly among highway segments and at different times of the day. Not only does the cost of expanding highway capacity vary widely (see Tables 11.7 and 11.8), but congestion levels change in different circumstances. The toll itself will influence the level of use and congestion on a highway, and thus any estimate of the optimal toll must allow for the effects of tolls on highway use as well as for the marginal costs of expanding roadway capacity. The only recent study attempting to measure both these effects of optimal congestion tolls is for San Francisco freeways.[59] In this study, two alternative assumptions about the value of delay were tested ($1.50 and $3.00 per hour, per person) as well as two different interest rates on highway investment (6 and 12 percent).

The results, presented in Table 11.12, show that the optimal toll varies from 0.1 cent to 38.5 cents per vehicle-mile in 1973 dollars, depending upon the time of day, the location of the freeway, and, to a

TABLE 11.12. Estimates of optimal long-run tolls and speeds on San Francisco area freeways (in 1973 dollars).

Interest rate (percent)	Freeway location	Value of time saved (dollars per person hour)	Peak hour, peak direction (7–8 A.M. & 5–6 P.M.)		Near peak, peak direction (6–7, 9–9 A.M. & 4–5, 5–7 P.M.)		Weekday daytime		Weekday night		Weekend	
			Speed (mph)	Toll (cents)	Speed (mph)	Toll (cents)	Speed (mph)	Toll (cents)	Speed (mph)	Toll (cents)	Speed (mph)	Toll (cents)
6	Rural-suburban	3.00	55.9	2.7	60.5	1.1	64.1	0.4	66.5	0.1	62.9	0.6
		1.50	51.8	3.1	58.9	0.8	63.4	0.3	66.3	0.1	61.9	0.4
6	Urban-suburban	3.00	54.9	3.3	60.0	1.2	63.9	0.5	66.5	0.1	62.6	0.7
		1.50	50.6	4.3	58.5	0.8	63.3	0.3	66.5	0.1	61.7	0.4
6	Central city	3.00	48.9	15.2	58.1	1.8	63.1	0.6	66.2	0.2	61.5	0.9
		1.50	47.7	13.3	58.0	0.9	63.1	0.3	66.2	0.1	61.4	0.5
12	Rural-suburban	3.00	52.7	5.2	59.1	1.5	63.5	0.5	66.4	0.1	62.0	0.8
		1.50	49.3	6.5	58.2	0.9	63.2	0.3	66.2	0.1	61.5	0.4
12	Urban-suburban	3.00	51.4	7.0	58.7	1.6	63.4	0.5	66.3	0.1	61.8	0.8
		1.50	48.3	9.5	58.0	0.9	63.1	0.3	66.2	0.1	61.4	0.5
12	Central city	3.00	47.7	26.7	58.0	1.8	63.1	0.6	66.2	0.2	61.4	0.9
		1.50	46.6	38.5	57.9	0.9	63.1	0.3	66.2	0.1	61.4	0.5

Source: Theodore E. Keeler and Kenneth A. Small, Automobile Costs and Final Intermodal Cost Comparisons, pt. 3 of The Full Costs of Urban Transport, ed. Theodore E. Keeler, Leonard A. Merewitz, and P. M. J. Risher (Berkeley: University of California, Institute of Urban and Regional Development, 1975), pp. 43–50.

lesser degree, the assumed values for time and interest rate. (The higher values of time increase the cost of congestion and make it desirable to invest in more highways.) At any given value of time or interest rate, the optimal toll is much higher during the peak hour and in the central city because the cost of providing downtown and peak-hour capacity is so much greater. Optimal tolls decrease rapidly during the off-peak hours and in suburban areas, typically reaching levels of 1 cent or less per vehicle-mile. If the estimates from San Francisco freeways are reasonably representative, congestion tolls would seem to be required only in the peak period and on highways in or near the centers of large metropolitan areas; otherwise, existing automobile-user taxes would be adequate.

A number of objections to congestion toll schemes, are often voiced, among which is concern about the costs of collection and enforcement. Since congestion tolls ideally should vary according to location and time of day, they cannot be collected by increased fuel, oil, or excise taxes. Thus, critics of tolling sometimes raise the specter of toll booths dotting a city, with the cost of motorists' delays while paying tolls and the salaries for toll collectors far outweighing any possible gains in reduced congestion. Plans have been suggested, however, that might permit toll collection and enforcement at reasonable cost. One proposal, which has thus far not proved feasible, is to equip automobiles with transmitters that broadcast a vehicle identification code to roadside receiving/billing machines so that the vehicle owner could be billed periodically according to the streets and the times of day he traveled; another is to equip cars with taxi-like meters whose rates would be controlled by roadside transmitters.[60]

A simpler and more economical means for assessing congestion tolls would be to use conventional toll booths only where access to a congested area is limited to a few major expressways, bridges, or tunnels (as in Manhattan). Increased parking charges in central areas might also be an effective surrogate for congestion tolls and could be easier to collect and enforce, particularly if the number of private parking lot operators is small. Increased parking charges, however, would affect trips destined for the congested area only, and would not be effective where a large volume of through traffic is attracted by lowered congestion levels. Increased parking charges might also give rise to "cruising" in lieu of parking, thus enhancing congestion. Perhaps the best remedy would be to require special licenses for operation in congested zones; monthly or daily licenses, sold at convenient locations (such as retailers, banks, or vending machines), would be displayed on the windshield, with color coding and large numerals to aid in enforcement.

Another objection to congestion tolls is that the commuting cost increase (tolls minus the reduction in travel time) will represent a larger percentage of poor travelers' incomes than of rich travelers' incomes. A preliminary study of Washington, San Francisco, and Boston suggests, however, that only a small fraction of poor households would be affected by congestion charges, since only the most congested downtown areas would be involved, and downtown workers typically have higher incomes than metropolitan averages; furthermore, poor workers are more likely than others to take transit. The revenue generated from congestion tolls could be used, moreover, to offset any regressivity if used to fund projects that help the poor.[61]

A related concern has been the effect that tolls might have on downtown economic activity; losses in retail sales and employment are particularly feared if shoppingtrips prove sensitive to automobile travel costs. But this problem might be alleviated if the tolls were applied to peak-period travelers only and left the cost of midday shoppingtrips unchanged. Shoppers and businesses might also benefit from the faster travel speeds and improved amenity of a downtown with fewer cars, although possibly not enough to offset a higher toll.

Despite the possible advantages of congestion toll schemes, there has been little practical experience with them. Singapore is the only city to actually apply on a large scale basis some form of congestion toll, in its case a central area licensing scheme. Singapore is a rapidly developing city-state with a population of 2.2 million, 70 percent of which lives within eight kilometers of the city center. In 1975, the government of Singapore imposed an area licensing requirement for all vehicles except commercial vehicles, buses, motorcycles, and carpools of four or more persons entering a six-square-kilometer zone in the center of Singapore between the hours of 7:30 A.M. and 10:15 A.M. The licenses were sold for 60 Singapore dollars per month (U.S. $26) or 3 Singapore dollars per day (U.S. $1.30) and were to be displayed on the windshield.[62] In addition, car parks were established outside the central area, from which express bus service was available to the downtown area, and the prices of all central-area parking spaces were doubled.

As expected, the Singapore licenses brought about a substantial decline (44 percent) in the total number of vehicles entering the central area during restricted hours; the number of automobiles and taxis declined by 73 and 65 percent, respectively, while the number of commercial vehicles, buses, and motorcycles and motor scooters increased by 120, 4, and 1 percent, respectively. But traffic speeds increased by only 22 percent in the central areas during restricted hours, perhaps because of the growth in truck traffic, while speeds increased by 10 percent on inbound radial roads and declined by 20 percent on the ring road around the central areas.[63]

Among households that owned cars, the percentage of workers who commuted to the zone by car fell from 53 to 43 percent.[64] Other automobile users changed their routes to avoid driving through the central area, as suggested by the higher congestion on the ring road. Even more significant was the fact that there was a 13 percent increase in the volume of traffic entering the central area in the half hour immediately preceding the restricted hours—so that the traffic flow and the level of congestion during that half hour exceeded those during the restricted hours. Also, by requiring the license only in the morning rush hours, conditions in the evening rush hours were worsened, as motorists who had avoided the central area on their way to work passed through on their way home and because some motorists, particularly on nonwork-trips, rescheduled travel to the central area in the afternoon.[65]

The average travel times for commuters who had used buses before licensing and who remained on buses afterward did decline, but the saving was only 1 minute (from 39 to 38 minutes). Average travel times for automobile commuters who chose to continue to drive actually increased by an average of 1 minute (from 29 to 30 minutes). Less surprisingly, the travel time of commuters who switched from automobile to bus increased by 9 minutes (from 29 to 38 minutes). The travel time savings of those who remained on buses may therefore have been completely offset by the losses of those who remained in automobiles or switched from automobiles to buses.[66]

The impact of the Singapore licensing scheme on the central-area business community is unclear. Although a survey revealed that most businessmen thought the scheme had reduced rents and increased vacancies in central-area commercial buildings, at least some businesses benefited from freer movement of commercial vehicles.[67] The problems and costs of vending licenses and enforcing the license requirement proved unexpectedly minor.

Singapore's equivocal experience with area licensing may be due to several unfortunate characteristics of the scheme adopted. For example, the charge for the central-area license may have been set too high, so that very few central-area automobile-users were left to benefit from the improved speeds during the restricted hours; similarly, congestion was almost surely overly increased in the hours surrounding the restricted period and on the ring road. (Singapore authorities subsequently extended the restricted hours in an effort to correct this problem.) The exclusion of trucks from the license requirement may have also been a mistake, as it limited the speed improvements achieved within the central area. Finally, if the license requirement had been imposed in the afternoon as well as in the morning, this might have prevented additional afternoon congestion from offsetting speed improvements in the morning.

Simulations of central-area licensing schemes generally suggest much more favorable results than those found in the Singapore demonstration, as long as the fees are set at the appropriate levels. For several years, area licenses or parking surcharges were seriously considered in London, and two detailed analyses of their effects, costs, and benefits have been completed. The first, conducted in 1967 for England's Ministry of Transport, predicted that a central-area license of six shillings (then U.S. $0.80) per day for a private car would reduce the number of vehicles entering Central London by 12 percent.[68] The savings in travel time from reduced congestion, minus the loss in convenience to those automobile-users forced to take transit or more circuitous routes, would amount to a net gain of £6–7 million (then U.S. $15–18 million) per year. Parking taxes were found to be about half as effective as central-area licenses in reducing automobile traffic or generating benefits. The second study, completed by the Greater London Council in 1974, examined only central-area licenses and estimated that a daily fee of 60 pence (U.S. $1.40) per automobile would reduce the number of automobiles entering central London by 45 percent and generate net transportation benefits of approximately £32 million (U.S. $75 million) per year.[69] Neither study estimated the benefits of environmental and energy improvements.

Similar results were obtained in a simulation of central-area licenses and parking surcharges for Boston in 1975. Several traffic-restraint schemes were investigated, including increasing the price of all nonresidential central-area parking spaces, requiring area licenses for the use of downtown expressways and local streets, and increasing tolls on several bridges and tunnels that provided access to the central area where tolls were also collected.[70]

All these policies produced net benefits (see Table 11.13) as long as the parking surcharge, tolls, or fees were set at the appropriate level. Partly because the central-area local streets are not convenient for through traffic, a $1.00 surcharge on nonresidential parking spaces produced the largest estimate of net benefits ($24 million per year in 1975 dollars). If no major improvements in central-area highway capacity were made, the net benefits of the parking surcharges were forecast to increase to $40–50 million per year (in 1975 dollars) over the next decade or two as growing incomes allowed for an increase in automobile ownership and use. Central-area licenses applied only to local streets were almost as beneficial as parking surcharges. Toll surcharges were least beneficial because several of the major highways entering the

TABLE 11.13.   Annual net transportation benefits from peak-period (worktrip) central-area traffic restraints in Boston, 1975 (in thousands of dollars).

| Central-area restraint policy | Time savings | | | | Costs | | Total net benefit |
| | Within central area | | Outside central area | | Inconvenience to diverted auto-users (5) | Increase in transit deficit (6) | (1) + (2) + (3) + (4) minus (5) + (6) |
	Autos (1)	Commercial vehicles (2)	Autos (3)	Commercial vehicles (4)			
Parking surcharge:							
$0.50	10,796	2,889	6,774	1,635	871	2,228	19,005
1.00	13,285	4,157	10,177	2,583	2,664	3,750	23,788
2.00	15,076	4,867	11,754	3,195	6,247	5,457	23,188
Area license, local street only:							
$0.50	12,129	3,574	6,268	1,583	1,572	2,262	19,720
1.00	12,529	4,454	8,803	2,325	3,879	3,760	20,472
2.00	12,161	5,303	11,413	3,204	8,610	5,566	17,905
Area license, all streets and ex-pressways:							
$0.50	15,110	4,858	−547	451	2,506	2,672	14,694
1.00	13,902	6,295	−4,210	243	6,404	4,603	5,223
Toll surcharge:							
$0.50	6,186	1,493	−2,311	−8	334	455	4,571
1.00	6,871	1,679	−3,644	40	533	560	3,853

Source: José A. Gómez-Ibáñez and Gary R. Fauth, "Downtown Auto Restraint Policies: The Costs and Benefits for Boston," *Journal of Transport Economics and Policy* 14 (1980):148.

central area had no tolls at all. The estimates of net benefits included only the gains and losses in travel time and convenience and did not evaluate administrative costs or environmental benefits.

Even though the net benefits of congestion toll schemes may be large, as the London and Boston simulations suggest, the distribution of benefits and costs may be politically unattractive.[71] From an economic standpoint, toll or license fees do not represent a real economic cost to society but rather a transfer of revenues from automobile users to a collecting agency; these revenues are then available for other uses by that agency, including compensating any constituents who lose because of the toll (that is, those for whom total toll and travel time expenses after tolling exceed travel time costs before tolling). However, if the constituents who pay the tolls are compensated in exact offsets, and this fact is recognized, it will completely defeat the purpose of the tolls; therefore, some constituents will almost surely be worse off after the fees are instituted (even though society as a whole is better off), and they will oppose the tolling scheme.

Many benefits from tolling, moreover, are uncertain and not readily visible. Travel time savings of a few minutes on each trip, while important in the aggregate, may not be large from the perspective of an individual traveler and may not be clearly identified in the traveler's mind with the pricing policy. In contrast, the costs of the policy to the traveler, in the form of a toll or fee, are obvious and more clearly caused by the policy.[72]

Thus, roadway pricing and congestion tolling schemes have many practical problems, and there remain many uncertainties about their effectiveness. The experience in Singapore suggests that such schemes, like other methods of reducing congestion, must be carefully implemented if they are to succeed. The prospects of inducing local politicians to support such policies also seem limited, at least until a successful demonstration dispels doubts about possible adverse results.

SUMMARY

Congestion, the major concern of early postwar urban public transportation policy, has continued to be a problem in many, if not most, U.S. metropolitan areas—though perhaps not quite to the same extent as before or as commonly imagined. The early postwar solution to urban traffic congestion was simply to build more highway capacity—in particular, to develop networks of high-performance expressways in, around, and through metropolitan areas. This capital-intensive solution became increasingly controversial as costs mounted and as concerns about the environmental and aesthetic effects of urban highway building became more pronounced.

Postwar urban highway building has not been pursued to the point of being unjustified in an economic sense. The available evidence suggests that only a few of the very costly and very centrally located facilities—mainly serving peak-hour commuter needs—may have gone beyond the economic margin where the costs of added capacity exceed the incremental benefits in reduced congestion. Even if fairly generous estimates are made for so-called external costs (such as environmental and aesthetic pollution), it is not obvious that the economically justified demand for urban highways would be markedly reduced. In fact, a reasonably compelling case might be made on economic grounds for selectively adding to urban highway capacity, particularly to alleviate many suburban bottlenecks.

Economic justification, though, is hardly the entire story. New highways built in U.S. metropolitan areas today are likely to confront substantial community opposition. Furthermore, the major source of funds for highway building and maintenance—fuel taxes—will almost surely decline in real value as long as these are fixed in cents per gallon rather than, say, assessed on an ad valorem basis. This real decline primarily reflects an erosion of value due to general price inflation, which is also steadily accelerating the costs of building urban highways. Thus, the wherewithal for building more urban highways is declining just as the costs of doing so are accelerating.

These political and inflationary considerations, among others, have intensified interest in recent years in alternative means of alleviating congestion. The alternatives proposed include improved traffic engineering, the imposition of tolls or fees for use of particular highway segments, and priority schemes that give preference in the use of high-performance urban highways to vehicles that use such facilities intensively (such as carpools and buses).

Of these alternatives, improved traffic engineering is almost surely the least controversial (though not totally without complications). Improved traffic engineering can usually create a net overall gain so as to benefit many at the expense of none or only a few—a quality that helps gain political acceptance.

Priority access schemes and congestion tolls, in contrast, have thus far almost invariably made a number of travelers worse off while helping others. Accordingly, priority access and toll schemes very often incur community opposition and political complications of some magnitude. Furthermore, if not well designed and implemented, these schemes can lead to situations in which total losses exceed gains. To a considerable extent, however, these undesirable characteristics of early experiments with priority schemes and congestion tolls are due to poor experiment design and management. It has become increasingly easy to identify applications of priority access or tolling schemes that minimize or eliminate such consequences;[73] for example, contra-flow bus priority lanes on expressways can be instituted so as to take advantage of capacity that otherwise would not be used. Similarly, implementing priority lanes when capacity is *added* to a freeway may provide the advantages of priority schemes without imposing losses on prior users.

The promise inherent in priority access, congestion tolls, and other such schemes to alleviate congestion, as well as the persistence and scale of congestion problems, dictates a public policy of continuing experimentation. The potential benefits of priority and tolling schemes are well in excess of the costs of implementation when these schemes are well designed and managed. And management and design can be expected to improve with experience.

Congestion is, moreover, a problem that can be alleviated, though perhaps not totally resolved. The basic trends toward lower density in residential- and work-location choices (as documented in Chapters 2 and 3) should help. Some inexpensive palliatives (traffic engineering, priority access, and tolls) should also be beneficial in many situations. If necessary, selective additional highway building *might* be economically justified in some urban areas. But it should also be remembered that congestion is *not* a problem that can or should be totally eliminated. The proper policy goal is attenuation, and that goal is well within the realm of the possible.

12

The Transportation Disadvantaged

PUBLIC POLICY DEVELOPMENTS

It is widely believed that poor, handicapped, and elderly persons who cannot use an automobile and do not have access to high-quality, low-cost public transportation cannot participate fully in society—especially given the dispersal of residences, workplaces, and shopping and recreational centers in U.S. metropolitan areas. It is therefore argued that public policies are needed to ensure a minimal level of urban transportation for everyone.

Historically, little effort was devoted to alleviating these special mobility problems. The poor, elderly, and handicapped were thought to benefit from existing transportation programs. Government assistance to urban mass transportation was often at least partially justified as a means to keep fares low and service extensive for the poor or for those who could not use an automobile. No special effort was made to target mass transportation assistance to help the disadvantaged, and little attention was given to alternative means of mobility for those who could not use conventional mass transit.

In the 1960s and the 1970s, however, the civil rights movement brought greater political awareness of the plight of the poor, elderly, and handicapped. In urban transportation, as in other areas, government programs proliferated to meet the problems faced by these people.

The first such programs were designed to help poor minority commuters and were stimulated by the McCone Commission's report on the causes of the 1964 riot in Watts (a black neighborhood near the center of Los Angeles). The McCone Commission blamed the riot on lack of employment, which, it was argued, was due in part to the inadequate and expensive public transportation connecting Watts with the suburban areas where jobs were increasingly concentrated.[1] Starting in 1966, the federal government funded a dozen demonstration projects in several metropolitan areas to test the hypothesis that improved bus service to outlying employment centers would reduce unemployment in inner-city neighborhoods.

The results of these demonstration projects were disappointing, and the projects were discontinued in the early 1970s. Most of the new routes suffered from low patronage, and the average operating cost per passenger (excluding project administration and promotion expenses) was about triple that of the national average for transit service at that time.[2] More significantly, there was little evidence that many jobs were found because of the new bus service, so that the cost of providing this service per job attachment was probably extraordinarily high.[3] When compared with racial discrimination or lack of skills and education, employment decentralization and inadequate or expensive public transportation appeared to be relatively minor causes of unemployment (or underemployment) among low-income central-city residents.[4] As the administrator of one demonstration project put it: "Some employers were using the transportation barrier as a convenient excuse for not hiring for other reasons."[5]

Starting in the late 1960s, a policy of reduced transit fares for the elderly spread rapidly among U.S. transit systems. In 1965, only five U.S. transit systems offered discount fares to the elderly; by 1970, the number had increased to 43, and by 1974, 145 systems offered such discounts.[6] In late 1974, the U.S. Congress made discount fares for the elderly virtually universal by requiring that any urban transit system receiving federal operating assistance charge elderly riders half or less of the base fare.

Some efforts have been made to expand discounts to other urban transportation modes and other mobility-disadvantaged groups. In West Virginia, for example, the state sells transportation vouchers at a discount to the handicapped and low-income elderly; these vouchers apply to any participating transportation carriers, including taxis or intercity buses, and are redeemed at face value by the state. The Commonwealth of Pennsylvania also operates voucher programs in several cities, but only elderly persons are eligible.

While discount fares undoubtedly help the elderly, they also reduce transit revenues and increase the need for subsidies, since fare reductions usually do not stimulate enough additional patronage to offset the reduced revenues per rider. Moreover, many elderly persons who have automobiles, who wish to travel to points not well served by transit routes, or who have physical handicaps that make it difficult to walk to transit stops or to board vehicles, find the discounts of little value. In most metropolitan areas, only a small percentage of the eligible elderly population even register for reduced-fare identification cards.[7]

Recognizing the limitations of transit-fare discounts, Congress passed legislation in 1973 encouraging door-to-door services for the elderly and the handicapped. The Urban Mass Transportation Act was amended to incorporate a small program of capital grants to private, nonprofit organizations (such as church groups and social service agencies) for the purpose of purchasing vehicles and equipment needed to provide special transportation services for elderly and handicapped persons.[8] Door-to-door services received even greater impetus from passage of the Rehabilitation Act of 1973, Section 504 of which states that "no otherwise qualified handicapped individual . . . shall, solely by reason of his handicap, be excluded from participation in, be denied the benefits of, or be subjected to discrimination under any program or activity receiving federal assistance." Transit operators, most of whom were subject to Section 504 because they received federal financial aid, interpreted this to mean that they must provide *some* service accessible to the handicapped, and usually opted for a special door-to-door system using vans or small buses.

By the late 1970s, several hundred door-to-door systems for the elderly and the handicapped were operating in U.S. metropolitan areas.[9] In most metropolitan areas, at least one operator provided vehicles equipped with hydraulic lifts or ramps for passengers in wheelchairs. Some of these operators charged nominal fares—often 25 cents—while costs typically averaged several dollars per ride.

Some groups representing the handicapped contend that these separate door-to-door services do not meet the requirements of Section 504 and insist that all conventional transit services must be made accessible to the handicapped through the modification of transit stations and vehicles. In 1978, the U.S. secretary of transportation issued federal regulations requiring modifications of bus and rail transit equipment to at least partially meet this goal.

One of these regulations requires that all buses purchased with federal capital grants after the fall of 1979 conform to a new "Transbus" design, developed by the Urban Mass Transportation Administration.[10] While Transbus was intended to improve operating performance, economy, and passenger comfort, in practice the only major difference between Transbus and the more advanced bus models being produced by American manufacturers is a feature to allow easier boarding by the physical handicapped: whereas the advanced bus models have floors 29–30 inches off the ground and "kneel" to 26 inches for easier boarding, Transbus has a floor 22 inches off the ground, kneels to 18 inches, and is equipped with either a ramp or a lift for wheelchair boarding. Bus manufacturers estimate that each Transbus would cost at least twice as much to build as the more advanced standard models.[11] Thus, development of Transbus could increase capital costs for buses by approximately $600 million per year and perhaps increase annual maintenance and operating expenses by several hundred million dollars more.[12]

As initially proposed in 1978, federal regulations to make rail transit and commuter railroad systems accessible to the handicapped would have required that over a 10- to 20-year period, every subway and commuter railroad station and at least one car in every train be able to accommodate passengers in wheelchairs. The U.S. Department of Transportation estimated the capital cost of the modifications needed to meet these standards at $1.5–1.7 billion, most of which would be for the installation of elevators in every subway station.[13] The American Public Transit Association contended that these capital costs were underestimated by a factor of two or three, and that the requirements would also increase the operating deficits of local transit authorities by slowing trains and buses and adding to maintenance needs.

As a result of the industry's complaints, the U.S. Department of Transportation amended the 1978 regulations, so that only the "most important" subway and commuter railroad stations—appproximately 40 percent of the total—must be accessible by wheelchair. Even so, the Department of Transportation and the U.S. Congressional Budget Office (apparently accepting the industry's criticism of the Department of Transportation's earlier figures) estimated that modifying only these key stations would require $1.2–1.7 billion in one-time capital expenditures and $14–49 million annually in extra operating expenses.[14]

The total bill for the discount transit fares for the elderly and door-to-door services for the elderly and handicapped put into effect in the late 1970s probably amounted to more than $100 million per year, and perhaps twice that much. Discount transit fares alone probably came to around $80 million per year, since the elderly accounted for about 7 percent of transit passengers, or approximately 400 million trips per year, and the average discount must have exceeded 19 cents per trip.[15] The bill for subsidized door-to-door services may have been almost as large as that for discount transit fares, although the exact outlays are impossible to estimate for lack of accurate nationwide data on the number and cost of door-to-door services in operation. If the regulations modifying conventional transit equipment are also put into effect, the annual cost of special programs for the mobility disadvantaged will increase by as much as one order of magnitude.

Despite the resources committed, these current and proposed programs help only a small portion of the mobility-handicapped population—specifically, the elderly and those who have difficulty climbing stairs (particularly individuals confined to wheelchairs). But, as pointed out in the next section, there are many other groups who might be considered transportation disadvantaged.

THE CHARACTERISTICS OF THE TRANSPORTATION DISADVANTAGED

In 1970, 20.1 million Americans (10 percent of the population) were 65 years old or older, 13.4 million (7 percent) had a physical or mental handicap that impaired their mobility, and 25.6 million (13 percent) had incomes below the poverty level. There is, however, considerable overlap among these three groups (see Figure 12.1). Consequently, only about 23 percent (45.7 million persons) of the American population in 1970 can be classified as poor, handicapped, or elderly.[16]

About 13 million residents of standard metropolitan statistical areas had incomes below poverty levels in 1970, while 9 million urban dwellers had handicaps that hindered their mobility, and 11.7 million were over 65 years old. The poor, handicapped, and elderly population in metropolitan areas in 1970 totaled approximately 26 million individuals, or 19 percent of the metropolitan population, assuming that the overlaps among the mobility disadvantaged in urban areas were similar to those in the nation as a whole.[17]

The handicapped. Of the estimated 9 million handicapped persons with mobility problems who resided in metropolitan areas in 1970, only a little over 7 million were potential beneficiaries of transportation policies to help the disadvantaged; the remaining 2 million were either institutionalized or so ill they could not leave their homes.[18] Even if the handicapped had accessible transportation services, the fact that as a group they have lower employment rates, lower incomes, and are often afflicted by mobility problems as they advance in age would also reduce their ability to travel. Overall, handicapped persons average about half as many trips per month as their nonhandicapped peers;[19] parity between the handicapped and nonhandicapped in tripmaking thus seems

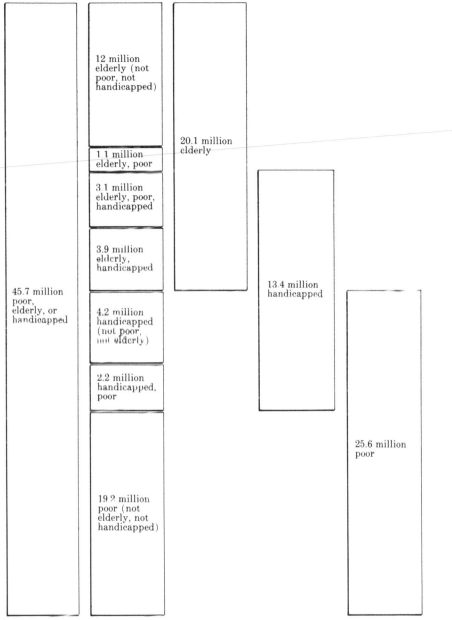

Figure 12.1. National population for 1970. (*Source:* Transportation Research Board, *Transportation Requirements for the Handicapped, Elderly, and Economically Disadvantaged,* National Cooperative Highway Research Program, Synthesis of Highway Practice, report no. 39 [Washington, D.C.: Transportation Research Board, 1976], pp. 8, 10, 11, 13.)

unlikely, regardless of the accessibility and availability of special transportation services for the handicapped.

In urban areas in 1970, 288,000 residents were estimated to be confined to wheelchairs, 271,000 had to use walkers, 222,000 were deaf, and 1.3 million were blind or had other serious visual problems (see Table 12.1). By far the largest single group of urban handicapped—3.7 mil-

TABLE 12.1.   Estimates of the numbers of handicapped persons who had difficulty using urban transportation in 1970.

	Living in metropolitan areas	National total
Acute conditions	354,000	490,000
Institutionalized	624,000	960,000
Chronic conditions:		
Visually impaired	1,309,000	1,982,000
Deaf	222,400	333,000
Use wheelchair	287,800	430,000
Use walker	271,000	410,000
Use other mobility aids:		
Special shoes	1,668,700	2,439,500
Cane or walking stick	1,459,000	2,216,500
Crutches	302,500	447,500
Leg or foot brace	166,600	244,500
Artificial leg or foot	83,700	122,000
Subtotal	3,680,500	5,470,000
Other mobility limitations	2,223,000	3,310,000
Total chronic conditions	7,993,700	11,935,000
Grand total (acute, institutionalized, and chronic)	8,971,700	13,385,000
Noninstitutionalized persons who are well enough to leave their homes	7,170,200	10,654,000

Source: Metropolitan population statistics estimated from national population estimates and from statistics on the frequency of handicaps in the elderly and nonelderly population found in Transportation System Center, *The Handicapped and Elderly Market for Urban Transportation,* report no. PB–224–821, prepared for the Urban Mass Transportation Administration (Springfield, Va.: National Technical Information Service, 1973).

lion in 1970—are those who use walking aids other than wheelchairs or walkers (that is, crutches, canes, braces, special shoes, or artificial legs). Another 2.2 million persons have other mobility problems, such as difficulty climbing steps or walking long distances due to arthritis. About 15–20 percent of the handicapped suffer from multiple illnesses or conditions, mainly combinations of vision or hearing problems with other mobility disabilities.[20] A survey of urban handicapped persons who are well enough to leave their homes also reveals that while the majority of handicapped persons have difficulty with stairs, walking a block or more, and waiting or standing, these problems do not affect every handicapped individual (see Table 12.2).

If automobile use and availability are included (and accepted as mobility criteria), two thirds or so of all handicapped persons may not experience serious difficulties with the current transportation system. In 1974, 41 percent of the urban handicapped well enough to leave their homes had driver's licenses, and 66 percent lived in households that owned automobiles (see Table 12.3). In addition, 64 percent of all urban handicapped persons reported that relatives or friends were willing to drive them where they had to go "as often as needed" or

TABLE 12.2.   Incidence of general mobility problems among handicapped people.

Mobility problem	Percent of handicapped[a]	Estimated number of handicapped (thousands)
Total number of handicapped	100.0	7,440
Difficulty going up or down stairs/inclines	64.9	4,825
Difficulty stooping/kneeling/crouching	60.6	4,508
Difficulty walking/going more than one block	56.9	4,231
Difficulty waiting/standing	56.2	4,184
Difficulty lifting or carrying weights up to 10 lbs.	47.3	3,522
Difficulty moving in crowds	41.4	3,079
Difficulty sitting down or getting up	40.5	3,011
Difficulty reaching/handling or grasping	33.5	2,493

Source: Grey Advertising, Inc., Summary Report of Data from National Survey of Transportation Handicapped People, report for the U.S. Department of Transportation, Urban Mass Transportation Administration (Washington, D.C.: U.S. Department of Transportation, 1978), p. 30.
[a] Percents add to more than 100 because of multiple general mobility problems among handicapped people.

TABLE 12.3. Availability of cars among urban handicapped people who can leave their homes, 1977.

	Percent of handicapped	Millions of handicapped
Ability to drive:		
Licensed	41	3.0
Not licensed	59	4.4
Car ownership (in household):		
Own car	66	4.9
Do not own car	34	2.5
Availability of car ride (as passenger):		
As often as needed or most of the time	64	4.7
Occasionally	26	1.9
Never when needed	11	0.8

Source: Grey Advertising, Inc., *Summary Report of Data from National Survey of Transportation Handicapped People,* report for the U.S. Department of Transportation, Urban Mass Transportation Administration (Washington, D.C.: U.S. Department of Transportation, 1978), p. 65.

"most of the time." Only 35 percent reported that rides were available only "part of the time" or "never when needed." Thus, out of 7.4 million urban handicapped persons who were well enough to leave their homes, probably no more than 2.6 million or so did not have some automobile service available. The actual number may even be smaller, since at least some of those who reported that friends and relatives were not able to drive them as often as needed may have been licensed drivers themselves. On the other hand, these statistics do not reflect the inconvenience to the handicapped, and to other members of the household, of having to rely on others for their transportation needs.

The mobility problems of many urban handicapped persons are also not so serious that they make conventional public transportation completely inaccessible. Both the handicapped and the nonhandicapped use conventional mass transportation for about 15 percent of their trips where transit service is available. However, taxis, vans, and walking are used more extensively by the handicapped than by the nonhandicapped, accounting for 3, 2, and 9 percent, respectively, of all trips by the handicapped and 1, 1, and 5 percent of all trips by the nonhandicapped. Nevertheless, for both the handicapped and the nonhandicapped, the private automobile is the most popular mode (by number of trips taken), although for the handicapped the automobile trip is more often taken as a passenger. Even in urban areas with mass transit, the automobile is used for 72 percent of all trips by handicapped persons compared with 78 percent of all trips by the nonhandicapped.

Assuming that physical disabilities affect those with and without access to the automobile proportionately, then the 2.6 million or so handicapped without access to the automobile includes about 800,000 persons who are visually impaired, 130,000 who are deaf, 170,000 who use wheelchairs, 160,000 who use walkers, and about 1.3 million who use other walking aids or have other mobility limitations. The deaf and visually impaired, who make up over one third of those handicapped without automobile access, might be able to use standard transit services. This leaves about 1.6 million who do not have access to automobiles and who have difficulty using transit services as now provided. It is these people, less than one quarter of the 7 million handicapped not confined, who would be the potential beneficiaries of policies designed to improve transit accessibility.

The poor. In 1970, 24.1 million persons in the United States were officially defined as poverty stricken; of these, about 13.1 million (54 percent) resided in metropolitan areas. The number of poor both inside and outside metropolitan areas has declined since the 1960s, due to growth in real per capita income. However, the poor are increasingly concentrated in urban centers (see Table 12.4). And even allowing for recent declines, the poor remain much more numerous than the handicapped or the elderly; partly as a consequence, the vast majority of poor persons (75 percent) are neither handicapped nor elderly.[21]

Those in low-income households make fewer trips than those in higher-income households (see Table 12.5). One of the reasons for this is that many of the poor are unemployed and thus do not make the worktrips that constitute about one quarter of the trips taken by the average U.S. household. Low-income persons also have less money to pay for the social, shopping, and recreational activities that often induce urban travel. Thus, low tripmaking rates by the poor may be more a function of lower rates of employment and incomes than a lack of affordable or accessible transportation services per se.

Low-income persons rely slightly less on the automobile and more on public transportation and walking than those in higher income brackets (see Table 12.5). Households with a 1969 income of $3,000–5,000 took 79 percent of their nonwalking trips by automobile, while households with incomes of $10,000–15,000 relied on automobiles for 89 percent of their nonwalking trips. In large metropolitan areas where public transportation service is better, low-income persons cut their automobile use even further. For example, in the Chicago metropolitan

TABLE 12.4 Persons below poverty level by place of residence, 1960, 1970, and 1975.

Place of residence	Millions of persons below poverty level				Percent of all persons below poverty level		
	1960	1970	1975	Percent change 1960–70	1960	1970	1975
In SMSAs:[a]							
In central cities	10.4	8.0	9.1	−23	27	33	35
Outside central cities	6.6	5.1	6.2	−23	17	21	24
Total SMSAs	17.0	13.1	15.3	−23	44	54	59
In nonmetropolitan areas	21.7	11.1	10.5	−49	56	46	41
Total, United States	38.7	24.2	25.8	−37	100	100	100

Source: U.S. Bureau of the Census, Consumer Income: Characteristics of the Population below Poverty Level, 1975, ser. P-60, no. 106 of Current Population Reports (Washington, D.C.: U.S. Government Printing Office, 1977), p. 23.
[a] Standard metropolitan statistical areas.

TABLE 12.5. Travel patterns by household income, 1969.

	Household income					
	Under $3,000	$3,000– $5,000	$5,000– $7,500	$7,500– $10,000	$10,000– $15,000	Above $15,000	All income
Average daily persontrips:							
Per person	1.0	1.7	1.8	2.2	2.2	2.4	2.0
Per household	2.2	4.8	5.9	8.0	8.1	9.5	6.2
Average daily personmiles:							
Per person	8.5	13.3	15.5	22.5	24.4	26.4	19.2
Per household	17.8	37.4	51.2	81.0	84.2	102.9	60.6
Average trip length in miles (round trip)	8.4	7.9	8.6	10.1	10.4	10.8	9.8
Percent of trips by purpose:							
Work	23.3	25.5	28.8	27.0	28.0	26.0	27.0
Family business	33.5	31.9	30.5	30.5	29.8	30.5	30.5
Education	16.3	16.5	12.9	14.1	15.9	16.0	15.2
Social	25.5	25.5	27.2	27.4	25.4	26.0	26.3
Percent of nonwalking trips made by automobile	77.9	79.2	85.6	86.6	88.8	90.5	86.3

Source: Calculated from data in James P. Leape, The Demand for Automobiles: An Analysis, senior honors thesis, Harvard University, 1977, pp. 43, 64.

area, households with incomes under $6,000 used automobiles for 74 percent of their trips and relied on mass transportation for more than 21 percent.[22]

Significant numbers of poor persons live in households that own cars, although automobile ownership rates are much lower among the poor than among higher-income groups. In 1970, less than 64 percent of the metropolitan families with incomes below $5,000 owned at least one car, whereas 94 percent or more of the families with incomes above $10,000 were car owners.[23] Automobile ownership rates among the suburban poor are high (probably because they have few alternatives), while automobile ownership is less common among the central-city poor. In 1970, approximately 7.2 million poor persons in metropolitan areas lived in households with at least one car, while 5.9 million poor persons (mostly central-city residents) lived in households without a car.[24]

Even the 7.2 million poor metropolitan residents who live in households that own a car may not be free of transportation difficulties. These families tend to own only one car, so that an automobile may not be available to all family members when needed. Car ownership may also impose a heavy financial burden on these households. Low-income families that own an automobile usually do save several hundred dollars per year in ownership and operating expenses by buying used cars and driving fewer miles per year than the typical household.[25] For example, the poor family owning one car in 1972–73 spent an average of about $800 on automobile expenses per year, or somewhere between 40 and 20 percent of its annual income, whereas moderate-income families owning one automobile spent an average of $1,000–1,200 per year or 5–10 percent of their income.[26]

The approximately 5.9 million poor metropolitan residents without cars in 1970 were not completely without transportation options. A substantial number of low-income persons without automobiles traveled in the cars of friends or relatives.[27] Low-income persons may also use public transportation or walk, especially since 4.4 million out of the 5.9 million carless urban poor in 1970 lived in central cities of metropolitan areas where these alternatives may have been viable. Of all urban households with 1969 incomes below $3,000, 66 percent resided within two blocks of a mass transportation line leading to a central business district, 93 percent lived within six blocks of such a transit line, and only 9 percent had no transit services available at all.[28]

Low-income carless persons also use taxis fairly extensively, especially in smaller metropolitan areas where little mass transportation service is available. Taxi fares are expensive and taxis are thus popularly thought to be a mode patronized by the well-to-do. But U.S. households with incomes below $4,000 in 1969, while accounting for only 10.7

percent of persontrips by all modes, accounted for 21.2 percent of all persontrips by taxi.[29] Taxis are presumably not a luxury for these households but rather a sensible means of economizing on total transportation costs by substituting an occasional taxi fare for the $800-or-more minimum annual outlay required to own and operate an automobile.

The elderly. Accepting the convention that persons aged 65 or over are elderly, there were approximately 20 million elderly persons in the United States in 1970, 11.7 million of whom resided in metropolitan areas. Because successive generations are larger and tend to live longer, the elderly population has been growing at an average annual rate of slightly more than 2 percent per year. By 1977, the number of elderly persons residing in metropolitan areas had grown to 14 million, divided almost equally between central cities and suburbs (see Table 12.6).

In 1970, approximately 20 percent of the urban elderly were handicapped, 5 percent were poor, and 15 percent were poor and handicapped; thus, a total of 40 percent of the urban elderly were physically handicapped, poor, or both. The proportion of elderly who are poor, however, has been falling rapidly, from 24.5 percent in 1970 to only 14.1 percent in 1977 (see Table 12.6).

Although elderly persons accounted for over 10 percent of the nation's population in 1970, they made only 5 percent of the trips taken nationwide. This is undoubtedly partly because so many elderly persons are retired, have low incomes, and suffer from physical disabilities. When the elderly do travel, they make about 90 percent of their non-walking trips by automobile and about 5–6 percent by mass transportation and taxicabs, as is the pattern among most adults (see Table 12.7). More of the elderly, however, take their automobile trips as passengers.

A large number of elderly persons can drive, however, and the share of elderly who have driver's licenses has been increasing rapidly. The percentage of men aged 60 to 69 who were licensed to drive increased from 66 to 83 percent between the early 1950s and 1970, while the percentage of women in that age group who were licensed increased from 18 to 42 percent during that same period.[30] Most gerontologists expect this trend to continue and perhaps accelerate, since the people now reaching 65 are not only healthier but grew up when driver's licenses were more common than they had been—especially for women.[31] It is estimated that in 1970, just under half of the metropolitan elderly, or 5–6 million persons, were licensed to drive, and the proportion has been increasing steadily.[32]

The elderly who are licensed drivers also travel significantly less than younger drivers, averaging only about 5,000 miles of automobile

TABLE 12.6. Elderly persons by place of residence and poverty level, 1970, 1975, and 1977 (thousands).

| | 1970 | | | 1975 | | | 1977 | | |
| | | Below poverty level | | | Below poverty level | | | Below poverty level | |
Place of residence	Total elderly	Thousands of elderly	Percent of total	Total elderly	Thousands of elderly	Percent of total	Total elderly	Thousands of elderly	Percent of total
Central cities of metropolitan areas	6,314	1,440	22.8	6,883	979	14.2	6,699	953	14.2
Outside central cities of metropolitan areas	5,432	908	16.7	6,833	668	9.8	7,301	639	8.8
Subtotal, metropolitan areas	11,746	2,348	20.0	13,716	1,647	12.0	14,000	1,592	11.4
Nonmetropolitan areas	7,507	2,361	31.5	7,946	1,670	21.0	8,468	1,584	18.7
Total, United States	19,253	4,709	24.5	21,662	3,317	15.3	22,468	3,176	14.1

Source: U.S. Bureau of the Census, Characteristics of the Low Income Population, 1970, no. 81 of Current Population Reports, ser. P-60 (Washington, D.C.: U.S. Government Printing Office, 1971); U.S. Bureau of the Census, Characteristics of Population below Poverty Level, 1975, no. 106 of Current Population Reports, ser. P-60 (Washington, D.C.: U.S. Government Printing Office, 1977); and U.S. Bureau of the Census, Characteristics of Population below Poverty Level, 1977, no. 119 of Current Population Reports, ser. P-60 (Washington, D.C.: U.S. Government Printing Office, 1979). Note that the number of persons is as of March in the following year.

TABLE 12.7. Travel patterns by age group, 1970.

| | Automobile | | | Percent of trips taken, by mode | | | | |
Age	Driver	Passenger	Total	Motorcycle and truck	Mass transit	Taxi	Other[a]	All modes
5–13	0.0	72.0	72.0	3.4	1.7	0.2	22.7	100.0
14–15	4.6	63.2	67.8	4.5	5.8	0.2	21.7	100.0
16–20	49.2	36.7	85.9	3.3	5.2	0.0	5.6	100.0
21–25	62.1	29.1	91.2	4.3	3.4	0.3	0.8	100.0
26–29	67.9	22.5	90.4	5.1	3.6	0.4	0.5	100.0
30–39	70.0	19.3	89.3	7.3	2.3	0.3	0.8	100.0
40–49	66.0	21.5	87.5	8.1	3.5	0.2	0.7	100.0
50–59	62.8	24.6	87.4	7.4	4.1	0.3	0.8	100.0
60–64	58.2	26.1	84.3	7.4	6.9	0.7	0.7	100.0
65–69	57.6	29.2	86.8	6.4	5.2	0.3	0.8	100.0
70 and over	50.2	41.0	91.2	2.6	4.7	0.4	1.1	100.0

Source: U.S. Department of Transportation, Federal Highway Administration, *Mode of Transportation and Personal Characteristics of Tripmakers,* report no. 9 of the *Nationwide Personal Transportation Study* (Washington, D.C. Federal Highway Administration, 1973), p. 31; and U.S. Bureau of the Census, *Statistical Abstract of the United States, 1978* (Washington, D.C.: U.S. Government Printing Office, 1978), p. 29.

[a] Includes school bus and airplane.

travel per year as compared with 10,000 miles or more for younger drivers.[33] This supports the theory that rates of travel among the elderly are not entirely due to lack of accessible transportation.

SOLUTIONS

While the requirement that there be some transportation aid or service for the disadvantaged has been widely accepted since the 1960s, a strong argument can be made that government should not be deeply involved in providing or promoting these services but rather ought to be concerned with improving the general welfare of the disadvantaged. Improving and subsidizing transportation or other services for disadvantaged persons may be a less efficient public policy than simply giving them added income and allowing them to determine how best to spend this money to improve their lives. Such an approach ensures that government aid is used to meet the most pressing needs of the poor, elderly, and handicapped as they themselves perceive their needs.

Special service programs have political advantages, however, in that they allow a large number of legislators, elected officials, and organizations that lobby on behalf of the disadvantaged to claim credit for establishing some programs to help. Furthermore, when the poor, elderly, and handicapped lobby for service programs, the local agencies, unions, and professional groups involved in providing the services often join them as allies. A program that simply gives money to disadvantaged persons, in contrast, might have few immediate supporters beyond the disadvantaged. Finally, programs that would provide income for the disadvantaged raise concerns about undermining incentives to work, while special services are seen as less threatening to the work ethic.

Improving automobile access. Current urban transportation policies for helping the transportation handicapped concentrate on improving accessibility to public modes, particularly to conventional mass transit. This focus on transit accessibility, however, may not well serve the diverse needs of all the transportation disadvantaged. An attractive alternative, for example, may be expanding access to the automobile. The automobile offers features, such as faster and more convenient service, not readily available otherwise, and these features may be particularly important to the elderly or physically handicapped who cannot walk far or who tire easily.[34]

One potentially inexpensive means of increasing automobile access would be to encourage mobility-disadvantaged individuals to obtain or keep driver's licenses. Virtually all elderly and poor persons who are not physically handicapped are physically able to drive. More significantly, over half the persons with physical handicaps are probably not precluded from driving, particularly those who are deaf; those who use special shoes, canes, crutches, or braces to walk; or those with other minor mobility-limiting disabilities.

Encouraging driving among the elderly and those with limited physical handicaps could pose safety problems, since these drivers may be less alert and have slower reflexes or poorer ability to judge speeds and distances. Several studies show, however, that elderly drivers compensate for their reduced abilities. Besides traveling only about half as many miles per year as younger drivers, elderly motorists also avoid situations—such as freeways, rush hour traffic, nighttime driving, or unfamiliar roads—that might tax their driving abilities.[35] These precautions keep the accident rates of the elderly comparable to those of the average driver (see Table 12.8). While elderly drivers have higher acci-

TABLE 12.8.   Automobile accident rates by driver age, 1972.

Age of driver	All accidents per one hundred drivers	Fatal accidents per one hundred thousand drivers	Accidents per million miles driven	Fatalities per million miles driven
All ages	25	60	28.8	0.069
Under 20	43	94	92.8	0.203
20–24	41	103	49.6	0.125
25–29	28	65	28.5	0.066
30–34	24	62	23.4	0.060
35–39	21	46	21.3	0.047
40–44	19	48	19.3	0.049
45–49	19	42	19.2	0.043
50–54	16	37	16.9	0.039
55–59	18	39	20.0	0.043
60–64	16	44	19.7	0.054
65–69	18	43	30.8	0.074
70 and over	13	62	27.3	0.134

Source: Involvement rates per driver are for 1972 as reported in National Safety Council, *Accident Facts 1973* (Chicago, Ill.: National Safety Council, 1973), p. 54. Accident rates per mile driven are based on 1969 estimates found in U.S. Department of Transportation, Federal Highway Administration, *Characteristics of Licensed Drivers,* report no. 6 of the *Nationwide Personal Transportation Study* (Washington, D.C.: Federal Highway Administration, 1973), p. 25.

dent rates per mile than middle-aged drivers (the safest age group), their safety records are significantly better than drivers in their twenties or teens.

The accident rates of elderly and physically handicapped persons might be decreased, moreover, through special training and testing procedures. For example, older drivers might be retrained every other year or so to compensate for declining motor skills and reflexes. Periodic retesting of older and handicapped drivers might also help keep dangerous drivers off the roads, particularly if the tests emphasize visual and reflex acuity as well as standard driving rules. Elderly or handicapped drivers with limited reflex abilities or other problems might also be granted restricted licenses, allowing them to drive only during the daytime or on local streets, for example.[36]

Automobile access might be further increased by government subsidization of vehicle modifications to enable some more seriously handicapped individuals to drive. The federal government (through the Veterans Administration) already pays veterans whose disabilities require modified vehicles up to $3,800 toward the purchase price of a first car and all of the cost of special equipment and modifications to that vehicle and to any subsequent car purchased.

The costs of modifying the vehicles vary greatly according to the specific disability. Some individuals require vehicles with only minor and inexpensive modifications—such as moving the brake or accelerator pedals—that may cost as little as $50. Veterans with amputated limbs usually require more elaborate equipment, including special controls. The most extensive modifications are needed for persons confined to a wheelchair; these can range from hand controls, a power seat, and a modified door for approximately $1,500 per vehicle, to a van with a hydraulic lift and special controls that costs $8,000 more than the normal vehicle purchase price.[37] Since automobiles typically last eight to ten years or more, the average annual government expenditure per driver is much lower than the cost of the modifications made to the average vehicle. Disabled veterans may also keep their cars longer than average because of the inconvenience of having the modifications made.

It is difficult to estimate how many handicapped persons might need and use subsidies for modifying vehicles. The primary beneficiaries would probably be among those confined to wheelchairs, since they require vehicles with the most extensive modifications and are most likely to be deterred by the cost if no subsidies are available. Vehicle modifications would not alleviate the mobility problems of all wheelchair-bound individuals (some undoubtedly have multiple disabilities or other problems that would make them unable to use even modified vehicles), but it has been estimated that about 116,000 people confined to wheelchairs in the United States could drive automobiles if the vehicles were suitably modified.[38] Other likely beneficiaries include some of the 272,000 urban residents who use walkers and the 3.7 million urban residents who use canes and similar walking aids. While many of these less severely handicapped persons drive already or need only the encouragement of training and licensing programs, some might require specially equipped automobiles.

The total cost of the program would depend on how generous the government subsidy was, as well as on the number of persons involved. A program that paid for the full costs of *both* acquiring and modifying vehicles for 116,000 wheelchair-confined persons considered potentially able to drive has been estimated by the Congressional Budget Office to be about $130 million per year (in 1979 dollars).[39] If the costs of vehicle modification alone were paid by government subsidies, the total costs would be cut by more than one half and perhaps by as much as two thirds. The costs might also be further reduced by virtue of the fact that some of these 116,000 already drive.

Improving transit access. Current public policy toward mobility-disadvantaged persons emphasizes increasing the accessibility of mass transit in three ways: (1) through government aid to reduce fares; (2) through subsidies to support more extensive service than is otherwise financially possible; and (3) through government-mandated modifications of transit vehicles and facilities to permit easier boarding by physically handicapped persons.

Lower fares and more extensive service offer significant benefits to several mobility-disadvantaged groups, particularly to the poor. Mass transportation is an attractive mode for low-income individuals, since it can offer reasonable service at a relatively low cost in heavily traveled corridors of large, high-density metropolitan areas. Subsidies to provide more extensive service are also helpful to the poor because the number of places that can be reached economically is increased.

One problem with relying too much on conventional mass transit to help the disadvantaged is the high cost of providing such service in low-density areas. Even with the substantial public aid currently provided, mass transit is often infrequent or nonexistent in small metropolitan areas or in nondowntown-oriented corridors in large metropolitan areas.

Moreover, very little of the current transit subsidies may actually help the handicapped, elderly, or poor. Poor persons tend to use transit for a larger percentage of their trips than middle- or high-income groups, but they also tend to travel less frequently. Consequently, the median income of mass transportation riders tends to be only slightly less than the median income of U.S. households, although it is significantly lower than the median incomes of automobile drivers and passengers. In 1969, 28 percent of transit users had household incomes below $5,000, while 36 percent had incomes above $10,000, including 18 percent above $15,000 (see Table 12.9). As the table shows, the poor make up a disproportionately large share of bus passengers but are underrepresented on subway and commuter rail lines. In 1976, the average operating subsidy required for bus passengers was 21 cents per trip, while the operating subsidies for rail transit and commuter rail lines averaged 35 cents and $1.25 per trip, respectively.[40] One study estimated that the trips taken by poor persons accounted for less than 10 percent of the 1976 national transit subsidies.[41]

If aid to the disadvantaged is a primary rationale for current transit

TABLE 12.9. Income distribution of travelers by mode, 1969.

	Percent of travelers with household incomes of:				
	Under $5,000	$5,000–$9,999	$10,000–$14,999	$15,000 or more	All incomes
All households in the United States	28.4	30.9	23.0	17.6	100.0
All travelers	12.1	42.0	29.6	16.2	100.0
Mass transportation passengers:					
All mass transport modes	27.4	37.0	18.0	17.7	100.0
Bus or streetcar only	31.7	37.5	15.7	15.0	100.0
Subway or elevated only	14.4	37.5	21.9	26.4	100.0
Commuter rail only	0.0	35.1	39.6	25.2	100.0
Taxi passengers	28.5	42.3	26.0	13.3	100.0
Automobile travelers:					
Driver	10.1	41.6	31.3	17.2	100.0
Passenger	12.7	43.2	29.1	15.1	100.0

Source: Calculated by José A. Gómez-Ibáñez and John Pucher from unpublished data gathered for the *Nationwide Personal Transportation Study* and supplied by the Federal Highway Administration. See José A. Gómez-Ibáñez, "Federal Assistance for Urban Mass Transportation" (diss., Harvard University, 1975), p. 210; and John Pucher, "The Income Characteristics of Transit Riders," technical report no. 1 (rev. ed.), Center for Transportation Studies, Massachusetts Institute of Technology, 1977, table 1–1.

subsidy programs, subsidies could be more heavily concentrated, at the very least, on those routes that poor persons patronize most heavily, such as inner-city routes in metropolitan areas. Even more focus could be achieved by charging the poor or handicapped lower fares than other passengers. This might be done through the use of identification cards or the distribution of transportation coupons analogous to food stamps. Policies that target transit subsidies more effectively may prove politically unattractive, however, partly because they conflict with the motivation to spread benefits widely among constituents.

Modification to make mass transportation stations and vehicles accessible to the physically handicapped are even less likely to be helpful than subsidized transit fares and service. Many of the physically handicapped persons for whom the station and vehicle modifications are intended have serious difficulty in reaching the stations and thus find the modifications of little use. For example, in 1977, although there were 157 lift-equipped buses on 22 routes in St. Louis (the U.S. city that has made the greatest effort to make its bus service accessible to wheelchair-confined persons), and roughly half of these were not malfunctioning because of maintenance problems, an average of only four bus riders per day used the lifts. All the stations in the new BART rail system in San Francisco are equipped with elevators for the handicapped, but only 500 persons use the elevators on an average day, and only 100 of these are wheelchair-bound. The new subway system in Washington, D.C., is also equipped with elevators; in its first eleven months of operation the system averaged approximately 26,000 daily riders, of whom only six, on average, were wheelchair users.[42]

Low-fare, door-to-door paratransit service. Publicly supported paratransit systems offering door-to-door service with automobiles, vans, or small buses have also been advanced as a solution to some of the problems of the mobility disadvantaged. According to one estimate, by 1976 over 3,000 such systems were in operation in the United States.[43]

Door-to-door paratransit avoids the difficulty that many physically handicapped persons have in reaching transit stops and often provides coverage to points not served by conventional transit. The problem with this type of service, however, is its high cost. In 1979, the Congressional Budget Office estimated total capital, maintenance, and operating costs for lift-equipped van service as being in the range of $2–4 per passenger-mile and between $16 and $25 per average trip.[44]

There are some disadvantaged groups, however, for whom paratransit may provide the only feasible service. This group may be small, probably primarily consisting of some fraction of the individuals who use wheelchairs or walkers and cannot drive even with specially

TABLE 12.10. Summary evaluation of means to improve the mobility of disadvantaged groups.

Means used to improve mobility	Physically handicapped					Poor who are not handicapped	Elderly who are not handicapped or poor
	Use wheelchair or walker	Use other walking aid (e.g., special shoes, cane, crutches, brace)	Blind	Deaf	Other mobility limitations		
Increase access to automobiles:							
Outreach and training programs to increase drivers	Secondary program	PRINCIPAL PROGRAM	Not helpful	Possibly helpful	PRINCIPAL PROGRAM	Moderately helpful	PRINCIPAL PROGRAM
Subsidies for vehicle modifications needed to permit independent driving	PRINCIPAL PROGRAM	Secondary program	Not helpful	Secondary program	Secondary program	Not helpful	Not necessary
Subsidies for automobile ownership and operating costs	Not necessary	Not necessary	Not helpful	Not helpful	Not necessary	Helpful but expensive	Not necessary
Increase access to mass transportation:							
Subsidies to lower fares	Not helpful	Secondary program	Secondary program	Secondary program	Secondary program	PRINCIPAL PROGRAM	Not necessary
Subsidies to expand service	Not helpful	Secondary program	PRINCIPAL PROGRAM	Secondary program	Secondary program	Secondary program	Not necessary
Modifications to vehicles and stations to help physically handicapped	Helpful but unnecessarily expensive	Helpful but unnecessarily expensive	Not helpful	Not helpful	Helpful but unnecessarily expensive	Not helpful	Not helpful
Subsidize door-to-door paratransit services	Secondary program	Secondary program	Secondary program	Secondary program	Secondary program	Secondary program	Not necessary

Source: Compiled by the authors.

equipped vehicles, and some of the deaf or blind. Paratransit service may also be advisable in low-density areas where provision of conventional mass transit service can be extremely costly.

SUMMARY

An overview of services to improve the mobility of the transportation disadvantaged is shown in Table 12.10. The most striking finding is that the most costly of the current programs to improve the mobility of the disadvantaged—modifications to transit vehicles and stations— is among the least effective. Moreover, this program provides assistance to only a small number of the transportation disadvantaged (mainly wheelchair users and those who have difficulty using stairs), while offering little to large groups of disadvantaged, such as the blind, the deaf, and the poor. Furthermore, other policies would better benefit wheelchair-bound individuals and those with walking difficulties, and at a far lower cost per person. In particular, improving access to the automobile may offer the largest gain at the lowest costs, both for the physically handicapped and the elderly. The high levels of automobile ownership and use among the transportation disadvantaged—even without special incentives or automobile accessibility programs—attest to the advantages of this alternative.

Although programs can be identified that offer more mobility at lower cost than current policies, the cost of significantly improving the mobility of disadvantaged persons is likely to be extremely high. Programs such as driver outreach and training may be relatively inexpensive, but subsidies for automobile modifications, reduced transit fares, or paratransit service could each cost hundreds of millions per year. Before such expensive programs are implemented, serious consideration should be given to whether the value of added mobility for disadvantaged persons would be commensurate with the cost. Income supplements or government programs to provide other (nontransportation) services might be a more suitable form of assistance—at least for some of the disadvantaged.

13

*Small-Car
Safety*

INTRODUCTION

If Americans drive smaller cars in the future than they have in the past, many urban transportation problems will be alleviated. Indeed, in order to effectively conserve energy and lower urban air pollution levels, there may be no alternative to substantially reducing the average size of private motor vehicles in the United States. While not central to solving land-use and congestion problems, smaller automobiles would make a contribution to ameliorating these difficulties as well. Enhanced mobility for the transportation disadvantaged also might be achieved more economically if the typical American automobile were smaller in size.

This small-car "solution" involves reducing the average gross weight of American cars by approximately 1,000 pounds. This may not substantially reduce the purchase price of American automobiles, as much of the reduction in weight would be achieved by substituting more expensive, sophisticated materials for heavier materials now in use, and might also involve more refined engineering in order to maintain performance and other qualities. To a considerable extent, downgrading the size of American automobiles will narrow, perhaps even eliminate, differences between the typical American and European vehicles.

It is difficult to fault a small-car solution to urban transportation problems on conventional grounds. If prices of energy, raw materials, and metals inflate more rapidly than other prices, the marketplace itself, even without support from regulatory or other considerations, could induce Americans to use smaller automobiles.

There is, in fact, only one argument commonly made against greater use of smaller cars: that these smaller vehicles are inherently less safe than larger ones. It is easy enough to understand the origins of such a view. It conforms with the common-sense observation that when small and large objects collide, all else being equal, the smaller object is likely to be damaged more than the larger. And there is considerable laboratory evidence to document this belief. Evidence also reveals that automobile fatality rates are higher in smaller cars and in foreign countries in which small cars are more prevalent than in the United States.

Automobile safety is a very complicated subject. For present purposes, only part of the automotive safety program is relevant—that for urban areas. The essential question for urban transportation analysts is whether the potential costs in reduced safety from greater use of small cars are likely to outweigh the many potential benefits. And if there is a safety problem connected to the use of small cars, can it be identified and corrected?

Greater use of small cars has safety implications in rural as well as in urban areas. A cursory look at traffic statistics reveals, in fact, that deaths from automobile collisions are more a rural than an urban phenomenon. On the other hand, small cars are used for a higher percentage of travel in urban than in rural areas, since the advantages of a small car are greater in cities and the disadvantages fewer. As shown in Table 13.1, 30 percent of urban residents own compact and subcompact vehicles as compared with 22 percent of rural residents. In addition, the urban share of total vehicle-miles of automobile travel has been growing over the years. In the United States in the 1970s, more than half of total car use took place in urban areas;[1] it is anticipated that urban vehicle-mileage may account for as much as two thirds of total automobile travel in the United States by the late 1980s.

The number of two-car families in the United States also continues to grow,[2] accompanied by a tendency for families to own one large and one small vehicle. This allows for more efficient use of vehicles, as the smaller vehicle, which is less expensive to operate, may be used for the majority of trips (such as one-person worktrips or shoppingtrips), while the larger vehicle may be reserved for those occasions, such as family outings, where there is a need for greater passenger capacity. Thus, the increase in number of multiple-car families should reinforce the tendency toward more intense utilization of small cars in urban

TABLE 13.1.   Motor vehicle ownership by class and by location of residence, 1975.

	Metropolitan areas[a]		Nonmetropolitan areas[a] (percent)	Percent of total motor vehicles
	Central cities (percent)	Suburban rings (percent)		
Subcompact	11.0	11.8	7.2	10.2
Compact	19.2	19.2	14.9	17.9
Intermediate	20.8	18.3	19.0	19.1
Standard	33.6	30.7	32.0	31.8
Luxury	5.5	5.8	4.0	5.2
Pickup truck	6.8	9.9	19.0	12.0
Passenger van	1.8	2.8	1.0	2.0
Motor home	0.2	0.2	0.3	0.2
Other[b]	1.0	1.2	2.3	1.5
Total motor vehicles	24.0	45.0	31.0	100.0

Source: From a survey of 3,149 households reported in Washington Center for Metropolitan Studies, Lifestyles and Household Energy Use: 1975 National Survey (Washington, D.C.: Center for Metropolitan Studies, 1975).

[a] Locational definitions follow those of the U.S. Bureau of the Census for standard metropolitan statistical areas.

[b] Not a passenger car, pickup truck, passenger van, or motor home.

areas. It is therefore significant that not only are the advantages of expanded use of smaller automobiles—reduced energy consumption, congestion, air pollution, and land-use requirements—greater in cities, but, as will be shown below, the costs of reducing safety disadvantages may well be less in an urban than in a rural setting.

THE AUTOMOBILE SAFETY PROBLEM IN GENERAL

The U.S. traffic safety record is as good as any in the world and is improving steadily (see Table 13.2 for a comparison of automobile fatality rates in different nations). The fact that the American and Canadian safety records are far superior to those in most European countries, combined with the fact that large cars are used to a much greater extent in both the United States and Canada, might suggest that the North American advantage in traffic safety derives from the greater use of large cars.

Such a conclusion, though, would be premature. For instance, the

TABLE 13.2. Traffic fatality rates in selected countries.

	Traffic fatalities[a] per 100 million vehicle-miles					
Country	1969	1971	1973	1974	1975	1976
Australia	7.7	7.2	6.6	6.0	5.9	5.2
Belgium	19.8	19.9	12.6	12.0	10.2	10.4
Canada	7.3	6.7	6.7	6.0	5.6	4.7
Finland	11.9	11.2	12.3	9.9	9.3	8.1
France	16.3	15.8	13.7	10.8	10.1	10.0
Germany	12.5	12.3	9.9	8.8	8.4	8.0
Italy	13.9	10.0	8.8	8.5	7.8	7.2
Japan	18.3	13.9	11.2	9.1	8.0	6.7
Netherlands	12.4	10.9	9.1	7.9	6.9	7.2
Norway	8.2	8.3	7.1	6.2	6.1	5.1
United Kingdom	6.4	5.9	5.2	4.9	4.5	4.4
United States	5.2	4.6	4.2	3.6	3.5	3.3

Source: Motor Vehicle Manufacturers Association, *Motor Vehicle Facts and Figures, 1979* (Detroit: Motor Vehicle Manufacturers Association, 1979), p. 64. Data on traffic deaths and travel vary significantly for the different countries. Every effort has been made to put the fatality rates for all countries on a comparable basis.
[a] Rate based upon deaths occurring within one year after the accident.

worst national fatality rate in Europe consistently belongs to Belgium, which is generally deemed to have an automobile mix more like that in the United States than almost any other European nation. Belgium is also largely urbanized, so that the high Belgian traffic fatality rate also runs counter to the U.S. experience that urbanized regions seem to have lower traffic death rates than more rural areas. Indeed, Sweden, which is more rural than most European countries, has one of the lowest automobile fatality rates in Europe, generally matched only by Britain and Norway.

What these international comparisons suggest is that automobile safety is influenced by many considerations. For example, driver training and experience, highway design standards, traffic law enforcement (especially as it relates to alcohol consumption), and other such factors may be considerably more important than automobile size in explaining geographic differences in traffic fatality rates. Good empirical insights into automobile safety problems therefore are likely to be achieved only by adopting a more focused approach, concentrating on intranational comparisons wherein large cultural differences are eliminated or reasonably well controlled.

Focusing on U.S. traffic safety data from the mid-1960s on, the death toll from traffic accidents in the United States has hovered in a range between 45,000 and 55,000 per year. This rough stability in the overall figure has been achieved by a steady decline in the death rate (for example, the number of deaths per 100 million vehicle-miles of travel or per 10,000 vehicles registered), offsetting a corresponding steady increase in the number of vehicles and vehicle-miles of travel. These broad trends, as well as much of the underlying detail, are shown in Table 13.3.

The overall fatality rate (per 100 million vehicle-miles) is almost twice as high, however, in rural as in urban areas. The mix of accidents is also dissimilar in urban and rural sectors, as shown in Table 13.4. In particular, pedestrian and bicycle injuries occur more commonly in urban than in rural areas, while collisions between motor vehicles resulting in fatalities are much more a rural phenomenon. Since the mid-1960s, for example, there have been roughly 15,000–18,000 traffic fatalities per year in urban areas as opposed to 30,000–37,000 per year in rural areas. Of the 15,000–18,000 yearly urban traffic fatalities, about 40 percent involve pedestrians and bicycles, accidents that would not be increased by the substitution of small for large automobiles, and even might be alleviated by such a substitution. Of the remaining 10,000 or so traffic fatalities per year occurring in urban areas, approximately 60 percent, or 5,000–6,000, would seem to involve collisions between motor vehicles, while the remainder mainly result from collisions between an automobile and a fixed object or from running off the road (included under noncollisions in Tables 13.3 and 13.4). There is also some evidence (see Table 13.5) that urban traffic fatality rates are somewhat inversely related to the size of a metropolitan area. But for nonfatal injuries, as contrasted with fatalities, the urban/rural relationship reverses somewhat. In 1977, 60 percent of the nonfatal injuries occurred in urban areas; moreover, the bulk of these occurred in multiple-car collisions.

In sum, of the approximately 50,000 annual traffic fatalities that occur in the United States, a bit over 10 percent would likely be exacerbated by greater use of small cars in urban areas. On the other hand, 12–13 percent of traffic fatalities—mainly those resulting from accidents in which pedestrians and cycle riders in urban areas were involved—*might* be helped by such a substitution. The overall safety problem that might arise from greater use of small cars in urban areas is thus bounded by the facts that a bit less than one third of total traffic fatalities are the result of urban automobile use, and that there are fewer multiple-car collisions—the type of accident most likely to be made worse by greater use of small cars—in urban areas.

TABLE 13.3. Traffic fatality rate by cause.

| | | | | | | Deaths from collision with: | | | | | | Death rates | | |
Year	Total deaths[a]	Pedes- trians	Other motor vehicles	Rail- road trains	Street- cars	Pedal- cycles	Animals, animal- drawn vehicles	Fixed objects[b]	Deaths from non- collision accidents[c]	Per 10,000 motor vehicles	Per million vehicle- miles	Per 100,000 popu- lation
1978	51,500	9,300	22,900	1,100	*	1,000	100	3,500	13,600	3.35	3.33	23.6
1977	49,510	9,100	21,200	902	3	1,100	100	3,400	13,700	3.33	3.35	22.9
1976	47,038	8,600	20,100	1,033	2	1,000	100	3,200	13,000	3.28	3.33	21.9
1975	45,853	8,400	19,550	979	1	1,000	100	3,130	12,700	3.33	3.45	21.5
1974	46,402	8,500	19,700	1,209	1	1,000	100	3,100	12,300	3.44	3.59	22.0
1973	55,511	10,200	23,600	1,194	2	1,000	100	3,300	15,600	4.28	4.24	26.5
1972	56,278	10,300	23,900	1,260	2	1,000	100	3,900	15,800	4.60	4.43	27.0
1971	54,381	9,900	23,100	1,378	2	800	100	3,800	15,300	4.68	4.57	26.4
1970	54,633	9,900	23,200	1,459	3	780	100	3,800	15,400	4.92	4.88	26.8
1969	55,791	10,100	23,700	1,495	2	800	100	3,900	15,700	5.19	5.21	27.7
1968	54,862	9,900	22,400	1,570	4	790	100	2,700	17,400	5.32	5.40	27.5
1967	52,924	9,400	22,000	1,620	3	750	100	2,350	16,700	5.35	5.50	26.8
1966	53,041	9,400	22,200	1,800	2	740	100	2,500	16,300	5.53	5.70	27.1
1965	49,163	8,900	20,800	1,556	5	680	120	2,200	14,900	5.36	5.54	25.4
1964	47,700	9,000	19,600	1,580	5	710	100	2,100	14,600	5.46	5.63	25.0

TABLE 13.3. (*Cont.*)

| Year | Total deaths[a] | Deaths from collision with: | | | | | | Fixed objects[b] | Deaths from non-collision accidents[c] | Death rates | | |
		Pedestrians	Other motor vehicles	Railroad trains	Streetcars	Pedalcycles	Animals/animal-drawn vehicles			Per 10,000 motor vehicles	Per million vehicle-miles	Per 100,000 population
1963	43,564	8,200	17,600	1,385	10	580	80	1,900	13,800	5.22	5.41	23.1
1962	40,804	7,900	16,400	1,245	3	500	90	1,750	12,900	5.12	5.32	22.0
1961	38,091	7,650	14,700	1,267	5	490	80	1,700	12,200	4.98	5.16	20.8
1960	38,137	7,850	14,800	1,368	5	460	80	1,700	11,900	5.12	5.31	21.2
1959	37,910	7,850	14,900	1,202	6	480	70	1,600	11,800	5.26	5.41	21.5
1958	36,981	7,650	14,200	1,316	9	450	80	1,650	11,600	5.37	5.56	21.3
1957	38,702	7,850	15,400	1,376	13	460	80	1,700	11,800	5.73	5.98	22.7
1956	39,628	7,900	15,200	1,377	11	440	100	1,600	13,000	6.07	6.28	23.7
1955	38,426	8,200	14,500	1,490	15	410	90	1,600	12,100	6.12	6.34	23.4
1954	33,586	8,000	12,800	1,269	28	380	90	1,500	11,500	6.07	6.33	22.1
1953	37,955	8,750	13,400	1,506	26	420	120	1,500	12,200	6.74	6.97	24.0
1952	37,794	8,900	13,500	1,429	32	430	130	1,450	11,900	7.10	7.36	24.3
1951	36,996	9,150	13,100	1,573	46	390	100	1,400	11,200	7.13	7.53	24.1
1950	34,763	9,000	11,650	1,541	89	440	120	1,300	10,600	7.07	7.59	23.0
1949	31,701	8,800	10,500	1,452	56	550	140	1,100	9,100	7.09	7.47	21.3

1948	32,259	9,950	10,200	1,474	83	500	100	1,000	8,950	7.85	8.11	22.1
1947	32,697	10,450	9,900	1,736	102	550	150	1,000	8,800	8.64	8.82	22.8
1946	33,411	11,600	9,400	1,703	174	540	130	950	8,900	9.72	9.80	23.9
1945	28,076	11,000	7,150	1,703	163	500	130	800	6,600	9.05	11.22	21.2
1944	24,282	9,900	5,700	1,663	175	400	140	700	5,600	7.97	11.42	18.3
1943	23,823	9,900	5,300	1,448	171	450	160	700	5,690	7.71	11.44	17.8
1942	28,309	10,650	7,300	1,754	124	650	240	850	6,740	8.58	10.55	21.1
1941	39,969	13,550	12,500	1,840	118	910	250	1,350	9,450	11.45	11.98	30.0
1940	34,501	12,700	10,100	1,707	132	750	210	1,100	7,800	10.63	11.42	26.1
1939	32,386	12,400	8,700	1,330	150	710	200	1,000	7,900	10.44	11.35	24.7
1938	32,582	12,850	8,900	1,490	165	720	170	940	7,350	10.93	12.02	25.1
1933–37[d]	36,313	14,480	8,630	1,600	300	540	270	1,030	9,460	13.50	15.61	28.5
1928–32[d]	31,050	12,300	5,700	1,850	450	*	*	700	9,100	12.10	15.60	25.2
1923–27[d]	21,800	*	*	1,200	480	*	*	*	*	11.10	18.20	18.7
1918–22[d]	12,700	*	*	*	*	*	*	*	*	13.90	*	11.9
1913–17[d]	6,800	*	*	*	*	*	*	*	*	23.80	*	6.8

Source: National Safety Council, *Accident Facts, 1979* (Chicago: National Safety Council, 1979).

[a] Totals may not quite equal the sum of the various types, because the estimates were generally made only to the nearest 10 deaths or to the nearest 50 deaths for certain types.

[b] Includes deaths from collisions with fixed objects such as walls and abutments, where the collision occurred while all wheels of the vehicle were still on the road.

[c] Classification is according to first injury- or damage-producing agent.

[d] Average for years shown.

* Data not available.

TABLE 13.4. Motor vehicle deaths and injuries by type of accident, 1977.

Type of accident	Deaths			Nonfatal injuries		
	Total	Urban	Rural	Total	Urban	Rural
Total	49,500	17,700	31,800	1,900,000	1,140,000	760,000
Collision with:						
Pedestrian	9,100	6,200	2,900	100,000	85,000	15,000
Other motor vehicle	21,200	6,400	14,800	1,360,000	870,000	490,000
Railroad train	900	400	500	4,000	3,000	1,000
Pedal-cycle	1,100	600	500	50,000	40,000	10,000
Animal or animal-drawn vehicle	100	*	100	6,000	2,000	4,000
Fixed object	3,400	1,900	1,500	80,000	50,000	30,000
Noncollision	13,700	2,200	11,500	300,000	90,000	210,000

Source: National Safety Council, *Accident Facts, 1978* (Chicago: National Safety Council, 1978), p. 45.
* Less than five.

THE SMALL-CAR SAFETY PROBLEM

When multiple-vehicle collisions occur, the chance of serious injury or death increases the lower the weight of the cars involved. The crash injury rate (defined as the ratio of injuries to crashes) is therefore higher when small cars are involved in an accident than when larger cars collide. Thus, unless small cars have a lower accident involvement rate (the ratio of the number of accidents to some exposure measure, such as registered vehicles or vehicle-miles), serious injuries or deaths resulting from multiple-car collisions will increase as the proportion of small cars in the automobile fleet grows.

Table 13.6 summarizes the effects of car size on serious injury rates in multiple-car collisions. This matrix is based on New York State accident data for the years 1969 through 1971, adjusted for differences in expected use of seat belts by people riding in vehicles of different weight.[3] On the basis of these data, it appears that persons in an accident involving a very large and a very small car have 60–80 percent higher serious injury rates than persons in accidents involving two large cars. The rate of serious injury for large-car occupants goes down when a large car hits a small car rather than another large car, but this safety gain is more than offset by higher injury rates for the occupants

TABLE 13.5. Motor vehicle accidents, injuries, and deaths by size of urban areas and by type of rural road, 1977.

Place	Fatal accidents	Injury accidents	Property-damage accidents	Injuries	Deaths Number	Deaths Rate[a]
Total	43,500	1,300,000	16,300,000	1,900,000	49,500	22.9
Urban area with populations of:						
Over 1,000,000	1,600	160,000	1,800,000	210,000	1,800	10.2
250,000–1,000,000	2,600	160,000	2,500,000	220,000	2,800	10.9
100,000–250,000	2,400	130,000	1,900,000	170,000	2,600	16.5
50,000–100,000	2,200	140,000	1,900,000	180,000	2,400	13.1
10,000–50,000	4,100	170,000	2,400,000	210,000	4,500	10.4
Under 10,000	3,300	110,000	1,300,000	150,000	3,600	15.6
Total urban area	16,200	870,000	11,800,000	1,140,000	17,700	10.9
Rural area:						
State roads	14,500	230,000	2,440,000	430,000	17,200	*
County roads	8,200	130,000	1,340,000	200,000	9,200	*
Controlled-access roads	2,800	40,000	280,000	70,000	3,300	*
Other	1,800	30,000	440,000	60,000	2,100	*
Total rural area	27,300	430,000	4,500,000	760,000	31,800	*

Source: National Safety Council, Accident Facts, 1978 (Chicago: National Safety Council, 1978), p. 45.
[a] Deaths per 100,000 population.
* Not applicable.

TABLE 13.6. Serious injury rates in two-car crashes in New York State (1969–71) adjusted for differences in expected safety belt use by different vehicle weight classes.[a]

Weight class of vehicle 2	Rate	Weight class of vehicle 1				
		1 (1,000– 1,999 lbs.)	2 (2,000– 2,749 lbs.)	3 (2,750– 3,249 lbs.)	4 (3,250– 3,999 lbs.)	5 (4,000– 5,499 lbs.)
1 (1,000– 1,999 lbs.)	Vehicle 1 rate	9.7				
	Vehicle 2 rate	9.7				
	Combined rate	9.7				
2 (2,000– 2,749 lbs.)	Vehicle 1 rate	11.5	7.1			
	Vehicle 2 rate	6.0	7.1			
	Combined rate	8.8	7.1			
3 (2,750– 3,249 lbs.)	Vehicle 1 rate	12.6	7.8	6.1		
	Vehicle 2 rate	4.7	5.6	6.1		
	Combined rate	8.7	6.7	6.1		
4 (3,250– 3,999 lbs.)	Vehicle 1 rate	13.8	8.5	6.6	5.2	
	Vehicle 2 rate	3.7	4.3	4.7	5.2	
	Combined rate	8.8	6.4	5.7	5.2	
5 (4,000– 5,499 lbs.)	Vehicle 1 rate	15.5	9.6	7.5	5.8	4.2
	Vehicle 2 rate	2.6	3.1	3.4	3.7	4.2
	Combined rate	9.1	6.4	5.5	4.8	4.2

Source: New York State Department of Motor Vehicles, An Analysis of Accidents in New York State by Make of Vehicle, report prepared for the U.S. Department of Transportation, National Highway Traffic Safety Administration, June 1972.
[a] Rates are per 100 million vehicle-miles.

of the small car. If two 3,500-pound cars are involved in an accident, for example, the rate of serious injury for occupants of each vehicle is 5.2 per 100 million vehicle-miles, for a combined overall average of 5.2. But if the same 3,500-pound car collides with a car weighing less than 2,000 pounds, the combined rate of injury increases to 8.8, reflecting a rate of only 3.7 for the occupants of the heavier car but 13.8 for occupants of the lighter car. Accidents involving two small cars are about as dangerous as accidents involving a small and a large car, although the risk is more evenly distributed among the occupants of the two vehicles. A transition from a large-car to a small-car fleet, therefore, will increase the possibility of injury in multiple-car collisions because the probability of a small car colliding with another small car will increase and because the probability of a small car colliding with a large car will be augmented during the change. The probability calculations in Table 13.7 demonstrate this point. For example, if the initial fleet mixture is, say, 20 percent small cars, 70 percent large cars, and 10 percent trucks (and assuming that vehicles of different size have the same accident involvement rates), 46 percent of all accidents will involve cars in a colli-

TABLE 13.7. Hypothetical changes in the composition of two-vehicle accidents with increasing small-car use.[a]

	Large cars predominate	Equal mix of large and small cars	Small cars predominate
Percent of motor vehicles on road by size:			
Small car	20.0	45.0	70.0
Large car	70.0	45.0	20.0
Truck	10.0	10.0	10.0
Percent of two-vehicle accidents involving:			
Car with larger car or truck	46.0	58.50	46.0
Small car with small car	4.0	20.25	49.0
Subtotal	50.0	78.75	95.0
Large car with large car	49.0	20.25	4.0
Truck with truck	1.0	1.00	1.0
Subtotal	50.0	21.25	5.0
Total	100.0	100.00	100.0

Source: Compiled by the authors.

[a] These calculations assume that the probability of a vehicle's being involved in a two-vehicle collision is independent of vehicle size. With 20 percent small cars, 70 percent large cars, and 10 percent trucks, for example, the proportion of automobile collisions involving a car and a larger car or truck equals $(0.2)(0.7) + (0.7)(0.2) + (0.2)(0.1) + (0.2)(0.1) + (0.1)(0.7) + (0.7)(0.1) = 0.46$.

sion with a larger car or a truck. This would hold true if the automobile mix were reversed (that is, if there were 70 percent small cars, 20 percent large cars, and 10 percent trucks). On the other hand, at an intermediate stage—say, at the point where there were 45 percent small cars and 45 percent large cars—58.5 percent of all accidents would involve collisions between a small car and a larger car or truck. As the proportion of small cars increases, moreover, the proportion of accidents involving two small vehicles increases rapidly. Thus, the percent of risky accidents (involving combinations of small and large vehicles or two small vehicles) increases steadily from 50 to 95 percent of all two-vehicle collisions as the percent of small cars in the fleet increases from 20 to 70 percent.

In contrast with the adverse evidence on injury rates in small cars when multiple-car collisions occur, there is some evidence that small cars are as safe, and possibly safer, than large cars during single-car crashes (a car hitting a fixed obstacle, running off the road, rolling over, and so on). A few studies have examined the vehicle weight/personal injury relationship and have found that, in the words of one such analyst, "there was not a statistically significant association between car weight and driver injury in single-car crashes."[4] A study of 221,000 personal injury accidents in France in 1969 showed that in single-vehicle accidents, the death rate in the lightest and "least speedy" cars was half that in the speediest cars.[5] Although some researchers believe that when a single car collides with a fixed object the passengers in a lighter car have a higher injury rate, the evidence is not overwhelmingly convincing. Most researchers agree that injury rates during one-car "off-the-road" accidents do not vary with vehicle weight or size.[6] In sum, there is no strong evidence that injury rates vary much by vehicle weight in single-vehicle crashes.

Small cars also do not appear to have a significantly higher accident involvement rate than large cars, although the evidence is somewhat conflicting. Some researchers have reported higher accident rates for small cars,[7] while others have shown small cars to have accident rates that were the same as or lower than those of larger vehicles.[8] Much of the difference in findings is attributable to lack of controls on other variables that might be expected to influence accident rates (for example, smaller vehicles are more often driven by younger, less experienced drivers).

Only one study of accident rates has controlled reasonably well for these other variables. This study was based on 8,911 questionnaires returned from a mailing to 28,209 California drivers and included data on number of accidents, estimated driving mileage, and relevant personal and vehicle characteristics. The major conclusions were that "there is no systematic relationship between vehicle size and frequency of accident involvement, when the known effects of age and quantitative exposure to risk are controlled for. Differences in driver characteristics (notably age) and vehicle usage as a function of vehicle make appear to invalidate apparent differences in accident rates among makes."[9] Unfortunately, even this study cannot be considered definitive, due to the low response rate, the lack of questionnaire validation, and the possible bias inherent in the self-reporting nature of the survey.

Perhaps the best summary of the accident involvement issue was provided by a member of the National Highway Traffic Safety Administration who noted that the question has not been "rigorously resolved." He speculated, however, that if all the significant variables (such as driver ages and characteristics, climate and geography, traffic law enforcement, and accident exposure) could be brought under control, any differences in accident rates between cars of different sizes would probably be small.[10]

Greater use of small cars in urban areas may reduce the number of deaths from automobile collisions with pedestrians and bicycle riders. Such deaths number roughly 11,000 per year, 65–70 percent of which take place in urban areas. Thus, while the number of fatalities in multiple-car collisions involving small cars may be greater, this may be offset by a reduction in the number of fatalities in accidents in which small cars hit pedestrians or bicycles. There is no conclusive data on the subject, however, so that the overall impact of increased use of small cars on traffic fatalities is conjectural.

There is some evidence, though, that pickups and vans are responsible for a disproportionately high percentage of pedestrian deaths.[11] In general, greater use of trucks and vans is considered to have had almost as much, if not more, of an adverse effect on recent U.S. traffic safety statistics as greater use of small cars.[12] Specifically, full-sized passenger cars have occupant fatality rates 50 percent lower than those of light trucks and 20 percent lower than those of vans, so that a shift from full-sized cars to trucks and vans has increased accident exposure.[13]

Any additional hazard inherent in small-car use may also be offset by more cautious driving or by greater use of seat belts. A considerable body of evidence and theory suggests that people choose a certain risk level in determining their driving habits.[14] Individuals stipulating and adopting a target risk for themselves also provides an alternative explanation for some of the adverse safety statistics associated with certain classes of vehicles, such as motorcycles, convertibles, sports cars, or two-door subcompacts; specifically, such a hypothesis would suggest that people driving or using such relatively risky vehicles do so knowledgeably and in the expectation of running a somewhat greater risk.

Although many owners of small cars, especially sports cars, may have been traditionally more willing to accept risks, if and as fuel prices or other forces induce a shift from large to small cars an increasing proportion of small-car users may try to compensate for any added risk by adopting more careful driving habits and other strategies. Some evidence that this has been the case is provided by the data on safety belt use by vehicle size in Table 13.8: drivers of subcompact and compact vehicles show significantly higher rates of safety belt use than drivers of larger cars. Moreover, the differences in safety belt use between subcompact and larger-car owners has increased in recent years,

TABLE 13.8. Survey of proportion of automobile occupants wearing safety belts.[a]

Dates	Automobile size	Wheelbase (inches)	Lap/shoulder belt (%)	Lap belt only (%)	Total (%)	Number of observations
9/77–6/78	Subcompacts	101	18.4	1.1	19.5	7,755
	Compacts	101–111	11.2	1.4	12.6	6,414
	Intermediate	111–120	9.1	1.2	10.3	10,266
	Full-sized	120	8.6	1.1	9.7	3,046
1964–77	Subcompacts	101	15.9	2.9	18.8	17,600
	Compacts	101–111	9.7	5.2	14.9	14,435
	Intermediate	111–120	6.5	4.8	11.3	10,887
	Full-sized	120	4.4	6.8	11.2	13,234

Source: Opinion Research, Inc., *Safety Belt Usage—Survey of Cars in the Traffic Population* (interim report), prepared for National Highway Traffic Safety Administration, U.S. Department of Transportation, December 1978.

[a] Survey sampled automobile occupants in traffic in and around 19 U.S. cities on all types of roads in urban, suburban, and rural areas.

perhaps in large measure because the small cars are now being used by a larger, more representative, and more risk-averse segment of the population.

In sum, if the small-car proportion of the total automobile fleet rises, so will the probability of more serious accidents,[15] particularly those involving multiple-car collisions between small cars and larger cars or trucks and small cars with other small cars. It should be stressed, however, that the sensitive portion of the total traffic fatality toll should be limited to multiple-car collisions, or, possibly, single-car collisions with fixed objects. At current annual rates, this would mean that about 15,000–25,000 fatalities nationwide might be involved (that is, sensitive to these influences) of which about 6,000–8,000 would be in urban areas. However, any rise in fatality exposure in multiple-car accidents from greater use of small cars would almost surely be offset to some extent by a reduction in pedestrian and bicycle deaths and increased caution (such as greater use of safety belts) among small-car users.

SOLUTIONS

Several measures can be taken to compensate for any increased traffic hazards created by greater use of small cars. Safety experts have a long list of policy actions that they generally recommend to reduce automobile fatalities and injuries. One such listing, ranked according to cost effectiveness, is shown in Table 13.9.

TABLE 13.9. Ranking of countermeasures to reduce automobile fatalities by decreasing cost-effectiveness in present-value dollars per total fatalities forestalled, 10-year total.

Countermeasure	Fatalities forestalled	Cost (millions of dollars)	Dollars per fatality forestalled
1. Mandatory safety belt usage	72,000	45.0	625
2. Roadway lighting	759	7.1	9,600
3. Driver-improvement schools for young offenders	1,980	36.3	18,400
4. Highway construction and maintenance practices	459	9.2	20,000
5. Upgrade bicycle and pedestrian safety curriculum offerings	649	13.2	20,400
6. Nationwide 55 mph speed limit	31,000	676.0	21,200
7. Driver-improvement schools	2,470	53.0	21,400
8. Regulatory and warning signs	3,670	125.0	34,000
9. Guardrail	3,160	108.0	34,100
10. Pedestrian safety information and education	490	18.0	36,800
11. Skid resistance	3,740	158.0	42,200
12. Bridge rails and parapets	1,520	69.8	46,000
13. Wrong-way entry avoidance techniques	779	38.5	49,400
14. Motorcycle rider safety helmets	1,150	61.2	53,300
15. Motorcycle lights on practice	65	5.2	80,600
16. Breakaway sign and lighting supports	3,250	378.0	116,000
17. Impact-absorbing roadside safety devices	6,780	833.0	123,000
18. Selective traffic enforcement	7,560	1,010.0	133,000
19. Combined emergency medical countermeasures	26,700	4,300.0	161,000
20. Combined alcohol safety action countermeasures	13,000	2,130.0	164,000
21. Citizen assistance of crash victims	3,750	784.0	209,000
22. Median barriers	529	121.0	228,000
23. Pedestrian and bicycle visibility enhancement	1,440	332.0	230,000
24. Tire and braking system safety critical inspection—selective	4,590	1,150.0	251,000
25. Clear roadside recovery area	533	151.0	284,000
26. Upgrade education and training for beginning drivers	3,050	1,170.0	385,000

Source: Energy Resources Council, *The Report by the Federal Task Force on Motor Vehicle Goals Beyond 1980*, vol. 2, draft report, Washington, D.C., September 1978, pp. 9–15.

This table makes it obvious why safety experts are almost unanimous in recommending increased use of safety belts as a major means of reducing automobile injuries and fatalities. Unfortunately, only 10–20 percent of automobile occupants apparently wear safety belts in the United States today. Even worse, some studies indicate that belt usage has been declining, despite the fact that the chance of a serious injury in a crash is about 40 percent lower for persons who wear a lap belt than for those who are unbelted. Belts that go around the shoulders as well as over the lap further improve the chances of escaping serious injury, although no definitive studies have been done thus far to estimate just what this additional improvement might be.[16]

As already noted, greater use of belts in small cars helps close the safety gap between small and large cars. It is not enough by itself, however, to close that gap totally. It has been estimated that the safety belt usage rate in small cars would have to rise from around an existing 20 percent rate to somewhere between 40 and 65 percent in order to offset the effect of a drop in average vehicle weight of 1,500 pounds.[17] Thus, the established rate of seat belt usage by small-car occupants would have to double or even triple in order to fully compensate for their increased exposure to fatalities and injury in multiple-car collisions.

A gain in seat belt use of this magnitude may eventually be brought about through federal government regulations, although past efforts to require belt use are not encouraging. Starting with the 1974 model year the National Highway Traffic Safety Administration (NHTSA) required that automobiles be equipped with ignition interlock systems so that the car would not start unless the seat belt were buckled, but motorists found these devices so inconvenient that the interlocks were frequently disconnected, and Congress ordered the agency to rescind the regulation in 1976. NHTSA then proposed that new cars be equipped with passive restraint systems—either automatic seat belts or air bags—starting with model years 1982 for large, 1983 for medium-sized, and 1984 for small cars. As the deadline approached, however, NHTSA was under pressure to delay the requirement and reverse the order in which restraints are introduced into large and small cars. If passive restraints are required, moreover, auto makers are more likely to use automatic belts than airbags since the latter are substantially less expensive. Automatic belts must be detachable for safety reasons, however, and thus many motorists may decide not to use them.

Another measure that would improve small-car safety would be to lower the "breakaway" point for highway signs, lighting supports, utility poles, and so forth. Even though, as noted above, some evidence suggests that small cars are not less safe, possibly even safer, than large cars when single-car crashes with fixed objects are involved, this may be primarily due to smaller cars not having as high an incidence of such involvements. Highway signs and posts, however, may not break away "adequately when struck by very light (e.g., subcompact) cars."[18] There is also some indication that light cars tend to overturn more often when they collide with concrete median barriers or with similar obstructions. As a result, the Federal Highway Administration is reexamining its highway safety standards for highway supports, poles, and barrier systems. The data presented in Table 13.9 suggest that these corrective actions are likely to be fairly expensive, compared with other measures (but the cost effectiveness might be improved if the number of small cars increases).

Another promising approach to improving the safety of small cars would be to reconsider vehicle design characteristics, not only for small cars but for large cars as well. When collisions occur, the risk to motor vehicle occupants is primarily a function of the weight, size, structural strength and configuration, and velocity of the vehicles (or objects) involved. "Crash worthiness" is a term used to describe the relative ability of a vehicle's passenger compartment to remain undeformed when a crash occurs. "Crush distance" is a measure of the amount of force a vehicle can absorb before the passenger compartment is penetrated and passengers are exposed to injury. If a small car collides with a larger vehicle, not only must it absorb more force, but it typically has less distance to crush before the passenger compartment is deformed. Furthermore, because of its limited crush space, the small car is less able to absorb the impact of another small car. Because they are heavier and therefore have more momentum, larger vehicles are said to be more "aggressive" in collisions.

One way to improve safety would be to achieve a better balance between aggressiveness and crash worthiness in the car fleet. According to a study performed by the Insurance Institute for Highway Safety, "what are needed are 'relatively sizeable but not heavy vehicles.' In particular, it would obviously be desirable from a safety standpoint if vehicle weight can be reduced without substantially reducing a vehicle's size. By using such an approach occupants could be afforded greater crash protection without adding to the kinetic energy that must be absorbed or dissipated in crashes."[19]

To attain a better balance in the car fleet, larger vehicles with a "longer crushing distance" could be made less aggressive by redesigning them so that "in front [they have] a structure enabling [them] to absorb energy . . . with an engine as far back as possible in the front part of the vehicle."[20] Smaller vehicles could be made more aggressive with "a high crushing effort, the peak of which should be as forward as possible, the lighter the vehicle."[21]

One private company working under government contract has developed a so-called research safety vehicle (RSV) that is capable of withstanding front impacts of 45–50 mph, side impacts of 40–45 mph, and rear impacts of 45–50 mph while providing occupant protection. This RSV weighs 2,673 pounds, and by conventional definition would be classified as a compact car. The additional safety features built into this car cost $729 (in 1977 dollars) of which $467 was for interior protection systems and the remainder mostly for structural modifications to better withstand frontal and side collisions.

Another relatively simple policy that would greatly alleviate any small-car safety problem would be to exclude use of the *very smallest* of the small cars. A reexamination of the data in Table 13.6 suggests that serious injury rates are substantially higher for cars just under one ton than for cars just above that weight. And cars just above one ton in weight offer almost as many benefits in terms of alleviating congestion, reducing energy consumption, and minimizing air pollution as do vehicles just under that weight. A policy, therefore, that encourages greater use of small cars just larger than the smallest subcompact range might yield most of the benefits derivable from small cars while keeping safety risks at a tolerable level.

In sum, there are many potential means of alleviating any additional safety problems that might be created by greater use of small cars. But some of these solutions might be quite costly. Unfortunately, those that are the least costly—particularly the greater use of seat belts—are likely to be the most difficult to achieve from a political or psychological standpoint. Perhaps the most relevant question, as suggested, is the extent to which the American public is actually motivated to reduce traffic fatalities and risks.

SUMMARY

All else being equal, greater use of small cars should somewhat intensify the traffic safety problem. However, it also seems that the extent of any such intensification can be easily overestimated or exaggerated, especially when drawing inferences mainly from laboratory experiments with car collisions. In automobile safety, laboratory evidence may not always provide a clear indicator of the underlying causes of accident rates, since, among other considerations, the human actors involved can modify results by adapting their behavior to fit different circumstances and risk exposures.[22]

Any traffic safety problems created in urban areas by greater use of small cars are thus likely to be at least somewhat attenuated by offsetting developments. To start, the kinds of serious traffic accidents that would be aggravated by greater use of small cars (multiple-car collisions and collisions of single cars with fixed objects) are more a rural than an urban phenomenon (by roughly a two-to-one margin). On the other hand, the classes of accidents (such as pedestrian and bicycle fatalities) most likely to be attenuated by greater use of small cars are a decidedly urban phenomenon (again by roughly a two-to-one margin). It is at least conceivable that these countervailing effects could simply balance one another, particularly if measured in terms of fatalities (as opposed to injuries). This does not mean, however, that the total effect of the growing use of small cars on overall traffic safety statistics is likely to net out to zero, because rural areas will almost surely be negatively affected.

It is not difficult, moreover, to identify policies that could offset any adverse effect generated by greater use of small cars. In particular, greater use of automobile seat belts would have such an effect. Indeed, if somehow the American public could be induced always to use seat belts when in automobiles, the safety gains would well outweigh any increased danger inherent in greater use of small cars.

It is also easy to identify automobile design modifications and size limitations that could alleviate small-car safety problems. Among the possibilities would be improving the crashworthiness of small cars to reduce the chances of serious accidents or fatalities in multiple-car collisions—particularly when two small cars crash, since the number of such accidents will increase with the greater use of small cars. Another relatively simple policy that might be pursued is limiting the use of the very smallest of the small cars, since the very smallest vehicles are significantly more dangerous and offer only minimal gains in fuel economy, pollution reduction, or other goals.

In general, the automobile safety problem is obviously very complex and multifaceted. The striking feature of the problem, in fact, as dramatically illustrated by international comparisons of traffic safety statistics, is the extent to which many variables other than car size are clearly at work. Highway design, driver experience and training, and a host of other variables are at least as influential as car size in determining automobile safety.

PART IV
CONCLUSION

14

The Role of
Public Policy

BASIC POLICY RECOMMENDATIONS

The simplistic notion of the early post–World War II years that the public responsibility for urban transportation was mainly to relieve congestion, where and when it appeared, has long since almost disappeared. The land use and aesthetics of urban areas are now also to be improved, or at least not too much demeaned, by transportation betterments and changes. In addition, energy consumption is to be reduced, urban air quality improved, and the mobility of the transportation disadvantaged enhanced.

Compromising and balancing these various and often conflicting policy goals is not easy. The difficulties are further compounded because changes in transportation not only interact with one another in a complex fashion but also affect the attainment of other social and economic policy goals. As a consequence, predicting the impact of any single policy initiative can be a very complicated undertaking. Policy recommendations made under such circumstances are almost necessarily undertaken with some uncertainty, even temerity.

At least one certainty, however, does emerge: the private automobile, in which 85–90 percent of all urban passenger trips in the United States were made in the 1960s and 1970s, will continue to be the principal urban transportation mode—at least for the remainder of the twentieth century. Indeed, under late-twentieth-century circumstances, the American attachment to the automobile is almost surely rational. The automobile offers many advantages not usually matched by other modes at a reasonable cost—advantages such as relatively high speeds, almost instant availability, door-to-door service, comfortable seating, and privacy. The automobile also enjoys several economies, the most important of which is that it is a do-it-yourself mode and thus saves on drivers' wages. If household incomes manage to rise faster than the cost of living, these advantages should increase over time. With higher incomes, more families will be willing and able to pay for the amenities of not only one automobile but increasingly two. Costs saved because of the do-it-yourself nature of the mode would also grow. Consequently, shifting large numbers of travelers to other forms of transportation could prove difficult or almost impossible.

Given this, it will be necessary to civilize the American automobile in order to solve many of the transportation problems that exist in American metropolitan areas. In particular, a massive shift from large to small automobiles holds the promise of ameliorating several problems created by the automobile, while preserving many of the features that make the automobile attractive. A shift to smaller and better engineered vehicles, for example, could halve average new-car fuel consumption in 10 years—an energy saving that could not be achieved by any other transportation policy under serious consideration.

A switch to reengineered and smaller automobiles will also relieve several other urban transportation problems to some extent. Such a transfer, for example, will substantially lessen the costs and complexities of reducing the air pollution generated by urban transportation. Small cars will require less space, particularly for parking, and thus will reduce somewhat the amount of urban land used for transportation purposes. The small automobile may also lessen traffic congestion, since slightly more small than large automobiles can be accommodated in a typical city street or expressway flow. Although small cars do create safety hazards, these are not very serious in urban driving, where the advantages of the small car are also greatest.

A second major policy for relieving urban transportation problems would be to stress, much more than in the past, carpooling and vanpooling, particularly as substitutes for the single-occupant automobile in worktrips. Of all trips in major metropolitan areas, about 25 percent are worktrips, and about 80–85 percent of these worktrips were made in private automobiles as of the late 1970s. Carpools and vanpools, used mainly for commuting, therefore can achieve only limited reductions in total urban transportation requirements. While modest compared with the reductions made possible by a shift to redesigned and smaller automobiles, a significant switch to carpools and vanpools should relieve congestion, improve urban travel times, lower concentrations of carbon monoxide in downtown areas during the peak hours, and reduce the number of parking spaces needed at workplaces and thus the total amount of land used for transportation purposes.

Increased use of carpools and vanpools appears feasible for work-trips because they offer the commuter many of the advantages of the private automobile at some potential savings in costs. Travel times, comfort, and other amenities can be similar to those of a private automobile, as long as the riders live and work close to one another and keep the same regular work hours. Because carpools and vanpools are do-it-yourself modes, they will not be too adversely affected by any increase in real incomes and wages. Furthermore, the do-it-yourself modes do not need empty backhauls or deadheading in order to be positioned for further use and to achieve reasonably effective utilization rates.

Carpooling also would allow for the use of much existing excess capacity in the system. For example, in the 1970s, only 1.2 persons on average typically traveled in automobiles being driven between home and work. Most of these cars could have carried at least two people without imposing major discomforts or greatly increasing costs.

Vanpools offer much the same labor and operating cost advantages as carpools but require procuring and deploying a new fleet of vehicles in lieu of or in addition to the private automobile fleet already in place. While this involves expenses and organizational problems of some magnitude, especially for scheduling and financing, the advantages of vanpooling—particularly in long-distance commuting to outlying or suburban workplaces—appear so substantial that an effort at implementation seems justified.

A third policy recommendation is to reduce transit costs by improving the productivity of conventional public transit. Like many other labor-intensive services, public transit has been handicapped by wages that escalate faster than prices. The same economic forces that have undermined the role of the domestic servant or household repairman have also been undermining the economics of public transit. In a modern society, it may simply be cheaper and easier to perform such functions with capital-intensive methods that either employ more consumer capital or make wholesale substitutions of new machines for old (in lieu, say, of labor-intensive repairs). In domestic service, the consumer capital takes such forms as washing machines, dryers, dishwashers, and disposals. In urban transportation, it takes the form of automobiles.

Unless means are found to improve the relatively poor productivity trends in public transit, the industry's workforce could become an endangered species, much like the household domestic.

There are many ways, however, in which transit productivity could be improved. Some of the more obvious such improvements involve better coping with the increasingly peaked diurnal cycle of the industry. Since most of the need for public transit occurs only during the four or so hours of the commuter rush, productivity improvements could be achieved by finding more alternative uses for transit drivers and operators during the off-peak hours, such as driving paratransit for the handicapped and elderly or doing office or maintenance work between the peaks. Other possibilities include greater use of express bus services and selective rush hour use of large vehicles that increase the number of passengers per operator. These productivity improvements are, moreover, far more likely to pass benefit/cost tests than almost any other kind of aid that might be rendered to public transit.

A fourth policy initiative would be to concentrate conventional public transit in those markets where it is most competitive and to tailor it more to the particular needs of those markets. Given the advantages of the automobile and the economics of mass transit, conventional mass transit is unlikely to increase significantly its share of total urban travel in the near future, at least at reasonable cost. There are, though, a few specific markets where public transit can compete with the automobile.

One such market is that for long-distance worktrips to the centers of the two dozen or so largest and most congested metropolitan areas. Although these trips constitute only a minor share of total urban travel, they account for a disproportionate share of the most serious urban transportation problems—traffic congestion and air pollution.

When serving long-haul commutes to the centers of large metropolitan areas, transit should be less timid about offering improved or premium service and charging commensurately higher fares. Many long-distance commuters to downtown areas have relatively high incomes and might be willing to pay for premium service to avoid driving in highly congested areas and paying expensive parking charges. The most striking evidence of this opportunity for public transit has been the success of express buses running from suburban residential areas to central (or, occasionally, suburban) workplaces. This type of service, often charging a premium fare, has been one of conventional transit's few growing markets and almost the only one where private unsubsidized operators have remained in business.

Another specialized market that has evidenced some prospects for growth is paratransit for the physically handicapped, the elderly, and others who cannot easily use automobiles or conventional public transit. In some lower-density areas it may be less expensive to provide paratransit than conventional public transit even for persons who can and normally do use public transit, including low-income people and the physically robust elderly. Overall, the specialized but highly diverse needs of the transportation disadvantaged would seem best met by a variety of initiatives, ranging from improvements in conventional transit to greater use of specially equipped automobiles.

Another market where transit seems capable of holding its own—especially if costs can be contained through productivity improvements—is serving short-haul worktrips and shoppingtrips to and from the inner-city neighborhoods and central business districts of older, more compact cities. The short distances involved in these trips and the high levels of traffic congestion often make transit competitive with the automobile in terms of travel time in these locales. These are also circumstances in which transit costs can be kept within reasonable bounds. Scattered evidence suggests that some transit systems in big cities make a modest operating profit on their inner-city runs; certainly the deficits are much lower than on suburban routes. Marketing and operating strategies that stress this strength should be at least relatively rewarding.

In general, a fundamental of good business strategy is to identify where the opportunities best match capabilities and then to pursue those opportunities intelligently. For transit, this means emphasizing conventional activities in the inner city and experimenting with express buses and paratransit in a few specialized applications. It even more certainly raises doubts about extending conventional transit into low-density suburban areas where prospective marginal revenues are likely to be well below marginal costs.

COST IMPLICATIONS

Many of the advantages and the disadvantages of reengineering the automobile, of shifting to carpooling and vanpooling, of greater use of express buses, and of the other recommendations summarized in the preceding section can be put in perspective by estimating the costs that these changes might impose on society. As a starting point, and to a rough order of magnitude, Americans spent almost $50 billion per year on urban commuting in the late 1970s.[1]

The costs of shifting to cleaner, more fuel-efficient automobiles are very difficult to estimate, since they depend, in part, on the extent of the improvements made and future technological developments. Experience with the 1970s federal regulations suggests that "civilizing" the automobile can be done at relatively low or no cost *if* shifts to smaller and lower-performance automobiles can be made acceptable to consumers. Air pollution control regulations have tended to increase the total lifetime cost (both capital and operating) of automobiles of any given size, but this increase has been partially offset by a concomitant shift to smaller automobiles that are cheaper to operate; similarly, more fuel-efficient cars tend to have a higher initial purchase price (due to more sophisticated engines, drivetrains, and materials), but this is offset to a significant degree by operating economies (even without downsizing). Several analyses project that, with expected downsizing, the real cost per mile of owning and operating an automobile will decrease in the early 1980s, even as the quality of the vehicle, from a social perspective, is improved.[2]

Such a projection, though, involves a considerable degree of optimism. At a minimum, reengineering and downsizing will result in inconvenience and poorer vehicle performance. For example, cleaner and more fuel-efficient cars probably will have slower acceleration. Smaller cars also have less cargo and passenger capacity, which make them less flexible and less useful for large family outings, vacations, or other similar purposes. It is suggestive, though, that approximately 40 percent of all U.S. urban households now own two cars, and the proportion is increasing. Many families thus can enjoy the cost advantages of small vehicles and the capacity advantages of larger vehicles by owning one of each. The speed with which the public has been shifting to small cars in response to increasing energy prices in recent years also suggests that small-car inconveniences may not be unduly troubling.

The other recommendations—carpooling, vanpooling, and selective improvements in conventional public transit—all involve reducing the number of cars in use, particularly for commuting. To estimate the financial impact of these policies, it must first be determined what reduction in automobile commuting is plausible and the approximate savings in automobile commuting costs that might result from such a reduction. As of the mid-1970s, about 87 percent of the urban workforce commuted to work in automobiles (see Table 3.1). Since only a few cars driven to work carried more than a driver (approximately one passenger for every five drivers, or 1.2 occupants on average in every commuter automobile), there were roughly 73 cars driven to work for every 100 employed persons in U.S. metropolitan areas. As of the late 1970s, this means that approximately 65 million persons commuted to work in 50–55 million automobiles in urban areas.[3]

As indicated in previous chapters (particularly Chapter 5), a very ambitious, multifaceted public policy program incorporating a variety of approaches to reducing automobile commuting might (under favorable conditions) lower the average number of cars driven to work by roughly one third—say, from 73 to 50 per 100 employees. Not only would improvement in conventional public transit services in older central cities be required to accomplish this but also extensive programs to promote vanpooling, carpooling, and express bus services. A one-third reduction would amount to roughly 16–18 million fewer automobiles driven to work on a typical weekday. This should translate into a substantial reduction in automobile operating costs and *possibly* some reduction in ownership costs as well (if there is a decline in the total number of cars owned by American households).

The likelihood of total automobile ownership costs diminishing is not great, however, because cars are owned for purposes other than commuting—recreation, shopping, and business trips, for example—that might justify continued ownership of automobiles at present levels. This would be especially true if those commuters who switched to vanpools, carpools, or express buses in lieu of driving an automobile were from households owning only one car. Since just under 60 percent of urban households own only one car, it is conceivable that a one-third reduction in automobile use for commuting could originate entirely from one-car families and therefore have minimal impact on total automobile ownership.

Operating-cost savings from reduced use of automobiles for commuting, in contrast, are almost certain. There would be a reduction in vehicle-miles of travel for worktrips almost proportional to the reduction in the number of automobiles used—the only offset arising from circuity in some carpooling and vanpooling trips. The extent of any operating savings would depend, of course, on exactly which types of cars were used less. If small automobiles increasingly dominate urban travel in American cities, savings will be less. On the other hand, any increase in the relative cost of energy will increase operating-cost savings. At a lower limit, it might be estimated that the typical automobile commuter trip would incur operating costs of at least 10 cents per mile and might quite easily incur as much as 15 cents per mile.

Operating-cost savings would also be influenced by the average length of the commuter trip shifted from automobile to other modes. In the late 1970s, the typical urban commuter trip was approximately 12 miles round trip. It is difficult to guess which trips, short or long, might be shifted from one mode to another. Public transit might be expected to be attractive for short trips, whereas vanpools or carpools might be more attractive for long commuter trips (see Chapter 5). Given this range of possibilities, the average commuter trip shifted from automobile to other modes might be placed between 10 and 15 miles round trip.

The higher figure also allows for some growth in the length of commuter trips, which has been the trend.

These numbers can be combined to construct a range of estimates for operating-cost savings achievable from reduced automobile commuting. If 18 million automobile trips of 10–15 miles each and incurring operating costs of 10–15 cents per mile were not taken, the annual savings would be somewhere between $4.5 billion and $10.1 billion (at 1979 price levels). A number roughly averaging these upper and lower estimates, $7.5 billion, would seem to be a good overall guess or estimate.

A reduction in automobile commuting might also yield cost savings by reducing the need for parking spaces at workplaces. It is difficult to estimate what the value of any such savings might be. Immediate savings would result from diminished demand for expansion of parking spaces at many existing employment sites. Additional parking can be quite expensive: capital costs of $2,000–3,000 per space are not uncommon and are often exceeded when parking structures are built at high-density locations. Even assuming a cost of only $500 per space, a very low estimate, urban transportation policies that reduced the need for commuter parking spaces by one third would be worth roughly between $500 million and $1 billion per year.[4] Without too much stretching, an estimate as high as $4–5 billion in savings per year might be justified.[5] On balance, a one-third reduction in urban automobile commuting should reduce automobile commuters' operating and parking costs by at least $8 billion annually and could easily reduce costs by as much as $10 billion or more per year.[6] To estimate what the net benefits to commuters of such a shift might be, however, these savings must be compared with the costs of implementing carpooling, vanpooling, and express bus programs as well as the costs of improving public transit enough to effectuate a reduction in automobile commuting.

An estimate of the costs of implementing alternatives to automobile commuting depends critically on which other transportation modes are used and to what extent. At one extreme, it might be assumed that all of the reduction in automobile use was achieved through carpooling. If, in the late 1970s, about 65 million urbanites commuted in a little over 54 million cars with an average automobile occupancy of 1.2, and every carpool contained only two workers, this would imply that 22 million commuters traveled to work in 11 million carpools. To reduce automobile use by one third through carpooling, the 65 million persons who commuted by automobile would have to travel in only 36 million cars and average automobile occupancy would have to increase to 1.8; in essence, this would require that 18 million additional two-person carpools would have to be formed (carrying 36 million commuters).

The main additions to costs from such a substantial increase in carpooling would be extra operating outlays associated with using more circuitous routings and any additional time costs imposed on commuters by such circuity or other schedule disruptions or delays created by carpooling. Estimating the value of time spent in commuting has always been speculative and controversial. The only standard suggestion is that the valuation should be related to the basic hourly wage level (or the hourly salary equivalent) of the individual worker. A good deal of uncertainty exists, however, as to whether commuting time should be valued at more or less than the individual's basic wage rate. Empirical research on traveler behavior suggests that the relationship depends very much on the individual and the specific circumstances involved.[7] For some individuals and some circumstances commuting may hold some recreational value (such as listening to the radio) or allow time for reflection and therefore is considered less onerous than time spent at work. On the other hand, driving to work on congested roads or commuting on a crowded bus or subway may be nerve-racking and unpleasant for many commuters and therefore worthy of a premium over their hourly salary equivalent. The valuation may also depend upon how much time is saved and how long the commuter trip is; it has been suggested, for example, that small changes in travel time are not noticed by commuters, and that the value (or cost) rises nonlinearly and disproportionately with increases in time after some basic threshold is passed (for example, 20 minutes or so on a one-way trip). Some observers even suggest that trips of less than 20–30 minutes are actually enjoyed by commuters and that substantial costs attached to commuting are only perceived as the length of the trip rises well above this threshold level. Most researchers agree, however, that the value of time is closely related to the wage rate and varies in the range between one third and twice that rate, depending on particular circumstances.[8]

It is not easy to estimate how much travel time might be lost in the aggregate by a large shift from single-occupant automobiles to carpools for worktrips. Commuting time would increase due to circuity and perhaps the need to wait for carpool members. Moreover, there might be some increase in travel time for shopping, personal business, or other nonworktrips that were formerly performed on the way to or from work. These increases would be partly offset, however, by gains to carpoolers and the remaining single-occupant automobile commuters because of reduced traffic congestion attributable to the decline in the number of automobiles used for commuting. Just what the net effect of all these forces might be is difficult to predict; it is conceivable that a substantial shift to carpooling might cause a net loss as great as 5–10 minutes each way per carpooler (assuming little offsetting traffic congestion reduction) or, at the other extreme, that the shift might have no effect at all, or might even slightly improve travel times (particularly for the commuters who continue to drive alone).

Even if the time loss per commuter is small, however, the total cost in travel time resulting from such a substantial increase in carpooling may be significant because of the number of commuters involved. Assuming a 5- to 10-minute round-trip time loss per carpooler, no gains for nonpoolers, 5-cents-per-minute value on commuting time (less than the 1980 U.S. minimum wage), and 34 million new carpoolers, the total cost in travel time would amount to between $2 billion and $4 billion per year.[9] But costs twice as large or no costs at all are also defensible as estimates for total travel time losses.

The operating costs of an increase in carpooling are far easier to estimate. Assuming a 15-mile round trip, that picking up an additional rider imposes 10 percent circuity, and that the pooling cars have operating costs in the 10- to 15-cent-per-mile range, the extra costs for the 17 million additional carpools would be in the range of $600 million to $1 billion per year. If picking up an additional rider added 20 percent circuity, then these operating costs would be roughly doubled.

Any estimates of the value of travel time and augmented operating costs associated with increased carpooling are largely speculative. Nevertheless, using the relatively conservative assumptions of a 5- to 10-minute round-trip time loss and a 20 percent increase in circuity for carpoolers, the additional travel time and direct operating costs associated with a two-and-a-half-fold increase in carpooling would amount to between $4 billion and $6 billion, or only about half as much as the $8–10 billion annual savings from a one-third or so reduction in automobiles used for commuting. This margin seems large enough to conclude safely that a substantial shift to carpooling would reduce aggregate urban commuting costs.

A similar analysis can be performed for vanpooling. To reduce the number of vehicles used to commute by one third, 65 million urban workers would have to travel to and from work in 37 million automobiles and vans. If average automobile occupancy in commuting remains at 1.2 and the average vanpool carries 8 persons (including the driver), then 3 million vanpools (carrying 24 million workers) and 34 million cars (carrying 41 million workers) would be required to achieve the target reduction in automobile use.

The cost of the increased travel time associated with vanpooling might be comparable to or perhaps a little less than that associated with carpooling. On the one hand, fewer persons will be inconvenienced (only 24 million new vanpoolers as compared to 34 million new carpoolers are needed to reduce automobile use by one third). On the other hand, the larger ride-sharing group required for vanpooling is likely to mean more circuity and delay per vanpool member than with carpooling. If the 24 million new vanpoolers average 10–20 minute delays per round trip at 5 cents per minute, the total time lost by vanpooling would amount to $3–6 billion per year.[10] Again, both higher and lower figures could be justified, given uncertainties about the delays of pooling, time savings from less traffic congestion, and the value placed on travel time.

The direct operating costs of vanpooling are likely to be higher than for carpooling. Assuming that vanpools travel longer distances than the average commuter trip to collect their full loads, round trips of approximately 20 miles per day might be typical. Assuming, too, that the vans are not used much for other purposes and that they would be larger than the typical compact or subcompact car, total costs (operating, depreciation, and so forth) of 30 cents per mile might be estimated. On this basis, the annual additional direct costs of 3 million new vanpools in lieu of private automobiles for commuting could be estimated to be $4.5 billion per year.[11] This figure may be too high to the extent that it ignores the value of the vans when employed in other uses by the household of the van driver. The effect of this omission is probably small, however, compared with the other uncertainties surrounding this calculation.

The vanpooling alternative would offer greater savings in total automobile operating costs than the carpooling alternative, since only 34 million automobiles (plus 3 million vans) would be used instead of 36 million automobiles. Assuming an operating cost of 10–15 cents per mile and a 20-mile round trip (since van drivers should be recruited from those commuting long distances), this added savings might amount to between $1 billion and $1.5 billion per year.[12]

In sum, the additional travel time and augmented operating costs associated with a shift to vanpooling are probably between $6 billion and $8 billion per year. While larger than those costs associated with carpooling, vanpooling costs are still likely to be less than the $8–10 billion of savings that could be achieved by reducing automobile commuting by one third. Thus, using vanpooling in place of a portion of today's automobile commuting should effectuate reductions in the total urban commuting bill, but not of quite so massive a size as carpooling.

The economics of conventional bus service replacing a full third of automobile commuting are not overwhelmingly favorable. A shift from automobiles to buses would probably increase travel time substantially, since buses do not travel as direct a route or at as convenient hours as a car or vanpool and because some time is likely to be spent walking to or from stops and waiting for the bus. A 15- to 20-minute delay per round trip per bus commuter seems probable at the minimum. The time spent commuting in buses may be considered more costly as well, since many people find walking to and from stops, waiting for buses, and traveling in a crowded bus with strangers less pleasant than time spent in their own cars or in a carpool. Assuming a value of 5 cents per minute of additional travel time and that 21 million workers would have to use buses in order to reduce the number of automobiles used for commuting by one third, the added travel time costs would be at least $4–5.25 billion annually.[13] Travel time costs of two or three times as much are also plausible if the bus service is not of good quality.

The direct operating costs of added bus service might also be high because most commuting occurs during peak travel hours, and a massive shift from automobiles to buses would require a substantial increase in the total fleet of public transit buses. For example, if the typical trip to work on an express bus takes about 30 minutes, then in any given rush hour one bus might complete only two trips (allowing for one deadheading trip back to start the route over). If every bus rider is provided a seat (so as to partially match the amenity levels of the automobile), then each bus could carry about 100 commuters during the two rush hours.[14] To carry 21 million more people by bus during the rush hours would therefore require approximately 210,000 additional buses in the system. Some of the additional demand for bus service *might* be absorbed by existing but less than fully utilized transit capacity, especially in cities that have rail transit. Some buses on short routes might also make more than two round trips per rush hour. Some of the shift in commuting from automobiles to buses should also occur in nonrush hours, since not everyone goes to work between 7:00 A.M. and 9:00 A.M. and returns between 4:00 P.M. and 6:00 P.M. If one half or one quarter of the shift occurred during off-peak hours or could be handled by existing excess transit capacity, then only 100,000–150,000 additional buses might be required. However, any such estimate (that only 100,000–150,000 new buses would be needed) is probably extremely optimistic, since mass transit in the late 1970s used approximately 53,000 buses and 10,000 rail transit cars to carry less than one third as many commuters.[15]

In the late 1970s, the purchase price of a new transit bus was about $90,000. Amortized over a 12-year life, 150,000 buses at $90,000 each would incur capital charges of $1.5 billion per year (in constant dollars) at a 5 percent discount rate, and about $2 billion per year at a 10 percent discount rate; the charge for 100,000 buses would obviously be two thirds as much. The annual cost of operating an urban transit bus (exclusive of capital charges) was typically about $65,000 per year in the late 1970s. Additional buses needed for rush hours only, however, might be brought on-stream at a somewhat lower annual charge; for example, their total annual mileage should be less than the average bus now in transit service, which operates not only during rush hours but to some extent during the off-peak hours as well. On this basis, the annual costs of operating additional transit buses might be reduced to approximately $40,000. At such a level, 150,000 additional buses would cost approximately $6 billion per year to operate.

Accordingly, even using assumptions advantageous to transit, bus service would almost surely be more expensive in a large-scale substitution than the automobile commuting it would replace. If only 15–20 minutes are lost per round trip, if only 100,000–150,000 additional buses are required, and if the discount rate is 5 percent, the added cost for additional bus service would be between $9 billion and $13 billion annually, exceeding the $8–10 billion yearly savings in automobile commuting expenses. Using far more plausible, less favorable assumptions, the time loss and direct costs of bus service would be higher and the net increase in aggregate transportation costs more substantial.

This same point can be made at a micro level by observing that one bus carrying 100 commuters would replace about 83 automobiles at a commuter automobile load level of 1.2 persons per car. Obviously, a bus—even a very expensive one fitted to meet a wide range of needs for the handicapped (at approximately $250,000)—would save on capital costs, since a typical bus and automobile last about the same number of years (ten) and 83 automobiles, if new, would cost (at late 1970s prices) over $300,000. A bus should also save somewhat on direct operating costs, since, even allowing for deadheading (empty returns) and some circuity to pick up passengers, the bus should not do much worse than quintuple the mileage required in its daily trips to accommodate the 100 commuters. However, the bus would have to go more or less the *longest* distance of any commuter served if it were to displace all automobile travel for the 100. Thus, if the 100 commuters averaged 10 miles per one-day worktrip and were uniformly distributed in a range from 5 to 15 miles, the bus would have to travel about 150 miles per day to serve this group of 100 commuters, as compared to 1,660 (20 x 83) miles of automobile travel. The direct automobile operating costs for fuel, oil, rubber, and so on would be at least 10 cents per mile and the bus costs should be no more than 50 cents; accordingly, these direct operating costs per day would be no more than $75 for the bus and at least $166 for the automobiles.

On the other hand, the bus requires a driver—possibly two if split shifts cannot be used. Furthermore, supervisors, clerks, and other personnel besides drivers must be employed so that a typical transit operation employs two to three people per bus in service. Even if only two employees per bus are required, on average, labor costs (including fringe benefits), can easily come to $40,000 per year at late-1970 wage levels. At 250 working days per year, labor costs can easily come to $160 per day, thus eradicating much of any advantage in direct operating costs for nonlabor items and capital costs. Add in the high probability that commuting by bus will take longer and be less comfortable, and the appeal of automobile commuting becomes clear.

Actually, as these numbers strongly suggest, a systematic large-scale substitution of buses for car commuting is neither feasible nor a particularly relevant comparison. Rather, buses could be expected to be used in lieu of automobiles in selected applications where they are particularly suitable (for example, express buses from moderate-density suburban residential areas to central workplaces and short-haul, inner-city worktrips). The costs of bus service should be lower in many of these applications, particularly in a transit system where excess capacity may already exist. Utilization of otherwise unutilized capacity in any system is always attractive economically; that, in fact, is the great advantage of carpooling.

The important point that emerges from these cost comparisons is that the savings from diverting commuters from private automobiles to other modes depend on which modes are substituted and where the substitutions are made. The greater the proportion of commuters who switch from automobiles to carpooling and, to a lesser extent, to vanpooling, the greater the savings. Buses are also an attractive alternative in certain circumstances, especially in older, compact central cities that have well-developed transit service. The ideal pattern would be for public transit to take on many of the shorter central-city trips now made by automobile while vanpools and carpools substitute for the automobile on longer distance commutes to less central or suburban employment locations. Clearly, though, there are distinct limits to how far these various substitutions can rationally proceed—and quite a bit of automobile commuting will remain in the system under almost any plausible assumptions.

MISPRICING, SUBSIDIES, AND THE URBAN TRANSPORTATION PROBLEM

If reengineered automobiles, ridesharing, and other such recommended solutions are so sensible and potentially economical, why didn't they develop earlier and why, even now, are they emerging only slowly? The answer is that many of these solutions have been strongly discouraged by extensive mispricing and subsidization of urban transportation activities. To a considerable degree, in fact, current problems in urban transportation are the result of mispricing—particularly the underpricing or subsidizing of urban automobile use. For example, urban motorists do not pay directly for the health damage or other difficulties they create by polluting the air. Congestion is excessive because highway users are not charged for the delays they impose on others or for the expensive increments to urban highway capacity required to keep urban peak-period downtown traffic flowing smoothly.

The policy response to these subsidies has been largely (although not exclusively) to create additional and, it has been hoped, countervailing subsidies. For example, when policy makers realized that urban automobile use was underpriced and subsidized, they responded by subsidizing public transportation as well, trying to create a more balanced use of the two modes. Initial federal programs to aid transit were also restricted to capital outlays only. This restriction created incentives for local governments to overcapitalize their transit systems, which, in due course, brought forth an additional federal aid program to subsidize operating expenses.

These subsidies may have created serious problems themselves by underpricing urban transportation in general relative to other goods and services. Indeed, many of the current problems of urban transportation (pollution, congestion, energy consumption) may well be a consequence of encouraging too much mobility. A policy that subsidizes one particular mode (for example, mass transit) to offset another subsidy (for example, for rush hour use of central-city expressways) may serve to increase the overall use of urban transportation and thereby exacerbate transportation-related problems The obvious alternative, which would greatly promote more rational use of urban transportation, would be to proceed in just the opposite direction: reduce or eliminate subsidies and mispricing wherever possible. A few suggestions toward achieving that end are proffered below.

Highway costs. The mispricing of urban highway use is perhaps the oldest and most seriously distorting of urban transportation subsidies (even though urban highways are not subsidized in the aggregate, since receipts from special highway-user taxes collected from urban motorists exceed or approximately equal the costs of constructing and maintaining the urban highway system). The difficulty, as related in Chapter 11, is that highway-user taxes are collected largely in the form of gasoline, vehicle, and other excise taxes that do not vary greatly with the location or type of facility used or the hour of travel. Certain types of highways are extraordinarily expensive to construct and maintain, notably the highways in the centers of large metropolitan areas designed principally to serve peak-period traffic. Consequently, users of those facilities are subsidized to a significant degree (albeit mainly by other urban motorists). The underpricing and overconstruction of peak-period highway capacity in downtown metropolitan areas obviously encourages individualistic automobile use and discourages such alternatives as carpooling, vanpooling, and increased transit use.

Mispricing of highway capacity is also exacerbated by legislation that often limits the application of highway-user taxes to highway capital expenditures, thereby creating incentives for excessive new construction. Furthermore, federal funds for highway building are often made available on so-called 90-10 matching formulas; the local government need only put up 10 cents to receive 90 cents more. These 10-cent dollars and easy availability of funds for new construction create incentives for expensive highway expansion. Federal highway aid is also earmarked for certain types of roads, such as the Interstate Highway System, which creates incentives to build these facilities rather than others. Similar restrictions on the use of state highway-user tax receipts are not uncommon.

Remedies to reduce the harm created by highway mispricing can be easily identified. For example, one-way streets, signal controls, expressway metering, and other sophisticated traffic-engineering techniques can be seen as a means of reducing any highway subsidy to peak-period users of congested facilities by increasing the effective capacity of these facilities at low cost. Priority lanes for carpools, vanpools, and transit vehicles also might help alleviate highway mispricing by reducing the amount of costly highway capacity allocated to what is often the most underpriced use, that by the single-occupant automobile. Experimentation with charges for use of the costlier sections of the urban highway system also seems worthwhile, including techniques such as increasing charges on already tolled facilities (such as bridges and tunnels) during the peak-traffic hours, central-area licenses, and higher central-area parking fees.

Federal urban highway aid should also be more available for maintenance and other noncapital purposes and should not be so closely tied to particular types of highways. Although some additional highway construction is probably worthwhile, much of the needed system has been built, and strong incentives for urban highway construction no longer seem all that appropriate. The possibility cannot be ruled out, moreover, that in many communities, expenditures on other transportation programs (such as transportation for the handicapped or improved transit service) might be more worthwhile. Such considerations argue for more general "transport" grants from federal sources to local agencies rather than the highly specific and single-mode grants that have been historically typical.

Environmental costs. As already noted (Chapters 8, 9, and 10), some automobile users may be subsidized to the extent that they do not pay for losses they create in health, aesthetics, and quiet or the full replacement or national security cost of the energy they consume. The environmental subsidy of the automobile has been substantially reduced in recent years, not so much by charging motorists taxes or fees equal to their environmental damages, but rather by mandating specific improvements or changes in new automobiles. The largest gains have probably been made in controlling automotive air pollution. Federal regulations governing new-car emissions have reduced the average pollution damage from over one cent per vehicle-mile in the late 1960s to perhaps one half as much by the late 1970s, with further reductions scheduled as cleaner cars make up more of the fleet. Reductions in automotive fuel consumption should also occur in the near future, as more small cars enter the U.S. automobile fleet. Some environmental costs have perhaps been lowered, too, through federal laws and regulations enacted in the 1960s and early 1970s that offer environmentalists and neighborhood groups opportunities to delay or prevent construction of what they deem to be objectionable facilities.

Despite some reductions, the environmental costs of urban transportation will remain a key policy issue. Particularly important will be setting future environmental standards or pollution taxes for automobiles so that the benefits gained from future environmental improvements are commensurate with the costs incurred. As environmental damages are more closely regulated, some changes—and more flexibility—in regulations may be advisable. For example, higher pollution standards might be demanded of cars sold and registered in urban areas than in rural areas, since the benefits of reduced pollution are greater in urban areas. Alternatively, manufacturers might be required to meet an average pollution standard on all new cars rather than the same standard on each vehicle, so that they could offer a variety of vehicles to the public, some exceeding and some falling short of the average fleet emissions standard. Automobiles might be periodically tested for pollution emissions, with those that pollute the most charged higher taxes than those that pollute least. By permitting producers and consumers to better equate the marginal costs and benefits of various compliance techniques, these changes should reduce the costs of achieving stipulated air quality goals.

Parking subsidies. Parking spaces provided free at many workplaces can also represent a substantial subsidy for automobile commutation. The exact magnitude of the subsidy is difficult to estimate, since the cost of providing parking spaces varies widely. In the late 1970s, the subsidy probably ranged from $100 to $1,000 per space per year (with the provision of free parking less common in situations where the cost per space approached the upper end of this cost range).

Charging for parking that is now free at workplaces would encourage carpooling and vanpooling, since these modes offer opportunities to share the parking fees.[16] Such charges for parking would also encourage mass transit use, although the substitution would be limited because transit service is not very competitive or economical at many of the suburban workplaces where free parking is now most prevelant. However, case studies of several downtown employers who converted from free to paid employee parking show substantial increases in carpooling and mass transit patronage.[17]

One way to reduce parking subsidies would be to include the cost of free parking space as taxable income paid to an employee. Under current tax laws, a free parking space at the workplace is a tax-exempt fringe benefit. Unlike most tax-exempt fringes (such as contributions by employers to health and insurance plans), exemption from parking costs is not obviously imbued with any clear social purpose.[18] Another alternative would be to revert to the tradition of compensating subsidies and allow employers greater latitude in giving tax-free financial assistance for other modes of commuting, such as pooling and mass transit. Certainly, the present widespread practice of providing parking as a tax-exempt fringe benefit seems anomalous and rather inconsistent with many other public policy initiatives.

Transit subsidies. By the late 1970s, government aid to mass transit amounted to several billion dollars per year, which covered approximately half of all transit operating costs and virtually all transit capital expenditures.

Transit subsidies are in part responsible for stabilizing and even slightly increasing transit ridership in the 1970s, but the cost per rider retained or gained has been extraordinarily high and only a small fraction of the new or retained transit riders represent potential or previous automobile drivers. Consequently, transit subsidies have had a disappointingly small impact on automobile use and alleviation of automobile-related problems.

Transit subsidies may even have reduced the ability of mass transit to compete with the automobile in the long run. The availability of subsidies on such a large scale may have weakened incentives for managers and unions to control costs and to make the productivity improvements that are critical to the long-term viability of mass transit. Subsidies may also have made it difficult to concentrate transit service in the market where it is most competitive—commuting trips to the centers of large metropolitan areas and short trips within central cities. To maintain broad political support for transit subsidies, Congress has given federal transit aid to many small metropolitan areas. And at the local level (in small and large towns) many transit authorities have maintained much more extensive route networks and schedules than are seemingly justifiable, mainly in order to gain still more public aid.

The special role that transit has to play in solving urban transportation problems is, moreover, one that need not depend so heavily on public largesse. If subsidies to mass transit were reduced, transit would still remain competitive with the automobile in the dozen or so densest, most congested metropolitan areas, where it now makes its largest contribution to solving urban transportation problems. Of course, and quite importantly, any impact from reducing transit subsidies would also be lessened if workplace parking subsidies and the underpricing of automobile use of congested centrally located highways were simultaneously eliminated.

One drawback to reducing transport subsidies to cars and trains is the possible effect on the transportation disadvantaged—especially on the poor. Poor persons, however, receive a surprisingly small percentage of current transportation subsidies, and many transit riders are not poor (particularly in large cities). In the same vein, the most heavily subsidized automobile users (those commuting downtown during the rush hours) typically have incomes that are much higher than average.[19]

Higher automobile- and transit-user charges can be mitigated, moreover, in many ways, such as car- and trip-pooling or greater use of smaller cars. Some problems might also be alleviated by policies such as those outlined in Chapter 12, for example, increasing the number of disadvantaged persons who can drive and selectively subsidizing transit and paratransit services that are particularly useful to the poor and those who cannot drive.

SUMMARY

The automobile will continue to dominate urban transportation in the United States for some while to come. Accordingly, it must be made more "urbane" or "civilized," so as to make it a more acceptable participant on the urban scene. The most obvious single step toward achieving that goal is to rescale the American car's dimensions, to make it smaller and more akin to its contemporaries found in other industrialized countries. A scaling down of the automobile, though, will not be enough in and of itself. In particular, the vehicle must be reengineered so as to emit fewer pollutants and to achieve more mileage from a given amount of fuel. In addition, a proliferation of smaller vehicles in the automobile fleet will require design modifications, probably in both larger and smaller vehicles, so that traffic safety is not unduly diminished through greater use of small vehicles.

For public transportation, by contrast, the primary goal will be reducing routine operating labor requirements, while still maintaining reasonable levels of service. This can be done in two rather different ways. The first and most promising is to develop do-it-yourself paratransit—that is, vanpooling and carpooling. The second is to reorganize or otherwise modify conventional mass transit so as to require fewer operating labor inputs; the possibilities for effectuating such a change range from use of more sophisticated scheduling techniques to simply expanding the scale of the typical transit bus (through, for example, articulation or second decking). It is hoped that by making these changes, conventional mass transit can lower its costs relative to the automobile and thereby make inroads on automobile commuting; if so, the total employment level and scale of transit operations might stabilize or even expand.

Transit can also be adapted to take better advantage of its market opportunities. Express bus service tailored more to specific trip patterns, especially in commutation from suburbs to central-city employment, perhaps represents the best such opportunity. Paratransit, whether do-it-yourself or professionally driven, represents another possibility, particularly in providing specialized services for those who do not have ready access to an automobile.

Many of these recommended changes will be hastened if urban transportation is priced more in accordance with its costs. Indeed, the current pattern of mispricing (particularly underpricing) is an important source of many of the congestion, pollution, and other problems commonly associated with urban transportation. Particularly important would be some attempt to correct the mispricing of peak-period highway capacity in the congested centers of large metropolitan areas. Further efforts to price or regulate automobile damage to the environment, as well as a reduction in parking and mass transit subsidies, would also be advisable.

The net effect of all these changes will likely be to leave the cost of traveling relatively unaffected from the viewpoint of the typical traveler, despite the removal of subsidies, while reducing the total costs and improving the performance of the urban transportation system from the perspective of society as a whole. The key to this is achieving *disciplined* use of the different transportation modes—having each do what it does best. In Western societies, market prices conventionally perform this discipline or allocative chore. The central public policy issue is whether society wishes to use market prices to a greater extent for this purpose or to proceed on the historical path of using arbitrary government allocations instead, with all the attendant waste of resources that almost surely will ensue.

APPENDIX
NOTES
INDEX

Appendix: Trends in Urban Residential Densities

To measure the degree of residential decentralization, economists and geographers estimate what are known as "urban population density functions." The estimation of these functions started with Colin Clark in the early 1950s and has been continued and extended by Clark and others since then.[1] Urban population density functions have been estimated for developed and developing countries going back to the nineteenth century.

Urban population density functions are most easily explained by graphics (see Figure A.1). In essence, the estimate is made by fitting a function (usually a negative exponential) to data on population densities for different parts of a city at different distances from the city center. Usually such data will not be exactly on a line or curve (as illustrated by the scatter of points shown in Figure A.1) so that statistical fitting is required.[2]

Two items of interest may be obtained from urban residential density functions. The first, usually denoted as D_0, is an estimate of the

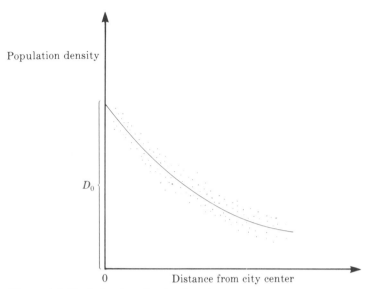

Figure A.1. Typical urban density function.

theoretical density (population per square mile) at the very center of the urban area; it is theoretical in the sense that such densities will typically not actually be observed, since the very center of the city is not normally devoted to residences. D_0 thus represents what the population density would be at the very center of the city if the patterns of population dispersion observable from data on the rest of the city are used to extrapolate a very centermost density; graphically, D_0 is the intersection of the fitted function with the vertical axis.

The other item of interest derived from urban population density functions, usually denoted by g for gradient, is a measure of the rate at which population densities decline away from theoretical central density reflected in D_0. Thus, a very high value of g means that the population drops off very rapidly from the center, while a small value of g indicates a very slow decline in population density with distance from the center.

A broad sampling of population density function estimates measured at various periods for various cities is shown in Table A.1. A remarkable uniformity is discernible, especially in the behavior of the density gradient. Specifically, with only a few exceptions—Tokyo being by far the most important—g has declined systematically over time in almost every city around the world for which estimates are available.

The estimates of the theoretical central density (D_0), on the other hand, are not as consistent. While in most cases the estimate of D_0 does

TABLE A.1. Estimates of population density functions over time for cities around the world.

Country or region	City	Year	$D_0{}^*$	g
New Zealand[a]	Christchurch	1911	15,400	1.00
		1936	15,400	.84
		1951	21,200	.83
	Wellington	1911	10,800	.75
		1936	9,600	.53
		1951	7,300	.48
Australia[a]	Brisbane	1901	6,600	.58
		1933	9,600	.47
		1947	14,300	.45
	Melbourne	1933	25,000	.35
		1954	13,700	.22
	Sydney	1911	10,000	.30
		1947	13,500	.19
		1954	9,300	.16
Far East[d]	Tokyo	1950	7,143	.063
		1955	9,337	.068
		1960	11,956	.073
		1965	22,218	.082
		1970	25,157	.081
	Sapporo	1965	23,506	.414
		1970	22,652	.231
	Hiroshima	1965	25,745	.173
		1970	14,341	.020

Country or region	City	Year	$D_0{}^*$	g
Continental Europe[a]	Berlin	1885	112,000	.68
		1900	158,000	.58
	Frankfurt	1890	55,000	1.16
		1933	34,000	.57
	Paris	1817	174,000	1.46
		1856	92,500	.59
		1896	143,000	.50
		1931	182,000	.47
		1946	69,500	.21
British Isles[a]	Birmingham	1921	40,100	.50
		1938	20,100	.29
	London	1801	104,000	.78
		1841	108,000	.58
		1871	86,500	.38
		1901	66,000	.23
		1921	44,300	.17
		1931	47,500	.17
		1939	32,000	.14
		1951	24,000	.12
		1961	20,500	.09

TABLE A.1. (Cont.)

Country or region	City	Year	D_0^*	g	Country or region	City	Year	D_0^*	g
United States[e]	Milwaukee	1880	17,107	.603	India[b]	Bombay	1881	93,470	.373
		1890	27,349	.572			1891	86,672	.325
		1900	35,681	.559			1901	61,580	.257
		1910	30,038	.485			1911	67,785	.235
		1920	26,384	.379			1921	71,444	.199
		1930	28,668	.348			1931	56,735	.172
		1940	25,275	.317			1941	69,095	.170
		1948	22,526	.292			1951	88,699	.128
		1954	17,097	.230			1961	96,635	.102
		1958	14,610	.199		Jamshedpur	1941	12,138	.477
		1963	12,610	.168			1951	11,520	.382
	Philadelphia[e]	1880	15,430	.186			1961	10,358	.232
		1890	17,596	.174		Hyderabad (Old City)	1951	49,862	.090
		1900	21,867	.174			1961	34,313	.324
		1910	25,019	.174		Madras	1951	60,888	.235
		1920	26,110	.155			1961	66,821	.235
		1930	23,962	.230					
		1940	23,094	.224					
		1948	20,574	.193					
		1954	17,658	.168					
		1958	16,172	.155	Latin America[e]	Mexico City	1950	69,000	.37
		1963	14,782	.143			1960	62,000	.27

City	Year	Density*	Gradient
Chicago[f]	1860	11,588	.570
	1870	27,348	.545
	1880	37,313	.485
	1890	33,451	.316
	1900	38,627	.257
	1910	38,627	.229
	1920	28,197	.156
	1930	28,120	.134
	1940	27,464	.130
	1950	24,605	.113
	1970	44,000	.17
São Paulo	1950	8,400	.14
	1960	12,000	.14
	1970	18,000	.12
Buenos Aires	1950	54,000	.21
	1960	37,000	.14
	1970	33,000	.12
Rio de Janeiro	1950	8,700	.09
	1960	10,000	.08
	1970	11,000	.07

Source: The original sources of the estimates for different countries are shown below. These have been adapted to place them on a directly comparable basis by Edwin Mills and Jee Peng Tan, "A Comparison of Urban Population Density Functions in Developed and Developing Countries," in Urban Studies (forthcoming).

a Colin Clark, Population Growth and Land Use (New York: St. Martin's Press, 1968).

b John E. Brush. "Spatial Patterns of Population in Indian Cities," Geographical Review 58 (1968): 362–391.

c Gregory K. Ingram and Alan Carrol, "The Spatial Structure of Latin American Cities," Journal of Urban Economics (forthcoming 1981).

d Edwin S. Mills and Katsutoshi Ohta, "Urbanization and Urban Problems," in Asia's New Giant: How the Japanese Economy Works, ed. H. Patrick and H. Rosovsky (Washington, D.C.: Brookings Institution, 1976), p. 744. Copyright © 1976 by the Brookings Institution.

e Edwin S. Mills, Studies in the Structure of the Urban Economy (Baltimore Johns Hopkins Press, for Resources for the Future, 1972).

f Bruce F. Newling, "Urban Growth and Spatial Structure: Mathematical Models and Empirical Evidence," Geographical Review 56 (1966): 213–225.

* Population per square mile.

TABLE A.2. Population density functions for 20 U.S. metropolitan areas, 1960–1970.

Metropolitan area	1960		1970		1970
	D_0	g	D_0	g	Population (thousands)
New York	31,606	.060	36,483	.083	16,207
Pittsburgh	4,745	.064	1,712	.032	1,846
Atlanta	5,193	.130	5,985	.126	1,173
Denver	10,625	.220	1,283	.013	1,047
Phoenix	3,159	.135	5,012	.174	863
Indianapolis	14,045	.336	1,558	.014	820
Columbus	24,248	.324	2,463	.069	790
San Antonio	8,086	.226	12,472	.286	773
Oklahoma City	1,209	.085	1,454	.149	580
Omaha	8,357	.254	2,577	.115	492
Toledo	9,168	.196	3,093	.114	488
Grand Rapids	11,048	.322	1,380	.044	353
Wichita	3,823	.208	4,652	.222	302
Charlotte	3,511	.250	1,691	.124	280
Fresno	1,275	.089	2,137	.101	263
Baton Rouge	6,768	.273	3,241	.181	249
Corpus Christi	1,598	.043	1,795	.111	213
Rockford	4,861	.328	3,858	.218	206
Binghamton	2,357	.161	953	.136	167
Kalamazoo	2,586	.262	2,158	.170	152

Source: Edwin S. Mills and Jee Peng Tan, "A Comparison of Urban Population Density Functions in Developed and Developing Countries," in *Urban Studies* (forthcoming).

decline, more exceptions occur than for g. In particular, rapidly growing cities can experience rising central densities over time.

Some of these same trends can be seen in population density function estimates for 20 U.S. metropolitan areas in 1960 and 1970, shown in Table A.2. Again, both D_0 and g usually declined between 1960 and 1970. However, the exceptions—New York City aside—tend to be cities located in the West or Southwest that are experiencing relatively rapid growth, such as Phoenix, San Antonio, Oklahoma City, Wichita, Fresno, and Corpus Christi. In New York City's case, the increase in D_0 and g between 1960 and 1970 may reflect the fact that Manhattan was far more vital in these years than the outlying boroughs, especially the Bronx and Brooklyn.

A more comprehensive overall comparison of average density gradients for six countries in differing stages of economic development is shown in Table A.3. Clearly, density gradients tend to be higher in less-developed countries than in developed or industrialized countries. But density gradients seem to be declining everywhere, at much the same pace.

TABLE A.3.   Comparison of average population density gradients among developed and developing countries.

Country	Year	Average density gradient
India (12 cities)	1951	.675
	1961	.652
Brazil (4 cities)	1950	.182
	1960	.171
	1970	.157
Japan (22 cities)	1965	.457
	1970	.391
Mexico (3 cities)	1950	.359
	1960	.335
	1970	.284
Korea (12 cities)	1966	.701
	1970	.670
	1973	.639
United States (20 cities)	1960	.199
	1970	.123

Source: Edwin S. Mills and Jee Peng Tan, "A Comparison of Urban Population Density Functions in Developed and Developing Countries," in Urban Studies (forthcoming).

Notes

1. The Evolution of Public Concerns and Policies

1. U.S. Department of Commerce, *Historical Statistics of the United States: Colonial Times to 1970*, bicentennial ed., pt. 2 (Washington, D.C.: U.S. Government Printing Office, 1975), p. 716.

2. Ibid., pp. 639–640.

3. John F. Kain, *Essays in Urban Spatial Structure* (Cambridge, Mass.: Ballinger, 1975), pp. 79–114.

4. U.S. Department of Commerce, *Historical Statistics of the United States*, pt. 2, p. 716.

5. Wilfred Owen, *The Metropolitan Transportation Problem* (Washington, D.C.: Brookings Institution, 1966).

6. Intercity trucks use high-performance highways, when available, more than other vehicles. In the truckers' view, if these high-performance facilities are paid for entirely by tolls, then an excise (unless rebated) on fuel and rubber consumed on such highways represents double taxation. Also, turnpike tolls tend to be more closely calibrated to the actual construction and maintenance costs of highway use by particular types of vehicles than are excises on gasoline, diesel tires, and so forth. Empirical evidence suggests that heavy diesel trucks are the beneficiaries of this (that is, they are undertaxed relative to the costs they impose).

7. This shortening of the congestion period, rather than its elimination, could be predicted on simple theoretical grounds. See Brian Martin and Martin Wohl, *Traffic System Analysis for Engineers and Planners* (New York: McGraw-Hill, 1967), pp. 164–175.

8. William Alonso, *Location and Land Use: Toward a General Theory of Land Rent* (Cambridge, Mass.: Harvard University Press, 1964); John F. Kain, "The Journey-to-Work as a Determinant of Residential Location," *Papers and Pro-*

ceedings of the Regional Science Association 9 (1962): 137-161; Richard Muth, *Cities and Housing* (Chicago: University of Chicago Press, 1969); Lowdon Wingo, Jr., *Transportation and Urban Land* (Washington, D.C.: Resources for the Future, 1961).

9. Lewis M. Schneider, *Marketing Urban Mass Transit* (Boston: Division of Research, Graduate School of Business Administration, Harvard University, 1965).

10. Jack Faucett Associates, "The Washington Area Metropolitan Rail System: A Current Perspective and a Preliminary Appraisal of Alternatives," a report prepared for the Congressional Research Service, Library of Congress, January 10, 1976; Melvin Webber, "The BART Experience—What Have We Learned?" *Public Interest*, no. 45 (Fall 1976): 79-108; Henry Bain, "New Directions for Metro: Lessons from the BART Experience," Washington Center for Metropolitan Studies, December 1976.

11. Malcolm Getz, "The Incidence of Rapid Transit in Atlanta" (diss., Yale University, 1973); Alan Altshuler, with James P. Womack and John R. Pucher, *The Urban Transportation System: Politics and Policy Innovation* (Cambridge, Mass.: MIT Press, 1979), ch. 8, pp. 252-316.

2. Metropolitan Location and Travel Trends

1. Edwin S. Mills and Jee Peng Tan, "A Comparison of Urban Population Density Functions in Developed and Developing Countries," *Urban Studies* (forthcoming).

2. Documentation of this point can be found in the appendix.

3. See John R. Meyer, John F. Kain, and Martin Wohl, *The Urban Transportation Problem* (Cambridge, Mass.: Harvard University Press, 1965); John F. Kain, "The Distribution and Movement of Jobs and Industry," in James Q. Wilson, ed., *The Metropolitan Enigma: Inquiries into the Nature and Dimensions of America's "Urban Crisis"* (Washington, D.C.: Chamber of Commerce of the United States, 1967); John R. Meyer, "Urban Transportation," in Daniel P. Moynihan, ed., *Urban American: The Expert Looks at the City* (Washington, D.C.: Voice of America Forum Lectures, 1970), p. 71; John F. Kain, "Postwar Changes in Land Use in the American City," in Kain, ed., *Essays on Urban Spatial Structure* (Cambridge, Mass.: Ballinger, 1975), p. 81.

4. Benjamin I. Cohen, "Trends in Negro Employment within Large Metropolitan Areas," *Public Policy* 19 (Fall 1971): 611-622; Alexander Ganz and Thomas O'Brien, "The City: Sandbox, Reservation or Dynamo?" *Public Policy* 21 (Winter 1973): 107-123.

5. Kain, *Essays on Urban Spatial Structure;* Robert A. Leone, "The Location of Manufacturing Activity in the New York Metropolitan Area" (diss., Yale University, 1971); and Franklin J. James, Jr., "The City: Sandbox, Reservation or Dynamo?: A Reply," *Public Policy* 22 (Winter 1974): 39-51.

6. John R. Meyer and Robert A. Leone, "The New England States and Their Economic Future: Some Implications of a Changing Industrial Environment," *American Economic Review: Papers and Proceedings* 68 (May 1978): 110-115.

7. Mills and Tan, "A Comparison of Urban Population Density Functions."

8. In Chicago between 1956 and 1970, for example, the average length of trips within the 1956 metropolitan study area boundaries grew by only 2 percent (from 4.2 to 4.3 miles). During that same period, though, the average length of all Chicago metropolitan area trips grew by 21 percent (from 4.2 to 5.1 miles), a change

reflecting the growth in the land area covered by the metropolitan area as well as decentralization.

9. U.S. Department of Transportation, Federal Highway Administration, *Highway Statistics,* various annual editions (Washington, D.C.: U.S. Government Printing Office, various years), table VM-1.

10. As measured in passenger-miles and reported in Association of American Railroads, *Yearbook of Railroad Facts, 1978 Edition* (Washington, D.C.: Association of American Railroads, 1979), p. 32.

11. Data for the 1970s are from the International Taxicab Association, Rockville, Md.

12. José A. Gómez-Ibáñez, "Federal Assistance to Urban Mass Transportation" (diss., Harvard University, 1975), p. 27.

13. Public transportation has been more successful in maintaining its share of work- and downtown-oriented travel largely because these trips offer the volume that makes high-quality public transportation service possible at a reasonable cost. Most worktrips are made during a few morning and evening hours, while nonwork travel is more evenly distributed over the day. Since the downtown area typically offers the highest concentration of metropolitan activity, the highest concentration of trips may be found there. Automobile use is also more time-consuming and expensive during the rush hours on trips to the downtown area.

14. The downtown area not only attracts large volumes of traffic because it contains a high concentration of metropolitan employment, but also because its central location and extensive highway system often make it a convenient route for through traffic. In Boston during the 1970s, for example, about half the cars entering a 2.5-square-mile downtown zone in the center of the metropolitan area were on through trips; this proportion became as high as 80 percent during peak hours. José A. Gómez-Ibáñez and Gary R. Fauth, "Downtown Auto Restraint Policies: Costs and Benefits for Boston," *Journal of Transportation Economics and Policy* 14, no. 2 (May 1980): 133–153; and Arnold M. Howitt, "Downtown Auto Restraint Policies: Adopting and Implementing Urban Transportation Innovations," ibid., pp. 155–167.

15. The averages reported in Table 2.8 hide substantial variations in speeds from route to route. For example, a slight overall average increase for a city may reflect increases on five and decreases on four of nine routes studied.

3. Government Programs to Revitalize Urban Mass Transportation

1. These statistics exclude bus or railroad passenger service that is primarily intercity in nature. See *Transit Fact Book, 1978–1979* (Washington, D.C.: American Public Transit Association, 1979), pp. 27, 43.

2. New York, Chicago, Boston, Philadelphia, and San Francisco are the only metropolitan areas with commuter rail services of any significance.

3. According to statistics collected by the International Taxicab Association, in 1970 the taxi industry carried 2.4 billion passengers and collected $2.2 billion in revenue; see John D. Wells et al., *Economic Characteristics of the Urban Public Transportation Industry,* report prepared by the Institute for Defense Analyses for the U.S. Department of Transportation (Washington, D.C.: U.S. Government Printing Office, 1976), p. 8–6. However, these taxi industry statistics may be inflated and may exaggerate the importance of the mode; see Alan Altshuler, "The Federal Government and Paratransit," *Paratransit,* special report no. 164

of the Transportation Research Board (Washington, D.C.: National Academy of Sciences, 1976), p. 92.

4. Table 3.1 shows that approximately 15.6 million workers commuted in carpools in 1975. Given that there are approximately 250 workdays per year and two trips per workday, the total number of commuting trips by carpool can thus be estimated at about 7.8 billion per year.

5. Commuter rail traffic grew from about four billion revenue passenger-miles per year in the late 1930s to a peak of about six billion in 1947 and then declined during the 1950s to about 4.5 billion per year, where it has more or less held ever since. See George W. Hilton, "The Decline of Railroad Commutation," *Business History Review* 36 (Summer 1962): 171–173; the Institute for Defense Analyses, *Economic Characteristics of the Urban Public Transportation Industry*, report to the U.S. Department of Transportation (Washington, D.C.: U.S. Government Printing Office, 1972), p. 7–22; and American Public Transit Association, *Transit Fact Book, 1978–1979* (Washington, D.C.: American Public Transit Association, 1979), pp. 27, 28, 43.

6. Hilton, "Decline of Railroad Commutation," p. 193.

7. American Public Transit Association, *Transit Fact Book, 1978–1979*, p. 43.

8. On average, each mode's revenues cover about half of operating costs. While data on capital costs are not available, revenues probably constitute a much smaller proportion of total costs for heavy rail vehicles and commuter railroads, since they are the more capital-extensive modes.

9. Public ownership was assumed in Detroit in 1922, New York in 1932, Cleveland in 1942, and Boston and Chicago in 1947.

10. Credit for beginning the movement for federal aid is often given to transportation planners for the City of Philadelphia. In 1956 and 1957, Mayor Frank Dilworth of Philadelphia proposed to Congress that the cities be allowed to use federal highway aid for mass transport projects. Dilworth was not joined by other mayors or others involved with city and mass transport interests until after the enactment of the Transportation Act of 1958. For a definitive history of the movement to get federal aid for transit from the 1950s to 1964 see Michael N. Danielson, *Federal-Metropolitan Politics and the Commuter Crisis* (New York: Columbia University Press, 1965). See also George M. Smerk, *Urban Transportation: The Federal Role* (Bloomington: Indiana University Press, 1965), pp. 140–178.

11. The capital grant program was passed not only because of low utilization of the capital loan program but also because organized labor joined the coalition of mass transportation supporters (in return for legislated guarantees that federal assistance would not reduce the numbers or worsen the working conditions of transportation workers).

12. In 1964, Congress initially authorized the expenditure of $375 million over three years. Congress authorized an increase of $300 million (to be spent over two years) in 1966, $190 million (over one year) in 1968, $3 billion (over five years) in 1970 and again in 1973, $7.9 billion (over six years) in 1974, and $7.5 billion (over five years) in 1978. Moreover, in 1970, Congress responded to industry complaints (that uncertainty about annual capital grant appropriations discouraged long-term capital planning) by putting the funding of the capital grant program on a special "contract authority" basis. Under this system, the agency administering the program could make legally binding commitments to fund projects on the basis of congressional authorizations, rather than having to wait for annual appropriations.

13. In 1978, a new, smaller capital grant program was established to supplement the original program. The new program provides grants for capital ex-

penses for buses only, to be distributed among metropolitan areas using a congressionally mandated formula based on urban population and population density. The new program was initially authorized at $1.4 billion to be spent over four years.

14. The U.S. Department of Transportation was not established until 1966, and it was not until 1968 that the department was given control of federal mass transportation assistance and UMTA was formed. Before 1968, federal aid to mass transportation was administered by the U.S. Department of Housing and Urban Development.

15. According to this hypothesis, ridership losses raised average costs, which in turn forced a fare increase and further ridership declines; a one-time infusion of new capital would stabilize costs and ridership and thus stop the continuing cycle of decline. Many of these arguments for the federal capital grant program were made in a 1961 report to the U.S. Department of Housing and Urban Development by the Institute of Public Administration. That report was eventually published as Lyle C. Fitch and Associates, *Urban Transportation and Public Policy* (San Francisco: Chandler, 1964).

16. UMTA reports that capital grants have been equally divided among bus transit (largely vehicle replacement), rail "modernization," and starts of new rail systems. Much of the rail "modernization" is apparently extension of lines on existing systems, so the split between replacement of existing capital and construction of new extensions or systems is probably fifty-fifty. See U.S. Congress, Congressional Budget Office, *Urban Mass Transportation: Options for Federal Assistance,* budget issue paper (Washington, D.C.: U.S. Government Printing Office, 1977), p. 9.

17. Estimated from data supplied by the U.S. Department of Transportation, Federal Highway Administration.

18. In 1975, a nationwide maximum of $200 million could be diverted, but none could be used for rail systems. As of 1976, the entire amount was divertible, and rail projects could be funded as well.

19. Since the commitment to build BART predated federal aid, local property and sales taxes were used to pay most of the capital costs; the federal government financed only the construction of some of the last segments and the purchase of rolling stock.

20. Melvin M. Webber, "The BART Experience—What Have We Learned?" *Public Interest,* no. 45 (Fall 1976): 84–88, 97–98.

21. See Martin Wohl, "An Analysis and Evaluation of the Rapid Transit Extension to Cleveland's Airport," working paper no. 708–43 (Washington, D.C.: Urban Institute, 1972); and George W. Hilton, *Federal Transit Subsidies: The Urban Mass Transportation Assistance Program* (Washington, D.C.: American Enterprise Institute for Public Policy Research, 1974), pp. 61–66.

22. The remaining 6 percent presumably had used other modes previously; see Hilton, *Federal Transit Subsidies,* pp. 66–67.

23. William B. Tye III, "The Capital Grant as a Subsidy Device: The Case Study of Urban Mass Transportation," *The Economics of Federal Subsidy Programs,* in *Transportation Subsidies,* pt. 6, U.S. Congress, Joint Economic Committee (Washington, D.C.: U.S. Government Printing Office, 1973), pp. 796–826.

24. Of course, even with these controls, some incommensurables always remain. On the one hand, the comfort of the ride may be superior on rail. On the other hand, the bus system may offer shorter waiting times at stops; since a bus carries fewer passengers than a rail transit car or train, a bus system operates more frequent service than a rail system of equivalent capacity. Bus systems may also re-

duce passenger transfers, since bus systems can offer "integrated" service where the residential collection, line-haul, and downtown distribution portions of the trip are all performed by the same vehicle.

25. Several studies came to similar conclusions about the travel volume necessary to support rail transit. See John R. Meyer, John F. Kain, and Martin Wohl, *The Urban Transportation Problem* (Cambridge, Mass.: Harvard University Press, 1965), pp. 299–306; Theodore E. Keeler and Kenneth A. Small, *Automobile Costs and Final Intermodal Cost Comparisons*, vol. 3 of *The Full Costs of Urban Transport*, ed. Theodore E. Keeler, Leonard A. Merewitz, and P. M. J. Fisher (Berkeley: University of California, Institute of Urban and Regional Development, 1975); and J. Hayden Boyd, Norman J. Asher, and Elliot S. Wetzler, *Evaluation of Rail Rapid Transit and Express Bus Service in the Urban Commuter Market*, report prepared by the Institute for Defense Analyses for the U.S. Department of Transportation (Washington, D.C.: U.S. Government Printing Office, 1973). A number of analysts dispute the results reported here, however, and argue that rail transit dominates bus transit at much lower traffic volumes. Generally, these analysts make assumptions about costs and operating practices that seem biased against the bus. For a review of these dissenting studies and their weaknesses, see Andrew M. Hamer, *The Selling of Rail Rapid Transit* (Lexington, Mass: Lexington Books, 1976), ch. 3.

26. Meyer, Kain, and Wohl, *The Urban Transportation Problem*, p. 86.

27. The PATCO line between Philadelphia and Camden, N.J., might be considered a new system rather than an extension since it is operated by a different agency from the one operating the older Philadelphia rail transit system. But the PATCO line was classified as an extension, because its main downtown station connects with the older system and because it is only a single 41-mile line. For a list of the rail transit extensions and systems begun between World War II and 1974 see José A. Gómez-Ibáñez, "Federal Assistance to Urban Mass Transportation" (diss., Harvard University, 1975), pp. 267–269.

28. For a critique of the rail transit systems planned in Atlanta and Washington, D.C., see Hamer, *The Selling of Rail Rapid Transit*, chs. 5 and 6; U.S. Congress, House Committee on the District of Columbia, *Washington Area Metro Rail System: Perspectives and Alternatives*, report prepared from the Library of Congress by Jack Faucett Associates, Inc., committee print serial S-4 (Washington, D.C.: U.S. Government Printing Office, 1976); and John F. Kain, "The Unexplored Potential of Freeway Rapid Transit in Regional Transportation Planning: An Atlanta Case Study," in Andrew Hamer, ed. *Unorthodox Approaches to Urban Transportation: The Emerging Challenge to Conventional Planning* (Atlanta: Georgia State University, Bureau of Business and Economic Research, 1972), pp. 38–51.

29. During the 1960s UMTA officials, who approved grants on a first-come, first-served basis, found themselves several billion dollars short for funding all of the capital grant applications received. Cities with major capital projects far down in UMTA's queue lobbied strongly for increased appropriations for the capital grant program.

30. Although these grants can be used for capital or operating expenses at local option, in practice the funds are used almost exclusively for operating outlays. Only 6 percent of these funds were used for capital outlays during the first two years of the program. See U.S. Department of Transportation, Urban Mass Transportation Administration, Office of Policy and Program Development, *Transit Operating Performance and the Impact of the Section 5 Program* (Washington, D.C.: Urban Mass Transportation Administration, 1976).

31. To discourage wasteful practices and the substitution of federal for local aid, local governments are required to maintain at least the level of operating subsidies they had previously funded and to match federal aid with an equal amount of their own assistance.

32. For a more detailed description of the uses of federal operating assistance in the first two years of the program see U.S. Department of Transportation, *Transit Operating Performance and the Impact of the Section 5 Program*, pp. 12–16, A–7.

33. The 1978 legislation increased the authorization for the original operating aid program by $1.8 billion to fund grants at $900 million per year through fiscal 1982. There were three new operating grant programs created by the 1978 legislation, authorized at a combined total of $1.97 billion over fiscal years 1979 through 1982. Two of the new programs were aimed at the large metropolitan areas where operating deficits are concentrated: one, authorized at $1 billion over four years, uses a formula that distributes 85 percent of the funds to urban areas with more than 750,000 persons, while the other, authorized at $550 million over four years, is for rail transit and commuter railroad expenses only and is distributed according to the number of rail route-miles and train-miles in each urban area. Partly to counterbalance the two new programs for large metropolitan areas, a third new operating grant program was established for small urban and rural areas only, authorized at $420 million over four years.

34. Other metropolitan areas that granted regional transit authorities similar taxing powers include Denver (1973), Chicago (1974), Louisville (1974), Cleveland (1975), and Houston (1978).

35. These statistics assume that operating assistance was sufficient to cover the shortfall between revenue and operating expenses, which seems reasonable, since most of the transit industry was publicly owned and operated by the 1970s. See American Public Transit Association, *Transit Fact Book, 1978–1979*, pp. 21, 22, 27.

36. Ibid., p. 31.

37. Between 1970 and 1977, the average transit fare in *current* dollars increased from 28 to 38 cents. Ibid., pp. 32–33.

38. Ibid., p. 30.

39. The cost of serving rush hour mass transportation trips is higher than the cost of serving midday trips because rush hour service requires more additions to capacity.

40. Between 1947 and 1960, when the mass transportation industry was declining and not receiving substantial public aid, unionized hourly rates for transit grew only 88 percent (in current dollars) while the average hourly wage in manufacturing grew 106 percent. From 1960 to 1968, when public aid was growing but still was not substantial, transit hourly wages increased slightly more rapidly than manufacturing wages: 44 versus 40 percent. From 1968 to 1973, the years of substantial aid increases, transit wage rates grew by 45 percent, while manufacturing wage rates grew only 37 percent. See U.S. Department of Labor, *Handbook of Labor Statistics–1975 Edition*, bulletin no. 1865 (Washington, D.C.: U.S. Government Printing Office, 1975), pp. 188, 226.

41. For a quantitative assessment of the effects of fare reductions in cities, see Keith M. Goodman and Melinda A. Green, *Low Fare and Fare-Free Transit: Some Recent Applications by U.S. Transit Systems*, report prepared by the Urban Institute for the U.S. Department of Transportation (Washington, D.C.: U.S. Department of Transportation, 1977).

42. The estimates of the change in transit patronage and the results of the sur-

vey of new riders are from Michael A. Kemp, *Reduced Fare and Fare-Free Urban Transit Services—Some Case Studies,* paper no. 1213-3 (Washington, D.C.: Urban Institute, 1974), pp. 19–27.

43. Eugene and Portland, Oregon; Salt Lake City, Utah; San Diego, California; Madison, Wisconsin; and Minneapolis, Minnesota.

44. The estimates of 30–50 cents per passenger are based on assumptions that one half to two thirds of the increase in operating deficits and all of the added patronage are due to service expansion and are based on data in Urban Mass Transportation Administration, Office of Policy and Program Development, *Increasing Transit Ridership: The Experience of Seven Cities* (Washington, D.C.: Urban Mass Transportation Administration, 1976).

45. Applicants were also to project operating costs of the capital project, to provide a financial plan for funding any operating deficits, and to explain any deviation from unspecified industry "norms" for operating efficiency. The 1972 criteria are in U.S. Department of Transportation, Urban Mass Transportation Administration, *Capital Grants for Urban Mass Transportation, Information for Applicants* (Washington, D.C.: Urban Mass Transportation Administration, 1972), pp. 18–33, esp. pp. 25, 28–29. The pressures leading UMTA to establish these criteria are described in Hilton, *Federal Transit Subsidies,* pp. 78–80.

46. The TSM plan must show that the local governments have considered a variety of low-cost measures to improve the productivity of their capital facilities, such as improving traffic signals and controls, providing transit and other high-occupancy vehicles priority in traffic, and discouraging private vehicle use in congested areas.

47. These regulations also required that construction contracts be negotiated with a fixed ceiling on the federal contribution, in order to discourage cost overruns.

48. For example, new designs for conventional bus and rail transit vehicles, improved subway construction techniques, and more exotic technologies such as automatic train control and fully automated transit systems.

49. For a description of UMTA's early RD&D programs see Hilton, *Federal Transit Subsidies,* pp. 13–50. For a description of UMTA's more recent RD&D programs see U.S. Department of Transportation, Urban Mass Transportation Administration, *Innovation in Public Transportation, Fiscal Year 1977* (Washington, D.C.: U.S. Department of Transportation, Urban Mass Transportation Administration, 1978).

50. Hilton, *Federal Transit Subsidies,* pp. 77–83.

51. Note that the percentages on the use of various transportation modes shown in Table 3.1 are for the year 1975, well after the OPEC price rise and Arab oil embargo.

52. Such schemes are described in more detail in Chapters 4 and 11.

53. See Meyer, Kain, and Wohl, *The Urban Transportation Problem,* pp. 299–306; and Keeler and Small, *Final Intermodal Cost Comparisons,* pp. 123–132. Since some costs, notably for highway construction and maintenance, may not be paid fully by the peak-hour automobile and mass transportation users (although Keeler and Small made every effort to allow for these), total cost comparisons may not provide totally accurate guidance to determine the situations in which mass transportation is competitive with automobiles. Highway costs constitute a larger portion of automobile than mass transportation total costs, and thus the results of these studies (especially Meyer et al.) may slightly underestimate the volumes required for mass transportation to capture a significant portion of the market.

54. Not all trips made by residents of high-density, low-income communities are easily served by mass transportation, however. Especially difficult to serve are trips to suburban workplaces or neighboring lower-density communities. The destinations of such trips are often so widely dispersed that convenient transit schedules are expensive to maintain. Another difficulty that may arise when serving low-income, high-density neighborhoods is crime. It has been suggested that the threat of crime when walking to and from stops or on mass transportation vehicles has reduced inner-city transit patronage in recent years. If true, and if crime continues to increase in inner-city neighborhoods, mass transportation may lose much of that market to other public transportation modes, such as taxis, which provide door-to-door service.

4. Improving Conventional Mass Transportation

1. See John W. Kendrick, *Postwar Productivity Trends in the United States, 1948–1969* (New York: Columbia University Press, 1973), p. 334; and John R. Meyer and José A. Gómez-Ibáñez, *Improving Urban Mass Transportation Productivity*, report to the U.S. Department of Transportation, Urban Mass Transportation Administration, 1977, p. 25. These figures are for the transit industry alone, although the productivity trends in commuter railroads were probably similar. The estimates of productivity growth provided here are for total factor productivity—that is, the ratio of outputs produced to all inputs consumed, including labor, capital, and intermediate goods.

2. For example, if output is measured, as it usually is, by number of passengers carried, then continuing to provide little-used services reduces productivity by cutting the output from a given amount of labor, capital, and other inputs.

3. This estimate assumes that it is socially beneficial to maintain transit service despite declining patronage, and thus the basic measure of output used is the number of vehicle-miles operated, rather than the number of passengers carried. See Meyer and Gómez-Ibáñez, *Improving Urban Mass Transportation Productivity*, pp. 33–35.

4. Kendrick, *Postwar Productivity Trends in the United States, 1948–1969*, p. 41.

5. Ibid., pp. 328–340.

6. The most significant exceptions are industries, such as medical services, that experienced extremely strong growth in total demand due to the growth of the population, gains in per capita income, or other helpful external forces.

7. A split shift is a daily work assignment that has a long unpaid break in the middle. In most cities, labor agreements restrict the use of split shifts by (1) limiting their proportion to 30–50 percent of total operating labor assignments, (2) specifying a limit to the permissible total length of any split shift (usually 11–13 hours), and (3) requiring premium pay for splits over a certain length (usually 10–12 hours).

8. These data were supplied under the condition that the transit property not be identified.

9. Sage Management Consultants, *Labor and Urban Transit Operations: Profile and Prospects*, report prepared for Transport Canada, Canadian Surface Transportation Administration, Urban Transportation Research Branch, 1978, p. 94.

10. Several transit authorities have negotiated changes in their labor contracts to allow some use of drivers who are only part-time transit employees. Robert E.

Lieb and Frederick Wiesman, "Survey of the Use of Part-time Employees in the Transit Industry," paper presented at the annual meeting of the Transportation Research Board, Washington, D.C., January 16, 1979.

11. At least one analyst is pessimistic about the potential for productivity gains from part-time labor. Charles Lave reports that several transit systems considering or implementing part-time labor estimate that this practice will reduce their labor costs by only 1.3–9 percent. Moreover, he estimates that the wage concessions required to gain labor's consent to part-time drivers might easily offset such small savings. However, he appears to underestimate the possibilities of part-time labor, which should offer more flexibility and opportunities for savings than simply changes in work rules governing split shifts. Lave's citing a 1.3–9 percent savings is also inconsistent with the 17–21 percent savings predicted for altered work rules in Toronto and San Diego. In calculating that wage concessions might offset these savings, Lave also assumes an unusually generous wage concession, in particular, that management will agree to raise *in perpetuity* the annual percentage increase in the wage rate, rather than the more common concession of a larger percentage increase only in the year of the work-rule change. With the former type of wage concession, the wage cost grows at a compound rate and eventually exceeds the labor savings of any work-rule change. See Charles A. Lave, "Is Part-Time Labor a Cure for Transit Deficits?" *Traffic Quarterly* 34 (January 1980): 61–74.

12. All of these possibilities for employing drivers during the off-peak hours would require significant restructuring of current labor practices. There might be opposition by firms and unions both outside and inside the industry; for example, both the taxi industry and the Teamsters' Union (which represents taxi drivers in several cities) might oppose the provision of taxi-like services by transit drivers.

13. See Meyer and Gómez-Ibáñez, *Improving Urban Mass Transportation Productivity*, pp. 100–106.

14. The economies in operating smaller buses on lightly traveled routes during the off-peak hours would have to be balanced against the cost of leaving the undersized vehicles idle during the peak hours.

15. In transportation industries other than mass transportation, a variety of different vehicles are used, selected to suit different circumstances. In contrast, the mass transportation industry uses a fairly standard 40-foot bus on almost all routes. Resistance to the introduction of vehicles of different sizes stems in part from the effect this would have on maintenance, training, and inventory expenses, which must be weighed against the benefits of selective use of larger and smaller buses.

16. Express operations increase average bus speeds by allowing some vehicles to skip less heavily used stops or to shift to faster parallel arterial streets or freeways for the nonstop portions of their routes. Adoption of express services may increase passenger waiting times, however, by lengthening headways at the skipped stops; the effect of longer headways can be minimized if the stops are lightly used or if headways are currently either very short or long enough that passengers arrive at the stop to meet a specific bus.

17. Bus priority and traffic management techniques contribute to increased bus speed and reliability largely by reducing the effects of traffic congestion. The possibilities include bus override of traffic signals, exclusive bus lanes on arterials and freeways, incremental changes in street design, or modification of street management techniques (such as eliminating one-way streets that often lead to increased car speeds but slower bus speeds).

18. For futher development of the advantages and disadvantages of these

schemes, see Meyer and Gómez-Ibáñez, *Improving Urban Mass Transportation Productivity,* pp. 109–124; John F. Kain, "How to Improve Urban Transportation at Practically No Cost," *Public Policy* 20 (Summer 1972): 335–358; and John F. Kain, "The Unexplored Potential of Freeway Rapid Transit in Regional Transportation Planning: An Atlanta Case Study," in *Unorthodox Approaches to Urban Transportation: The Emerging Challenge to Conventional Planning,* ed. Andrew Hamer (Atlanta: Georgia State University, Bureau of Business and Economic Research, 1972), pp. 38–51.

19. In recent years, several transit properties decreased off-peak fares in an attempt to reduce the difference between peak and off-peak use. Since transit use is not too sensitive to fare changes, these off-peak discounts resulted in substantial revenue losses and were usually quickly discontinued. Raising peak period fares may be a more practical means of encouraging more balanced peak and off-peak use, since it should increase total transit revenues. However, for political reasons, any such peak-period fare increase would probably have to be introduced as part of a package of general fare increases or in place of such increases.

20. On the other hand, an increase in peak mass transportation fares unmatched by an equivalent markup for parallel automobile travel could be counterproductive, adding to highway congestion when least desired.

21. Two exceptions to this tendency toward uniform fares have been the widespread adoption of discounts for elderly and handicapped passengers and the implementation of fares that vary with distance using automatic ticket-vending and collecting equipment on the subway systems in San Francisco and Washington, D.C.

22. Interlining describes the practice of scheduling one vehicle and driver to serve several transit routes, usually in an effort to improve equipment and labor utilization.

23. Contracting out is not commonly done in the transit industry. Nevertheless, the industry has had some limited experience with contracting, which suggests that the practical problems might not be insuperable. For example, a few of the smaller transit properties contract with other firms for the performance of limited maintenance and, less commonly, administrative functions.

24. See E. S. Savas, "Municipal Monopolies vs. Competition in Delivering Public Services," *Urban Analysis* 2 (1974): 93–116.

25. The private and public carters do not operate identical services, so cost comparisons are difficult. One difference that leads to an expectation that private carting costs would be lower is that the private carters collect only from multifamily dwellings and commercial establishments, so the amount of refuse collected at each stop is about twice as large as the amount collected by the public agency's refuse collectors. On the other hand, there are also several service differences that would suggest that private carting costs should be higher; for example, private carters collect refuse from behind the building (while public collection is usually from curbside) and have more widely scattered customers. Ibid., p. 98.

26. Ibid., pp. 98–99.

27. Ibid., pp. 107–112.

28. Meyer and Gómez-Ibáñez, *Improving Urban Mass Transportation Productivity,* p. 131.

29. For a description of these private transit management companies, see David B. Vallenga, "Can Professional Transit Management Improve Our Urban Transit Systems?" *Proceedings of the Transportation Research Forum* 14 (1973): 345–350.

30. A system similar to this exists between Conrail and several transit author-

ities for the provision of suburban commuter railroad services. The major difference between this and the procedure suggested here is that the contracts with Conrail are negotiated subject to arbitration and without competitive bidding.

31. Contracting out would be less attractive where local mass transportation authorities and transit unions have worked out their own satisfactory solutions to the problems of peak-hour labor and vehicle needs. In such circumstances, it may not even be advisable to contract out for maintenance and administrative tasks, since these tasks might provide off-peak employment for transit workers needed as drivers in the peak hours only.

32. The benefits and problems of route-by-route bidding schemes are described in detail by Roger Schmenner in "Bus Subsidies: The Case for Route-by-Route Bidding in Connecticut," *Policy Analysis* 2 (Summer 1970): 421–428.

33. This suggestion has been made by Ray A. Munday in "The Economic Use of Subsidies for Urban Mass Transportation," *Transportation* 5 (1976): 128–129.

34. Kendrick, *Postwar Productivity Trends in the United States, 1948–1969,* pp. 110–111; and Meyer and Gómez-Ibáñez, *Improving Urban Mass Transportation Productivity,* pp. 8–10.

5. Dial-a-Ride, Pooling, Taxis, and Futuristic Public Transportation

1. U.S. Department of Housing and Urban Development, Office of Metropolitan Development, Urban Transportation Administration, *Tomorrow's Transportation: New Systems for the Urban Future* (Washington, D.C.: U.S. Government Printing Office, 1968).

2. "Separation" simply means keeping trains at safe distance from each other.

3. U.S. Congress, Office of Technology Assessment, *Automatic Train Control in Rail Rapid Transit* (Washington, D.C.: U.S. Government Printing Office, 1976), pp. 110–111.

4. Ibid., p. 119.

5. Ibid., p. 116.

6. For example, the initial capital costs of the ATC components of Washington's new METRO system are estimated, probably optimistically, at $100 million. If half of the cost is attributable to ATO and ATS, then an annual savings of $4.4 million in operating expenses per year would be required to justify automation beyond ATP, assuming a 30-year life and an 8 percent interest rate. If the average annual total cost of an employee is $30,000, such a savings would require a net reduction of 150 employees or 0.27 per vehicle (if the completed METRO system operates with 556 vehicles). Such savings are seldom experienced by rail systems with ATO and ATS, and where they are, the labor force reductions may be due to less extensive off-peak service rather than automation.

7. For a detailed assessment of current experience with automated guideway systems see U.S. Congress, Office of Technology Assessment, *Automated Guideway Transit: An Assessment of PRT and Other New Systems,* report prepared at the request of the Senate Committee on Appropriations, Transportation Subcommittee (Washington, D.C.: U.S. Government Printing Office, 1975). For a more optimistic but cursory review of the prospects for automated guideways, see U.S. Congress, Office of Technology Assessment, *Impact of Advanced Group Rapid Transit Technology* (Washington, D.C.: U.S. Government Printing Office, 1980).

8. For descriptions of PRT proposals, see J. Edward Anderson, ed., *Personal Rapid Transit* (Minneapolis: University of Minnesota, Department of Audio Vis-

ual Extension, 1972); and J. Edward Anderson, ed., *Personal Rapid Transit II* (Minneapolis: University of Minnesota, Department of Audio Visual Extension, 1974).

9. Assessments of dual-mode potential are plagued by the difficulty of developing accurate estimates of the performance and, particularly, the cost of such untried systems. Such difficulties (along with probable double-counting of benefits) undermine the optimistic assessments of Peter Benjamin et al., "Analysis of Dual Mode Systems in Urban Areas," 3 vols., report by the Transportation Systems Center for the U.S. Department of Transportation, December 1973.

10. U.S. Department of Housing and Urban Development, *Tomorrow's Transportation,* p. 59.

11. For a description of the federal role in promoting dial-a-ride, see Alan Altshuler, "The Federal Government and Paratransit," in *Paratransit,* special report no. 164 by the Transportation Research Board of the National Academy of Sciences (Washington, D.C.: National Academy of Sciences, 1976), pp. 89–104.

12. Taxi fares are used as a measure of taxi costs largely because cost data are not readily available and because taxis, unlike dial-a-ride, are usually not publicly subsidized, so fares must cover costs.

13. Bert Arrillaga and George E. Mochanier, "Demand Responsive Planning Guidelines," reported by the Mitre Corporation to the U.S. Department of Transportation, April 1974; Myron H. Ross, "Dial-a-Ride: Boon or Bane?" *Transportation Research Forum Proceedings,* vol. 18 (1977); and Reid Ewing and Nigel Wilson, "Innovations in Demand Responsive Transit," report for the U.S. Department of Transportation by the Center for Transportation Studies, Massachusetts Institute of Technology, November 1977, table 2.

14. Most of these analyses compared dial-a-ride costs to bus costs, not taxi costs. See, for example, Joseph Stafford et al., *Economic Considerations for Dial-a-Ride,* Massachusetts Institute of Technology, Urban Systems Laboratory report no. USL-TR-70-11 (Cambridge, Mass.: MIT Urban Systems Laboratory, 1971); and J. Hayden Boyd, Norman J. Asher, and Elliot S. Wetzler, "Non-Technological Innovation in Urban Transit: A Comparison of Some Alternatives," unpublished, February 1976.

15. Computerized assignment was first used in a Haddonfield, N.J., dial-a-ride demonstration in the early 1970s and later tested more extensively in a Rochester, N.Y., demonstration sponsored by UMTA between 1976 and 1977. While the costs at the Haddonfield demonstration were much higher than local taxi fares, no evaluation of computerized assignment's contribution to the Haddonfield performance was made. However, Chris Hendrickson has analyzed the Rochester demonstration carefully and has found that computerized assignment probably reduced waiting and travel times slightly, but also increased costs by approximately 70 cents per passenger. Improvements in computers may make computerized assignment more attractive in the future, but at present Hendrickson concluded that computerization offers few advantages, largely because of limitations in the assignment programs, the cost of computers, and the need to preserve backup manual dispatching capability in the event of machine failure. See Chris T. Hendrickson, "Evaluation of Automated Dispatching for Flexibility Routed Paratransit Service," in *Paratransit 1979: Proceedings of a Workshop,* special report no. 186 of the Transportation Research Board, National Academy of Sciences (Washington, D.C.: National Academy of Sciences, 1979), pp. 56–62; and George E. Mochanier, *Summary Evaluation of the Haddonfield Dial-a-Ride Demonstration,* report no. UMTA-VA-06-0012-75-3, prepared by the Mitre Corpora-

tion for the U.S. Department of Transportation, Urban Mass Transportation Administration, May 1975.

16. A service improvement created by dial-a-ride may also be of value. In the longer run, too, dial-a-ride could make it easier to achieve labor economies through attrition if one dial-a-ride vehicle can do the work of more than one conventional bus during the off-peak.

17. Transit costs are from American Public Transit Association, *Transit Fact Book, 1978 Edition* (Washington, D.C.: American Public Transit Association, 1978), pp. 21, 24. The taxi fares are for Kalamazoo, Battle Creek, and Grand Rapids and are taken from Ross, "Dial-a-Ride: Boon or Bane?" Again, any taxi cost advantage might be partly attributable to the fact that in most communities taxi drivers are paid a lower hourly wage than transit drivers, often only 60 percent as much.

18. Only in a few large U.S. cities, most notably Washington, D.C., are there no limits on the numbers of taxi firms or medallions. For a description of typical limits on entry to the taxi industry and a detailed review of the arguments for and against their abolition, see Ronald F. Kirby et al., *Paratransit: Neglected Options for Future Mobility* (Washington, D.C.: Urban Institute, 1974), pp. 65–70, 89–99; and Sandra Rosenbloom, "Taxis, Jitneys, and Poverty," *Transaction* 7 (February 1970): 47–54.

19. Two important institutional barriers exist to vanpooling (but not to carpooling). Vanpools can encounter regulatory problems with state public service or utility commissions and also sometimes have difficulty in acquiring insurance. More and more states, though, have established insurance rates for multiple-use vans. Similarly, most public service or utility commission objections to vanpooling can be overcome by simply restricting them to commutes with origins outside the areas of existing franchised public transit. Pooling tends to be more advantageous for longer distance commutes, so this restriction is not too limiting.

20. As of late 1977, the FHWA had funded a total of 92 carpool demonstration projects in 30 states and 85 urban areas at a total cost to the federal government of $14 million. Frederick A. Wagner, "Evaluation of Carpool Demonstration Projects," paper presented at the annual meeting of the Federally Coordinated Program of Research and Development in Highway Transportation, Columbus, Ohio, November 1977, p. 11.

21. William L. Berry, *On the Economic Incentives for Commuter Carpooling* (diss., Harvard Business School, 1975). Commuters probably prefer homogeneity in all forms of public transportation, although their preference is likely to be stronger where the riding groups are smaller and long-lasting as in carpooling and vanpooling.

22. The percentages come from responses to a survey question about carpooling, reported in Alan M. Voorhees and Associates, Inc., and Behavioral Sciences Corporation, "A Study of Techniques to Increase Commuter Vehicle Occupancy on the Hollywood Freeway: Final Report," prepared for the California Department of Transportation, 1974, p. 89; and as cited in Berry, *On the Economic Incentives for Commuter Carpooling.*

23. For example, a sample of carpoolers on the Hollywood Freeway commuted an average of 19 miles one way, while a sample of nonpoolers commuted an average of only 17 miles. Average automobile occupancy is generally found to rise systematically with length of commute. 3M found that its few failures or near failures in vanpooling were on shorter commutes.

24. This worry, though, may be exaggerated, as ridesharing typically appeals

most to long-distance commuters not well served by transit.

25. See Gregory K. Ingram, "Reductions in Auto Use from Carpools and Improved Transit," discussion paper no. D76-10, Department of City and Regional Planning, Harvard University, October 1976, p. 24; and Moshe Ben-Akiva and Terry J. Atherton, "Short Range Travel Demand Predictions: Analysis of Carpooling Incentives," *Journal of Transport Economics and Policy* 11 (September 1977): 241.

26. Ben-Akiva and Atherton, "Short Range Travel Demand Predictions," p. 238.

27. Similar results were independently estimated by Ingram in simulations of the effects of carpooling incentives in Washington, D.C., Boston, Los Angeles, and Chicago; see Ingram, "Reductions in Auto Use from Carpools and Improved Transit."

28. For a list of those in operation in 1976, see Interplan Corporation, *Transportation Systems Management: State of the Art*, prepared for the U.S. Department of Transportation, Urban Mass Transportation Administration (Washington, D.C.: U.S. Government Printing Office, 1977), pp. 75–76.

29. Ibid.

30. Frederick J. Wegmann, Arun J. Chatterjee, and Stanley R. Stokey, "Evaluation of an Employer-Based Commuter Ridesharing Program," photocopied manuscript, Department of Civil Engineering, University of Tennessee, Knoxville, July 1977.

31. Berry, *On the Economic Incentives for Commuter Carpooling*, p. 117.

32. 3M identifies the following benefits to itself: reduced congestion at 3M installations; reduced demand for parking; reduced capital expenditures for automobile-related facilities; and more efficient use of land at 3M installations. As benefits to users, 3M suggests money savings; reduced risks and tension in commuting; and greater availability of cars for use by other family members, thereby increasing mobility and social-economic opportunities. Among benefits to nonusers, 3M suggests reduced congestion and parking demand in and around 3M installations; benefits to the general public, such as reduced congestion on streets and highways, reduced land use for automobile-related facilities; a positive effect on the environment (for example, less air and noise pollution); and reduced energy consumption.

6. Automobile Futures: Some Speculations on Ownership and Fleet Composition

1. The figures cited are for the seven-year period from December 1972 through December 1979.

2. In the intercity travel market, automobile ownership decisions will also be affected by competition from airlines, railroads, and buses. Air travel is energy-intensive, but the introduction of more fuel-efficient aircraft should gradually attenuate this disadvantage. Railroad passenger fares are also unlikely to increase so long as Congress is willing to fund the subsidies required to keep fares and ridership roughly stable. Although thus far there has been no public assistance to intercity buses, improved fuel efficiency in new buses may well prove sufficient for buses to hold their market position.

3. U.S. Bureau of the Census, *Population Estimates and Projections: Projections of the Number of Households and Families, 1975–1990*, Current Population

Reports, Special Studies, ser. P-25, no. 607 (Washington, D.C.: U.S. Government Printing Office, 1975), p. 14.

4. See, for example, Damian Kulash, "Forecasting Long Run Automobile Demand," in *Strategies for Reducing Gasoline Consumption through Improved Motor Vehicle Efficiency*, Transportation Research Board, special report 189 (Washington, D.C.: Transportation Research Board, 1977), pp. 14–19; R. P. Smith, *Consumer Demand for Cars in the U.S.A.* (London: Cambridge University Press, 1975), pp. 27–41; Sorrel Wildhorn, Burke K. Burright, John H. Enns, and Thomas F. Kirkwood, *How to Save Gasoline: Public Policy Alternatives to the Automobile* (Cambridge, Mass.: Ballinger, 1976), p. 301; and Wharton Econometric Forecasting Associates, Inc., *An Analysis of the Automobile Market: Modeling the Long-Run Determinants of the Demand for Automobiles*, report to the U.S. Department of Transportation, February 1977, vol. 1, ch. 3.

5. John F. Kain and Gary R. Fauth, *The Effects of Urban Structure on Household Auto Ownership Decisions and Journey to Work Mode Choices, Phase II*, report to the U.S. Department of Transportation, May 1976.

6. The forecast of a 2–3 percent average annual growth in automobile ownership between the late 1970s and 1985 is well within the range of predictions made by several analysts. For example, the Federal Task Force on Motor Vehicle Goals Beyond 1980 estimated a 2 percent average annual growth rate for the 1980s, while Wharton Econometric Forecasting Associates predicted a growth rate of 1.8 percent between 1980 and 1985. See Energy Resources Council, *Report by the Federal Task Force on Motor Vehicle Goals Beyond 1980*, vol. 2 (Washington, D.C.: Energy Resources Council, 1976), p. 7–3; and Wharton Econometric Forecasting Associates, Inc., *An Analysis of the Automobile Market*, vol. 1, p. 1–6.

7. Federal Task Force on Motor Vehicle Goals Beyond 1980, *Report*, p. 13–3; and Wildhorn, Burright, Enns, and Kirkwood, *How to Save Gasoline*, p. 216.

8. Changes in fuel economy, gasoline prices, and taxes may cause a change in the rate at which older cars are scrapped. In particular, if new models are substantially less expensive to own and operate, new-car sales should increase as older, more costly models are retired earlier. A gas-guzzler tax, however, might cause a decline in sales of larger new cars, delaying the replacement of some older vehicles. All of these changes in new-car sales and in scrappage rates will be tempered, furthermore, by compensating changes in the prices of used cars. For example, the introduction of newer, more fuel-efficient models should cause used-car prices to fall, reflecting their diminished attractiveness, and thus make it more costly to trade in an older car early.

9. J. D. Murrell, "Light Duty Automotive Fuel Economy—Trends through 1979," Society of Automotive Engineers, technical paper no. 790225, presented in Detroit, March 1979, p. 7.

10. See, e.g., Kulash, "Forecasting Long Run Automobile Demand," p. 18.

11. There is some fragmentary evidence that this effect is small and that additional income may be spent buying a more luxurious car of the same size. For example, in an analysis of the determinants of the choice of size of car in one-car families, income had a relatively small and statistically not significant coefficient for all but luxury standard cars. See James P. Leape, *The Demand for Automobiles: An Analysis*, undergraduate honors thesis, Harvard University, April 1977, pp. 152–153, 158–160.

12. Ibid., p. 58.

13. See, for example, ibid., pp. 152–160; Charles F. Manski and Leonard Sherman, "An Empirical Analysis of Household Choice among Motor Vehicles,"

Transportation Research 14A (October–December 1980): 349–366; N. Scott Cardell and Frederick C. Dunbar, "Measuring the Societal Impacts of Automobile Downsizing," *Transportation Research* 14A (October–December 1980): 423–434; and Charles A. Lave and Kenneth Train, "A Disaggregate Model of Auto Type Choice," *Transportation Research* 13A (1979): 1–9.

14. For an early exposition of these interrelationships and the problems in estimating them empirically, see John F. Kain, "The Journey to Work as a Determinant of Residential Location," *Papers and Proceedings of the Regional Science Association*, vol. 9, 1962, pp. 137–161. See also Boris S. Pushkarev and Jeffrey M. Zupan, *Public Transportation and Land Use Policy* (Bloomington: Indiana University Press, 1977).

15. Cambridge Systematics, Inc., "A Behavioral Model of Automobile Ownership and Mode of Travel," prepared for the Office of the Secretary, U.S. Department of Transportation, October 1974.

16. Steven R. Lerman, "Neighborhood Choice and Transportation Services," in *The Economics of Neighborhood*, ed. David Segal (New York: Academic Press, 1979).

17. John F. Kain, Gary R. Fauth, and Jeffrey Zax, *Forecasting Auto Ownership and Mode Choice for U.S. Metropolitan Areas*, research report R77-4, Program in City and Regional Planning, Harvard University, Cambridge, Mass., December 1977.

18. John F. Kain and Gary R. Fauth, "The Impact of Urban Development on Auto Ownership and Transit Use," paper prepared for the Allied Social Science Association, annual meeting, December 28–30, 1977, p. 31.

7. Land Use

1. See, for example, George M. Smerk, *Urban Mass Transportation: A Dozen Years of Federal Policy* (Bloomington: Indiana University Press, 1974).

2. For a particularly eloquent statement of this argument, see A. R. Karr, "Mass Transit Gets Short Shrift," *Wall Street Journal*, December 30, 1977, editorial page.

3. "Learning from Europe's Cities," *Transatlantic Perspectives*, June 1979 (publication of the German Marshall Fund of the United States).

4. George W. Hilton, "Rail Transit and the Pattern of Modern Cities: The California Case," *Traffic Quarterly* 21, no. 3 (July 1967): 379–393; George M. Smerk, "The Streetcar: Shape of American Cities," *Traffic Quarterly* 21, no. 4 (October 1967): 569–584; Samuel B. Warner, Jr., *Streetcar Suburbs: The Process of Growth in Boston, 1870–1900* (Cambridge, Mass.: Harvard University Press, 1962); and Edward S. Mason, *The Street Railway in Massachusetts: The Rise and Decline of an Industry* (Cambridge, Mass.: Harvard University Press, 1932).

5. U.S. Bureau of the Census, *Selected Characteristics of Travel to Work in Twenty Metropolitan Areas: 1976*, ser. P-23, no. 72 of the Current Population Reports, Special Studies (Washington, D.C.: U.S. Government Printing Office, 1978), pp. 13–18.

6. John B. Lansing and Gary Hendricks, *Automobile Ownership and Residential Density* (Ann Arbor, Michigan: Survey Research Center, Institute for Social Research, University of Michigan, June 1967), pp. 21–101; and John B. Lansing, Eva Mueller, and Nancy Barth, *Residential Location and Urban Mobility* (Ann Arbor: Survey Research Center, Institute for Social Research, University of Michigan, June 1964), pp. 73–81.

7. See, for example, Edwin S. Mills, *Studies in the Structure of the Urban Economy* (Baltimore: Johns Hopkins University Press, 1972); and Gerald S. Goldstein and Leon N. Moses, "Transportation Controls and the Spatial Structure of Urban Areas," *American Economic Review* 65 (May 1975): 289–294.

8. Researchers who have developed and refined models of residential location decisions include the following: Robert M. Haig, *Major Economic Factors in Metropolitan Growth and Arrangement* (New York: Regional Plan of New York and Its Environs, 1927); Richard V. Ratcliff, *Urban Land Economics* (New York: McGraw-Hill, 1949); Lowdon Wingo, Jr., *Transportation and Urban Land* (Washington, D.C.: Resources for the Future, 1961); William Alonso, *Location and Land Use* (Cambridge, Mass.: Havard University Press, 1964); Robert H. Strotz, "Urban Transportation Parables," in *The Public Economy of Urban Communities*, ed. Julius Margolis (Washington, D.C.: Resources for the Future, 1965), pp. 127–169; Richard F. Muth, *Cities and Housing* (Chicago: University of Chicago Press, 1969); Edwin S. Mills, "Transportation and Patterns of Urban Development: An Aggregative Model of Resource Allocation in a Metropolitan Area," *American Economic Review* 57 (May 1967): 197–241; idem, *Studies in the Structure of the Urban Economy;* Gregory K. Ingram et al., *The Detroit Prototype of the NBER Simulation Model* (New York: National Bureau of Economic Research, 1972); Robert M. Solow, "Congestion Cost and the Use of Land for Streets," *Bell Journal of Economics and Management Science* 4 (Autumn 1973): 603–618; and idem, "On Equilibrium Models of Urban Location," in *Essays in Modern Economics*, ed. J. M. Parkin (London: Longman's, 1973).

9. This model assumes that housing of every type (for example, with particular structural and neighborhood characteristics) is available at every distance from the metropolitan center. In fact, however, choices are more limited, especially in the short run, because buildings are relatively durable and immobile and their structural and neighborhood characteristics are difficult to change. The limited availabilty of houses of particular types means that actual location shifts will be less regular or uniform than those predicted by this model.

10. See, for example, Muth, *Cities and Housing*, pp. 31–33, or Alonso, *Location and Land Use*, pp. 108, 114.

11. This prediction is developed by Malcolm Getz in *The Incidence of Rapid Transit in America* (diss., Yale University, 1973), and in "A Model of the Impact of Transportation Investment on Land Rents," *Journal of Public Economics* 4 (February 1975): 57–74.

12. Three distinct models have been developed to explain the location choices of businesses: (1) the "classical" or Weberian model; (2) the central-place model; and (3) extensions of the monocentric model of residential-location choice. Each model focuses on only a few of the potentially important determinants of workplace-location choice. The classical model—developed in Alfred Weber, *Alfred Weber's Theory of the Location of Industries*, tr. and ed. C. J. Friedrich (Chicago: University of Chicago Press, 1928); Edgar Hoover, *The Location of Economic Activity* (New York: McGraw-Hill, 1948); Walter Isard, *Location and Space Economy* (Cambridge, Mass., MIT Press, 1956); Leon Moses, "Location and the Theory of Production," *Quarterly Journal of Economics* 72 (May 1958): 259–272; and elsewhere—concentrates on the role that freight transportation of outputs and inputs and the economies of scale in the production process play in location choice.

The central-place model focuses on the impact on location choice of the need to transport products from manufacturing plants to retailers and of consumer shoppingtrips to the retailers. It was developed in Walter Christaller, *The Cen-

tral Places of Southern Germany, tr. C. Baskin (Englewood Cliffs, N.J.: Prentice-Hall, 1966); August Losch, *The Economics of Location,* tr. William Woglom (New Haven: Yale University Press, 1954); William L. Garrison, Brian J.L. Berry, Duane F. Marble, John B. Nystuen, and Richard L. Morrill, *Studies of Highway Development and Geographic Change* (Seattle: University of Washington Press, 1959); Brian J.L. Berry, "Commercial Structure and Commercial Blight: Retail Patterns and Processes in the City of Chicago," University of Chicago, Department of Geography, research paper no. 85, prepared for the Community Renewal Program of the City of Chicago, 1963; Brian J.L. Berry, *Geography of Market Centers and Retail Distribution* (Englewood Cliffs, N.J.: Prentice-Hall, 1967); and elsewhere.

The extensions of the residential-location model concentrate on the role of commuting cost changes in business-location decisions and were developed in Strotz, "Urban Transportation Parables," pp. 165–169; Robert M. Solow, "On Equilibrium Models of Urban Location," pp. 2–16; and elsewhere.

The workplace-location model described here contains elements of the classical and central-place models, but since changes in commuting costs are central to the present discussion, principal reliance is on the extensions of the residential-location model. For a more complete review of the several workplace-location models, see José A. Gómez-Ibáñez, "Transportation Policy and Urban Land Use Control," Harvard University, Department of City and Regional Planning, discussion paper no. D75-10, 1975, pp. 22–36.

13. The effect of commuting cost changes on employment will be diminished if landlords are able to capture all or part of the benefit from any transportation improvement in the form of higher land rents in the central area. The landlords' share in the benefit will depend on the elasticity of demand for the area's products and the number of opportunities to substitute labor or other factors for land in the production process. As with land rent changes in the residential area, however, the landowners in the production area are unlikely to absorb all the effect of a commuting cost change in altered rents.

14. It should be noted that the methods used to finance a public transportation improvement may also have an impact on the costs to various groups and therefore on the land-use effects. For example, if a new highway or transit facility creates large capital or operating deficits for a local government and these are paid in the first instance by downtown property owners in the form of higher property taxes, the favorable effects on downtown employment that might otherwise be created by the improvement could be largely offset. (In the longer run, though, the increased taxes might be "absorbed" in lower property values, depending on the relevant supply and demand elasticities.) On the other hand, if the increased costs are assessed against the users of the facilities in the form of fares or tolls, the impact will depend on whether these higher direct costs are offset by time or other savings for users. In short, determining the cost impact of a public transportation improvement can involve a complex analysis of how the improvement is financed.

15. One employment effect of a transportation change not considered here is the creation of jobs for the construction of any improved transportation facility. Such direct employment effects may be viewed as particularly important from a political standpoint. See Regina Herzlinger, "Costs, Benefits and the West Side Highway," *Public Interest* 55 (Spring 1979): 77–98. The land-use implications of such employment would depend on where the workers resided, which in turn would be conditioned by the actual location of the jobs, how long the jobs lasted, and so forth. Jobs can also be directly eliminated by transportation construction, due to land acquisition or temporary obstruction of access to existing shopping

centers. Standard location models ignore these considerations, which in many instances may be quite substantial (perhaps overriding the offsetting and therefore small net influences analyzed in location-theory models).

16. For evidence that firms in population-serving industries locate close to residences, see Edgar Hoover and Raymond Vernon, *Anatomy of a Metropolis* (Cambridge, Mass.: Harvard University Press, 1959); Berry, *Geography of Market Centers and Retail Distribution;* and J.D. Forbes, "Central Place Theory—An Analytical Framework for Retail Structures," *Land Economics* 48 (February 1972): 15–22. A model that does incorporate this residence-workplace interaction was developed by Ira S. Lowry, *A Model of Metropolis,* Rand Corporation, publication no. RM-4035-RC (Santa Monica, Calif., 1964). Some of the implications, as well as the problems, of this model are discussed below.

17. Walter Isard and V. Whitney argue, for example, that the advent of the automobile reduced shoppingtrip costs and, as a result, shifted some retail sales from small towns to the central cities of larger metropolitan areas. Although they do not explicitly consider the effect of the automobile on the internal structure of cities as such, the analogous intraurban development would appear to be the supplanting of many small "strip-type" local shopping districts by larger "regional" shopping centers, as has occurred in the past three decades. See Isard and Whitney, "Metropolitan Site Selection," *Social Forces* 27 (1949): 263–269.

18. Some types of population-serving firms will be more sensitive than others to changes in shoppingtrip costs. The locations of firms that sell less frequently purchased and more expensive items (such as cars, furniture, and major appliances) are likely to be relatively insensitive to such changes because shoppingtrip costs are only a small portion of the total costs of purchasing these goods. Conversely, the locations of firms that sell frequently purchased, relatively inexpensive items (such as food) may be particularly sensitive to changes in shoppingtrip costs.

19. Lowry, *A Model of Metropolis.*

20. Daniel Brand, Brian Barber, and Michael Jacobs, "Techniques for Relating Transportation Improvements and Urban Development Patterns," *Highway Research Record,* no. 207 (1967): 53–67; Stephen M. Putnam, "Urban Land Use and Transportation Models: A State-of-the-Art Summary," *Transportation Research* 9 (1975): 187–202.

21. For a typical application of a Lowry-type model to forecast transportation improvements, see Stephen H. Putnam, "Urban (Metropolitan) Impacts of Highway Systems," in *The Urban Impacts of Federal Policies,* ed. Norman J. Glickman (Baltimore: Johns Hopkins University Press, 1979), pp. 376–397.

22. This concern is especially relevant because location theory provides little guidance for the appropriate equation forms or empirical values for such highly simplified employment and population functions as are used in EMPIRIC. In practical applications of EMPIRIC, the equation forms and empirical values that best replicate past changes are usually selected.

23. Gregory K. Ingram, John F. Kain, and J. Royce Ginn, *The Detroit Prototype of the NBER Simulation Model* (New York: National Bureau of Economic Research, 1972).

24. Mills, *Studies in the Structure of the Urban Economy.*

25. Kenneth A. Small, "Transportation Goals and Land Use Policy: The Case of Central City Decline," paper presented at the Eastern Economic Association Annual Meeting, Boston, May 10–12, 1979.

26. While Small does focus on behavior that might be important in determining the impact of a transportation improvment on land use, his analysis omits (as

he himself recognizes) some important considerations. In particular, Small (like most of his predecessors) does not analyze the financing and tax incidence effects of public transportation improvements. Rather, he argues that these "should be comparitively small if, as is usually the case, the locals' share is a small fraction of the total project cost." While this may be a reasonably good generalization about capital costs for transportation improvements, it does not sufficiently address the incidence of operating costs, particularly for transit extensions or improvements. Small's emphasis on transportation impacts may also have led him to indulge in what some critics consider a double counting of some transit benefits.

27. John R. Meyer, John F. Kain, and Martin Wohl, *The Urban Transportation Problem* (Cambridge, Mass.: Harvard University Press, 1965), ch. 3.

28. Ibid., ch. 2, pp. 44–47.

29. Tom Muller et al., *Economic Impact of I-295 on Richmond Central Business District* (Washington, D.C.: Urban Institute, 1977), pp. 32–38. Another important intercity statistical study of the effects of transportation on metropolitan land-use change is David Harrison, Jr., "Transportation Technology and Urban Land Use Patterns," Harvard University, Department of City and Regional Planning, research report no. R76-2, 1976. Harrison examines the statistical relationship between the density of new development and the available transportation for several U.S. metropolitan areas over the decades from the late 1880s to the mid-1900s. Harrison's analysis has no clear implications for the impact of current transportation policies, however, since it concentrates on the effects of major changes in transportation technology, such as the introduction and proliferation of the automobile.

30. Identified by Mahlon Straszheim in *An Econometric Analysis of the Housing Market* (New York: National Bureau of Economic Research, 1975), p. 216.

31. For a comprehensive summary of these transit studies, see Robert L. Knight and Lisa L. Trygg, "Land Use Impacts of Rapid Transit: Implications of Recent Experience," a report prepared by deLeuw, Cather & Co. for the U.S. Department of Transportation, August 1977.

32. Alan Aboucher, "The Analysis of Property Values and Subway Investment and Financing Policies," Institute for the Quantitative Analysis of Social and Economic Policy, working paper no. 7306 (Toronto: University of Toronto, 1973), mimeographed; D. N. Dewees, "The Effect of a Subway on Residential Property Values in Toronto" (Toronto: Institute for Policy Analysis, University of Toronto, 1975), mimeographed; Gordon W. Davies, "The Effect of a Subway on the Spatial Distribution of Population," research report no. 7404 (London, Ontario: Department of Economics, University of Western Ontario, 1974), mimeographed.

33. Warren G. Heenan, "The Influence of Rapid Transit on Real Estate Values in Toronto," presentation to a workshop-conference on transit and redevelopment sponsored by the Institute for Rapid Transit in cooperation with Boston College, June 15, 1966, in Toronto, mimeographed; Warren G. Heenan, "The Impact of Transit: Real Estate Values," paper read at the Fourth International Conference on Urban Transportation, 1969; James H. Kearns, "The Economic Impact of the Gonge Street Subway," address to the American Transit Association, 83rd annual meeting, September 1964, New York City, mimeographed; T. R. Wacher, "The Effects of Rapid Transit Systems on Urban Property Development," *Chartered Surveyor*, March 1970.

34. Abouchar, "Analysis of Property Values."

35. Davies, "The Effect of a Subway on the Spatial Distribution of Population."

36. Dewees, "The Effect of a Subway on Property Values," pp. 8–44.

37. Knight and Trygg, "Land Use Impacts," pp. 8–43.

38. The prodevelopment policies that followed the introduction of the Toronto rapid transit system included "(1) aggressive marketing of air rights and available excess land parcels by the transit commission; (2) allowance of liberal floor area ratios (in some cases increased from 3:1 to 12:1) and density bonuses by the city, especially around stations; (3) encouragement of coordinated design efforts with developers desiring direct access from office retail or apartment buildings; and (4) city zoning classification changes in certain districts, notably near metropolitan area transit stations, to permit much higher intensity development." Robert L. Knight and Lisa L. Trygg, "Evidence of Land Use Impacts of Rapid Transit Systems," *Transportation* 6 (1977): 235.

39. BART's impact has been studied more than that of any other U.S. system. Among the more significant reports on these impact studies are Michael Dyett, David Dornbusch, et al., *Land Use and Urban Development Impacts of BART: Final Report,* prepared for the U.S. Department of Transportation and the U.S. Department of Housing and Urban Development, October 1978; Melvin Webber, "The BART Experience—What Have We Learned?" *Public Interest,* no. 45 (Fall 1976): 79–108; Highway Research Board, *Impact of the Bay Area Rapid Transit System on the San Francisco Metropolitan Region: Proceedings of a Workshop Conference, February 9–11, 1970,* special report no. 3 (Washington, D.C.: Transportation Research Board, 1970); and Institute of Urban and Regional Development, *Overview and Summary: BART Impact Studies Final Report Series* (Berkeley: University of California, 1973). For a good bibliography of BART impact studies, see Knight and Trygg, "Land Use Impacts," pp. 226–230.

40. See Dyett, Dornbusch, et al., *Development Impacts of BART.*

41. Ibid., pp. 36–39.

42. A reduction in transit times may provoke a larger shift to transit in the long run than the short run because in the long run travelers can change the location of their workplaces and residences to take better advantage of the new transit service. Figure 7.1 incorporates these long-run possibilities, however, since modal response curves are typically based on cross-sectional studies of traveler choices. See Edward Weiner, "Modal Split Revisited," *Traffic Quarterly* 23, no. 1 (1969): 5–27.

43. Dyett, Dornbusch, et al., *Development Impacts of BART,* pp. 48–55, 70–79, 105–107.

44. Knight and Trygg, "Land Use Impacts," p. 60.

45. Ibid., p. 147.

46. Most of this work has been performed by David Boyce in collaboration with various students and associates. Perhaps the best overall summary of this work can be found in David Boyce et al., *Impact of Rapid Transit on Suburban Residential Property Values and Land Development: Analysis of the Philadelphia-Lindenwold High-Speed Line,* prepared for the Office of the Secretary, U.S. Department of Transportation (Philadephia: University of Pennsylvania, Regional Science Department, 1972).

47. Knight and Trygg, "Land Use Impacts," pp. 149–180.

48. Despite all these difficulties, it may still be worthwhile for policy analysts to consider larger-scale land-use impacts when evaluating alternative transportation policies. Such consideration might, at the very least, motivate the research necessary to improve understanding of transportation's effects on central-city and suburban growth.

8. Energy

1. The importance of these variables is suggested by the fact that Canada's energy consumption is even higher than that of the United States when measured on a per capita or percent of GNP basis. See J. Darmstadter, J. Dunkerley, and J. Alterman, *How Industrial Societies Use Energy: A Comparative Analysis* (Baltimore: Johns Hopkins University Press for Resources for the Future, 1977); also see Hans H. Landsberg et al., *Energy: The Next Twenty Years,* report by a study group sponsored by the Ford Foundation and administered by Resources for the Future (Cambridge, Mass.: Ballinger, 1979), pp. 83–88.

2. Gordon J. MacDonald, "Long Term Availability of Natural Resources," in *Alternatives for Growth,* ed. Harvey McMains and Lyle Wilcox (Cambridge, Mass.: Ballinger, 1978), ch. 4, pp. 43–78.

3. John R. Meyer, "Discussion of 'Long Term Availability of Natural Resources,'" in *Alternatives for Growth,* ch. 5, pp. 79–84.

4. Meyer, "Discussion of 'Long Term Availability of Natural Resources,'" table V-1, p. 81; Landsberg et al., *Energy: The Next Twenty Years,* pp. 83–88.

5. Better insulation, greater use of solar (particularly passive) energy, and so on might be expected, over time, to reduce the use of nonrenewable energy sources for space heating. See Robert Stobaugh and Daniel Yergin, eds., *Energy Future* (New York: Random House, 1979), pp. 183–215.

6. The debate on whether to use coal or nuclear energy for the generation of electricity has been finessed in constructing Table 8.1 by assuming that these two fuels would equally fill any void created by not using liquid hydrocarbons to produce electricity.

7. The usual forecast made in the 1970s of U.S. energy consumption in 1990 was 100-plus quads, with coal accounting for 10–14 quads of the increase, nuclear energy accounting for 7–8 quads of the increase, hydroelectric power accounting for 1–3 quads of the increase, and oil accounting for 8–10 quads of the increase. Obviously, an increase in oil consumption implies considerable importation of oil into the United States.

8. The U.S. government's energy policy has vacillated among these three options. As originally stated by President Nixon in 1974, U.S. energy policy stressed the third option: expanded supply. Subsequently, President Carter in his national energy policy message of April 1977 shifted the focus to the first two options, substitution and conservation. Carter returned to a greater emphasis on expanding supply with his revised energy policy announced in July 1979.

9. This is not to deny the possibility that transit could be made more energy efficient. Many of the suggestions advanced in Chapter 4 for improving conventional transit's productivity would conserve energy as well. Similarly, greater use of flywheels in rail transit could save energy. See John R. Meyer and José A. Gómez-Ibáñez, *Improving Urban Mass Transportation Productivity,* report to the U.S. Department of Transportation, Urban Mass Transportation Administration, 1977. The energy efficiency of transit will depend, though, on many public policy decisions yet to be made, and the total potential for transit energy saving seems minuscule compared with the possibilities for reducing automobile energy needs.

10. Another reason for stressing energy conservation in the areas of space heating and automobiles is that many industrial and commercial users have probably already come closer to achieving optimum energy use, since industrial and commercial users have long had more incentive and knowledge to achieve energy economies than individual householders. Certainly, industrial users made larger

percentage reductions in energy consumption after the OPEC price increases than most other users, suggesting that if energy use was not optimized initially, they were quick to adapt when the incentives were strengthened. Without doubt, most commercial modes of transportation are closer to optimum energy use than private modes. Truck, airline, railroad, and bus companies have a reasonably long and constructive history of substituting newer and more fuel-efficient technologies as these became available. The main impact of increased fuel prices on commercial transport's use of energy may be to only slightly accelerate the introduction of fuel-efficient technologies as they become available or to bring on long-available fuel economizing measures that previously did not pay.

11. At least when the electricity is generated by oil or coal; see William Hamilton, "Energy Use of Electric Vehicles," *Transportation Research* 14A (October–December 1980): 416.

12. For a description of current electric vehicle technology see Edward A. Campbell, "Return of the Electric Motor Vehicle," *Traffic Quarterly* 33, no. 1 (January 1979): 29–43.

13. Forecasts of future electric vehicle technology are summarized in Kenneth Train, "The Potential Market for Non-Gasoline Powered Automobiles," *Transportation Research* 14A (October–December 1980): 406; and U.S. Congress, Office of Technology Assessment, *Technical Report,* vol. 2 of *Changes in the Future Use and Characteristics of the Automobile Transportation System* (Washington, D.C.: U.S. Government Printing Office, 1979), pp. 345–352.

14. Train, "The Potential Market for Non-Gasoline Powered Automobiles," p. 406.

15. Campbell, "Return of the Electric Motor Vehicle."

16. See Train, "The Potential Market for Non-Gasoline Powered Automobiles"; and Steven D. Beggs and N. Scott Cardell, "Choice of Smallest Car by Multi-Vehicle Households and the Demand for Electric Vehicles," *Transportation Research* 14A (October–December 1980): 389–404.

17. Hamilton, "Energy Use of Electric Vehicles."

18. See Table 3.1.

19. U.S. Congressional Budget Office, *Urban Transportation and Energy: The Potential Savings of Different Modes,* report prepared for the Senate Committee on Environment and Public Works, serial no. 95–8 (Washington, D.C.: U.S. Government Printing Office, 1977).

20. In the households where the former driver sells his car, however, there should be no such offset and even a reduction in nonwork automobile trips by household members.

21. For the purpose of calculating fleet average, Title III, Sect. 503 of the Energy Policy and Conservation Act of 1975 provides that the total number of passenger automobiles produced by a given manufacturer shall be divided into two categories: (1) passenger automobiles that are domestically manufactured, and (2) passenger automobiles that are not domestically manufactured. The average fuel economy is to be calculated separately for each category, as if each were produced by a different manufacturer. The act states that "an automobile shall be considered domestically manufactured in any model year if at least 75 percent of the cost to the manufacturer of such automobile is attributable to value added in the United States." During the 1978 and 1979 model years only, the act allowed manufacturers to count some imported cars as part of their domestically manufactured fleet. The number of imported cars that can be counted as domestically manufactured in those years is set by a very complex formula, but is essentially one half the number of cars imported by that manufacturer in model year 1974.

22. The light-duty truck standards impose different requirements on vehicles with four-wheel and two-wheel drive, and make allowances for manufacturers producing specialty vehicles or with peculiar hardships. In 1977, standards of 17.2 miles per gallon for two-wheel drive and 15.8 miles per gallon for four-wheel drive were promulgated for model year 1979 trucks weighing less than 6,000 pounds. In 1978, standards were issued for the 1980 and 1981 model years, covering trucks weighing up to 8,500 pounds and requiring averages of 16 and then 18 miles per gallon for vehicles with two-wheel drive and 14 and then 15.5 miles per gallon for vehicles with four-wheel drive. Light-duty truck standards in the range of 19.7–27.4 miles per gallon have been proposed, but not promulgated, for model year 1985 light-duty trucks.

23. Barry D. McNatt, II. T. MacAdams, and Robert Dullan, "Comparison of EPA and In Use Fuel Economy of 1974–1978 Automobiles," report prepared for the U.S. Department of Energy, Office of Transportation Programs, October 1979.

24. Sorrel Wildhorn et al., *How to Save Gasoline: Public Policy Alternatives for the Automobile* (Cambridge, Mass.: Ballinger, 1976), pp. 14–142.

25. Energy Resources Council, *The Report by the Federal Task Force on Motor Vehicle Goals Beyond 1980*, vol. 2 (Washington, D.C.: Energy Resources Council, 1976), pp. 5–17 through 5–25.

26. The average fuel economy of new cars increased from 14.2 miles per gallon to 20.1 miles per gallon between model years 1974 and 1979. J. D. Murrell calculates that if the weight distribution of 1979 new cars had been the same as the weight distribution of 1974 model new cars, the average fuel economy of the 1979 models would have been only about 17.5 miles per gallon. Thus, 2.6 miles per gallon (20.1 minus 17.5) of the fuel economy savings between 1974 and 1979 might be attributed to weight and related size changes, while 3.3 miles per gallon (17.5 minus 14.2) might be attributed to other sources. See J. D. Murrell, "Light Duty Automotive Fuel Economy—Trends through 1979," Society of Automotive Engineers, technical paper no. 790225, 1979, p. 4.

27. Some of the variance in fuel economy reported in Table 8.6 is due to differences in weight *within* the weight class. Since the weight classes are very narrow, however, most of the fuel economy differences are probably due to factors other than variations in weight.

28. Wildhorn et al., *How to Save Gasoline*, pp. 62–64.

29. The description of near-term drivetrain, transmission, and engine modifications relies extensively on U.S. Congressional Budget Office, "Preliminary Assessment of Post 1985 Automotive Fuel Economy Standards," April 1980.

30. Honda has offered a small stratified-charge engine, but Ford Motor Company abandoned its plans for a larger stratified-charge engine in 1980, partly because it appeared to offer less promise than diesel engines.

31. The gap in performance between a diesel and gasoline engine of equivalent displacement appears to have narrowed recently due to technological improvements in the diesel. Still, the diesel is more sluggish than a comparably sized gasoline engine and, to achieve equivalent performance, the diesel engine must be turbocharged or increased in size with some attendant loss in its fuel advantages.

32. As explained in more detail in the next chapter, the diesel can easily meet the final statutory standards for hydrocarbons and carbon monoxide, as well as the interim 2.0 gram per vehicle-mile nitrogen oxides standard, but it may not be able to meet the ultimate 1.0 gram nitrogen oxide standard without difficulty. Unlike the gasoline engine, the diesel also emits substantial quantities of particu-

lates that have been regulated only since 1980. The technological capabilities for meeting future proposed particulate standards are still uncertain.

33. For a description of these technologies, see Jet Propulsion Laboratory, *Do We Need A New Engine?* Automotive Technology Status and Projections, report no. 78–71, prepared for the U.S. Department of Energy (Pasadena, Calif.: Jet Propulsion Laboratory, 1978).

34. For a review of evidence on the price elasticity of gasoline demand in motor vehicles, see Robert S. Pindyck, "The Characteristics of the Demand for Energy," in *Energy Conservation and Public Policy*, ed. John C. Sawhill (Englewood Cliffs, N.J.: Prentice-Hall, 1979), pp. 22–45; and William C. Wheaton, "The Long Run Structure of Transportation and Gasoline Demand," photocopied draft, Massachusetts Institute of Technology, Department of Economics, April 1980, p. 7.

35. See Table 6.4.

36. Between 1960 and 1973, the number of miles traveled per automobile per year slowly increased from about 9,400 to 10,000. In 1974, annual mileage per automobile dropped suddenly to 9,448; by 1977, it had climbed back to 9,839, but still had not hit the 10,000 level.

37. The three studies are F. G. Adams, H. Graham, and J. M. Griffin, "Demand Elasticities for Gasoline: Another View," discussion paper no. 279, Department of Economics, University of Pennsylvania, June 1974, as cited by Pindyck, "Demand for Energy," pp. 39–40; Robert S. Pindyck, *The Structure of World Energy Demand* (Cambridge, Mass.: MIT Press, 1979); and Wheaton, "Long Run Gasoline Demand." Wheaton attributes most of the elasticity to reduced automobile ownership and use rather than to improved fuel economy of the vehicle, whereas Pindyck shows the opposite finding. This discrepancy is probably partly due to specification problems identified by Wheaton but also to imperfect statistical control for other variables besides energy prices that influence automobile use and fuel economy across countries.

38. One possible offset would be if the consumers find small, fuel-efficient cars so uncomfortable that they drive less.

39. N. Scott Cardell and Frederick C. Dunbar, "Measuring the Societal Impacts of Automobile Downsizing," *Transportation Research* 14A (October–December 1980): 423–435.

9. Air Pollution

1. Stationary sources are largely industrial, but also, by convention, represent all sources of air pollution other than highway vehicles, so that so-called stationary sources usually include such nonstationary polluters as airplanes and railroads.

2. See U.S. Environmental Protection Agency, Office of Air Quality Planning and Standards, *1976 National Emissions Report, National Emissions Data System of the Aerometric and Emissions Reporting System*, report no. EPA-450/4-79-019 (Research Triangle Park, N.C.: U.S. Environmental Protection Agency, 1979), pp. 30, 86.

3. Defining the "base case" for determining the costs and benefits of a depollution or energy conservation program can prove very difficult. The standard approach is to take *actual* performance in some precontrol base year and measure *observed* changes (in emissions, costs, fuel consumed) in subsequent controlled periods. See National Academy of Sciences and National Academy of Engi-

neering, *Air Quality and Automotive Emission Control,* vol. 4, *The Costs and Benefits of Automobile Emission Control,* prepared for the Senate Committee on Public Works (Washington, D.C.: U.S. Government Printing Office, 1974). Another approach would be to adopt a historical counterfactual and estimate what circumstances would have been *without* the control program; benefits and costs would then be estimated by the difference between the counterfactual and results observed under the control program. See Edwin S. Mills and Lawrence J. White, "Government Policies toward Automotive Emissions Control," in *Approaches to Controlling Air Pollution,* ed. Ann F. Friedlaender (Cambridge, Mass.: MIT Press, 1978), pp. 348–409. Specifying the counterfactual base line is something of a subjective exercise, since cause and effect may be difficult to disentangle. For example, Mills and White argue that emissions controls had little to do with improvements in automobile fuel efficiency that followed the application of the 1970 Clean Air Act Amendments, but rather were the result of "higher fuel costs after 1973" (p. 350). However, emissions controls clearly decreased fuel efficiency in the mid-1970s and thereby undoubtedly intensified the effects of higher fuel prices, thus motivating more rapid acceptance of automotive changes that conserved on fuel. Similarly, Mills and White argue that any fuel economies attributable to incentives created by automotive emissions regulations in the early years of the program "should not be included in [benefit] calculations [measuring] the future worth of the program because these economies would not disappear if the program disappeared." This presumption is hardly obvious, however, and depends on just how the program effectuates fuel economies; for example, fuel injection and stratified-charge engines, technologies that yield a *joint* product of greater fuel efficiency and reduced costs for achieving emission targets, might not be worth their added initial costs for fuel economy reasons *alone.*

4. The discerning reader will have noted that policy (5) essentially speeds up traffic, in direct opposition to policy (4), which slows down traffic. Contradictions of this kind are not uncommon in air pollution policy and reflect the inadequacy of the information base on which decisions are based.

5. Experience with central-area control schemes in Singapore suggests the possibility of such a relocation. (See Chapter 11.)

6. This particular configuration is called TASSIM (for Transport and Air Shed Simulation Model) and comes from Gregory K. Ingram, Gary R. Fauth, and E. Kroch, "Cost and Effectiveness of Emission Reduction and Transportation Control Policies," *Revista Internazionale di Economia dei Transporti,* April 1975, pp. 17–47.

7. Ibid.

8. These two policies were set up so as to be mirror images of each other: centralization was defined as a 20 percent increase in central residential and workplace densities; decentralization was defined as a 20 percent reduction in those densities.

9. National Academy of Sciences and National Academy of Engineering, *Air Quality and Automotive Emission Control.*

10. The largest damage in dollar terms imposed by automobile air pollution is that reflected in residential property values. The effects on human health come second, although the range is large due to to lack of reliable data on the effects of air pollution on human mortality and morbidity as well as the difficulty in assigning a dollar value to pollution-induced deaths and illnesses. To put the automobile air pollution costs in perspective, the National Academy study estimates that pollution from all sources combined probably did between $15 billion and $20 billion in damage in 1970 when measured in 1973 prices.

11. For reviews of these empirical estimates, their strengths and weaknesses, see Mills and White, "Government Policies toward Automotive Emissions Control," pp. 348–409; and Daniel L. Rubinfeld, "Market Approaches to the Measurement of the Benefits of Air Pollution Abatement," in *Approaches to Controlling Air Pollution*, ed. Friedlaender, pp. 240–273.

12. The choice of the year 2010 as a cut-off point is admittedly arbitrary, but this horizon seems a realistic one for a long-term public project such as air pollution control.

13. A potential major advantage of assessing effluent fees or fines according to the amount of emissions cars produce during periodic tests, rather than using standards to control emissions, is that it could create incentives to maintain control devices more effectively. See Mills and White, "Government Policies toward Automotive Emissions Control," p. 394. Effluent fees have several other advantages as well, as noted below.

14. Although the NAS/NAE estimates of the costs and benefits of automobile emission controls have many defects and contain many uncertainties, as the members of the NAS/NAE panel observe repeatedly in their report, their estimates are nevertheless the best available. As Mills and White put it, "The best estimate of the costs and benefits of the current program come from the NAS/NAE report" ("Government Policies toward Automotive Emissions Control," p. 378). Mills and White argue, though, that the NAS/NAE results are biased toward overestimation of benefits because they count some post–1970 fuel economies as benefits. However, as pointed out in note 3 of this chapter, the Mills and White conclusion itself depends on some assumptions of dubious validity (in particular, that technologies jointly producing fuel economy and reduced air emissions would be continued without the air emissions justification). Furthermore, the NAS/NAE estimates build on and are largely consistent with most other estimates of the costs and benefits of automotive emissions control programs, particularly the so-called RECAT report, which is the only other large-scale effort besides the NAS/NAE study to attempt a comprehensive estimate of the automobile emissions-control program's benefits and costs.

15. It does not automatically follow, though, on economic efficiency grounds, that a program with these low-cost strategies is necessarily rational. The NAS/NAE benefit/cost study focused only on automobile emissions control, and its results are subject to this limitation as well as to the more general limitations of benefit/cost analysis. The same amount of money spent on other health, safety, or clean air programs, might have as much potential for cost-effective air depollution as the automotive emissions standards. It might prove more cost effective in most U.S. cities (Los Angeles being the most important probable exception) to reduce total NO_x in the atmosphere through greater emphasis reducing emissions from stationary or other nonautomotive sources—that is, corrective actions at airports or stricter standards for large stationary sources may be cheaper ways of reducing NO_x emissions than very strict standards for automobiles.

16. An extensive discussion of these and other policy options can be found in both the NAS/NAE report and in Mills and White, "Government Policies toward Automotive Emissions Control."

17. *The Costs and Benefits of Automobile Emission Control*, p. 117–118. These estimates also placed the average per car lifetime saving of such a switch in mix at $106 per car, far below the estimates of the NAS Committee on Motor Vehicle Emissions. Any such saving for pollution control would have to be interpreted as a reduction in the *highest* cost estimates shown in Tables 9.5 and 9.6.

18. This, moreover, would be *without* requiring a change of catalyst in catalytic mufflers at 50,000 miles. If all catalyst vehicles were required to change cata-

lysts at 50,000 miles, total annual costs would rise to $10–11 billion (in 1974 dollars).

19. As of the early 1980s, automobile manufacturers considered a 1.5 gpm NO_x standard to be achievable, while some government administrators and environmentalists shifted from seeking a target of 0.4 to 1.0 for NO_x. To the extent that this shift in targeted standards and manufacturers' perceptions persists, the above discussion might be more accurate if 1.5 and 1.0 were substituted wherever 2.0 and 0.4 now appear.

20. Again without catalyst changes. With complete catalyst change, the figure rises to $6–7 billion per year (in 1974 dollars).

21. Estimating the costs or benefits from a relaxation of emissions standards is an extremely difficult task. Illustrative of the complexity is the confusion of even so careful an analysis as that of Mills and White ("Government Policies toward Automotive Emissions Control"). They criticize the NAS/NAE report (p. 363) for not providing estimates of benefit reductions that would result from freezing emissions standards at the interim 1975 level, though the NAS/NAE report does provide an estimate of the present value of discounted costs that might be saved by such a policy ($41 billion). By contrast, Mills and White (p. 379) apply somewhat less rigorous standards to their own speculations, supplying neither cost nor benefit estimates for reduction in emission standards. Rather they simply assert: "Our guess is that the program should aim at 80–85 percent abatement instead of 95 percent [and] this conclusion is independent of the criticism that the program has achieved abatement at needlessly high cost." A major difficulty is that no one knows exactly what the shape of the "dosage-response curve" is that relates emissions to air quality, though virtually everyone agrees that it is probably not linear and therefore not easily interpolated from existing point estimates.

22. This possibility is supported by the "NO_x Technical Analysis" that accompanied EPA's November 1973 proposed revisions for the NO_x automobile emission standards. For data on the relative contribution of mobile and stationary sources to NO_x emissions in different metropolitan areas, see U.S. Environmental Protection Agency, *1976 National Emissions Report: National Emissions Data System of the Aerometric and Emissions Reporting System.*

23. Again, with no catalyst changes anywhere as cars age. See *Air Quality and Automotive Emission Control.*

24. The consumer incentive could become a particularly attractive feature if deterioration of control devices with use becomes a major problem. As standards have been tightened, *relative* increases in emissions have become greater as cars age; a model year 1980 car, for example, will spew forth 20 percent or so greater emissions per mile when 10 years old than when new, while a 1970 model is only about 10 percent worse when old than when new. This greater relative deterioration of 1980 over 1970 cars though, is mainly a function of higher initial standards. Thus, even a 10-year-old model year 1980 car will not pollute as much as a brand new 1970 car. See U.S. Environmental Protection Agency, *Mobile Source Emission Factors* (Washington, D.C.: U.S. Government Printing Office, 1979). Whether it "pays" to enforce higher standards on older vehicles is a controversial subject and depends, among other considerations, on perceptions about the regressiveness inherent in imposing clean-up costs on owners of used cars who are relatively poor. See Leonard P. Gianessi, Henry M. Peskin, and Edward Wolff, "The Distribution Implications of National Air Pollution Damage Estimates," and Nancy Dorfman, "Comments," in *The Distribution of Economic Well-Being,* ed. F. Thomas Juster (Cambridge, Mass.: Ballinger, 1977). Another consideration is the rate at which durability of control devices might be improved. It must be remembered here that while *relative* deterioration has increased as standards

have improved, *absolute* levels of deterioration have declined, so that the total emissions attributable to decay of control devices has also declined.

25. Mills and White, "Government Policies toward Automotive Emissions Control," p. 394.

26. Ibid., p. 395.

27. In the context of cleaner air, for example, larger amounts spent on cleaning up stationary sources of pollution might be more efficient; or, alternatively, if the public policy focus is on reducing the health hazards of automobile use, various campaigns to improve highway safety might be more cost effective.

10. Aesthetics and Other Community Concerns

1. Partly because automobiles are relatively minor noise sources, there have been no major analyses of automobile noise costs comparable to those for trucks. Two major efforts to estimate the impact of truck noise are Jon P. Nelson, *Economic Analysis of Transportation Noise Abatement* (Cambridge, Mass.: Ballinger, 1978); and U.S. Environmental Protection Agency, *Background Document for Medium and Heavy Truck Noise Emissions Regulations,* report no. EPA-550/9-76-008 (Washington, D.C.: Environmental Protection Agency, 1976).

2. For a brief description of the Ldn index and its relation to other noise measures, see Nelson, *Transportation Noise Abatement,* pp. 19-26.

3. U.S. Environmental Protection Agency, *Truck Noise Emissions Regulations,* pp. 4-18 and 4-25; and U.S. Environmental Protection Agency, *Population Distribution in the U.S. as a Function of the Outdoor Noise Level,* report no. 550/0-74-009 (Washington, D.C.: Environmental Protection Agency, 1974), p. 25.

4. The role of these factors in determining highway noise levels is explained in Bolt, Beranek, and Newman, Inc., *Highway Noise: Generation and Control,* National Cooperative Highway Research Program, report no. 173 (Washington, D.C.: Transportation Research Board, 1976); and Nelson, *Transportation Noise Abatement,* pp. 21-22.

5. People's reaction to noise is reflected in the fact that the Ldn for a highway usually increases with the log of the traffic volume on the highway rather than in proportion to the traffic volume. For examples of formulas to predict a highway's Ldn on the basis of traffic volumes see Bolt, Beranek, and Newman, *Highway Noise,* p. 54.

6. For a critical review of the studies of the relationship between property values and noise, see Nelson, *Transportation Noise Abatement,* pp. 79-123, 186; and Raymond B. Palmquist, "Theoretical and Empirical Issues Concerning the Use of Property Value Changes in the Evaluation of Public Projects" (diss., University of Washington, 1978), pp. 14-24, 77-109.

7. This procedure is similar to the one adopted by Nelson to calculate the benefits of truck noise abatement in *Transportation Noise Abatement,* pp. 184-187. Nelson assumes a 10 percent interest rate in amortizing his values, whereas a 5 percent interest rate has been used here on the basis that this lower interest rate abstracts from inflation effects and more accurately represents a real rate of return on capital.

8. See U.S. Environmental Protection Agency, "Motor Carriers Engaged in Interstate Commerce," 39 *Federal Register* 38208 (October 29, 1974), Title 40, *Code of Federal Regulations,* pt. 202; and U.S. Environmental Protection Agency, "Compliance with Interstate Motor Carrier Noise Emission Standards," 40 *Federal Register* 42432 (September 12, 1975), Title 49, *Code of Federal Regulations,* pt. 325.

9. The EPA also retained the right to set new standards below 80 dBA after 1982. See U.S. Environmental Protection Agency, "Transportation Equipment Noise Emission Controls—Medium and Heavy Trucks," 41 *Federal Register* 15538 (April 13, 1976), Title 40, *Code of Federal Regulations*, p. 205.

10. See data for option "E" in U.S. Environmental Protection Agency, *Background Document for Medium and Heavy Truck Noise Emissions Regulations*, report no. EPA-550/9-76-008 (Washington, D.C.: Environmental Protection Agency, 1976), p. 4–32.

11. Even though the federal government collects only about one third of the total tax revenues eventually used for all highway purposes, it collects and disburses most of the money used for highway construction—especially in urban areas. In contrast, state highway funds tend to be used more for maintenance and other nonconstruction purposes (see Chapter 11).

12. See U.S. Federal Highway Administration, "Noise Standards and Procedures," 38 *Federal Register* 15953 (June 19, 1973), Title 23, *Code of Federal Regulations*, pt. 772.

13. David Segal, "The Economic Benefits of Depressing an Urban Expressway: The Case of Boston's John Fitzgerald Expressway," forthcoming in *Transportation Research Record*, 1981.

14. A major reason for this redevelopment is Quincy Market, a widely proclaimed and successful undertaking of the Rouse Corporation.

15. [Boston] Metropolitan Area Planning Council, Central Transportation Planning Staff, *Central Artery/I-93 Corridor, Central Area Planning Study*, report for the Massachusetts Department of Public Works, March 1978. After the election of a new governor in 1978, the Commonwealth withdrew its support for this proposal.

16. The aesthetic problems were assumed to be a function of the distance of the property from the highway, since both the view of the highway and the potential views of the harbor decline with distance. However, this assumption probably exaggerates the estimated effect of the highway's visual blight on property values in two ways. First, the independent effects of highway air and noise pollution on property values were not isolated; since pollution is probably inversely correlated with distance from the highway, the estimated property value changes are due to aesthetic problems created by noise and air pollution as well as the ugliness of the elevated structure and the loss of the harbor view. Second, and probably more serious, a visually obtrusive highway is likely to increase property values further away from the highway as well as decrease property values close by, since the further properties are made relatively more desirable. To the extent that the highway transfers value from properties close by to those further away, an analysis of how property values decline with proximity to the highway will overestimate the overall net loss in property values caused by the highway. See Segal, "The Economic Benefits of Depressing an Urban Expressway."

17. Ibid.

18. As reported in Chapter 11, air pollution and congestion costs rarely exceed one cent per vehicle-mile, though they can rise sharply for centrally located facilities (like the Fitzgerald Expressway) during the rush hours.

19. A good account of this can be found in Regina Herzlinger, "Costs, Benefits and the West Side Highway," *Public Interest*, no. 55 (Spring 1979): 77–98.

20. The "3c" planning process was initially dominated by state highway departments that, not surprisingly, recommended extensive additional highway construction. See Thomas A. Morehouse, "The 1962 Highway Act: A Study in Artful Interpretation," *Journal of American Institute of Planners* 35 (May 1969): 160–168. Nevertheless, the "3c" requirements somewhat legitimized the

complaints of highway opponents and offered a forum for voicing concerns.

21. For a more detailed account of the requirements and effects of NEPA and Section 4(f) of the Department of Transportation Act of 1970, see Alan A. Altshuler and Robert W. Curry, "The Changing Environment of Urban Development Policy," *Urban Law Journal* 10 (1976): 1–47; U.S. Council on Environmental Quality, *Environmental Quality: The Fifth Annual Report of the Council on Environmental Quality* (Washington, D.C.: U.S. Government Printing Office, 1974), p. 389; and U.S. Council on Environmental Quality, *Environmental Quality: The Sixth Annual Report of the Council on Environmental Quality* (Washington, D.C.: U.S. Government Printing Office, 1975), pp. 629, 638–639.

22. For a description of these transportation planning requirements and the opportunities they offer for opponents of transportation projects, see Altshuler and Curry, "The Changing Environment of Urban Development Policy."

23. Allen D. Manvel, "Land Use in 106 Large Cities," paper prepared for the consideration of the National Commission on Urban Problems, research report no. 12 (Washington, D.C.: U.S. Government Printing Office, 1968).

24. Other studies of the relationship between automobile use and the amount of land used for transportation in a city arrive at results more or less consistent with those just cited. Using data older than those collected by the National Commission on Urban Problems but doing some comparisons over time as well as comparisons of different cities at one point in time, for example, Niedercorn and Hearle arrived at more or less equivalent conclusions. Bartholomew also preformed a similar study in the mid-1950s; his sample consisted of very few major cities and a large number of small ones, and it is therefore suggestive (especially in light of the somewhat weaker findings just reported for a larger sample that included more small cities) that he found much the same relationships between land use and transport choices. See John Niedercorn and Edward Hearle, "Recent Land-Use Trends in Forty-Eight Large American Cities," Rand Corporation, memorandum no. RM-3664-FF, June 1963; Harland Bartholomew, *Land Use in American Cities* (Cambridge, Mass.: Harvard University Press, 1955); John Lansing, *Transportation and Economic Policy* (New York: Free Press, 1966); World Bank, "Urban Transport: Sector Policy Paper" (Washington, D.C.: World Bank, 1975); and Organization for Economic Cooperation and Development, "Urban Transportation and the Environment: Background Reports" from a seminar held July 10–12, 1979 (Paris: Organization for Economic Cooperation and Development, 1979).

25. In cities with over two million in population, garages typically account for at least one third of total downtown parking spaces. By comparison, cities with populations of 100,000 will have only a little over 10 percent or so of their downtown parking spaces in garages. See Wilbur Smith and Associates, *Parking in the City Center* (Detroit: Automobile Manufacturers Association, 1965), p. 6.

26. David J. Harrison, Jr., "Transportation Technology and Urban Land Use Patterns," research report no. R76-2, Harvard University, Department of City and Regional Planning, 1976.

11. Traffic Congestion

1. The "equivalents" measure buses, trucks, and other large vehicles in terms of standard automobile space requirements.

2. For a description of speed/volume relationships on various types of roads,

see Highway Research Board, *Highway Capacity Manual,* special report no. 87 (Washington, D.C.: Highway Research Board, 1965).

3. Traffic engineers and planners can simulate reasonably well the way motorists respond to congestion by altering their choice of route. (The ability to switch routes complicates highway assessment, though, by making it difficult to analyze changes in any particular highway segment in isolation.) The degree of flexibility that travelers have in adjusting their hours of travel to congestion is more poorly understood than route choice, however, and thus it is difficult for planners to predict the extent to which motorists will slow the growth of congestion by altering their time of travel.

4. The study is Ann F. Friedlaender, *The Interstate Highway System: A Study in Public Investment* (Amsterdam: North-Holland Publishing Company, 1965). The FHWA has also completed an analysis of the benefits and costs of the Interstate Highway System. The Federal Highway Administration study does not make separate estimates for the urban portions, although it does reach conclusions similar to those of Friedlaender about the benefits and costs of the combined urban and rural portions. See U.S. Congress, House of Representatives, Committee on Public Works, *Benefits of Interstate Highways,* report prepared by the U.S. Department of Transportation, Federal Highway Administration, committee print no. 91-41 (Washington, D.C.: U.S. Government Printing Office, 1970).

5. Friedlaender, *The Interstate Highway System,* pp. 113–115, 136–138.

6. These estimates assume that the present allocation of freight shipments between trucks and railroads is more or less optimal. Some transportation economists suggest, however, that government regulation of freight rates has allowed trucks to capture a substantial volume of freight shipments that could be carried more economically by railroads. Friedlaender estimates that if shipments are currently misallocated, both the rural Interstate and two-lane road systems produce substantial net losses (Friedlaender, *The Interstate Highway System,* p. 114).

7. Friedlaender assumed, based on FHWA 1961 estimates, that the system would cost $41 billion to complete in 1961 dollars. In 1975, the FHWA revised its figures and estimated that the system would cost $89 billion in 1973 dollars. Deflating to 1961 dollars by using the consumer price index, the FHWA's revised estimate amounts to $59.9 billion.

8. The FHWA forecast that 78 billion vehicle-miles of travel would take place on urban Interstates in 1977 (exluding toll roads and segments completed before 1957), while actual traffic volumes (including toll roads and segments completed before 1957), amounted to 142 billion vehicle-miles. The FHWA overestimated rural Interstate travel somewhat, forecasting 155 billion vehicle-miles in 1977 compared to the actual 126 billion. See Friedlaender, *The Interstate Highway System,* p. 48; and Motor Vehicle Manufacturers' Association, *Motor Vehicle Facts and Figures 1979* (Detroit: Motor Vehicle Manufacturers Association, 1979), p. 58.

9. Since no forecasts were available for traffic volumes without the Interstate System, Friedlaender made a somewhat arbitrary assumption that without the Interstate System all urban traffic would have grown at 3 percent per year—the rate forecast by the FHWA for traffic growth on other major urban roads *with* the Interstates. Friedlaender assesses the sensitivity of her results with comparisons of a few alternative assumptions about traffic growth, although she does not fully adjust for the different congestion levels implied. For example, Friedlaender states that if urban traffic is assumed to have grown at a 9 percent rate

without the Interstates instead of 3 percent, the present value of the net benefits would almost double (increasing from $13.442 billion in 1961 dollars to $23.659 billion in 1961 dollars, using a 5 percent discount rate). She assumes, however, that the speed improvements offered by the Interstates would be the same, regardless of the traffic growth rate without the Interstates, and therefore may underestimate the increase in benefits with a 9 percent growth rate. See Friedlaender, *The Interstate Highway System*, pp. 45–51, 114.

10. The mere "option" of having the access available, especially for emergency services, might be of some value even if it were never actually needed. For this option-pricing case, see Burton Wiesbrod, "Collective-Consumption Services of Individual-Consumption Goods," *Quarterly Journal of Economics*, no. 312 (August 1964): 471–477.

11. For analyses of scale economies in highway construction, see John R. Meyer, John F. Kain, and Martin Wohl, *The Urban Transportation Problem* (Cambridge, Mass.: Harvard University Press, 1965), pp. 200–204; Herbert Mohring, *Transportation Economics* (Cambridge, Mass.: Ballinger, 1978), pp. 140–146; Theodore E. Keeler and Kenneth A. Small, *Automobile Costs and Final Intermodal Cost Comparisons*, vol. 3 of *The Full Costs of Urban Transport*, ed. Theodore E. Keeler, Leonard A. Merewitz, and P. M. J. Fisher (Berkeley: University of California, Institute of Urban and Regional Development, 1975), pp. 19–30; and Marvin Kraus, "Scale Economics Analysis for Urban Highway Networks," photocopied, Boston College, Department of Economics, no date.

12. These economies may be small, though, since right-of-way acquisition averages only about 10 percent of total costs in rural areas and 25 percent in urban areas. In urban areas, moreover, small additions to the right-of-way width may cause disproportionate increases in costs if they required the removal or relocation of additional structures or utilities.

13. Federal highway aid could not be used to provide relocation assistance to displaced persons and businesses until 1962.

14. Kiran Bhatt, Michael Beesley, and Kevin Neels, *An Analysis of Road Expenditures and Payments by Vehicle Class, 1956–1975* (Washington, D.C.: Urban Institute, 1977), pp. 175–186.

15. For example, Bhatt, Beesley, and Neels, *Road Expenditures and Payments*, excluded a portion of the state fuel tax receipts in those states (such as California) where part of the state fuel tax is designated as a general sales tax; similarly, a portion of the local property tax on motor vehicles was excluded in states or localities where taxes are levied on other property.

16. Ten percent is in excess of the usual real rate of return deemed appropriate when using price deflated measures of benefits and costs.

17. Similar concentrations of traffic in peak hours are found on other Boston urban expressways and arterials, although the degree of peaking varies slightly among facilities. Patterns in other communities vary, depending on local conditions, but generally also reveal much the same peaking.

18. For two- to four-lane expressways, the capacity of the expressway is roughly proportional to the number of lanes. See Highway Research Board, *Highway Capacity Manual.*

19. The assumption of a $2 million per lane-mile capital cost is based on the figures in Table 11.8. The calculations assume no scale economies, which is appropriate for an elevated highway like the Fitzgerald.

20. The FHWA reported that in 1975, maintenance expenditures per lane-mile averaged $1,837 on the Interstate System. See U.S. Department of Transportation, Federal Highway Administration and American Association of State Highway

and Transportation Officials, Committee on Maintenance, "Maintenance Aid Digest," MAD-13, October 1977, photocopied, p. 6. Since urban expressways like the Fitzgerald are heavily traveled (and often have special structural characteristics such as being elevated) maintenance costs per lane-mile are probably many times higher than this average.

21. During one morning and one evening hour, traffic volumes in any one direction on the Fitzgerald exceed 4,800 vehicles, the maximum one-way volume of a six-lane expressway when capacity is defined at 1,600 vehicles per lane-hour. These extra vehicles are included in the vehicles requiring a third lane in each direction. If a fourth lane in each direction were added to maintain the 35–40 mph speeds even in those two peak hours, then the average cost of peak-period users would be substantially higher than 8–13 cents per vehicle-mile.

22. If the construction costs were $2 million per lane-mile, the costs of serving the remaining Fitzgerald users averaged 1.9 cents per vehicle-mile (at 5 percent) and 3.2 cents per vehicle-mile (at 10 percent), assuming a capacity of 1,767 vehicles per lane-mile. With a capacity of 1,600 vehicles per lane-mile, the comparable figures are 2.0 and 3.3 cents per vehicle-mile. If costs per lane-mile are scaled upward, these "average-user costs" rise, but so would those for the peak-hour users, with the ratio of the two probably little affected.

23. It is suggestive, though, that several urban bridges, tunnels, and a few metropolitan expressways (for example, in Boston and Chicago) either come close to covering costs or generate surpluses from toll charges (especially if allowances were made for the gas taxes generated by the use of these facilities as well as their toll receipts).

24. The external costs that petroleum use imposes on society have only recently begun to be considered, and most of the calculations made to date are highly speculative. For a pioneering effort to assess these costs, see *Energy Future*, ed. Robert Stogbaugh and Daniel Yergin (New York: Random House, 1979), pp. 9, 16–55.

25. National Academy of Sciences and National Academy of Engineering, *Air Quality and Automotive Emission Control*, vol. 4, *The Costs and Benefits of Automobile Emission Control*, prepared for the Senate Committee on Public Works (Washington, D.C.: U.S. Government Printing Office, 1974).

26. Urban motorists are probably responsible for nearly all of national automobile air pollution damage, since automobile air pollutants seldom cause annoyance or harm at the concentrations found in rural areas.

27. Keeler and Small, *Automobile Costs and Final Intermodal Cost Comparisons*, pp. 52–55; Theodore E. Keeler and Kenneth A. Small, "On the Environmental Costs of the Various Transportation Modes," working paper, University of California, Institute of Urban and Regional Development, 1974.

28. David Segal, "The Economic Benefits of Depressing an Urban Expressway," forthcoming in *Transportation Research Record*, 1981.

29. For a history of the federal highway aid program and changes in the restrictions on use of federal tax receipts, see U.S. Congressional Budget Office, *Highway Assistance Programs: A Historical Perspective*, background paper (Washington, D.C.: U.S. Government Printing Office 1978).

30. For a review of some of the issues involved in removing restrictions on the use of federal highway aid, see U.S. Congressional Budget Office, *Transportation Finance: Choices in a Period of Change*, budget issue paper (Washington, D.C.: U.S. Government Printing Office, 1978). The case for allowing nonhighway uses of federal highway-user tax receipts is more complicated and problematic, however, especially if the taxes are truly viewed as user charges and if other govern-

ment regulations and policies reduce the degree to which some classes or urban highway users are subsidized.

31. At other times and places, some reduction in the real or constant dollar user tax-level might be justified. This probably would not mean a reduction in current-dollar taxes, however, as long as there is any significant inflation.

32. For an overview of signal timing and control techniques, see Highway Research Board, *Highway Capacity Manual*, pp. 126–128; Louis J. Pignataro et al., *Traffic Control in Saturated Street Networks*, National Cooperative Highway Research Program, report no. 194 (Washington, D.C.: Transportation Research Board, 1978).

33. The capital outlay is usually negligible because most of the required signals and hardware are already in place, lacking only computerized control. Capital costs of recently installed computerized control systems in Toronto amounted to only $5 million for a total of 864 intersections, while in San Jose, Calif., and Whichita Falls, Tex., capital costs were only $1 million for 60 intersections and $128 thousand for 77 intersections, respectively. See Barbara J. Keyani and Evelyn S. Putnam, *Transportation System Management: State of the Art*, report prepared by Interplan Corporation for the U.S. Department of Transportation, Urban Mass Transportation Administration (Washington, D.C.: U.S. Government Printing Office, 1976), p. 5.

34. Fred A. Wagner and Keith Gilbert, *Transportation System Management: An Assessment of Impacts*, report prepared by Alan M. Voorhees, Inc., for the U.S. Department of Transportation, Urban Mass Transportation Administration (Washington, D.C.: U.S. Government Printing Office, 1978), p. 37.

35. Highway Research Board, *Highway Capacity Manual*, p. 114.

36. Clearly, on-street parking, when and where the street capacity is not needed (and the parking does not interfere with other activities such as emergency access), can be exceedingly cheap.

37. The real trade-off is between enforcement costs and outlays for off-street parking. Enforcement may have a large political cost that is deemed insurmountable by some officials.

38. One-way streets can increase speeds by as much as 10 miles per hour with higher travel volumes, according to Roberta Remak and Sandra Rosenbloom, *Peak Period Traffic Congestion: Options for Current Programs*, National Cooperative Highway Research Program, report no. 169 (Washington, D.C.: Transportation Research Board, 1976), p. 47.

39. Some of the disadvantages of one-way streets and the difficulties in measuring traffic capacity gains from one-way streets are outlined in Highway Research Board, *Highway Capacity Manual*, pp. 325–326.

40. Remak and Rosenbloom, *Traffic Congestion*, p. 47.

41. Keyani and Putnam, *Transportation System Management*, pp. 14–16.

42. Ibid., p. 7.

43. These figures are for the late 1970s; for typical costs, see ibid.; Wagner and Gilbert, *Transportation System Management*, p. 34; and Remak and Rosenbloom, *Traffic Congestion*, pp. 47–48.

44. Since only a few new roadways had opened and traffic management efforts had not started during the 1950s, the study attributed the Central London capacity increases largely to growing driving skills and to improvements in the acceleration, braking, visibility, and maneuverability of automobiles.

45. J. M. Thomson, "The Value of Traffic Management," *Journal of Transport Economics and Policy* 2 (1968): 3–32, esp. pp. 5, 9, 29. See also T. M. Ridley and E. D. Turner, "The Value of Traffic Management: A Reply," *Journal of Trans-*

port Economics and Policy 2 (1968): 367–383; and J. M. Thomson, "The Value of Traffic Management: A Rejoinder," *Journal of Transport Economics and Policy* 2 (1968): 383–388.

46. In some circumstances, however, a bus operating on an arterial street can require three or four times as much street capacity as a car.

47. The evidence on this point is limited and conflicting. For different views, see William D. Whitney, "Small Car Speeds and Spacings on Urban Expressways," *Highway Research Board Bulletin,* no. 351 (1962): 18–23; and Ministry of Transportation, *A Study of Trends in the Design of Vehicles with Particular Reference to Travel Use in Towns* (London: Her Majesty's Stationery Office, 1967).

48. Thomson, "The Value of Traffic Management," pp. 9–10.

49. See Chapter 4.

50. For detailed descriptions of various high-occupancy vehicle priority techniques and their benefits and costs see Transportation Systems Center, *Priority Techniques for High Occupancy Vehicles: State-of-the-Art Overview,* report for the Technology Sharing Program of the U.S. Department of Transportation (Washington, D.C.: U.S. Department of Transportation, 1975); Public Technology, Inc., *Manual on Planning and Implementing Priority Techniques for High Occupancy Vehicles: Technical Guide,* report prepared for the U.S. Department of Transportation (Washington, D.C.: Public Technology, Inc., 1977); Herbert S. Levinson, Crosby L. Adams, and William F. Hoey, *Bus Use of Highways: Planning and Design Guidelines,* National Cooperative Highway Research Program, report no. 155 (Washington, D.C.: Transportation Research Board, 1975), and Herbert S. Levinson et al., *Bus Use of Highways: State of the Art,* National Cooperative Highway Research Program, report no. 143 (Washington, D.C.: Transportation Research Board, 1973).

51. Successful bus priority ramps are in operation on the North Central Expressway in Dallas and on I-35W in Minneapolis; bus and carpool priority ramps have operated for several years on several Los Angeles freeways. Analysts of the California Department of Transportation, an agency with much experience in operating carpool priority lanes, estimate that they can get 85–90 percent compliance on carpool priority ramps with the normal level of enforcement employed on any high-volume freeway section, supplemented by periodic intensive enforcement, particularly just after the priority ramp is opened; see Robert G.B. Goodell, "Experience with Carpool Bypass Lanes in the Los Angeles Area," photocopied, California Department of Transportation, October 1975, p. 7.

52. For a summary of recent experience with contra-flow lanes, see Transportation Systems Center, *Priority Techniques,* Appendix A; and John R. Meyer and José A. Gómez-Ibáñez, *Improving Urban Mass Transportation Productivity,* report to the Urban Mass Transportation Administration, U.S. Department of Transportation (Springfield, Va.: National Technical Information Service, 1977), pp. 114–118.

53. Moreover, the benefits from improved transit driver and vehicle productivity may further reduce the minimum volume necessary to justify contra-flow operations; see Meyer and Gómez-Ibáñez, *Urban Mass Transportation Productivity,* pp. 117–118.

54. For description of the Los Angeles, Miami, and Boston projects and results see Howard J. Simkowitz, "A Comparative Analysis of Results from Three Recent Non-Separated Concurrent-Flow High Occupancy Freeway Lane Projects: Boston, Santa Monica, and Miami," paper presented at the 57th annual meeting of the Transportation Research Board, Washington, D.C., January 1978; Daniel Brand, John Attanucci, Howard Morris, and Charles Kalauskas, "The Southeast

Expressway Reserved Lane for Buses and Carpools," paper presented at the 57th annual meeting of the Transportation Research Board, Washington, D.C., January 1978; and John W. Billheimer, Robert Bullmer, and Carolyn Fratessa, *The Santa Monica Freeway Diamond Lanes: An Evaluation*, report prepared by Systan, Inc., for the U.S. Department of Transportation (Cambridge, Mass.: Transportation System Center, 1977).

55. Simkowitz, "Three Recent Non-Separated Concurrent-Flow High Occupancy Freeway Lane Projects," pp. 16–17.

56. See Chapter 5. Also see William L. Berry, *On the Economic Incentives for Commuter Carpooling* (diss., Graduate School of Business Administration, Harvard University, 1975).

57. The California Department of Transportation opposed two-person carpools using the priority lane on the Santa Monica Freeway, out of fear that the response would be so great that travel times in the priority lane would deteriorate to the level of the regular lanes, defeating the purpose of the priority system. If two-person carpools are that readily formed, however, on a freeway like the Santa Monica, with four lanes or more in each direction, two lanes might be designated for the exclusive use of carpools and buses, rather than only one lane for buses and three-person carpools. Alternatively, the metered access to the Santa Monica Freeway might have been adjusted to keep flows at the desired levels.

58. Herbert D. Mohring, "Urban Highway Investments," in Robert Dorfman, ed., *Measuring Benefits of Government Investments* (Washington, D.C.: Brookings Institution, 1965).

59. Many studies have estimated the congestion toll assuming that traffic volumes and highway capacities would remain at constant levels after the toll had been applied, but only the San Francisco study estimated the congestion toll after traffic volumes and highway capacity had been adjusted. The San Francisco study can be found in Keeler and Small, *Automobile Costs and Final Intermodal Cost Comparisons*, pp. 43–50. For other pioneering efforts to measure the delay costs of additional vehicles, see Alan A. Walters, "The Theory and Measurement of Private and Social Costs of Highway Construction," *Econometrica* 29 (October 1961): 676–699; Herbert D. Mohring, "Relationship between Optimum Congestion Tolls and Present Highway User Charges," *Highway Research Record*, no. 47 (1967): 1–14; and Donald N. Dewees, "Simulations of Traffic Congestion in Toronto," *Transportation Research* 12 (1978): 153–161.

60. Among those who propose such tolling schemes is Walters in "Cost of Highway Congestion"; also see William S. Vickery, "Pricing in Urban and Suburban Transport," *American Economic Review* 53 (May 1963): 452–465. Great Britain's Road Research Laboratory has worked on developing inexpensive tolling devices. According to J. Michael Thomson, the work in the Road Research Laboratory has shown that the cost per car for the necessary special meters or transmitters could be as low as $5.00 each if they were manufactured on a large scale. One difficulty that Thomson notes, which has not been resolved, is how to deal with those vehicles that only occasionally come into the congested centers of metropolitan areas. If those automobiles are required to install the special equipment, then the aggregate cost for equipment becomes very high. If they are not required to install the special equipment, then enforcement becomes a problem. See J. Michael Thomson, "Methods of Traffic Limitation in Urban Areas," in *The Automobile and the Environment: An International Perspective*, ed. Ralph Gakenheimer (Cambridge, Mass.: MIT Press, 1978), pp. 176–180.

61. Damian J. Kulash, *Income Distributional Consequences of Roadway Pricing*, paper no. 1212-12 (Washington, D.C.: Urban Institute, 1974), p. 25.

62. As of December 31, 1975, the license fee was raised to 80 Singapore dollars per month (U.S. $35) and four Singapore dollars per day (U.S. $1.73).

63. Peter L. Watson and Edward P. Holland, *Relieving Traffic Congestion: The Singapore Area License Scheme*, World Bank Staff Working Paper no. 21 (Washington, D.C.: World Bank, 1978), pp. 41–61.

64. Ibid., pp. 103, 106.

65. Ibid., p. 158.

66. The World Bank's evaluation of the Singapore licensing scheme does not calculate the net overall change in commuter travel time and does not provide enough data on the volumes of travelers who made different types of trips before and after the licensing scheme to construct an estimate. Ibid., pp. 96, 103, 131–133.

67. Ibid., pp. 210–227.

68. J. M. Thomson, "An Evaluation of Two Proposals for Traffic Restraint in Central London," *Journal of the Royal Statistical Society*, ser. A, vol. 130 (1967): 327–377.

69. Estimated net benefits were higher in the second study partly because they include times savings to persons traveling to or from noncentral-area destinations while the estimates of the earlier analysis do not. See Greater London Council, *Supplementary Licensing* (London: Greater London Council, 1974).

70. Gary F. Fauth, José A. Gómez-Ibáñez, Arnold M. Howitt, John F. Kain, and Hugh C. Williams, *Central Area Auto Restraint: A Boston Case Study*, report for the U.S. Department of Transportation, Urban Mass Transportation Administration, research report no. R78-2, Harvard University, Department of City and Regional Planning, 1978; José A. Gómez-Ibáñez and Gary R. Fauth, "Downtown Auto Restraint Policies: The Costs and Benefits for Boston," *Journal of Transport Economics and Policy* 14 (1980): 133–153.

71. The U.S. Department of Transportation has shown considerable interest in sponsoring a demonstration of congestion tolls or roadway pricing in a major U.S. city to resolve some of the uncertainties about benefits and costs, but without much success. See Tom Higgins, "Road Pricing—Should and Might It Happen?" *Transportation* 8 (1979): 99–113; and Bert Arrillaga, "Comment: Road Pricing—Should and Might It Happen?" *Transportation* 8 (1979): 115–118.

72. For a full explanation of the problems of getting congestion toll schemes adopted and implemented, see Arnold M. Howitt, "Downtown Auto Restraint Policies: Adopting and Implementing Urban Transport Innovations," *Journal of Transport Economics and Policy* 14 (1980): 155–167.

73. The superiority of traffic engineering may simply reflect greater experience in implementing such schemes so that gains consistently exceed losses and any redistribution is minimized or, at least, not too noticeable.

12. The Transportation Disadvantaged

1. California Governor's Commission on the Los Angeles Riots, *Violence in the City—An End or a Beginning?* (Los Angeles, 1965), p. 65; for a discussion of these proposals, see John F. Kain and John R. Meyer, "Transportation and Poverty," *Public Interest* 18 (Winter 1970): 75–76.

2. Based on a survey of 12 demonstration projects funded between 1966 and 1971, the cost averaged $1.11 per passenger; see U.S. General Accounting Office, letter to Carlos G. Villerreal, administrator of the Urban Mass Transportation Administration of the U.S. Department of Transportation, dated January 1972,

reprinted in U.S. Congress, House Appropriations Committee, *Department of Transportation and Related Agencies Appropriations for 1973*, 92d Cong., 2d sess., 1972, pt. 2, pp. 656–659.

3. Local sponsors of some demonstration projects claimed significant employment gains, but the U.S. General Accounting Office found that these claims usually were not well documented. The sponsor of a demonstration project in New York, for example, reported that 69 percent of the passengers using the new service to go to work said they could not get to work if the service were discontinued. The local sponsor did not ask whether those passengers would be unable to find other, comparable jobs if the service were discontinued. See U.S. General Accounting Office, letter to Carlos C. Villerreal, pp. 656–659; and Tri-State Transportation Commission, *Public Transport Services to Non-CBD Employment Concentrations, Progress Report No. 3* (New York: Tri-State Transportation Commission, 1969), p. 23.

4. In a special 1970 census of employment of low-income area residents, less than 5 in 1,000 persons who said they were not in the labor force but wanted, might have wanted, or would have wanted a regular job listed transportation problems as the principal reason they were not looking for work. See U.S. Department of Commerce, Bureau of the Census, *1970 Census of Population and Housing*, Vol. PHC (3)-1: *Employment Profiles of Selected Low-Income Areas, United States Summary—Urban Affairs* (Washington, D.C.: U.S. Government Printing Office, 1972), p. 64.

5. Thomas H. Floyd, "Using Transportation to Alleviate Poverty: A Progress Report on Experiments under the Mass Transportation Act," paper presented at the Conference on Transportation and Property, American Academy of Arts and Sciences, Brookline, Mass., June 7, 1968, p. 17.

6. Institute of Public Administration, *Transportation for Older Americans: A State of the Art Report*, prepared for the Administration on Aging, National Technical Information Service (Springfield, Va.: Institute of Public Administration, 1975), pp. 143–144.

7. In Washington, D.C., for example, the regional transit authority estimated that it issued a total of 50,000 reduced-fare identification cards to the elderly and 8,600 reduced-fare identification cards to the handicapped. These figures represent only about one quarter of the elderly population in the metropolitan area and (if the proportion of handicapped is the same in Washington, D.C., as in the nation as a whole) about one fifteenth of the handicapped. Estimates of the numbers of reduced-fare identification cards issued were provided in a telephone interview with Mr. Fox, Washington Metropolitan Transit Authority, Washington, D.C., September 6, 1979.

8. This program is authorized under Section 16(b)2 of the Urban Mass Transportation Act. The federal government will pay up to 80 percent of project capital costs, but will not pay any operating expenses. Nonprofit organizations apply for these federal grants through their state's designated coordinating agency, usually a state's department of transportation. Authorized federal funding levels for Section 16(b)2 grants averaged about $20 million per year through the 1970s.

9. See System, Inc., *Paratransit Integration: State of the Art Report*, prepared for the Transportation Systems Center, U.S. Department of Transportation (Washington, D.C.: U.S. Department of Transportation, 1978).

10. *Federal Register*, vol. 42, no. 185, September 23, 1977, pp. 48,339–48,340.

11. As of late 1980, American bus manufacturers had refused to bid on Transbus contracts, citing the technical difficulties and costs of producing such a vehicle.

12. The $600 million annual capital cost is based on $125,000 extra per bus and a nationwide fleet of approximately 50,000 buses, 10 percent of which are retired each year. Maintenance and operating costs would also increase because the Transbus has more sophisticated equipment (particularly the ramps and lifts), and because the low floors make maintenance of the engine, drivetrain suspension, and other systems more difficult.

13. U.S. Department of Transportation, "The Economic Impacts of U.S. Department of Transportation Regulations Implementing Section 504 of the Rehabilitation Act of 1973—the Costs and Benefits of the Handicapped in Federally Assisted Transportation Programs," *Federal Register,* vol. 43, no. 111, June 8, 1978, p. 25,052.

14. U.S. Congressional Budget Office, *Urban Transportation for Handicapped Persons: Alternative Federal Approaches* (Washington, D.C.: U.S. Government Printing Office, 1979), p. 55.

15. The average discount should have been at least half the average transit fare (38 cents in 1978). For statistics on national transit fares and ridership by ages, see American Public Transit Association, *Transit Fact Book 1978* (Washington, D.C.: American Public Transit Association, 1978), and U.S. Department of Transportation, Federal Highway Administration, *Mode of Transportation and Personal Characteristics of Tripmakers,* report no. 9 of the *Nationwide Personal Transportation Survey* (Washington, D.C.: U.S. Department of Transportation, 1973), p. 32.

16. Statistics on the number of poor, elderly, and handicapped Americans in 1970 can be found in U.S. Department of Transportation, Transportation Systems Center, *The Handicapped and Elderly Market for Urban Mass Transit,* report no. PB-224-821, prepared for the Urban Mass Transportation Administration (Springfield, Va.: National Technical Information Service, 1973); U.S. Bureau of the Census, *General Population Characteristics, United States Summary,* vol. PC(1)-B1 of 1970 Census Population (Washington, D.C.: U.S. Government Printing Office, 1973), pp. 263, 315; and Transportation Research Board, *Transportation Requirements for the Handicapped, Elderly, and Economically Disadvantaged,* National Cooperative Highway Research Program Synthesis of Highway Practice, report no. 39 (Washington, D.C.: Transportation Research Board, 1976), pp. 7–13.

17. Statistics on the poor and elderly population can be found in U.S. Bureau of the Census, *General Population Characteristics, United States Summary,* p. 314. A recent report estimates that 7.4 million persons with mobility handicaps reside in urbanized areas, excluding those who cannot leave their homes. If the ratio of handicapped persons who can leave their homes to those who cannot is the same in urbanized areas as it is in the nation as a whole, approximately 9.4 million handicapped persons lived in urbanized areas in 1970. For statistics on the numbers of handicapped see Transportation Systems Center, *The Handicapped and Elderly Market;* and Grey Advertising, Inc., *Summary Report of Data from National Survey of Transportation Handicapped People,* report for the U.S. Department of Transportation, Urban Mass Transportation Administration (Washington, D.C.: U.S. Department of Transportation, 1978).

18. Of course, some of the institutionalized handicapped persons may not be so seriously ill as to be unable to benefit from transportation services. Nevertheless, the figure of roughly 7 million beneficiaries has been confirmed by two other studies. A 1977 survey estimates that 7.4 million of the handicapped persons residing in urban areas were well enough to go out. See Grey Advertising, Inc., *Survey of Transportation Handicapped.* Data on the incidence of various handicaps col-

lated in a second study imply that 7.2 million handicapped persons who could go out lived in metropolitan areas in 1970. See Table 12.2 and Transportation Systems Center, *The Handicapped and Elderly Market.*

19. Handicapped individuals who can leave their houses report taking an average of 29 trips per month compared to 55 trips for the nonhandicapped; see Grey Advertising, Inc., *Survey of Transportation Handicapped,* p. 30.

20. Ibid., p. 20.

21. These statistics are based on the national data summarized in Figure 12.1.

22. Chicago Area Transportation Study staff report, "1970 Travel Characteristics: Trip Length," no. CATS-372-4, 1975, p. 25.

23. Calculated from data in U.S. Bureau of the Census, *Metropolitan Housing Characteristics: United States Summary,* vol. HC(2)-1 of *1970 Housing Census* (Washington, D.C.: U.S. Government Printing Office, 1972), pp. 5, 22, 39, 56, 73.

24. Estimates of the number of metropolitan residents who live in households below the poverty line and who do not own cars are not available in the publications of the U.S. Bureau of the Census. The above calculations assume that 55 percent of the poor persons who live in central cities are carless and 30 percent of those who live in the suburbs are carless, as based on the data described in note 23.

25. See George Katona, Lewis Mandell, and Jay Schmiedeskamp, *1970 Survey of Consumer Finances* (Ann Arbor: University of Michigan, Survey Research Center, 1971), pp. 61–63, 68; U.S. Department of Transportation, Federal Highway Administration, *Automobile Ownership,* report no. 11 of *Nationwide Personal Transportation Study* (Washington, D.C.: Federal Highway Administration, 1974), p. 26; and James P. Leape, *The Demand for Automobiles: An Analysis,* senior honors thesis, Harvard University, 1977, pp. 35–66.

26. Calculated from data in U.S. Department of Labor, Bureau of Labor Statistics, *Consumer Expenditure Survey: Integrated Diary and Interview Survey Data, 1972–1973; Total Expenditures and Income for the United States and Selected Areas,* BLS bulletin no. 1992 (Washington, D.C.: U.S. Government Printing Office, 1978), pp. 24, 25, 30, 31. The burden of car ownership on poor families is undoubtedly exaggerated somewhat because of limitations in the measurement of income (such as exclusion of money transfers and in-kind receipts), particularly for families with incomes below $3,000 in 1972–73.

27. For example, 36 percent of the nonwalking persontrips made by Washington, D.C., households with incomes below $6,000 in 1968 were as automobile passengers, presumably driven by friends or relatives. Peter Tufano, *The Utilization of Taxicab Services by the Urban Poor,* senior honors thesis, Harvard University, 1979, p. 79.

28. Rolan M. Hatley, *Availability of Public Transportation and Shopping Characteristics of SMSA Households,* report no. 5 of *Nationwide Personal Transportation Study* (Washington, D.C.: Federal Highway Administration, 1972), pp. 8, 11.

29. Estimated by Tufano, *The Utilization of Taxicab Services by the Urban Poor,* p. 43, as calculated from data in Arthur Webster, Edward Weiner, and John D. Wells, *The Role of Taxicabs in Urban Transportation* (Washington, D.C.: U.S. Government Printing Office, 1974), p. 3–12.

30. U.S. Department of Transportation, Federal Highway Administration, *Characteristics of Licensed Drivers,* report no. 6 of the *Nationwide Personal Transportation Study* (Washington, D.C.: Federal Highway Administration, 1973), p. 18.

31. Martin Wachs and Robert Blanchard, "Lifestyles and Transportation

Needs of the Elderly in the Future," *Transportation Research Record* 618 (1977): 19–22.

32. This rough estimate is based on the nationwide licensing rates for different age groups applied to the age and sex distribution of metropolitan elderly residents as of 1970.

33. U.S. Department of Transportation, Federal Highway Administration, *Characteristics of Licensed Drivers*, p. 25.

34. Surveys show that elderly individuals who are licensed to drive or have access to a car are well satisfied with their mobility, while those without cars take fewer trips and are less pleased with their transportation. See Institute of Public Administration, *Transportation for Older Americans: A State of the Art Report*, report for the U.S. Administration on Aging and the U.S. Department of Health, Education and Welfare (Springfield, Va.: National Technical Information Service, 1975), p. 163.

35. Ibid., pp. 164–165.

36. Possible modifications for driver's licenses for the elderly are described in ibid., pp. 176–194.

37. Cost estimates are approximate only and are based on telephone interviews with Anthony Graziano of the Prosthetics Department of the Boston Regional Office of the U.S. Veterans Administration, June 28 and July 2, 1979.

38. Congressional Budget Office, *Urban Transportation for Handicapped Persons*, p. 40.

39. This assumes that 80 percent of the 116,000 wheelchair-confined persons could be accommodated in small "adapted" cars costing about $5,500 with a useful life of six years, and that the other 20 percent would require vans equipped with a lift costing about $15,000 with a useful life of nearly 10 years. Ibid., p. 64.

40. John R. Pucher, *Equity in Transit Financing: The Distribution of the Costs and Benefits of Transit Subsidies among Income Classes* (diss., Massachusetts Institute of Technology, 1978), p. 48.

41. Ibid., pp. 77, 121.

42. David Young, "Accessibility: A Problem of Time and Money," *Mass Transit* 5, no. 10 (October 1978): 32, 34.

43. Institute of Public Administration, *Transportation for Older Americans*, p. 16.

44. Congressional Budget Office, *Urban Transportation for Handicapped Persons*, p. 60. These estimates are consistent with the figures in Chapter 5, which show that for dial-a-ride systems without lifts, operating costs alone commonly amounted to about $1.00 per passenger-mile in the late 1970s.

13. Small-Car Safety

1. In the United States in 1976, 55.2 percent of total vehicle-miles traveled were on urban roads.

2. In 1970, 35.6 percent of metropolitan area families in the United States had two or more cars, while in 1975, 36.9 percent of metropolitan area families owned two cars. Motor Vehicle Manfacturers Association, *Motor Vehicles Facts and Figures, 1978* (Detroit: Motor Vehicle Manufacturers Association, 1978), p. 39.

3. People riding in small cars apparently use seat belts more often than those riding in large cars, thus partially offsetting any extra hazard inherent to small car use. See Table 13.8.

4. B. J. Campbell and D. W. Reinfurt, "Relationship between Driver Crash

Injury and Passenger Car Weight," as cited in Donald F. Mela, "How Safe Can We Be in Small Cars?" *Proceedings of the Third International Congress on Automotive Safety*, vol. 2 (Washington, D.C.: National Motor Vehicle Safety Advisory Council, U.S. Department of Transportation, 1974), p. 48-4. See also J. K. Kihlberg, E. A. Narragon, and B. J. Campbell, *Automobile Crash Injury in Relation to Car Size*, report no. VJ-1823-R11 (Ithaca, N.Y.: Cornell Aeronautical Laboratory, 1964), p. 66.

5. Claude Berlioz, "Comparison of the Aggressiveness of Different Vehicles and the Safety They Afford," in *Report on the Third International Technical Conference on Experimental Safety Vehicles* (Washington, D.C.: National Highway Traffic Safety Administration, U.S. Department of Transportation, 1972), pp. 2-5 through 2-6.

6. See Mela, "How Safe Can We Be in Small Cars?" pp. 48-2 through 48-5, for a good summary of the research to date.

7. See B. J. Campbell and D. W. Reinfurt, *Crash Rates by Vehicle Make, Based upon Mileage or Registration Exposure*, University of North Carolina Highway Safety Research Center, Chapel Hill, N.C. (forthcoming); University of Michigan Highway Safety Research Institute, *Acquisition of Information on Exposure and on Nonfatal Crashes, Final Report*, vol. 4, report to the U.S. Department of Transportation, May 1971, pp. 226–229; and A. K. Dutt and D. W. Reinfurt, *Accident Involvement and Crash Injury Rates by Make, Model and Year of Car: A Follow-up*, University of North Carolina Highway Safety Research Center, Chapel Hill, N.C., June 1977, pp. 1, 2, 83.

8. New York State Department of Motor Vehicles, *An Analysis of Accidents in New York State by Make of Vehicle*, report prepared for the U.S. Department of Transportation, National Highway Safety Administration, Washington, D.C., June 1972, pp. 27–35; Kihlberg, Narragon, and Campbell, *Injury in Relation to Car Size*, p. 67; and Mela, "How Safe Can We Be in Small Cars?" p. 48–5.

9. H. W. Case, A. Burg, and J. D. Baird, "Vehicle Size and Accident Involvement: A Preliminary Study," *Journal of Safety Research* 5, no. 1 (March 1973): 26–35.

10. Telephone interview with Donald F. Mela, National Center for Statistics and Analysis, National Highway Traffic Safety Administration, U.S. Department of Transportation, September 7, 1979. The only substantial evidence of different accident rates for different vehicles applies to vehicles other than passenger cars. There seems to be some consensus that motorcycles and tractor trailer trucks, for example, have substantially higher fatal-crash involvement rates than other vehicles. See Leon S. Robertson and Susan P. Baker, "Motor Vehicle Sizes in 1440 Fatal Crashes," *Accident Analysis and Prevention* 8 (1976): 168–169; Barry Felrice, "Safety in the Year 2000: How Much is Enough?" paper presented at the American Institute of Planners Conference on Future Urban Transportation, Aspen, Colo., June 1979; and Mela, "How Safe Can We Be in Small Cars?"

11. Felrice, "Safety in the Year 2000," p. 7.

12. Felrice, "Safety in the Year 2000"; and Henry H. Wakeland, "Available System Design Philosophies in the Small Car Crash Safety Problem," in *Third International Congress on Automotive Safety*, vol. 1 (Washington, D.C.: National Motor Vehicle Safety Advisory Council, U.S. Department of Transportation, ca. 1974).

13. This shift from large cars to vans and trucks may be an unintended side effect of government regulations on air pollution and fleet mileage targets, which in the late 1970s, were less rigorously applied to trucks and vans than to automobiles.

14. Samuel Peltzman, *The Regulation of Automobile Safety* (Washington, D.C.: American Enterprise Institute for Policy Research, 1975).

15. As long as accident involvement is not sensitive to weight differences.

16. Mela, "How Safe Can We Be in Small Cars?" p. 48-11.

17. Ibid., pp. 48-13 through 48-15.

18. Felrice, "Safety in the Year 2000," p. 14.

19. Insurance Institute for Highway Safety, *To Prevent Harm* (Washington, D.C.: Insurance Institute for Highway Safety, 1978), pp. 32–33.

20. Phillipe Ventre, "Homogeneous Safety and Heterogeneous Car Population?" in *Report on the Third International Technical Conference on Experimental Safety Vehicles, June 1972* (Washington, D.C.: National Highway Traffic Safety Administration, U.S. Department of Transportation, 1972), p. 2-56.

21. Ibid., p. 2-56.

22. Peltzman, *The Regulation of Automobile Safety.*

14. The Role of Public Policy

1. Total direct costs of automobile commuting (including vehicle ownership but excluding parking) were in the vicinity of $35 billion to $40 billion per year; transit operating expenses were about $5 billion annually (see Table 3.2); capital costs for transit were in the vicinity of $1 billion per year; parking, unrecouped externalities, and so on (see Chapter 10) could easily account for $5 billion more annually.

2. See Chapter 6.

3. As of the end of the 1970s, just under 100 million people were employed in the United States. Assuming that employment in urban and rural locations divides roughly in proportion to population, approximately 70–75 percent—say, 70–75 million persons—worked in urban or metropolitan areas. If 73 percent of these 70–75 million were driving to work (as shown in Table 3.1), 50–55 million cars were involved. For estimates of the U.S. workforce in the 1980s, see U.S. Department of Labor, Bureau of Labor Statistics, *Employment Projections for the 1980s,* bulletin 2030, 1979.

4. If a parking space lasts 40 years with no scrap value and no annual maintenance costs, the annual savings from eliminating 18 million parking spots would be $525 million at a 5 percent discount rate and $920 million at a 10 percent discount rate. Some of these savings might simply represent transfers of funds rather than real cost reductions to society, since a reduction in demand for land for parking might reduce land prices elsewhere (such as at the periphery of urban areas).

5. Assuming a cost of $1 per day for parking, and 18 million fewer commuter automobiles, $4.5 billion could be saved over 250 working days.

6. Society would reap additional benefits from any reduction in pollution and aesthetic or other social costs not now recouped from automobile drivers.

7. M. E. Beesley, "The Value of Time Spent in Travelling: Some New Evidence," *Economica* 32 (May 1965): 174–185; G. Kraft and T. Domencich, *Free Transit* (Lexington, Mass: D. C. Heath, 1970), pp. 4–40; and Reuben Gronau, "The Value of Time in Passenger Transportation: The Demand for Air Travel," occasional paper no. 109 (New York: National Bureau of Economic Research, 1970).

8. Beesley, "The Value of Time Spent in Travelling"; Kraft and Domencich,

Free Transit; and Gronau, "The Value of Time in Passenger Transportation."

9. (5–10 minutes lost) × (5 cents per minute) × (34 million new carpoolers) × (250 weekdays per year).

10. (10–20 minutes delay per round trip) × (5 cents per minute) × (24 million new vanpoolers) × (250 weekdays per year).

11. (30 cents per van-mile) × (20 miles round trip) × (three million new vanpools) × (250 weekdays per year).

12. (10–15 cents per mile) × (20 miles round trip) × (three million fewer automobiles) × (250 weekdays per year).

13. (15–20 minutes delay per round trip) × (5 cents per minute) × (21 million new bus riders) × (250 weekdays per year).

14. This figure of 100 commuters per bus is consistent with performance in the early 1970s, when roughly 5 million workers commuted in a fleet of about 50,000 public buses. For data on the total ridership and vehicle fleet of the transit industry, see American Public Transit Association, *Transit Fact Book, 1979* (Washington, D.C.: American Public Transit Association, 1979).

15. If mass transit carried 21 million new commuters, that would amount to about 10 billion additional transit commuting trips per year. In the late 1970s, mass transit carried about 8 percent of all urban commuters (see Table 3.1) or about 6 million workers for 3 billion commuting trips per year. Mass transit's total patronage was then about 5.6 billion persontrips per year, but this figure includes many noncommuters who do not travel during peak hours and thus do not affect the number of vehicles required. American Public Transit Association, *Transit Fact Book, 1978.*

16. William L. Berry, *On the Economic Incentives for Commuter Carpooling,* (diss., Graduate School of Business Administration, Harvard University, 1975), argues persuasively that sharing of parking charges is one of the strongest incentives for creating carpools.

17. See Don H. Pickrell, "Free Parking and Urban Transportation," Program in City and Regional Planning, discussion paper, Harvard University, April 1980.

18. A good discussion of the advantages and disadvantages of policies to equalize or eliminate employer subsidies of different transportation modes can be found in Pickrell, "Free Parking and Urban Transportation."

19. See Altshuler et al., *The Urban Transportation System: Politics and Policy Innovation* (Cambridge Mass.: MIT Press, 1979), chs. 8, 9.

Appendix: Trends in Urban Residential Densities

1. The original work on population density functions is Colin Clark, "Urban Population Densities," *Journal of the Royal Statistical Society* 114 (1951): 490–496.

2. For the reader interested in more detail on the technical aspects of urban population density functions and their measurements, good explanations can be found in Edwin S. Mills and Jee Peng Tan, "A Comparison of Urban Population Density Functions in Developed and Developing Countries," *Urban Studies* (forthcoming).

Index